Innovation in the Asia Pacific

Thomas Clarke · Keun Lee
Editors

Innovation in the Asia Pacific

From Manufacturing to the Knowledge Economy

Springer

Editors
Thomas Clarke
Centre for Business and Social Innovation
University of Technology Sydney
Sydney, NSW
Australia

Keun Lee
Department of Economics
Seoul National University
Seoul
Korea (Republic of)

ISBN 978-981-10-5893-6 ISBN 978-981-10-5895-0 (eBook)
https://doi.org/ 10.1007/978-981-10-5895-0

Library of Congress Control Number: 2017948208

Printed on acid-free paper

This Springer imprint is published by Springer Nature
The registered company is Springer Nature Singapore Pte Ltd.
The registered company address is: 152 Beach Road, #21-01/04 Gateway East, Singapore 189721, Singapore

Preface

This book is the work of academics from around the world researching innovation who are members of the Asia Pacific Network which organises the annual Asia Pacific Innovation Conference (APIC).

The Asia Pacific Innovation Network was formed in 2010 to bring together scholars in the Asia Pacific region interested in the legal, managerial and economic aspects of innovation. Research interests include innovation policy including basic research, applied research and implementation of innovation; intellectual property; market design to promote alternative energy and other innovations; innovation for sustainability; and innovation in legal and other social institutions.

The successive APIC Conferences have circumnavigated the Asia Pacific with conferences in Melbourne, Australia 2010; Singapore 2011; Seoul, Korea 2012; Taipei, Taiwan 2013; Sydney, Australia 2014; Hangzhou, China 2015; Fukuoka, Japan 2016; and Wellington, New Zealand 2017.

For their help and guidance in the development of this work, we would thank all of the participating members of APIC, and especially like to thank the members of the APIC Board including Reiko Aoki of the Japan Fair Trade Commission, Shou-Ling Jang of the National Taiwan University, Sadao Nagaoka, Professor of Tokyo Keizai University, and Wu Xiaobo and Can Huang of Zhejiang University.

Most of all we are grateful for the inspiration of Beth Webster, General Secretary of APIC and Director of the Centre for Transformative Innovation, Swinburne University of Technology, Australia. With remarkable energy, intelligence and determination, Beth has built APIC from its foundations to the robust international research body it is now.

Sydney, Australia — Thomas Clarke
Seoul, Korea (Republic of) — Keun Lee

Contents

Contributors

John Chelliah University of Fiji, Lautoka, Fiji

Thomas Clarke Centre for Business and Social Innovation, University of Technology Sydney, Sydney, NSW, Australia

Rainer Frietsch Fraunhofer Institute for Systems and Innovation Research, Karlsruhe, Germany; Institute for Policy and Management, Chinese Academy of Sciences, Beijing, China

Ping Gao Information School, Capital University of Economics and Business, Beijing, China

Soheyla Gholamshahi Centre for Business and Social Innovation, UTS, Sydney, Australia

Horst Hanusch Institute of Economics, University of Augsburg, Augsburg, Germany

Yasushi Hara SciREX Center, National Graduate Institute for Policy Studies, Tokyo, Japan

Albert G. Hu China Europe International Business School, Shangai, China; National University of Singapore, Singapore, Singapore

Yee Kyoung Kim KISTEP, Seoul, Korea (Republic of)

Keun Lee Department of Economics, Seoul National University, Seoul, Korea (Republic of)

Michael Lester Centre for Business and Social Innovation, UTS Sydney, Ultimo, Australia

Guanyu Liu Information School, Capital University of Economics and Business, Beijing, China

Peter Neuhäusler Fraunhofer Institute for Systems and Innovation Research, Karlsruhe, Germany; Innovation Economics, Berlin University of Technology, Berlin, Germany

Junichi Nishimura Faculty of Economics, Gakushuin University, Tokyo, Japan

Hiroyuki Okamuro Graduate School of Economics, Hitotsubashi University, Tokyo, Japan

Elizabeth Pattinson University of Technology Sydney, Sydney, Australia

Jochen Schweitzer Centre for Business and Social Innovation, University of Technology Sydney, Sydney, Australia

Keiichiro Suenaga Meiji University, Tokyo, Japan; Josai University, Sakado, Japan

Jue Wang Nanyang Technological University, Singapore, Singapore

Peng Zhang National Bureau of Statistics of China, Beijing, China

Lijing Zhao National Bureau of Statistics of China, Beijing, China

Chapter 1
Introduction: Fast Cycle Innovation in the Asia Pacific

Thomas Clarke and Keun Lee

Abstract This chapter introduces the central thesis of the book that while the Asia Pacific has become the centre of world manufacturing, it now faces a greater challenge in how to transform both its manufacturing and service economy to achieve the potential of a knowledge economy. This innovation towards a knowledge economy involves a continuous process impacting upon every aspect of industry and society. Knowledge economies are economies in which growth is dependent on the quantity, quality, and accessibility and usefulness of ideas, creativity and information, rather than simply increasing the material means of production. The chapter introduces the technological trajectories of national innovation systems in the Asia Pacific, and examines the basis of fast cycle innovation. It explores the implications of the internationalisation of innovation, and the importance of sustaining investment in research and innovation. The significance of a culture of innovation is highlighted, and how this might contribute to rapidly changing techno-economic paradigms in the Asia Pacific.

Keywords Innovation systems · Fast cycle · Technological paradigms

Innovation is the key to the continued success of the economies of the Asia Pacific. According to the OECD (2015: 2) innovative economies are "more productive, more resilient, more adaptable to change and better able to support higher living standards." Innovation may be broadly defined as "The design, invention, development and/or implementation of new or altered products, services, processes, systems, organizational structures, or business models for the purpose of creating new value for customers and financial returns for the firm" (US Department of Commerce 2012).

T. Clarke (✉)
Centre for Business and Social Innovation, University of Technology Sydney, Sydney, NSW, Australia
e-mail: t.clarke@uts.edu.au

K. Lee
Department of Economics, Seoul National University, Seoul, Korea (Republic of)
e-mail: kenneth@snu.ac.kr

T. Clarke and K. Lee (eds.), *Innovation in the Asia Pacific*,
https://doi.org/10.1007/978-981-10-5895-0_1

Innovation is not an isolated or limited activity, and promoting an innovative culture and commitment to continuous innovation is the secret of dynamic industries and companies. As the OECD (2010) states "Innovation is a continuous, pervasive activity that takes place throughout the economy. Firms constantly change products and processes, collect new knowledge, and develop new ways of working" (2010: 34).

This book is focused upon the innovative economies of the Asia Pacific examining how advances achieved in manufacturing can be translated into developing knowledge economies. Knowledge economies may be defined as economies in which growth is dependent on the quantity, quality, and accessibility and usefulness of ideas, creativity and information, rather than simply the material means of production. Schumpeter first recognized the importance of knowledge in the economy in his reference to 'new combinations of knowledge' at the heart of innovation and entrepreneurship (Schumpeter 1934: 57). Later Penrose with her view of dynamic capabilities identified the immense increase in the value of transferable knowledge in the economy to the firm "the rapid and intricate evolution of modern technology often makes it necessary for firms in related areas around the world to be closely in touch with developments in the research and innovation of firms in many centres" (Penrose 1995: xix). The knowledge based economy focuses on the development of knowledge capital, but also the technological trajectories of national innovation systems, a core concept of Schumpeterian economics since Freeman (2008). The most distinctive element of the present trajectory of innovation in the Asia Pacific is the fast cycle capability demonstrated in different ways. As Lee and Lim (2001) suggest the economies of the Asia Pacific have projected significant industries forward rapidly to international competitiveness through three different means. There can be accelerated following of the forerunners (often compressing generations of discovery and application of techniques into just a few years (World Bank 1993). In other Asian industries whole stages have been skipped leading to the most advanced technology. Finally in the most successful Asian industries new path creation has not only allowed catch up, but taking the lead in key technologies. It is a fascination with this phenomena of fast cycle capability in the Asia Pacific that informs the contributions to this work.

The Internationalisation of Innovation

The scope of innovation has broadened as more industry sectors engage in continuous innovation, in technological innovation but also organisational and marketing innovation. Innovation is associated with high technology industries, but is relevant also in medium and low technology industries. As the complexity and costs of innovation have increased, innovation has become more open as firms partner to share costs, discover complementary expertise, gain access to new technologies and knowledge, and join innovative networks often around open source software.

This collaboration is often the key to innovation with companies working with external partners, suppliers, customers and universities. The degree of openness influences access to knowledge, and while firms often seek to retain their core capabilities, open innovation can involve less risk and cost than in-house development, with a larger base of ideas and technologies to draw upon. Along with this greater openness the geography of innovation is expanding with the dramatic increase in R&D expenditure and innovation in the Asia Pacific, which has become an essential element in global information and communication technology innovation value chain (OECD 2010). Multinational corporations account for approximately half of the world's total R&D expenditure, and whilst most internationalisation of R&D by multinational corporations still takes place within the main OECD countries, China, India, Japan, Singapore and Taiwan feature prominently among the top 12 locations attractive for multinational R&D (Chandra et al. 2009: 89). The development of knowledge networks and markets becomes critical to the innovation process with the transfer of intellectual property, know-how, and software: "Becoming ever more closely integrated into fast-evolving regional and global production and knowledge networks. Extending and deepening their capacities in science, technology (S&T) and innovation …moving up the value chain, differentiating their economies and contributing to advances in science and technology in order to tackle societal grand challenges" (OECD 2013a: 11, b).

Science, technology and innovation are increasingly becoming internationalised as communication and mobility has advanced immeasurably, and common needs and dilemmas are increasingly recognised. In a world of constrained resources and growing environmental threats science, technology and innovation are explicitly recognised as vital drivers for sustainability in addressing the sustainable development challenges including climate change (UNESCO 2016: xx). Ideas, science and technology are becoming more mobile as cloud computing and supercomputing offer collaborative solutions to the handling of big data globally as in the Human Genome Project, or the Human Brain Project. Science as with music provides a universal language that can be shared across borders, for example there are 10,000 scientists from 60 countries working together at the European Laboratory for Particle Physics (CERN) in Switzerland (Aebischer 2016: 4).

Global investment in research and development has grown faster than the global economy, with UNESCO estimating world expenditure on research and development reached PPP$ 1478 billion in 2013 (UNESCO 2016: 24). The OECD defines research and experimental development (R&D) in a broad sense: "Research and experimental development (R&D) comprise creative work undertaken on a systematic basis in order to increase the stock of knowledge, including knowledge of man, culture and society, and the use of this stock of knowledge to devise new applications" (OECD 2002: 30). As high income countries have reduced their public investment, lower income countries have increased theirs. The North-South divide in research and innovation is narrowing, with both North-South collaboration increasing, but also South-South collaboration developing (UNESCO 2016: xx).

However, the reality is that the large multinational corporations that dominate global value chains are ready to distribute production throughout the world, and may be prepared to adapt and augment their R&D overseas, but they are still inclined to keep investment in core knowledge in their home country. "R&D and other forms of knowledge-related investment are traditionally less globalized than other forms of investment; although multinational firms often locate their production or services related activities such as sales and customer support abroad, they are more reluctant to do the same for investment in knowledge. This is changing but there is still a tendency to keep investment in knowledge 'at home'" (UNESCO 2016: 62). This has caused some Asian economies to make major investment commitments in stimulating their home-grown innovation with significant results.

Investment in Research and Innovation

The emerging commitment to innovation is clear in the UNESCO (2016) *Science Report—Towards 2030* with Japan retaining its position as a leading economy in terms of gross domestic expenditure on research and development (GERD), but being joined by the Republic of Korea and China as economies committed to investment in research and development, and with India now striving to join the ranks of the leading countries in the world in investment. Table 1.1 indicates that the Republic of Korea government is now committing the most funding to GERD with the equivalent of 0.95% of GDP, followed by Germany, France and the USA.

In terms of business financing of expenditure on research and development the pattern of Asian economies powering ahead is even more pronounced with three Asian countries in the top five investors including the Republic of Korea, Japan and China (Table 1.2). The United States remains the world's greatest investor in research and development as a country with $396.7 billion dollars of total expenditure on research and development in 2013, however the combined spend of China, Japan and the Republic of Korea amounts to $496.2 billion in total (Table 1.3). When taking into account the rapid build-up of India's innovative economy, and the sustained investment in research and development of the other leading economies of South East Asia including Taiwan, Singapore, Thailand, Malaysia, Hong Kong, and the Philippines it does appear that innovation is moving Eastwards.

Table 1.1 GERD Financed by Government as a share of GDP 2005–2013 (%)

	2005	2013
Republic of Korea	0.60	0.95
Germany	0.69	0.85
France	0.79	0.78 (2012)
USA	0.77	0.76
Singapore	0.66	0.77 (2012)
Russia	0.66	0.76
Japan	0.55	0.60
UK	0.53	0.44
China	0.35	0.44

Source Adapted from: UNESCO (2016: 28)

Table 1.2 GERD Financed by business as a share of GDP 2005–2013 (%)

	2005	2013
Republic of Korea	2.02	3.26
Japan	2.53	2.64
USA	1.73	1.92
Germany	1.68	1.91
China	0.91	1.60
France	1.27	1.44
UK	1.00	1.05
Italy	0.53	0.68
Russia	0.73	0.68

Source Adapted from: UNESCO (2016: 29)

Table 1.3 World share of expenditure on R&D: GERD in PPP$ billions 2007–2013

	2005	2013
USA	359.4	396.7
China	116.0	290.1
Japan	139.9	141.4
Germany	69.5	83.7
Republic of Korea	38.8	64.7
France	40.6	45.7
India	31.1	42.8 (2011)
UK	37.2	36.2
Brazil	23.9	31.3

Source Adapted from: UNESCO (2016: 26)

How Asia has become the driver of economic growth and innovation in the global industrial economy is increasingly apparent in the rates of investment in research and development distributed among the regions (Table 1.4). North America no longer has the clear domination of the innovation agenda it retained until the end of the 20th century, meanwhile the commitment of China and India to research and development quadrupled from 5 to 20% of global investment in a decade of rapid and often spontaneous growth.

With the total global investment in R&D approaching 2 trillion dollars in 2016, in purchasing power parity (PPP) values, this investment is being driven by Asian countries (including China, Japan, South Korea and India) accounting for over 40%

Table 1.4 World share of business R&D, 2001–2011 (%) in PPP$

	2001%	2011%
North America	40.7	29.3
Japan and the Asian Tigers	22.2	21.7
China and India	5.1	19.9
Western Europe	24.3	19.7

Source Adapted from: UNESCO (2016: 59)

Table 1.5 Distribution of total global R&D investment

	2014%	2015%	2016%
Asia (including China, Japan and India)	40.2	41.2	41.8
China	19.1	19.8	20.4
USA	26.9	26.4	26.4
Europe	21.5	21.3	21.0
Russia	3.1	2.9	2.8
South America	2.8	2.6	2.6
Middle East	2.2	2.3	2.3
Africa	1.0	1.1	1.1

Source Adapted From: R&D 2016 Global R&D Funding Forecast, Industrial Research Institute

of these investments (Table 1.5). The United States which for nearly a century led the world in R&D now accounts for 26.4% of investment, and Europe accounts for 21% (R&D 2016: 3).

The OECD exercises the necessary caution regarding translating too readily R&D into innovation and a dynamic economy: "R&D statistics are not enough. In the context of the knowledge based economy, it has become increasingly clear that such data need to be examined within a conceptual framework that relates them both to other types of resources and to the desired outcomes of given R&D activities. This link may be made for example, via the innovation process or within a the broader framework of intangible investment," which covers not only R&D and related science and technology activities but also "expenditure on software, training, organisation etc.…It is also of interest to analyse R&D data in conjunction with other economic variables, such as value added and investment data" (OECD 2002: 14).

Other indicators of knowledge generation reinforce the view that the Asia Pacific is challenging to become the centre of global innovation:

- In terms of developing human capital the EU remains the world leader in the number of researchers with 22.2%, but China (19.1%) has overtaken the United States with 16.7% (UNESCO 2016: 33).
- While the EU still leads the world with publications (34% of the total) followed by the United States on 25%, the rate of publication in China has risen meteorically from 5% of the world total in 2004 to 20% in 2014 (UNESCO 2016: 35).

Broadening and Deepening the Innovation Culture

China, India, Japan, Korea and Australia

Applying different innovation strategies China, India, Japan, Korea and Australian have advanced their economies. In each of these countries the broad institutional regime has played an important role. In China and India, in particular utilising innovation strategies to tap global knowledge, reverse engineering, and exploiting the knowledge of their population diaspora, as well as developing information and communication technologies, has accelerated the innovation process (Dahlman 2009). Though China and other Asian economies have achieved a lot in a short time (for example China has produced its first large passenger aircraft the ARJ21-700 with a capacity for 95 passengers,) there remains a sense of there being some significant way to go for them to successfully transition from being the manufacturing centre of the world economy to being the centre of the global knowledge economy. As UNESCO reports despite the massive injection of funds for better trained researchers and more sophisticated equipment, China has yet to produce many cutting-edge breakthroughs in technology. "Few research results have been turned into innovative and competitive products and China faces a … deficit in its intellectual property balance of payments. Many Chinese enterprises still depend on foreign sources for core technologies and intellectual property. Just 4.7% of GERD goes on basic research, compared to 84.6% on experimental development" (UNESCO 2016: 50). Japan while continuing as one of the most R&D intensive economies in the world, has relatively reduced investment in information and communication technologies. The Fukushima nuclear plant explosion has shaken the national confidence in science, and the most recent national plan for science and technology put forward three key areas of recovery and reconstruction from the Fukushima disaster, green innovation around renewable energy, and life innovation (UNESCO 2016: 51). Similarly, in the face of growing competition, increasing pollution and demands for sustainability, Korea is pursuing a low carbon, green growth policy, and has allocated seed funds for the creative economy. Having relied on large conglomerates to foster growth in the industrial economy where most private investment in R&D was focused, "The challenge will be for the country to produce its own high-tech start-ups and to foster a creative culture in SMEs. Another challenge will be to turn the regions into hubs for creative industries by providing the right financial infrastructure and management to improve their autonomy" (UNESCO 2016: 51). Turning to a brief analysis of the policy and performance of four of the leading economies of Asia China, India, Japan and Korea, there are great advances to record, but also significant challenges yet to be overcome in terms of broadening and deepening the culture and practice of innovation.

China

The Chinese government injected RMB 4 trillion (US$ 576 billion) into the economy in the post 2008 aftermath of the global financial crisis, targeting investment at airports, motorways and railroads, which combined with rapid urbanisation across the country. McKinsey portrays the Chinese edge in mass innovation as consisting of China's vast and dynamic domestic market offering an edge in customer focused innovation; China's manufacturing eco-system enabling efficiency-driven innovation as the world's largest manufacturer; and accelerated learning for engineering based innovation, facilitating technology transfer in such industries as communications equipment, wind power, and high speed rail (2015: 8).

The Chinese economy has now reached a 'new normal' of slower but steadier growth with GDP increasing less than 7% in 2016 the lowest rate in two decades. Having become the factory of the world, China began to lose this status as higher wages and more stringent environmental regulations made it less competitive than countries with lower wages and less environmental protection. This signalled the urgency of the need to transform China's economic development model from being labour, investment, energy and resource intensive into an economy based on higher technology and innovation (Cao 2016: 621). Though in this transformation the rate of growth has reduced, the GDP per capita has continued to increase exponentially from $7624 in 2008 to $12,609 in 2014 (in constant 2011 PPP$) (World Bank 2015). A renewed commitment to science, technology and innovation has led to outstanding achievements including the Shenzhou space program, and in supercomputing. Major gaps in information and communication technology have been filled, together with advances in energy, environmental protection, advanced manufacturing, and biotechnology. Major leaps forward in medical sciences have included participation in the Human Genome Project, and Human Variome Project, an international effort to catalogue genetic variation throughout the world in order to improve diagnosis and treatment (Cao 2016: 625).

As the efforts continue at building an indigenous innovation capability 'turning China into an innovation-oriented nation,' there is the possibility of China overtaking the United States in the output of scientific publications; in 2005 china produced 66,151 publications and the US 267,521, but by 2014 China produced 256,834 publications and the US 321,846 according to the Web of Science. Yet despite the evident successes, China has experienced challenges in translating science and technology into higher performance in innovation in the domestic economy. Chinese business continues to rely primarily on foreign sources of core technologies, with a deficit of $10 billion in the intellectual property balance of payments composed of royalties and licence fees which the US insists should be much higher (Ghafele and Gilbert 2012). Concerns about the modest level of innovation at the most senior levels of government in China led to a major review and a new *National Medium and Long-term Plan for the Development of Science and Technology* with a series of goals to achieve by 2020 including:

- raising investment in R&D to 2.5% of GDP;
- raising the contribution of technological advances to economic growth to 60%;
- limiting China's dependence on imported technology to no more than 30%.

China is well on the way to achieving these targets, and accompanying them is a series of 16 mega-engineering programs covering advanced manufacturing, transportation, agriculture, environment, energy, ICTs, and space channelling resources to selected areas. This is coinciding with a top-down reform process in the Chinese Academy of Sciences and a national reform of public institutions of health, education, research and culture. The outcome of this comprehensive effort to make the Chinese economy more innovative remains to be seen (Cao 2016: 620). Added to the drive for innovation, is the massive China 'Belt and Road' strategic initiative to build infrastructure aimed to link 65 countries with China from Asia, Europe, and

Africa, intended to stimulate economic growth in its poorer hinterland and utilise excess industrial capacity.

However, as the OECD cautioned and the Chinese government has increasingly recognised the recent path of rapid industrialisation and urbanisation may not be sustainable due to the excessive consumption of energy and raw materials, and the resulting environmental degradation which also leads to damage to human health. Furthermore, there is the growing inequality in China with uneven distribution of the benefits of economic growth across the regions, between urban and rural populations, and between the super-rich and the poor (although there are some signs that this is being checked), and finally the large migration flows and rapid urbanisation has put strains on the social fabric as well as the environment (OECD 2008). China has now to convincingly commit to achieve sustainable development in economic, environmental and social dimensions.

India

With continuous economic growth (at a highly variable rate), the systemic reduction of widespread poverty, improvements in the economy, and a greater flow of both inward and outward investment, India has emerged as an innovative economy becoming the world leader in the export of computer and information services, and the centre of 'frugal' innovation. On the other side of the ledger though is growing inequality, high inflation, and increasing current debt, with the phenomena of jobless growth (Mani 2016: 599). India's economy is dominated by a service sector representing 57% of GDP, with a manufacturing sector only contributing 13% of GDP. The new Modi government in India is attempting to shift the economy towards an East Asian growth model encouraging export-oriented manufacturing. This involved disbanding the Planning Commission which had pursued a series of medium-term government plans for India for over six decades, and replacing this with a National Institute for Transforming India (NITI). India is building capability in high-tech industries including space technology, pharmaceuticals and computer and information technology services. For example, for its maiden voyage to Mars, India developed the Mangalyaan probe at a fraction of the cost of the NASA Maven probe and they arrived within three days of their American rival. India has also participated in the CERN nuclear research program in Switzerland (Mani 2016: 602). Finally India has aspirations to become a global hub for nanotechnology

The Indian government is investing in aircraft design, nanotechnology and green energy sources, using ICT skills to narrow the urban-rural divide, and is encouraging the private sector to commit more resources to R&D with generous incentives. Half of business R&D in India is distributed across just three industries of pharmaceuticals, automotive and IT, and the R&D is concentrated in a handful of large firms in each sector. In pharmaceuticals five firms account for 80% of R&D, in automotive two firms dominate, Tata and Mahindra, and in IT there are three dominant firms of Infosys, Tata Consultancy Services, and Wipro. These industries are heavily concentrated in six Indian states (from a total of 29 states) which account for half of R&D and three quarters of foreign direct investment (Mani 2016: 602). Foreign multinationals are playing an increasing role in innovation in India, as at the same time Indian companies have made major acquisitions overseas and acquired knowledge assets. The industrial base of India is in almost every sense highly concentrated, however in a small way counterbalancing this, India has become a centre of frugal innovation—developing products and processes with the same features as the original, but simpler and costing significantly less to produce. This has proved effective in the health sector as in medical devices, such as the portable electrocardiogram (ECG) machine, and been adopted in a wide range of other sectors including health services and financial services. Characteristics of frugal innovation include:

- most products and services typifying frugal innovation have come from large firms
- manufactured items require dedicated R&D;
- diffuse rates of new products have varied, with some like the Tata micro-car not being accepted by the market;
- frugal innovation does not succeed when key features of products are removed;
- frugal services tend not to involve R&D, simply an innovation in supply chains (Mani 2016: 607).

Japan

The inspiration for innovation in Asia for the second half of the 20th century were the burgeoning consumer electronics, automotive and engineering industries of Japan, which not only dominated world markets (including those of Europe and the United States) in the 1970s and 1980s, but navigated a path for the Asian Tiger economies of South Korea, Taiwan, Singapore and Hong Kong to be followed by the newly industrialised countries of Thailand, Malaysia, Philippines, and Indonesia which the World Bank celebrated in *The East Asian Economic Miracle: Economic Growth and Public Policy* (1993). The unprecedented and durable success of Japanese exports based on price, technology and quality took both Europe and US markets by surprise. In 1960 the US produced 52% of all new cars in the world, and Japan made just 1%. By 1990 Japanese production had soared to 28% of the world total while the US share had reduced to 17%. In consumer electronics the Japanese advantage was greater still with Japanese producers developing successive waves of new consumer products. In January 1992 President Bush (senior) made an ill-fated visit to Tokyo accompanied by the CEOs of GM, Ford and Chrysler, who were by then comprehensively outcompeted by the Japanese automotive industry, to learn more about Japanese management methods (Burstein 1993: 31). The fundamentals of the Japanese system that were lacking in the American economy included high quality basic education and training systems, long term investment horizons, continuous improvement, flexibility and commitment to quality in manufacturing, and national support for critical industries (Burstein 1993: 38). However, the price of the decades of rapid growth of the Japanese economy was immense asset-price inflation and financial engineering with widespread speculation. The bursting of the Japanese financial bubble was well advanced by 1992, and though successive government efforts to revive the economy to its former glory were made a prolonged stasis occurred.

The vigorous strategy of Prime Minister Abe to stimulate the Japanese economy commenced in 2013, included a comprehensive strategy on energy systems, health next-generation infrastructure and regional development, and improving the national innovation system, revised in 2014 to specify cross-cutting technologies to achieve the strategy including information and communication technologies, nanotechnology, and environmental technology. Central to this strategy is the promotion of university-industry collaboration, including a large programme launched to support high-risk, high-impact R&D, entitled *Impulsing Paradigm Change through disruptive Technologies* (ImPACT) (Sato and Arimoto 2016: 645). Strategic innovation is conceived as addressing major socio-economic challenges including infrastructure management, resilient disaster prevention and agriculture. A particular focus in Japan is raising the proportion of women researchers which in 2013 was only 14.6%, the lowest proportion of women researchers of any member of the OECD, and similarly the efforts to enhance the participation of women across the economy, in combatting Japan's ageing demographics. Japan has a greater demographic challenge than any other developed country with a working age population reducing from 86.99 million people in 1997 to 76.2 million in 2017 (Tani 2017).

In the aftermath of the 2011 triple disaster (earthquake, tsunami and nuclear explosion) Japan experienced its first trade deficit since 1980, due partly to a fall in exports and increase in the cost of oil and natural gas imports. This trade deficit has continued due to the weaker competitiveness of Japanese manufacturers, and the legacy of the transfer of Japanese factories overseas. Yet technology exports grew by 53% between 2008 and 2013, with technology imports remaining constant. Meanwhile reshoring of Japanese firms production is occurring due to the depreciation of the yen, and the relative social stability at home together with reliable infrastructure. Japanese industry is attempting to combine its traditional strengths with a future-oriented vision, in fields such as environment, infrastructure, mobility, robotics, together with promoting creative industries such as digital content, online services, tourism and Japanese cuisine looking towards a new landscape for Japanese innovation.

Korea

The commitment to technological progress and developing an educated and skilled workforce in Korea has made it a benchmark for successful economic development with GDP per capita growth from US$ 255 in 1970 to US$ 25,976 in 2013 (Yim and Lee 2016: 661). Following an export-oriented development strategy Korea successfully made the transition from a developing to a developed economy (Dahlman 2009). Yet with competition with Japan and China intensifying, exports slipping, and the increasing demand for green growth, Korea needs to embark on a new developmental model. Successive governments have now targeted low carbon technology and green growth, together with the creative economy, for example between 2008 and 2011 the government invested US$28 billion in the following priority areas:

- Advancement of key industries, such as the automobile, shipping and semi-conductor industries;
- Core technology for the development of new industries;
- Knowledge-based service industries;
- State-driven technology, such as space, defence and nuclear power;
- Issue-driven areas such as new diseases and nanodevices;
- Global issues such as renewable energy and climate change;
- Basic and convergent technology, such as intelligent robots and biochips (Yim and Lee 2016: 662).

In the pursuit of rapid technological progress the Republic of Korea is now investing a higher gross domestic expenditure on R&D of 4.15% than any other country with the exception of Israel (Table 1.6), with some concerns expressed that the government focus on industrial research and innovation needs greater emphasis on basic scientific research. Despite this new emphasis on basic research, industrial production and technology still represented two thirds of GERD in 2013. While the Korean economy is striving to become more creative and entrepreneurial the structure of the economy remains dominated by conglomerates such as Samsung and LG in electronics and Hyundai in vehicles which drive export earnings and account for three-quarters of private sector investment in R&D, a higher share even than before. As the OECD (2014: 16) comments:

"The Korean innovation system is in many respects highly developed. That system has helped to underpin Korea's rapid industrialisation. However, long-standing policy emphases on manufacturing and large firms are today in question. Structural problems such as the relatively weak innovation performance of

Table 1.6 Distribution of GERD/GDP leading economies 2002–2013 (%)

	2002	2013
Israel	4.17	4.21
Republic of Korea	2.27	4.15
Japan	3.12	3.49
Finland	3.26	3.32
USA	2.55	2.81
OECD average	2.15	2.40
China	1.07	2.02

Source Adapted from: UNESCO (2016: 26), OECD (2015) Main science and technology indicators

SMEs, a lagging services sector and limited domestic job creation among the industrial conglomerates have led to a shift in policy priorities. This shift is crystallised in the current government's Creative Economy Strategy. This Strategy entails a far-reaching set of measures aimed at fostering cutting-edge innovation and consolidating a knowledge-based economy increasingly driven by high-value services."

The aspiration remains to transform the Korean regions into hubs for creative industries through providing the right financial infrastructure and management with innovative new products, services and business models (Yim and Lee 2016: 674; OECD 2014).

Australia

Australia is experiencing the profound problems of moving from a very successful resources economy to an emerging knowledge economy. Australia has a dynamic and flexible economy with a high level of human resources and strong research organisations facilitating the rapid take-up of knowledge from around the world. This imported knowledge combined with local knowledge and capability supports a 'fast-user' strategy. There is a high level of public sector R&D and successful niche markets in some advanced manufacturing sectors, telecoms, wine, and application of new technology in knowledge based services. Australia is a world leader in mining and agricultural technology, and with the resources of a large continent has enjoyed a prolonged export boom to Asia of fuel, minerals and agricultural commodities. This has brought with it the 'curse of resources' a two-speed economy with mining growing faster than the rest of the economy resulting in slower growth and less competitiveness in other sectors. As the long boom slows with the coming to completion of China's urbanisation and industrialisation, Australia has to forge a future in newly emerging knowledge industries.

Though Australia has now the record for the longest sustained economic growth of any advanced industrial countries, this was accompanied by a recent fall in productivity growth, and doubts regarding the innovative capacity of the economy (ISA 2016). There is evidence that Australia performs well at knowledge creation ranking 8th out of 36 OECD countries in its contribution to the top 1% of cited papers per million people, and the Australian universities have trended upwards in research metrics and teaching reputation (DOI 2016). However though Australia's research infrastructure, skills and networks have significant outputs and are internationally respected, there is widespread recognition that the transfer of knowledge needs to be improved. Australia is failing to translate its strong research base into commercialisation, and relationships and collaborations between industry and research organisations are not well developed. There are some sectors such as mining, advanced manufacturing, financial services and scientific and technical services in which Australian businesses have high levels of innovation, however many businesses in Australia demonstrate little radical innovation (DOI 2016).

However innovative entrepreneurship is notable in Australia with the Global Entrepreneurship Monitor study estimating Australia's entrepreneurial activity at 13.1% of the adult population, which places it among the highest of the developed economies. In terms of high shares of small business start-ups (less than 50 employees), Australia has a high level of activity with start-ups (less than two years old) contributing 1.44 million full time equivalent jobs between 2006 and 2011. While the innovation system facilitates start-ups, lack of investment funds often limits further growth of these small companies, and there is a need for more targeted equity finance in the innovative entrepreneurial eco-system (OCE 2016). The recent success of Australian enterprise software company Atlassian which listed on the NASDAQ in 2015, and reached a market capitalisation of $7 billion by 2017, has enthused the Australian software community that world class innovation can occur locally.

Schumpeterian Analysis: Leaping Techno-economic Paradigms

The two central theoretical questions addressed in this work concern how certain economies of the Asia Pacific achieved rapid progress in technology and innovation, and secondly how may the economies sustain and advance this progress? These are also very practical questions that confront both governments and business throughout the region. For example, President Xi Jinping speaking on the future of the Chinese economy has reflected on the dangers of becoming caught in the *middle income trap*. This is the slowing of growth as developing economies become trapped between low-wage manufacturers and high-wage innovators because their wages are too high to compete with low-wage exporters and their level of technological capability is too low to allow them to compete with the advanced economies (Lee 2013: 5; World Bank 2010, 2012). The middle income trap has stranded economies, such as Brazil and Argentina, which previously were making good progress at catching up with the advanced economies. *Catch-up* is a process by which a late-developing country narrows the gap in income and technological capability with leading countries. For example, in terms of gross domestic product per capita there was rapid catch-up between Korea and Taiwan and other countries during the period 1960 to 2010. In 1960 the per capita income of Korea and Taiwan was about $150, significantly lower than that of Brazil ($208) or Chile ($550). However after some decades of changing economic fortunes by 2010 GDP per capita in Korea ($20,540) and Taiwan ($18,588) far exceeded Brazil ($10,992) and Chile ($12,639) in constant US$ (Lee 2013: 7–8).

It was Joseph Schumpeter in his work *The Theory of Economic Development* (1934) who first highlighted the dynamic mechanisms of innovation and creative destruction that drives such differences in economic fortunes. Neo-Schumpeterian perspectives on this phenomena of economic catch-up have focused on innovation and technological capabilities as the enabling factors. If the main factor for catch-up in the 1970s and 1980s was capital accumulation, in the later 1980s and 1990s the accumulation of technological capabilities is most relevant. It is the countries that made significant investment in the development of R&D and skill formation that sustained catching up, while those not making this investment fell further behind (Lee 2013: 25; Nelson and Winter 1982). Learning is central to catch-up based on rapid innovation, and Jaffe et al. (1993) suggest technological innovation can be regarded as the exploitation of the available knowledge stock to generate new knowledge. In this way latecomers to innovation in the Asia Pacific have benefited from the flow of knowledge from advanced economies to facilitate more effective local research and innovation.

Neo-Schumpeterian analysis offers concepts of *technological regime* (Nelson and Winter 1982: 258) and *technological paradigm* (Dosi 1982; Clarke and Clegg 2000). The concept of technological regime refers to distinctive innovative processes across technological sectors, and distinguishes science based innovation from cumulative innovation. Breschi et al. (2000) propose four fundamental elements in technological regimes:

- Technological opportunity
- Appropriability of innovations
- Cumulativeness of technological advances
- Properties of the knowledge base.

Technological regime expresses the characteristics of sectors of technology, but can also express the characteristics of the knowledge bases of countries and firms (Lee 2013: 26). This relates to the broader concept of the national system of innovation (Freeman 2008). Lundvall (1992: 2) defines the national system of innovation as the "elements and relationships which interact in the production, diffusion and use of new, and economically useful, knowledge…and are either located within or rooted inside the borders of a nation state." The national innovation system (NIS) refers to the efficiency of a country in establishing a system of learning and innovation, that is the acquisition, creation, diffusion and utilisation of knowledge: how efficiently companies, universities and research laboratories in an economy acquire external knowledge, or create new knowledge, and how this knowledge is diffused and utilised by other institutional actors, "Differences in the NIS are hypothesised to affect the direction and speed of a nation's innovation and eventually lead to different levels of competitiveness between nations" (Lee 2013: 26).

Analysis of innovation and development can proceed at three levels: the national system of innovation; sectoral systems of innovation examining different industries; and at the level of the firm. At each of these levels, different modes of learning and innovation may apply. Two contrasting modes of innovation proposed by Jensen et al. (2007) are the science, technology, innovation (STI) formal mode based on the production and use of codified scientific and technical knowledge; and the doing, using and interacting (DUI) which relies on informal processes of learning and experience-base know-how. Differences in national innovation systems and in modes of innovation impact on the capacity to catch-up of countries and firms. Lee (2013) examines this capacity at the country, sector and firm levels in terms of:

- Technological specialisation—the choice of which technologies or sectors to focus on for catch-up growth;
- Whether latecomers should specialise in short-cycle (emerging) technologies, or in longer cycle technologies; and whether a latecomer will do well to target high-quality (original) patents for catch-up growth;
- The learning and creation of knowledge, whether by indigenous creation and diffusion of knowledge or through reliance on foreign knowledge;
- Choosing between a concentrated growth strategy, or a diversified growth strategy.

The early explanations of the rapid economic growth of the newly industrialised economies (NIEs) concerned the role of government versus markets in catching-up (Chang 1994). A more traditional technology based view of development suggested that the NIEs catch-up with advanced economies by assimilating and adapting obsolete technologies of the advanced countries, consistent with a product life-cycle theory (Vernon 1966). Catching-up is conceived as relative speed in a race along a unidirectional process (Perez and Soete 1988). However, Lee and Lim (2001: 460) suggest another and more promising possibility:

"…In the catching-up process, the latecomer does not simply follow the path of technological development of the advanced countries. They perhaps skip some stages or even create their own distinctive path, which is different from the forerunners. This observation is consistent with the emerging literature on leapfrogging. For example, Perez and Soete (1988) observes that every country is a beginner in terms of the newly emerging techno-economic paradigm, which implies the possibility of leapfrogging by latecomers like NIEs. The idea of leapfrogging is that some late-comers may be able to leap-frog older vintages of technology, bypass heavy investments in previous technology system, and catch-up with advanced countries (Hobday 2005). The increasing tendency toward globalization and development of information technology makes the leapfrogging argument ever more plausible."

Hence the traditionally conceived flight path of the flying geese to become an advanced economy involved treading a long and difficult path of industrial and structural transformation from labour intensive industries (typified by textiles), to non-differentiated scale driven industries (steel, basic chemicals, and heavy machinery), to differentiated assembly based industries (automobiles, electric, electronic goods), and finally to the Schumpeterian R&D intensive industries (specialty chips, biotechnology, and new materials) (Fig. 1.1).

In the 1990s and early 2000s the Asian Newly Industrialised Economies (NIEs) of Singapore, Hong Kong, Taiwan and Republic of Korea were swiftly catching up with Japan in R&D intensive industries, and were stepping up their investment in R&D. The ASEAN-4 countries (Thailand, Malaysia, Indonesia, and the Philippines) were still largely in the factor driven industries and non-differentiated

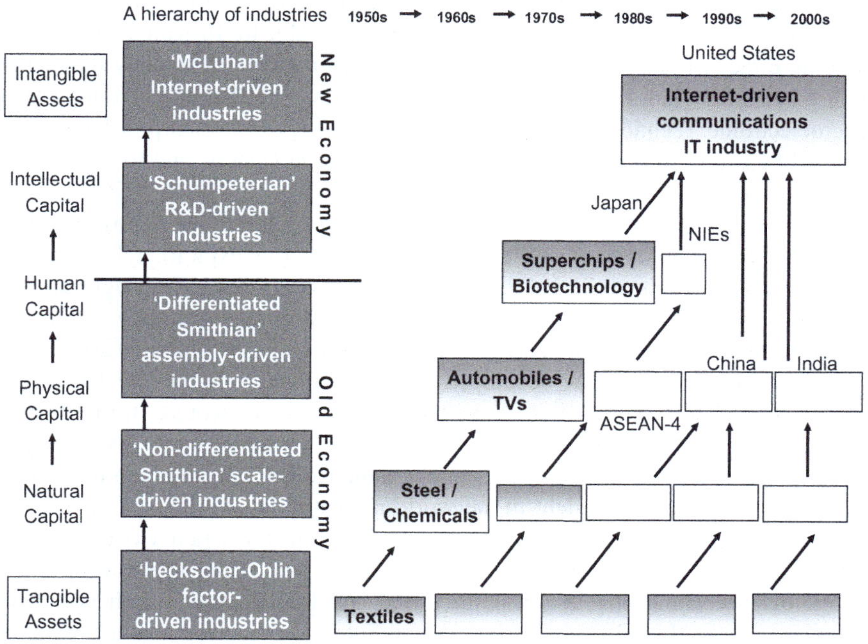

Fig. 1.1 Leaping techno-economic paradigms. Adapted from Ozawa et al. (2001): 'The internet revolution' *Journal of Economic Issues* 35(2): 289–298

scale driven industries, though they entered with some success the labour-intensive, standardized low-end segments of the assembly based differentiated industries of computer chip assembly and low-end consumer electronics. Meanwhile Taiwan and the Republic of Korea have demonstrated their capacity for leap frogging into innovation in high technology industries, and now China and India too have illustrated this ability for rapid catch-up in selected fields of technology. As mentioned earlier Lee and Lim (2001) indicate three different patterns of catch-up:

(a) A path-following catch-up, with latecomers following the same path taken by forerunners;
(b) A stage-skipping catch-up referring to latecomer firms following the path, but skipping some stages and saving time;
(c) A path-creating catch-up which refers to latecomer firms exploring their own path of technological development.

Lee (2013) offers examples of stage skipping and path-creating from the recent experience of Korean industry. When Samsung considered the potential of the memory chip business (dynamic random access memory chips or D-RAM), as a latecomer they would be competing with the established industries of the United States and Japan who were moving from 16 K-bit D-Ram to 64 K-bit D-Ram.

The Korean government advised Samsung to begin with 1-Kbit D-Ram, but private companies had the prerogative of skipping from 1-Kbit to 16-Kbit D-Rams, and entering directly the 64 K-bit D-Ram market. Samsung entered directly the market with 64 K-bit D-Ram memory chips after purchasing the design technology from Microelectronic Technology, and production technology from Sharp in Japan. This enabled Samsung to save time in its catch up with the leaders, and to become the market leader in the 2000s.

Another example of a bold strategy in an emerging industry employing a new generation of technologies is an illustration of path-creating exploiting the paradigm shift, such as analogue to digital technology. Korea could not have caught up with Japan, if Samsung and LG had not focused on digital technology, while the Japanese companies kept with analogue products for a longer time (Lee 2013: 167–169). The Japanese analogue developed high definition TV in the late 1980s, and offered to transfer technologies related to this product to Korean firms. Instead Korean firms developed the leap-frogging digital technology for HD TV through a public-private R&D consortium. This initiated the Korean hegemony in the display industry which remains evident in the world market today.

Such strategic opportunities for technological transformation exist more frequently with technologies with short cycle times, that is the speed with which technologies become obsolete, and the speed and frequency at which new technologies emerge (Lee 2013: 18). Latecomers intent on leapfrogging technologies can target these short cycle technologies as they have not invested heavily in existing technologies as incumbents already in the industry have done. Short cycle technologies are more readily disrupted and latecomers can leverage greater opportunities to advance creating faster localisation of knowledge-creation and the possibility of higher profitability from differentiation.

National Innovation Systems in the Asia-Pacific

Let us now turn to a brief introduction to the contributions to this book, and the theoretical and empirical issues considered. In the first chapter of Part One of this book on National Innovation Systems, Hanusch and Hara compare OECD countries' preparations for the future: out of innovations created in the present the potential of a firm, region or economy are prepared. They examine the 'future preparedness' in terms of the development model of 'Comprehensive Neo-Schumpeterian Economics' (CNSE) based on (a) on the notion of future-orientation penetrating all spheres of socio-economic life in developed as well as in developing countries; (b) on the principle of innovation as the main driving force and the engine of future-orientation and development. Future orientation is characterised on indicators including the real, public and financial sectors of the economy. They suggest that development is a "complex process of evolution and transformation, rather than a simple transition along a steady state growth path" (Castellacci 2004).

This analysis builds on qualitative and quantitative growth factors and processes based on networks and collaborations between firms, governments, universities and research institutions, including cluster models and eco-system models. Hanusch and Hara insist "There exists no continuous growth process ending in a long term equilibrium. Growth is characterized by punctuated equilibria, induced by structural change or socio-economic transformations having their origins in marginal as well as disruptive innovations primarily in the technological field. Technological innovations propelling industry dynamics and economic growth obviously are a major source of economic development. But, technological innovations are not the only driving force, nor can industry development occur in a vacuum. Instead, development is accompanied and influenced by novelty and change shaping also the monetary realms of an economy as well as the public sector." They conclude that there is no general pattern of a useful masterplan in the membership states of the OECD, and that on the contrary diversity to a high degree pictures the reality shown in the data.

In the second chapter in Part One on National Innovation Systems (NIS), Lee and Kim analyze the NIS of East Asia and Latin America, and thereby to show the sources of the divergent economic performance in these groups of countries. This divergence between East Asia and Latin America reflects that these two regions selected different policy priority in knowledge development; the priority was given to technology in East Asia whereas it was given to science in Latin America. The main characteristic of R&D expenditure in Latin America is that universities and public labs are taking up most of the R&D but they are decoupled from the demands from the private sector. The role of Latin America's private sectors remains weak, and the difference in corporate R&D among the East Asian countries and Latin American countries are substantial.

East Asia and Latin America initially imported foreign technologies, but only East Asia has been able to build up its indigenous technological capabilities. One of the reasons for this difference is that in East Asia, the domestic corporate sectors were the main agents of technology imports, whereas the trans-national corporations were the main agents for production in Latin America. R&D investment by TNCs in Latin America was mainly carried out in their home countries, and the TNCs sought to protect their technologies by confining it within the boundary of the TNCs (Hanson 2011: 54). "This resulted in the divergence in the development of indigenous technological capabilities between the two regions. East Asia built up its technological capabilities by investing in its own R&D activities, whereas the Latin American countries were trapped in productive capabilities with few in-house R&D activities."

Emerging new technologies in short cycle fields present better growth prospects, and the possibility of higher profitability associated with less collision with the technologies of advanced countries and the presence of first-mover advantages. This divergence in technological specialization can be considered as one explanation how the Asian countries went beyond the middle income trap situation in the mid-1980s, whereas Latin American countries failed to overcome the trap. "Overall, the emergence of digital technologies replacing analogue technologies seems to have served as a critical window of opportunity for some latecomers, especially Korea over Japan. Digitalization of many products has been undertaken for several decades since the mid-1980s, from the emergence of the digital calculator, followed by watches, fixed line telephones, mobile phones, cameras, and TVs. Digitalization of products and production processes implies lesser disadvantages for the latecomers because the functions and quality of products are determined more by electronic chips and less by skills of the engineers, which is more critical in analogue products." The view of Lee and Kim based on short or long cycle times also differs from the traditional recommendation to focus on trade-based specialization, which is more suitable for low-income countries, because it argues that middle-income countries need to specialize in technological sectors that rely less on existing technologies, and look at the greater opportunities associated with new technologies. It is also complementary to the growth identification and facilitation framework of Justin Lin (2012). "We are suggesting a distinctive policy argument that claims that sustained industrial catch-up requires not only an entrance into mature industries, but also leapfrogging into emerging industries that are new to both the advanced and developing countries."

In an analysis of an evolutionary approach to innovation in the next chapter, Suenaga examines how several countries and firms in the Asia Pacific move from imitating developed countries to generating innovation? Neo-classical economics often assumes that only one production curve exists for the whole economy of a country, when actually there are various production curves depending on the industry, product, and process, and the introduction of a new production curve involves high risk. "Innovative, risk-taking entrepreneurs are required for the introduction of a new production curve, even in developing countries."

With reference to the production capability required to improve productivity, i.e., to shift the production curve upwards, when workers and technicians accumulate production experience, they develop increased expertise, resulting in improved productivity. In production, "learning to learn" (Stiglitz 1987), that is understanding the importance and centrality of learning, is vital. Economies and firms in the Asia Pacific have realized technological changes by engaging not only in simple imitation but also in 'creative imitation' (Kim and Nelson 2000). An example involves adapting technologies to their environments and applying them to other industries.

What is the relationship between innovation and the division of labour? Smith (1776: 9) points out the following three effects of the division of labour: (1) an increase in productivity, (2) saving time, and (3) the invention of machines. Smith's discussion specifically concerns the division of labour in a workshop, however the division of labour between factories or industries also stimulates an increase in productivity and the invention of machines.

The ideas of Smith and Schumpeter appear to contradict one another at first glance: Smith's 'division of labour' and the 'new combinations' which Schumpeter regards as a key factor in economic development. Suenaga inquires whether the main factor involved in economic development is a 'dividing' or a 'combining' one? The views of Smith and Schumpeter are not contradictory he argues but complementary. Specialization in particular processes is made possible by the division of labour, yet the possibility of a new combination is also born during these processes, and this encourages a further division of labour by extending the market. Suenaga (2015) refers to this pattern of economic development as 'Smithian = Schumpeterian development.'

Singapore and Hong Kong are two small highly successful economies in Asia that illustrate very divergent paths of catching up and innovation as Jue Wang reveals in the next chapter in Part One. Singapore and Hong Kong have a similar history: both developed from British colonies and experienced an upgrade of industrial structure from labor intensive industries such as textile and clothing to high tech industries such as electronics and to banking and financial services (Young 1992). The two city states have comparable economic performance and competitiveness and are often placed close to each other in various rankings such as the Global Competitiveness Report (WEF 2017), World Competitiveness Yearbook (IMD 2017), and Global Innovation Index (GII 2016). The GDP per capita in these two economies was almost identical until the 2000s. Singapore's economic growth slowed down in the late 1990s but quickly recovered and surpassed Hong Kong in 2004 and even overtook the US in 2011. With its recent success in finance and other sectors, Singapore is presently ahead of Hong Kong on many indicators.

Although there are many similarities, the differences in the development trajectory of these two cities are clear, the most important distinction is the role of the government. Singapore is noted as a government-made city-state for the high level of government intervention in various aspects of the society (Mok 2005). By contrast, Hong Kong adopts a "positive non-intervention" policy that favors the free economy and minimizes the power of government in influencing the market. The difference is reflected in the innovation policy in these two economies. The Singapore government has actively implemented a series of strategies and allocated substantial funds to promote innovation and entrepreneurship. While a similar set of policies and programs are in place to drive research and innovation in Hong Kong, the scale is much smaller.

The Singapore government is actively involved in the economic development of the nation: since independence in 1965, the state has planned and implemented several economic development strategies, promoting labor-intensive export-oriented manufacturing in the 1960s–1970s, foreign invested high-tech industries in the 1980s, R&D and value-added activities in the 1990s (Wong 2001; Yeung 2000). Through the regulated labor market, taxation and financial incentives, and state-owned enterprises, the state successfully led industrial restructuring (Huff 1995). The strong state and active intervention is regarded as a distinctive feature of the national competitiveness of Singapore (Yeung 2000).

The outstanding economic performance of Singapore and other Newly Industrialized Countries (NICs) in East Asia in the 1980s and 1990s can be attributed to the strong state and active interventionist industrial policy by the governed market theory (Wade 1990), Hong Kong is an exception, with equally successful economic growth but less active industrial policy. State invention in Hong Kong varies in different periods of time. In the 1960s and 1970s, due to the limited financial resources and conservative nature of the state, Hong Kong was regarded as demonstrating laissez-faire capitalism with a non-interventionist economic philosophy and low public expenditure. The features of this system included free trade, no restrictions on imports or currency, low taxes, small government, little state borrowing, regular budget surpluses, no long-term state planning or market intervention (Goodstadt 2005; Sharif 2012).

Beginning in the 1980s, the Hong Kong government adopted a new state intervention strategy that Jue Wang describes as positive non-interventionism—with no resource allocation but responding to industries' with regulations. Public expenditure still remained low. After the change in sovereignty in 1997, the government was under pressure to perform and became more interventionist oriented (Cheung 2000). Hong Kong was perceived to be less successful in technology development than Taiwan and Singapore, and there was a calling for greater government involvement in areas such as science parks, government R&D subsidy and expansion of university engineering research activities (Davies 1996). Several state initiatives to promote industrial development and the economy were announced in this period, although the scope and scale were rather limited compared with other NICs.

In the final Chapter of Part One Clarke, Chelliah and Pattinson offer a comparative survey of the contrasting innovation systems of the Asia Pacific. While Asian economies have achieved rapid industrial progress, as they reach the global technological frontier they need to develop new institutional capabilities for sustaining international competitiveness. Foundational institutions including education, research, law and finance require coordination around coherent national innovation systems to sustain commitment to innovative products and processes. Technological innovation is more likely to succeed "when the elements of the broader environment surrounding firm's activities are well articulated into a system, than in situations where each element works largely in isolation…The overall innovation performance of an economy depends not so much on how specific formal institutions (firms, research institutes, universities) perform, but on how they interact with each other as elements of a collective system of knowledge creation and use, and on their interplay with social institutions (such as value, norms and legal frameworks)" (Dodgson 2009: 592). The national innovation system essentially facilitates how knowledge is generated and accumulated in the economy to serve as the catalyst and fuel for innovation (Yim and Nath 2005).

National innovation systems evolve over time with institutional development supporting the development of capabilities to match the level of technology and industry. Figure 1.2 illustrates the historical strategic trajectory of upgrading skills and innovation system development. Beginning in Asia in the 1950s with a focus on building the basic assembly capabilities, there is a progression through to the manufacture of components and mass consumer goods. An important stage is the design and manufacture of original equipment (OEM), often intended for local markets. Achieving global positioning with products that have been designed and manufactured by Asia firms followed (ODM), and now Japan's Toyota is joined for example by Korea's Samsung and China's Huawei with world leading own brands

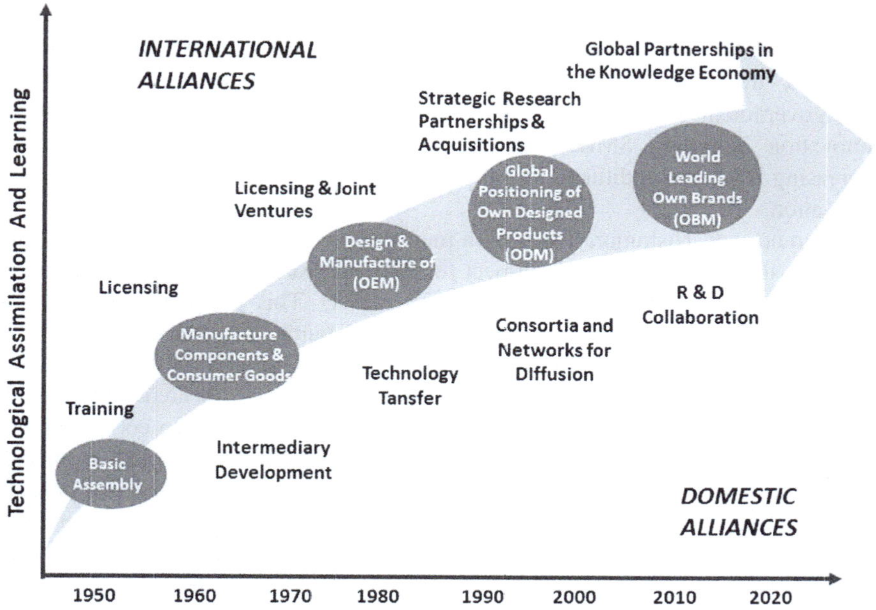

Fig. 1.2 Strategic trajectory for upgrading skills and innovation system development. *Source* Dodgson et al. 2008), Hobday (2005), Gereffi (1999)

(OBM). Throughout this progression, it is important to build national innovation systems that can promote the development of intermediary producers, technology transfer, and help build production networks and R&D collaboration. As Asian firms internationalise the acquisition of advanced training, the award of licences, formation of joint ventures, development of strategic alliances, lead ultimately to key overseas acquisitions, and leadership in global partnerships. The significance of the national innovation systems is in not only helping to create this advance of capabilities, but in diffusing the capabilities in the economy (Dodgson 2009: 595).

Diverse Modes of Innovation in the Asia-Pacific

The different modes of innovation are examined in Part Two of the book, beginning with the chapter of Okamuro and Nishimura on the performance of R&D consortia. Collaborative R&D projects among private firms, universities, and public research institutes attract increasing attention as an effective means of promoting innovation (Hemmert et al. 2014). Especially for SMEs, such collaboration provides important opportunities to access and obtain advanced scientific knowledge generated at universities and public research institutes (Motohashi 2005). Yet efficient governance of R&D consortia is a difficult task because they include academic and business partners that possess different interests and incentives, which in extremes can lead to free-riding and opportunistic behaviour. The governance of R&D consortia matters for innovation performance (Mora-Valentin et al. 2004). The government support for R&D consortia for example in order to promote innovation involving SMEs may impact on project performance directly by increasing R&D expenditures, but also indirectly through project monitoring and evaluation.

Okamuro and Nishimura focus on a major support program for R&D consortia in Japan, the Consortium R&D Project for Regional Revitalization (CRDP) by the Ministry of Economy, Trade and Industry (METI). This program aims at commercializing scientific seeds of universities and public research institutes. The consortiums to be supported have to include at least one private firm and a university. The government (METI) concludes a commissioned research contract with the project management organization, which in turn is expected to coordinate the consortia partly by concluding joint research contracts with all project members. METI selects R&D consortia to be financially supported based on project proposals and evaluates the performance of subsidized projects after the first year (midterm evaluation) and the second year (final evaluation). Various follow-up supports may be offered to several projects even after the funding period. In this way project leadership and public monitoring may be important for project performance, as internal and external disciplines.

Few studies of R&D consortia have empirically addressed the effect of project governance. Specifically, the effect of project monitoring by the government has scarcely been investigated. The literature of innovation management has long recognized the role of innovation champions in private R&D (e.g. Chakrabarti 1974), but the role of project leadership in R&D consortia remains poorly explored. Focusing on the effects of project leadership and public monitoring, this chapter empirically examines the determinants of project performance of publicly funded R&D consortia in Japan using original survey data, to investigate the contribution of project leadership and public monitoring to generating innovation.

In the following chapter Hu, Peng and Lijing examine the relationship of patents to technology innovation. The development of patents is conventionally regarded widely as a significant part of the innovation process in many modes of innovation. Patents are often used as an indicator of technology innovation, and China's patenting surge raises the question whether China has become as innovative as her patent numbers suggest? If patents measure innovation output, a measure of inputs to the innovation process is R&D expenditures. China's R&D spending has more than kept pace with the rapid growth of GDP in China. R&D as a share of GDP increased from 1.4 in 2007 to 1.8% in 2011, which was not far from the OECD average. However, patent numbers have been growing even faster than the increase in R&D expenditure. The number of invention patents granted to resident, non-individual applicants per 10 million dollars of R&D expenditure (in 2011 purchasing power parity prices) was 3 for China and 2 for the U.S. in 2007. In four years, the ratio for China rose to 6.3, and that for the U.S. increased more modestly to 2.4. While not impossible, it would seem unlikely that this large and widening disparity in patents to R&D ratio can be explained by the difference in the productivity of R&D of the two countries.

The objective of this chapter is to explore both innovation and non-innovation-related explanations of China's patenting surge and to discuss their policy implications. "The conventional role of patents lies in preventing copying and pre-empting unauthorized entry, the need for which rises when new technologies are created, thus implying a tight connection between technology innovation and patenting." Recent experience in developed countries, particularly the U.S., indicates that applying for patents has also been driven by firms' concerns that an unfavorable court ruling over the ownership of intellectual property could inflict significant financial damages on them. This has led firms to build up a war chest of patents that might increase their bargaining power in anticipation of such intellectual property disputes. The propensity to apply for patents can increase, when the underlying rate of technology innovation has not significantly, but when developments in legal institutions and public policy change the firms' perception of the need for such strategic maneuvers.

The comparison of resident patent applications filed at national patent offices is subject to a home bias. For large countries, the domestic market represents the largest opportunity for inventors to realize the returns to their inventions, and thus the inventors tend to seek out patents in their home country first. Hu, Peng and Lijing focus on the comparison between China, Japan and South Korea. China's USPTO patent applications, although growing at a faster rate, are still outnumbered by those of Japan and South Korea.

Hu (2010) investigated two hypotheses in explaining the foreign patenting surge in China: market covering and competitive threat. With foreign companies more deeply engaged with the Chinese economy, returns from protecting their intellectual property in China have increased. As domestic Chinese firms' ability to imitate foreign technology gains strength and competition between foreign firms intensifies in the Chinese market, such competitive threat heightens the urgency to protect intellectual property. Using a database that comprises SIPO and USPTO patents, he found support for the competitive threat hypothesis. Li (2012) investigated the impact of Chinese government's patent subsidy programs on China's patenting surge, using province-level aggregate data for the period from the mid 1990s to 2007. His results showed that patent applications increased after a province launched a patent application fees subsidy program.

Investigating the rapid growth of Chinese patent applications at the USPTO, Branstetter et al. (2015) found that much of the surge of Chinese patenting in the U.S. has been driven by multinational corporations' R&D activity in China, rather than indigenous Chinese firms' inventions. China's extraordinary patenting ascent in recent years has taken place against a backdrop of increasing technological sophistication of Chinese firms and Chinese government proactively promoting the acquisition of intellectual property. Chinese firms have been aggressively applying for patents as a result of their newly acquired capability to invent new technologies and their response to the government incentives and other strategic considerations.

While the former is most likely to be a result of conscious R&D effort, the latter would have increased the propensity to patent independent of technology innovation.

Hu, Peng and Lijing conclude the Chinese patenting surge adds to the on-going debate and discussion of the role of the patent system in technology innovation, and in economic development in general. What kind of patent system can best serve the development needs of China deserves greater attention of academics and policy makers than it currently receives. In particular, a greater appreciation of the less innocuous effect of rapidly growing patent right claims, especially those that could erect barriers for future technology innovation, is needed.

Innovation is increasingly delivered through strategic alliances and partnerships, and collaboration is growing between firms within and outside the Asia Pacific region. Schweitzer in a chapter on contracting and innovation culture in alliances suggests how characteristics of network capitalism can be interpreted as indicators of joint innovation culture including:

- the nature of contractual agreements between partners;
- the alignment of their innovation objectives;
- the ambiguity inherent in their mutual contributions to the partnership.

Innovation partnerships generally may result to be bureaucratic, market, clan, or adhocracy, Schweitzer discusses how in an Asia Pacific context, innovation partnerships are limited by the extent of codification and diffusion of information and the social embeddedness of economic transactions. He highlights how the understanding of innovation in Schumpeters' (1934) term incorporates five types of activity:

- new production methods
- new sources of supply
- the creation of new products
- the capitalisation of new markets
- and organising business in new ways.

This latter type especially contains new methods of creating value through collaborative innovation including through partnerships, strategic alliances, joint ventures, and technology/patent relationships that allow firms combining own competencies with those of other firms (Gudergan and Schweitzer 2008). Examples in Asia Pacific include firms such as Nissan, Samsung or the Dongfeng Motor Group and outside the region companies like SEEK, Apple, Cisco, HP, Dell, Procter and Gamble and many others that have successfully collaborated (Tapscott and Williams 2008).

Specific alliances are often described very broadly, so that it is nearly impossible to differentiate them from other types of inter-firm relationships and economic transactions like for example supplier relationships. As "hybrid" organizational forms they are a way to manage exchanges or relationships that are more complex than a standard market exchange since they involve purposive linkages (Kale et al. 2000), exchange, sharing or co-development (Gulati 1995), yet they do not merit full integration (Gulati 1998; Williamson 1991; Zenger and Hesterly 1997). Hence, we see innovation alliances as a unique form of organization, which in its simplest form can be defined as a group of stakeholders intentionally organized to accomplish an overall, common innovation goal, which is explicit or implicit, carefully considered and established through a strategic planning process.

Schweitzer's focus is on examining the alliance contractual nature and culture as key aspects for effectively managing innovation partnerships in the Asia Pacific context, developing a conceptual framework that is embedded in economic perspectives of network capitalism (Boisot and Child 1996; Tung and Worm 2001), organizational control theory (Ouchi 1980) and theoretical developments on organizational culture (Cameron and Quinn 2011) and alliance contracts and contractual complexity (Reuer et al. 2006). The objective is to add to the academic dialogue about contractual aspects and culture within Asia Pacific innovation alliances.

In the following chapter in their analysis of the technological innovation systems and information technology industry sustainability, Liu and Gao offer a comparative study of China's telecommunications industry. The international technology industry has experienced an accelerated growth curve as late-coming countries join the wave of technology innovation, transforming from imitating the leaders to promoting their own indigenous technology innovations, particularly South Korea and China. For example, in China with wireless mobile technology since the 2008 indigenous 3G mobile technology—TD-SCDMA was adopted, the telecommunications industry has expanded rapidly. With sustained indigenous technology innovation, Chinese companies such as Huawei and ZTE, have grown into important players in the global market, with the sustainability of the Chinese industry considerably improved. Liu and Gao define here sustainability here in an operational sense as "the capacity to endure." Their focus is upon the technological innovation system as a key driver of socio-technical change, examining the relationship between technology innovation, sustainable socio-technical change and industry sustainability.

Liu and Gao investigate the theoretical frameworks on socio-technical change and highlight the system perspective developed by Leavitt and Bass (1964) and applied by Lyytinen and Newman (2008), which divides the relevant organisational field into four interacting and aligned components—task, structure, actor and technology (Fig. 1.3) each of these components is interconnected, and the dynamic between them can be both incremental and punctuated. "According to this model, sustainable socio-technical change then could be viewed as persistent technological change achievement (tasks) with sustained change of the dynamic social (people and structure) and technical environment (technology)".

At the level of the technological innovation system according to Carlsson et al. (2002) this is constituted by three elements—actors, relationships and institutions. Actors include organisations along the value chain, universities and research institutions, as well as public agencies, venture capital, and industrial alliance. Both formal and informal relationships between these actors are significant, such as problem-solving networks, buyer-supplier networks, and research networks.

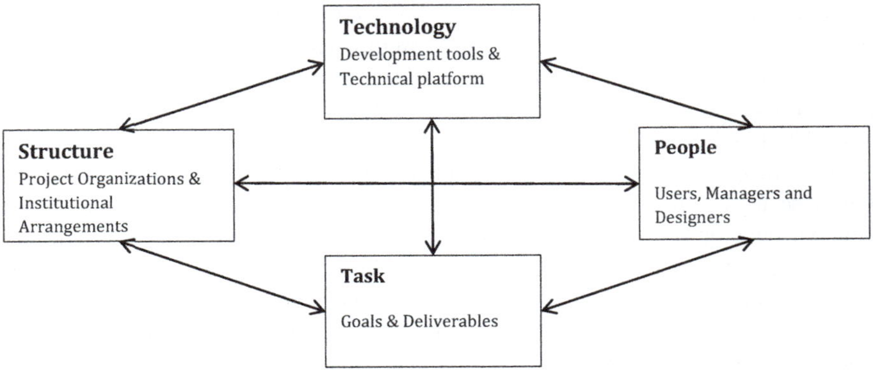

Fig. 1.3 Model of socio-technical change (adopted from Lyytinen and Newman 2008). *Source* Adapted from Lyytinen and Newman (2008)

Finally, institutions such as culture, norms, laws, regulations and routines need to be identified as the 'rules of the game.' In their chapter Liu and Gao examine how the technological innovation system by impacting socio-technical change can influence the sustainability of industry. Their analysis of technology innovation in China's telecommunications industry provides a rich explanation of how new technology is developed and diffused.

In their analysis of the Structures and Strategies of Chinese Companies in Key Enabling and Advanced Manufacturing Technologies, Frietsch and Neuhauser suggest "Without any doubt the most dynamic country of the past decade in terms of its economic development and its science and innovation system is China." Responding to the competitive technological challenge of China, and also the USA, Japan and South Korea, the European Union has chartered a strategic path to becoming the Innovation Union. Key enabling technologies (KETs) to be focused upon were identified in the seventh framework programme (FP7) of the European Union, comprising:

- nanotechnology
- photonics
- industrial biotechnology
- advanced materials and
- micro- and nano-electronics.

Supporting these KETs are Advanced Manufacturing Technologies (AMTs), process technologies including production apparatus, equipment and procedures for the manufacture of specific materials and components. Frietsch and Neuhauser examine where Chinese companies are in terms of competitiveness in these Key Enabling Technologies compared to Europe, asking where Chinese innovation is occurring, and which technology markets are they addressing?

Examining the international share of patent applications in Key Enabling Technologies they indicate that the USA has a steep decline from more than 35% of the total in 2002, to 23% in 2012. Japan increased its share to 30% in recent years overtaking the USA in 2007, and Germany ranks third with 15% in 2009, but some decline since. In contrast there was a surge in Chinese patent applications to 7% in 2012, and Korean applications also increased between 2007 and 2010 to just below the Chinese rate. However there is a difference in focus between the countries: "Further differentiating the patent applications by technological subfields reveals the Japanese focus on microelectronics, photonics and advanced materials, while the USA is strong in industrial biotechnology and nanotechnology. Germany has a strong position in AMT, as do France and the UK. China focuses on photonics and microelectronics at the transnational level, which puts it in direct competition with Japan." While China may not be ready for international competition in many technological fields, with the exception of microelectronics and photonics, they can focus on their huge national market where they are in competition with Japan and the USA. China will enter the international market in years to come with the considerable experience gained in their domestic market.

Organisational and Human Dimensions of Innovation

In Part Three of the book the organisational and human dimensions of innovation in the Asia Pacific are examined, beginning with Clarke and Gholamshahi's analysis of the significance of human capital for the development of knowledge-based economies. In the OECD countries, more than half of GDP is accounted for by knowledge-based industries, including the main producers of high-technology goods, high and medium technology manufacturing, and knowledge intensive services such as finance, insurance, business, communication and social services. This is manifest in the rising human capital levels of the population in OECD countries as measured in educational attainment, and in the increased demand for highly educated and highly skilled workers.

The challenge for the Asia Pacific is to develop the human, social and institutional capital necessary for successfully competing in the knowledge economy. The *Forum for the Future* (2016) suggests a five capitals model of human capital, social capital, finance capital, manufacturing capital and natural capital. Defining human capital as people's health and well-being, knowledge, skills and motivation, and defining social capital as the institutions which sustain and develop human capital in partnership with others for example families, communities, businesses, unions, schools and voluntary organizations including the values and behaviours that allow these social forms to operate). Human capital is one of these five interdependent forms of capital, and is not a separate, substitutable item in itself (that is human capital works with and complements other forms of capital). Human and social capital become ever more critical as the knowledge economy progresses. Hoff and Stiglitz insist, "Development is no longer seen primarily as a process of capital accumulation but rather as a process of organizational change" (2001: 389). The Asian Development Bank in a report on *Moving Towards Knowledge-Based*

Economies (2007) suggests a new a new paradigm for economic development "It is even envisaged that knowledge can eventually become a means of mass production —similar to manual labour in the industrial economy—once web-based information and communication technologies (ICTs) have reached worldwide penetration levels, allowing individuals to work and provide routine knowledge in a virtually networked (global) environment" (ADB 2007: ix).

However the development of human capital involves an interplay of supportive institutions, endowments and policies. In terms of the educational component of human and social advance, many developing countries have cultures that place a very high value on educational attainment (though in some cultures this commitment is heavily gender biased). Education is of central importance in many of the cultures of Asia, for example the desire for learning, and the belief in personal development through education is more profound in Chinese culture than in the West. The Chinese mode of learning has an ancient lineage and involves a classical approach to literature and science, but traditionally is accompanied by a pedagogy of rote learning of codified knowledge, an approach that will scarcely equip China for effective participation in a rapidly transforming global economy. Recognising this, the government proposed a change in the mission of the Chinese universities from 'the cultivation of knowledge' to the 'cultivation of talents and creativity' (Clarke 1999). Yet the rhetoric of policy may not be matched by the rigour of practice in China. In contrast India with a strong emphasis on mathematics and technical skills in its educational system is in some ways better prepared for a knowledge based economy. However it is important to recognise the significance of human capital development in human terms not simply economic terms, as Sen argues we should evaluate development in terms of "the expansion of the 'capabilities' of people to lead the kind of lives they value—and have reason to value."

The development on innovation across a very wide canvas is portrayed in the final chapter of the book by Michael Lester in The Creation and Disruption of Innovation? The disruptive impact of new digital networked technologies upon the transformation of enterprises and industries extends to a disruption of the processes of innovation itself, encompassing the nature of innovation concepts, theory, research and practice. This suggests we need to rethink our ideas on innovation as we enter what has been described as the second machine-age of big data, super computers and broadband communication (Brynjolfsson and McAfee 2014). The chapter highlights the disruption of conventional wisdom on innovation processes examining the new wave of entrepreneurial start-ups in the digital age. Unprecedented opportunities exist it is claimed in the rapid expansion of creative innovation and entrepreneurship with a social as well as economic purpose. New product technology platforms and open source software have reduced the technological barriers and risks to product innovation. The evolution of big data combined with powerful data algorithms creates the capacity to discern patterns in complexity integral to the creation of new knowledge. Big data tools are being applied across all scientific disciplines and industries and businesses.

The institutional foundations of this innovation and growth are examined and the importance of inclusive and open institutions stressed for accelerating innovation, conceiving of innovation as the knowledge-based outcome of complex linkages and interactions between actors and institutions including universities, businesses and government (Freeman 1995). This suggests a systems approach to the wide institutional relationships including education, taxation, law and other institutions including governments in shaping the markets of the future.

Digital transformation is also impacting established industries most notably the growing finance sector where derivative products of complex quantitative construction, and automated trading with high frequency algorithms is changing the nature of the industry. Processes of disintermediation and consolidation of industries are occurring simultaneously, for example as Amazon has restructured and consolidated large parts of the retail industry in the United States. The wider impact of increasing returns to scale are illustrated with reference to the Beijing Genomics Institute, the world's largest genetic research centre which now produces a quarter of the world's genomic data acting as a universal reference library, made viable by the rapidly falling costs of mapping the human genome.

The importance of an innovation focus and culture in enterprises rather than simply investment in research and development is stressed. This is part of open innovation with increasing collaboration both within firms and with external networks, using these relationships to leverage resources. Research collaboration is reinforced with standards, alliances and consortia. The development of innovation districts offer opportunities for encounters between inventors of knowledge, entrepreneurs who commercialise knowledge, and institutions that facilitate this process.

The perennial question remains 'who will win the innovation race' and it appears possible that innovation may now prove a new source of competitive advantage for China, Korea and other Asian economies, in the way in which Japan led innovation in key sectors in earlier decades. China has made great strides in building science and technological capabilities, and is on track to becoming the world's top R&D spending country by 2019, though there remain some serious doubts regarding the institutional openness of the Chinese economy and society, without which nurturing a culture of creativity will be much more difficult.

New Digital Frontiers of Innovation in the Asia Pacific

Looking to the future, as the innovative economies of the Asia Pacific continue to grow rapidly, they are becoming more integrated into the global economy. As substantial inbound foreign direct investment into the region continues, outbound foreign direct investment from the Asia Pacific has become significant, as China and India have followed Japan into making major investments in mature western markets. Meanwhile complex international production and value chains have become centred in the Asia Pacific including for the most sophisticated information and communication products (while control of the most valuable activities including finance, design, and marketing remain firmly based in the multinationals headquarters in the West) (Gerreffi et al. 2005; Clarke and Boersma 2017). But new digital frontiers of innovation now are being actively negotiated in the Asia Pacific. For example, under its RIE2020 policy, Singapore is organizing its R&D investments into four thematic domains that reflect major national challenges and economic opportunities: Advanced Manufacturing and Engineering; Health and Biomedical Sciences; Urban Solutions and Sustainability; and Services and Digital Economy (GII Report 2016: 139).

Successive Kondratieff long waves of sustained innovation and economic growth have been driven by general purpose technology, such as steam power, oil, motor vehicles, and plastics. The development of information and communication technologies with the development of microprocessors has driven the latest wave since the late 1960s delivering the information society. With the speeding up of technological progress there are multiple candidates for the central driver of the next wave of innovation including mobile telephony, the Internet, nanotechnology and bioengineering, however at the centre of these technological advances has been the innovations in telecommunications, computing and broadcasting encompassed in broadband technology. Broadband speeds and performance/price ratio are now doubling every 12 to 15 months, following Moore's Law. The rapid trajectory of broadband will deliver devices and services yet unimaginable. In several Asian economies, this inflection point is already being reached. Rather than playing catch-up, Asian economies have been setting the pace in the development of both fixed and mobile broadband networks. Korea proved an early leader in the deployment of fixed broadband, and Japan led in the early stages of mobile broadband deployment. China pioneered Internet Protocol Television, and China now has the largest base of broadband users, while India has deployed broadband in support of its growing software outsourcing industry (Kelly 2009).

The new models of business enterprise feasible with broadband technology promise a new industrial revolution. Emerging digital business eco-systems disrupt traditional value chains. McKinsey suggests three types of eco-system emerging for businesses with different sources of value creation and competition:

- *Linear value chains*
  Linear value chains dominated for most of the 20th century, comprising value adding steps with the goal of producing and selling products, most notably with automotive assembly.
- *Horizontal platforms*
  Horizontal platforms gained prominence due to the rise of personal computing and the Internet, cutting across value chains. Companies with horizontal platforms own hard assets and sophisticated architecture, with value added software and technology stacks.
- *Any-to-Any Platforms*
  Any-to any platforms have emerged recently such as Uber and Airbnb which operate based on existing platforms, but are themselves asset-light while providing valuable services internationally (Greenberg et al. 2017).

The transcendence of new business eco-systems with their distinctive business models is nowhere clearer than in the domination of the US stock exchanges by platform-oriented companies: in March 2017 Apple ($732 billon) Alphabet (Google) ($581 billion) Microsoft ($497 billion), Amazon ($403 billion), and Facebook ($396 billion) claimed five of the six largest corporations by market capitalisation (Greenberg et al. 2017). This dramatic shift towards investing in platform companies is already occurring in the Asia Pacific with Alibaba (listed on the New York Stock Exchange reaching a market capitalisation of $278 billion in 2017, and Tencent reaching a market capitalisation of $277 billion. The digital eco-systems of Alibaba and Tencent are larger than Amazon's, and are advancing digital payments systems and fintech applications including WeChat and Alipay that are among the world's largest and most sophisticated digital payment systems which appear destined to replace major international financial institutions (Zapron and Meertens 2017).

The transformation to a digital world is accelerating rapidly, with the exponential increase in data flows internationally far exceeding any increase in international trade. Online connectivity is becoming universal with estimates of 26 billion connected devices in the world by 2020 providing the infrastructure for the Internet of Things (Greenberg et al. 2017). This compounding connectivity combines to promote further innovation and connection Arthur (2009). In Germany the confluence of these multiple trends has come to be known as *Industry 4.0*. That is as robotics, 3D printing, data analytics, the Internet of Things, and digital fabrication are joined together, they integrate the physical and virtual worlds in productive endeavor:

"The term *Industry 4.0* refers to the combination of several major innovations in digital technology, all coming to maturity right now, all poised to transform the energy and manufacturing sectors. These technologies include advanced robotics and artificial intelligence; sophisticated sensors; cloud computing; the Internet of Things; data capture and analytics; digital fabrication (including 3D printing); software-as-a-service and other new marketing models; smartphones and other mobile devices; platforms that use algorithms to direct motor vehicles (including navigation tools, ride-sharing apps, delivery and ride services, and autonomous vehicles); and the embedding of all these elements in an interoperable global value chain, shared by many companies from many countries. These technologies are often thought of separately. But when they are joined together, they integrate the physical and virtual worlds. This change enables a powerful new way of organizing global operations: bringing the fungibility and speed of software to large-scale machine production. Under the *Industry 4.0* model, product design and development take place in simulated laboratories and utilize digital fabrication models. The products themselves take tangible form only after most of the design and engineering problems have been worked out. The networks of machinery that have engendered industrial society become hyper-aware systems of highly flexible technology, responding rapidly not just to human commands but to their own perceptions and self-direction" (Geissbauer et al. 2016; PWC 2016).

The Internet and the open science movement have provided a platform for the sharing of information and collaboration internationally. "This growth in interconnectedness, information-sharing and data-reuse has helped to develop a modern approach to science... The focus of scientific discovery has shifted from basic research to 'relevant' or big science, in order to solve pressing developmental challenges." (Neupane 2016: 6). Sharing data across web-based platforms enables the global scientific and innovation community to build on raw data sets through collaboration, for example in the big data set generated for climate change projections developed utilising global scale models, employing large datasets compiled in different parts of the world to focus on local problems (Cooney 2012). Sharing metadata in virtual knowledge banks enables local projection of weather patterns and the cultivation of crops for particular climatic conditions. Utilising metadata, computer networks and online collaboration can help the focus on "the bigger picture and how research can be applied to address challenges that could ultimately threaten human existence, such as global pandemics, water, food and energy insecurity or climate change" (Neupane 2016: 6).

In this context the exercise of artificial intelligence becomes viable and necessary. Artificial Intelligence (AI) is a science and a set of computational technologies that are inspired by—but operate differently from the ways people use their nervous systems and bodies to sense, learn, reason, and take action. While the rate of progress in AI has proved unpredictable, there have been significant advances in recent years. "Once a mostly academic area of study, twenty-first century AI enables a constellation of mainstream technologies that are having a substantial impact on everyday lives. Computer vision and AI planning, for example, drive the video games that are now a bigger entertainment industry than Hollywood. Deep learning, a form of machine learning based on layered representations of variables referred to as neural networks, has made speech-understanding practical on our phones and in our kitchens, and its algorithms can be applied widely to an array of applications that rely on pattern recognition. Natural Language Processing (NLP) and knowledge representation and reasoning have enabled a machine to beat the Jeopardy champion and are bringing new power to Web searches" (Stanford 2016a: 5).

As the Stanford University study suggests presently AI is changing people's daily lives, in ways that improve human health, safety, and productivity. We have to find how to deploy AI-based technologies in ways that promote democratic values such as freedom, equality, and transparency, for example:

- Transportation, where a few key technologies have catalyzed the widespread adoption of AI. Autonomous transportation will soon be commonplace and, as most people's first experience with physically embodied AI systems, will strongly influence the public's perception of AI, as cars become better drivers than people
- Improvements in safe and reliable hardware will spur innovation over the next fifteen years. Similarly, Home/Service Robots, will be used in homes, primarily in the form of vacuum cleaners.

- In Healthcare there has been a forward leap in collecting useful data from personal monitoring devices and mobile apps, from electronic health records (EHR) in clinical settings and, to a lesser extent, from surgical robots designed to assist with medical procedures and service robots supporting hospital operations (Stanford 2016a: 6–7, b).

While impressive, these technologies are designed for particular tasks. Each application typically requires years of specialized research. In similarly targeted software applications, substantial increases in the future uses of AI technologies, including self-driving cars, healthcare diagnostics and targeted treatments, and physical assistance for elder care will be possible. AI and robotics may also be applied in industries such as agriculture, food processing, and factories (Stanford 2016a, b).

Innovation for Sustainability

In negotiating the frontiers of innovation there will be a need to commit to sustainable directions in environmental and social terms. The imperative for innovation to be sustainable will be increasingly recognised. Achieving global sustainability environmentally and socially will be the greatest inspiration for innovation. At present the total population of Asian countries constitutes approximately 55% of the world's population and the total gross domestic product of Asia reflects over 32% of the world's total GDP (Eurostat 2014). The economic growth of emerging economies in Asia is rapidly increasing and has attracted vast manufacturing facilities of multinational companies. A result of this massive industrial development is that Asian countries' environmental burden is high and Asian countries' CO_2 emissions from fuel combustion constitute 67% of the world's CO_2 emissions (IEA 2013). The widespread and committed implementation of eco-innovation in Asian countries will contribute to achieving global sustainable development as well as green growth (Jang et al. 2015: 12587). This is necessary to maintain the ecology of the planet which provides for all forms of life.

"The Earth's natural capital yields an annual dividend of resources that form the bedrock of the human economy and the life support system for the planet's inhabitants. However, as the world's population grows, its cumulative consumption is increasingly biting into that productive capital" (Hackmann and Boulton 2016: 12). The impact of human activity is transmitted globally through the oceans, atmosphere, and economy. Conversely these global systems have a local impact that varies according to geography in a complex relationship between social and biological and geophysical processes that have reconfigured the ecology of the world. "On account of multiple interdependences and non-linear, chaotic relationships that unfold differently depending on context, this coupling means that attempts to address a problem affecting one aspect of this ecology necessarily have implications for others" (Hackmann and Boulton 2016: 12). This presents a central challenge to decouple economic growth from any further damaging environmental impact. It is possible to achieve this with the emergence of new renewable forms of energy and other sustainable technologies.

Successive United Nations Conferences climaxing in the COP 21 agreement in Paris in 2015 have committed to sustainable development, which was originally defined as "A process of change in which the exploitation of resources, the direction of investments, the orientation of technological development, and institutional change are all in harmony and enhance both current and future potential to meet human needs and aspirations" (WCED 1987).

While helping to alleviate more than four hundred million people from poverty, the Chinese construction and industry boom badly damaged the environment (UNESCO 2015: 621). Outdoor air pollution alone contributed to 1.2 million premature deaths in China in 2010, nearly 40% of the world total (Lozano et al. 2012). McKinsey highlights that China's leading cities have built vast potential innovative capacity but have not improved the quality of life factors that attract top talent, substantially lagging global peers on lifestyle metrics, for example air quality in Beijing has an atmospheric pollutant count of 83 (of particulates smaller than 2.5 micrometers), and Shanghai 52, presenting respiratory health hazards to the population, while Silicon Valley is at 10 and Boston at 6 (McKinsey 2015: 117).

Policies are beginning to be introduced across Asia Pacific countries for a substantial development of innovation based on firm ecological principles (Jang et al. 2015). The advancing phenomena of eco-innovation may be defined as "All efforts from relevant actors that introduce, develop, and apply new ideas, behaviours, products and processes and contribute to reducing environmental burdens or ecologically specified sustainability targets" (Rennings 2000). Eco-innovation is a broad concept, comprising:

- innovation in pollution control (new, better, or cheaper abatement technology);
- green products;
- cleaner process technologies;
- green energy technology and transport technologies, and
- waste reduction and handling techniques (Kemp and Pontoglio 2011).

Eco-innovation creates and develops extensive new business opportunities and benefits by preventing or reducing the negative impacts of fossil fuels or other toxic emissions or pollution, or optimizing the use of natural resources. Eco-innovation involves the application of environmental technologies to operationalise the concepts of eco-efficiency and eco-industry (Sarkar 2013). At the beginning eco-innovation focused mainly on production and processes, but has expanded considerably to include management systems, creating new markets, organizations, institutions and social eco-innovation (Charter and Clark 2007; OECD 2009; EIO 2015) (Table 1.7).

As discussed by Horbach (2008) the determinants of the adoption of eco-innovation include supply, demand and policy influences. The supply side is composed of the requisite technological capabilities for eco-innovation, and the possibilities for resolving appropriation and market characteristics. Since

Table 1.7 Determinants of eco-innovation

Elements contents	
Supply	Technological capabilities (knowledge capacities)
	Appropriation problems and market characteristics
	Supply-led demand
Demand	Expected market demand (demand-pull hypothesis)
	Social awareness of the need for clean production; environmental
	Consciousness and preferences for environmentally friendly products
Institutional and political influences	Environmental policy instrument
	Institutional structures

Source Adapted from Horbach (2008)

eco-innovation often provides products not existing before, or even imagined, such as solar panels and electric cars, the supply of the new products can in itself initiate demand. The market demand pull follows when consumers realise there are ecologically sound products available, and this can help build the consciousness of the need for environmentally friendly products. Finally there are the institutions and political influences that support eco-innovation that will facilitate innovation networks and information flows (Jang et al. 2015; Newell 2010). In their review of the adoption of eco-innovation policy Jang et al. (2015) suggest that Singapore, Japan and the Republic of Korea are at the most advanced stage, and that Malaysia, China, Thailand and Indonesia are at intermediate stages, while the other Asian countries are still initiating policies for eco-innovation. This will be the greatest challenge facing the Asia Pacific—how to continue progress in innovation and deliver environmentally and socially sustainable growth.

References

Aebischer, P. (2016). Universities Increasingly Global Players, *UNESCO Science Report—Towards 2030*, UNESCO Publishing, pp. 3–5.

Arthur, W. B. (2009). *The nature of technology: What it is and how it evolves*. New York, NY: Simon and Schuster.

Asian Development Bank. (2007). *Moving towards knowledge-based economies*.

Boisot, M., & Child, J. (1996). From fiefs to clans and network capitalism: Explaining China's emerging economic order. *Administrative Science Quarterly, 41*(4), 600–628.

Branstetter, L., Li, G., & Veloso, F. (2015). The Rise of International Coinvention. In *The Changing Frontier: Rethinking Science and Innovation Policy* (pp. 135–168). University of Chicago Press.

Breschi, S., Malerba, F., & Orsenigo, L. (2000). Technological regimes and schumpetarian patterns of innovation. *Economic Journal, 110*(463), 388–410.

Brynjolfsson, E., & McAfee, A. (2014). *The second machine age: Work, progress, and prosperity in a time of brilliant technologies*. W.W. Norton

Burstein, D. (1993). *Turning the tables: A machiavellian strategy for dealing with Japan*. Simon Schuster.
Cameron, K. S., & Quinn, R. E. (2011). Diagnosing and changing organizational culture: Based on the competing values framework. John Wiley & Sons.
Cao, C. (2016). China, *UNESCO Science Report—Towards 2030*. UNESCO Publishing, pp. 620–641. http://en.unesco.org/unesco_science_report.
Carlsson, B., Jacobsson, S., Holmén, M., & Rickne, A. (2002). Innovation systems analytical and methodological issues. *Research Policy, 31*(2), 233–245.
Castellacci, F. (2004). A neo-Schumpeterian approach to why growth rates differ. *Revue Economique, 55*, 1145–1169.
Clarke, T. (1999). The development of management education in China. *Education and Training, 41*(6/7), 273–276.
Clarke, T., & Clegg, S. (2000). *Changing paradigms: The transformation of management knowledge for the 21st Century*. London: Profile Books.
Clarke, T., & Boersma, M. (2017). The governance of global value chains: Unresolved human rights, environmental and ethical dilemmas in the apple supply chain. *Journal of Business Ethics, 143*(1), 111–131.
Chandra, V., Erocal, D. Padoan, P., & Brage, C. A. (2009). Innovation and growth: Chasing a moving frontier. OECD/World Bank.
Chang, H. J. (1994). *The political economy of industrial policy*. London: Macmillan.
Chakrabarti, A. K. (1974). The role of champion in product innovation. *California management review, 17*, 58–62.
Charter, M., & Clark, T. (2007). *Sustainable innovation*. Franham, UK: The Center for Sustainable Design.
Cheung, A. B. (2000). New interventionism in the making: Interpreting state interventions in Hong Kong after the change of sovereignty. *Journal of Contemporary China, 9*(24), 291–308.
Cooney, C. M. (2012, January). Downscaling climate models: Sharpening the focus on local-level changes. *Environmental Health Perspectives, 120*(1).
Dahlman, C. (2009). Different innovation strategies, different results: Brazil, Russia, India, China and Korea (the BRICKs). In V. Chandra, D. Erocal, P. Padoan, & C. A. Brage (Eds.) (2009) *Innovation and growth: Chasing a moving frontier* (pp. 131–168). OECD/World Bank.
Davies, H. (1996). High IQ and low technology: Hong Kong's key to success. *Long Range Planning, 29*(5), 684–690.
Dodgson, M. (2009). Asia's national innovation systems: Institutional adaptability and rigidity in the face of global innovation challenges. *Asia Pacific Journal of Management, 26*(3), 589–609.
Dodgson, M., Gann, D. M., & Salter, A. (2008). *The management of technological innovation: strategy and practice*. Oxford University Press on Demand.
DOI (Department of Industry, Innovation and Science). (2016). *Australian innovation system report 2016*. Canberra: Australian Government.
Dosi, G. (1982). Technological paradigms and technological trajectories. *Research Policy, 11*, 147–162.
EIO (The Eco-Innovation Observatory) (2015). *Methodological Report*, http://www.ecoinnovation.eu.
Eurostat. (2014). Asia-Europe Meeting (ASEM), A statistical portrait. Luxembourg, Luxembourg: Eurostat.
Forum for the Future. (2016). *The five capitals model—a framework for sustainability*. https://www.forumforthefuture.org/sites/default/files/project/downloads/five-capitals-model.pdf.
Freeman, C. (2008). *Systems of Innovation*. Edward Elgar.
Freeman, C. (1995). The 'National System of Innovation' in historical perspective, Cambridge. *Journal of Economics, 19*, 5–24.
Geissbauer, R., Vedsø, J., & Schrauf, S. (2016). A strategist's guide to industry 4.0. *Strategy-Business.com* (Summer, 83).

Gereffi , G. (1999). International trade and industrial upgrading in the apparel commodity chain. *Journal of International Economics, 48*, 37–70.

Gereffi, G., Humphrey, J., & Sturgeon, T. (2005). The governance of global value chains. *Review of International Political Economy, 12*(1), 78–104.

Ghafele, R., & Gibert B. (2012). Promoting intellectual property monetization in developing countries: A review of issues and strategies to support knowledge-driven growth, policy research working series 6143. Economic Policy and Debt Department, Poverty Reduction and Economic Management Network, World Bank.

GII (Global Innovation Index). (2016). *Winning with global innovation*, WIPO.

Goodstadt, L. F. (2005). *Uneasy partners: The conflict between public interest and private profit in Hong Kong*. Hong Kong University Press.

Gulati, R. (1995). Social structure and alliance formation patterns: A longitudinal analysis. *Administrative science quarterly, 40*, 619–652.

Gulati, R. (1998). Alliances and networks. *Strategic management journal, 19*, 293–317.

Greenberg, E., Hirt, M., & Smit, S. (2017, April). The global forces inspiring a new narrative of progress, *McKinsey Quarterly*.

Gudergan, S. P., & Schweitzer, J. (2008). Alliances. In S. Clegg, & J. R. Bailey (Eds.), *International encyclopedia of organization studies* (pp. 51–55). Thousand Oaks, CA: Sage Publications.

Hackmann H., & Boulton, G. (2016). Science for a sustainable and just world: A new framework for global science policy. *UNESCO Science Report—Towards 2030*. UNESCO Publishing, pp. 12–14.

Hanson, M. (2011). *Economic development, education and transnational corporations*, London: Routledge.

Hemmert, M., Bstieler, L., & Okamuro, H. (2014). Bridging the cultural divide: Trust formation in university–industry research collaborations in the US, Japan, and South Korea. *Technovation, 34*(10), 605–616.

Hobday, M. (2005). Firm-level innovation models: perspectives on research in developed and developing countries. *Technology Analysis & Strategic Management, 17*(2), 121–146.

Horbach, J. (2008). Determinants of environmental innovation—New evidence from German panel data sources. *Research Policy, 37*, 163–173.

Hu, A. G. (2010). Propensity to patent, competition and China's foreign patenting surge. *Research Policy, 39*(7), 985–993.

Huff, W. G. (1995). The developmental state, government, and Singapore's economic development since 1960. *World Development, 23*(8), 1421–1438.

IEA (International Energy Agency). (2013). *CO_2 emissions from fuel combustion* (p. 2013). IEA: Paris, France.

ISA (Innovation and Science Australia). (2016). Performance review of the Australian innovation, science and research system, Australian government.

Jaffe, A., Trajtenberg, M., & Henderson, R. (1993). Geographic Localization of Knowledge Spillovers as Evidenced by Patent Citations. *The Quarterly Journal of Economics, 108*(3), 1 August 1993, 577–598.

Jang, E. K., Park, M. S., Roh, T. W., & Han, K. J. (2015). Policy instruments for eco-innovation in Asian countries. *Sustainability, 7*, 12586–12614.

Jensen, M., Johnson, B., Lorenz, E., & Lundvall, B. (2007). Forms of knowledge and innovation. *Research Policy, 36*, 680–693.

Kale, P., Singh, H., & Perlmutter, H. (2000). Learning and protection of proprietary assets in strategic alliances: Building relational capital. *Strategic management journal, 21*(3), 217–237.

Kapron, Z., & Meertens, M. (2017). *Social networks, e-commerce platforms, and the growth of digital payment eco-systems in China: What it means for other countries*. Better than Cash Alliance.

Kelly, T. (2009). Broadband as a platform for economic, social and cultural development: Lessons from Asia. In V. Chandra, D. Erocal, P. Padoan, & C. A. Brage (Eds.) (2009) Innovation and growth: Chasing a moving frontier (pp. 229–245). OECD/World Bank.

Kemp, R., & Pontoglio, S. (2011). The innovation effects of environmental policy instruments—A typical case of the blind men and the elephant? *Ecological Economics, 72*, 28–36.

Kim, L., & Nelson, R. (2000). *Technology, learning and innovation*. Cambridge University Press.

Leavitt, H. J., & Bass, B. M. (1964). Organizational psychology. *Annual Review of Psychology, 15*, 371–398. Leavitt.

Lee, K. (2013). *Schumpeterian analysis of economic catch-up: Knowledge, path-creation, and the middle-income trap*. Cambridge University Press.

Lee, K., & Lim, C. (2001). *Technological regimes, catching-up and leapfrogging: Findings from the Korean industries*. Research Poilcy.

Li, X. (2012). Behind the recent surge of Chinese patenting: An institutional view. *Research Policy, 41*(1), 236–249.

Lin, J.Y. (2012). A Framework for Rethinking Development and Policy, World Bank.

Lundvall, B. A. (1992). *National systems of innovation*. London: Anthem Press.

Lyytinen, K., & Newman, M. (2008). Explaining information systems change: A punctuated soci-technical change model. *European Journal of Information Systems, 17*, 589–613.

McKinsey Global Institute. (2015). *The China effect on global innovation*. McKinsey Company.

Mani, S. (2016). India, *UNESCO Science Report—Towards 2030*. UNESCO Publishing, pp. 598–620. http://en.unesco.org/unesco_science_report.

Mok, K. H. (2005). Fostering entrepreneurship: Changing role of government and higher education governance in Hong Kong. *Research Policy, 34*(4), 537–554.

Mora-Valentin, E. M., Montoro-Sanchez, A., & Guerras-Martin, L. A. (2004). Determining factors in the success of R&D cooperative agreements between firms and research organizations. *Research Policy, 33*(1), 17–40.

Motohashi, K. (2005). University–industry collaborations in Japan: The role of new technology-based firms in transforming the National Innovation System. *Research policy, 34* (5), 583–594.

Nelson, R., & Winter, S. (1982). *An evolutionary theory of economic change*. Cambridge, MA: Harvard University Press.

Neupane, B. (2016). A more developmental approach to science. *UNESCO Science Report—Towards 2030*. UNESCO Publishing, pp. 6–8.

Newell, R. G. (2010). The role of markets and policies in delivering innovation for climate change mitigation. *Oxford Review of Economic Policy, 26*, 253–269.

OCE (Office of the Chief Economist). (2016). Australian innovation system report, department of industry, innovation and science, Australian Government.

OECD. (2002). *Frascati manual—proposed standard practice for surveys on research and experimental development*. OECD. http://www.oecd-ilibrary.org/science-and-technology/frascati-manual-2002_9789264199040-en.

OECD. (2008). *China, OECD Reviews of innovation policy*. OECD.

OECD. (2009). *Sustainable Manufacturing and Eco-Innovation: Towards a Green Economy*. OECD.

OECD. (2010). *The OECD innovation strategy: Getting a head start on tomorrow*. OECD.

OECD. (2013a). *Innovation in Southeast Asia*. OECD Reviews of Innovation Policy OECD.

OECD. (2013b). *Knowledge Networks and Markets,* OECD Science, Technology and Industry Policy Papers No 7, OECD.

OECD. (2014). *Industry and technology policies in Korea*. Paris: OECD.

Ouchi, W. G. (1980). Markets, bureaucracies, and clans. *Administrative Science Quarterly, 25*(1), 129–141.

Ozawa, T., Castello, S., & Phillips, R. J. (2001). The internet revolution, the "McLuhan" stage of catch-up, and institutional reforms in Asia. *Journal of Economic Issues, 35*(2), 289–299.

Penrose, E. (1995). *The theory of the growth of the firm* (3rd ed.). Oxford: Oxford University Press.

Perez, C., & Soete, L. (1988). Catching up in technology: entry barriers and windows of opportunity. In G.Dosi et al. (Eds.), *Technical Change and Economic Theory* (pp. 458–479). London: Francis Pinter.

PWC. (2016). *Industry 4.0: Building the digital enterprise*. PWC. https://www.pwc.com/gx/en/industries/industries-4.0/landing-page/industry-4.0-building-your-digital-enterprise-april-2016.pdf.

Rennings, K. (2000). Redefining innovation—Eco-innovation research and the contribution from ecological economics. *Ecological Economics, 32*, 319–332.

Reuer, J. J., Ariño, A., & Mellewigt, T. (2006). Entrepreneurial alliances as contractual forms. *Journal of Business Venturing, 21*(3), 306–325.

Sarkar, A. N. (2013). Promoting eco-innovations to leverage sustainable development of eco-industry and green growth. *International Journal of Ecosystem Ecological Science, 3*, 171–224.

Sato, Y., & Arimoto, T. (2016). Japan, *UNESCO Science Report—Towards 2030* (pp. 642–659). UNESCO Publishing.

Schumpeter, J. (1934). *The theory of economic development*. Harvard Economic Studies: Harvard University.

Sharif, N. (2012). Facilitating and promoting innovative entrepreneurship in Hong Kong: Theory and practice. *Canadian Journal of Administrative Sciences, 29*, 139–153.

Smith. (1776). *The wealth of nations*. LONDON: Methuen.

Stanford. (2016a). *Artificial intelligence and life in 2030, One hundred year study on artificial intelligence*. Report of the 2015 Study Panel, September.

Stanford. (2016b). *One hundred year study on artificial intelligence (AI100)*. Stanford University. Accessed August 1, 2016. https://ai100.stanford.edu.

Stiglitz, J. (1987). Learning to learn, localized learning and technological progress. In P. Dasgupta & Stoneman (eds.), *Economic Policy and Technological Performance* (pp. 125–153). Cambridge University Press.

Suenaga, K. (2015). The emergence of technological paradigms: The evolutionary process of science and technology in economic development. In *The Evolution of Economic and Innovation Systems* (pp. 211–227). Springer International Publishing.

Tani, S. (2017, April 3). Japan Inc. in Grips of deepening labor shortage. *Nikkei Asian Review*. http://asia.nikkei.com/Politics-Economy/Economy/Japan-Inc.-in-grips-of-deepening-labor-shortage.

Tapscott, D., & Williams, A. D. (2008). *Wikinomics: How mass collaboration changes everything*. Penguin.

Tung, R. L., & Worm, V. (2001). Network capitalism: The role of human resources in penetrating the China market. *International Journal of Human Resource Management, 12*(4), 517–534.

UNESCO. (2016). *UNESCO Science Report—Towards 2030*. UNESCO Publishing. http://en.unesco.org/unesco_science_report.

Vernon, R. (1966). International investment and international trade in the product cycle. *The International Executive, 8*(4), 16.

Wade, R. (1990). *Governing the market: Economic theory and the role of government in East Asian industrialization*. Princeton University Press.

Williamson, O. E. (1991). Comparative economic organization: The analysis of discrete structural alternatives. *Administrative science quarterly*, 269–296.

Wong, P. K. (2001). The role of the state in Singapore's industrial development. *Industrial Policy, Innovation and Economic Growth: The Experience of Japan and the Asian NIEs*, 503–569.

World Bank. (1993). *The East Asian miracle: Economic growth and public policy*. Oxford University Press.

World Bank. (2010). *Exploring the middle income trap: World Bank East Asia Pacific economic update: Robust recovery, rising risks* (Vol. II). Washington, DC: World Bank.

World Bank. (2012). *China 2030: Building a modern, harmonious, and creative high-income society*. Washington, DC: World Bank.

World Bank. (2015, March). *World Bank development indicators*. Washington, DC: World Bank.

WCED. (World Commission on Environment and Development). (1987). *Report of the World commission on environment and development: Our common future*. http://www.un-documents.net/our-common-future.pdf.

Yeung, H. W. C. (2000). State intervention and neoliberalism in the globalizing world economy: lessons from Singapore's regionalization programme. *The Pacific Review*, *13*(1), 133–162.

Yim,D., & Lee, J. (2016). *UNESCO Science Report Towards 2030 in Korea*. UNESCO, 660–675.

Yim, D. S., & Nath, P. (2005). *National innovation systems in the Asian context*, *10*(1).

Young, A. (1992). A tale of two cities: factor accumulation and technical change in Hong Kong and Singapore. *NBER macroeconomics annual*, *7*, 13–54.

Zenger, T. R., & Hesterly, W. S. (1997). The disaggregation of corporations: Selective intervention, high-powered incentives, and molecular units. *Organization Science*, *8*(3), 209–222.

Part I
National Innovation Systems

Chapter 2
Preparing for the Future: The OECD-Countries in Comparison

Horst Hanusch and Yasushi Hara

Abstract In modern growth or development theory innovation is a crucial factor which pushes the dynamics of an economy and determines its success in the future. Out of innovations, created in the present, the potential for the future of a country are prepared, deciding how its economic fitness and competitiveness will emerge. Future-orientation is in a natural way connected with innovativeness of a firm, a region or a country and shapes the strength and the specifics of the process of development. Looking around the world economy, one can observe a variety of countries which exist at different levels of development. Each of them has to master its economic future, choosing its own specific development strategy. How the various countries, belonging to different continents and cultures, will succeed in this endeavour is surely one of the most exciting and important issues of coming decades. In this global context our study is focusing on "future preparedness" of a specific group of countries, the OECD countries. The origin of this group dates back to 1960, when 18 European countries and the United States as well as Canada created in Paris an organization dedicated to global development. Today the group consists of 34 member countries which span the globe from North to South America, to Europe and the Asia-Pacific region. They include many of the world's most advanced countries but also emerging ones like Mexico, Chile and Turkey. The concept of "future preparedness" gets its analytical and empirical relevance when it is placed and investigated within a specific development model. Such a model determines the theoretical basis of the study and provides the necessary ingredients for an empirical application. In our study we will use "Comprehensive Neo-Schumpeterian Economics" (CNSE) as an analytical framework (Hanusch and Pyka 2007a). This approach is based (a) on the notion of future-orientation penetrating all spheres of socio-economic life in developed as well as in developing countries; (b) on the principle of innovation as the main driving force and the

H. Hanusch (✉)
Institute of Economics, University of Augsburg, Augsburg, Germany
e-mail: horst.hanusch@wiwi.uni-augsburg.de

Y. Hara
SciREX Center, National Graduate Institute for Policy Studies, Tokyo, Japan
e-mail: ya-hara@grips.ac.jp

T. Clarke and K. Lee (eds.), *Innovation in the Asia Pacific*,
https://doi.org/10.1007/978-981-10-5895-0_2

engine of future-orientation and development. Based on the concept of CNSE the central aim of our study is to gain new insights and findings concerning the "future preparedness" of the OECD-countries. To meet this target we (a) rely on the notion of "future-orientation" as a basic prerequisite for being prepared to master the future; (b) try to bring this concept of "future preparedness" on a concrete basis by using indicator analysis embedded in the framework of CNSE; (c) investigate patterns of similarities in the set of indicators; (d) show how these patterns look like by applying cluster analysis; (e) draw some conclusions from the patterns concerning the status and variety of future-orientation in the group of OECD-countries. Future-orientation will be described and characterized in total by 45 indicators, focusing on the real (16), the public (21) and the financial sector (8) of an economy. The indicators reflect many different activities in the various countries related to innovation and the "emerging future" within the concept of CNSE. Dependent on data availability, the indicator sets comprise different years mainly in the period between 2006 and 2012.

Keywords Development models · Comprehensive Neo-Schumpeterian economics · Indicator analysis of Future-Orientation · Future-Oriented country analysis (FCA)

Introduction

In modern growth or development theory innovation is a crucial factor which pushes the dynamics of an economy and determines its success in the future. Out of innovations, created in the present, the potential for the future of an economy are prepared, deciding how its economic fitness and competitiveness will emerge. So, "future preparedness" is in a natural way connected with innovativeness of a firm, a region or a country and shapes the strength and the specifics of the process of development.

Looking around the world economy, one can observe a variety of countries which exist at different levels of development. Each of them has to master its economic future, choosing its own specific development strategy. How the various countries, belonging to different continents and cultures, will succeed in this endeavor is surely one of the most exciting and important issues of coming decades.

In this global context our study is focusing on "future preparedness" of a specific group of countries, the OECD-countries. The origin of this group dates back to 1960, when 18 European countries and the United States as well as Canada created in Paris an organization dedicated to global development. Today the group consists of 34 member countries which span the globe from North to South America, to Europe and the Asia-Pacific region. They include many of the world's most advanced countries but also emerging ones like Mexico, Chile and Turkey.

The concept of "future preparedness" gets its analytical and empirical relevance when it is placed and investigated within a specific development model. Such a model determines the theoretical basis of the study and provides the necessary ingredients for an empirical application.

In our study we will use "Comprehensive Neo-Schumpeterian Economics" (CNSE) as an analytical framework (Hanusch and Pyka 2007a). This approach is based (a) on the notion of future-orientation penetrating all spheres of socio-economic life in developed as well as in developing countries; (b) on the principle of innovation as the main driving force and the engine of future-orientation and development.

We will see that CNSE is able to provide the conceptual framework for studying and picturing the future-oriented features for the OECD-countries. In such a framework economic agents as well as political institutions have to be open to the future, characterized by discontinuous dynamics driven by novelties in all fields of the socio-economic system which include a permanent influx of change and transformation in an economy. At any time there exists in the economy a potential of futuristic occurrences, of issues related to time to come. In total that situation may be described as a nation's "emerging future". It can be influenced or even determined by creating and shaping the future-orientation or its preparedness for future events embodied in the process of development. In this way, a kind of "future resilience" is built up which may provide a certain surveyor's rod to get an idea about the ability of a country to master the challenges and/or to harvest the opportunities which will happen in coming times.

In other words, to get a good depiction of a country's readiness to cope with its economic future questions like the following have to be asked: How do countries handle their economic future? Does there exist a certain pattern of future preparedness in different countries? Can specific similarities or dissimilarities between single countries be observed and satisfactorily explained?

To answer these questions for the group of OECD-countries a "Future-Oriented Country Analysis" (FCA) is carried out. For such an analysis certain procedural steps have to be followed: (a) applying the concept of "future preparedness" on a concrete basis by using indicator analysis embedded in the framework of CNSE; (b) investigating patterns of similarities in the set of indicators; (c) showing how these patterns look like by applying cluster analysis; (d) drawing some conclusions from the patterns concerning the status and variety of "future preparedness" in the group of OECD-countries.

"Future preparedness" in our FCA study will be described and characterized in total by 45 indicators, focusing on the real (16), the public (21) and the financial sector (08). The indicators reflect many different activities in the various countries related to innovation and the "emerging future" within the concept of CNSE. Dependent on data availability, the indicator sets comprise different years mainly in the period between 2006 and 2012.

In the succeeding we will proceed as follows.

At first, we will discuss briefly the Neoclassical and the Schumpeterian approaches which represent the main types of growth and development models in the literature. This discussion gives us the theoretical background for deciding which one shall be used as the analytical frame for our indicator analysis. We will come to the conclusion that Comprehensive Neo-Schumpeterian Economics (CNSE) is the right conceptual frame. The next section incorporates the main part of our study, namely the indicator based empirical investigation of "future preparedness" of the OECD countries, using the framework of CNSE. The results of the study are shown and discussed in the following section. At the end some concluding remarks will be drawn.

Theoretical Background

Neoclassical economics offers an easily understandable description of an economy if you are looking for a theoretical framework for an empirical study. In this approach at the micro-level agents act as "*homines oeconomici*" characterized by perfect rationality. That means they have full information concerning the current situation of their decisions and they build up rational expectations with respect to future events. Under these circumstances they are able to allocate their resources in such an optimal way that individual utility or profit is maximized according to existing restrictions.

The shift from micro- to macroeconomics is also a relatively simple one. All the results on the micro level of an economy, determined by rational behavior, are aggregated to a macro level using the representative household or firm as a useful transformation concept.

In this theoretical framework however, problems arise as soon as changes in the fundamental assumptions are made in order to picture the functioning of an economy in a more realistic manner. Time, for instance, is a crucial element in explaining the dynamics of an economy. As long as time is handled as a mathematical category, no difficulties arise in the perfect neo-classical world. Even long lasting processes can easily be followed on the development path until a steady state equilibrium is reached. Traditional growth theory is full of explanations for this result. Primarily it is determined by defining technological progress as an external phenomenon, falling like "manna from heaven", and through decreasing marginal factor productivities. Even "new growth theory"—which brought revolutionary insights into the orthodox neoclassical explanation of growth by introducing innovative activities and their feedback effects—still is bound to argue in a concept of general equilibrium as long as time is interpreted in a mathematical sense using a neoclassical frame.

Analysis and explanation of reality are changing fundamentally, however, if time is characterized in a historical perspective. Then, growth and development shine up as a "complex process of evolution and transformation, rather than a simple transition along a steady state growth path" (Castellacci 2014). The determining factors of such an evolutionary process are change and the pursuit of novelty. Both are creating the basis of a future-oriented development which is characterized by true uncertainty in a non-perfect world.

One of the first economists who focused on these essential features of a capitalistic economy was Joseph A. Schumpeter. In his famous book *Theory of*

Economic Development (1912) he revealed the role of innovations and risk taking entrepreneurs as main driving forces of economic development in a historical time perspective. After a long period of intellectual ignorance, Schumpeter's approach gained growing importance in literature in the last four decades as Neo-Schumpeterian Economics (NSE). NSE builds up on traditional Schumpeterian thinking, improved by stressing besides quantitative aspects also qualitative growth factors and processes based on formal or informal networks as well as collaborations between firms, governments, universities and research institutions (Saviotti and Pyka 2008). In the literature you may also find the denotations network (cluster) model, Silicon Valley or eco-system model (Wallace 2013).

The growth path in NSE is characterized by unbalanced dynamics combined with processes of catching up, falling back, forging ahead and leap-frogging. There exists no continuous growth process ending in a long term equilibrium. Growth is characterized by punctuated equilibria, induced by structural change or socio-economic transformations having their origins in marginal as well as disruptive innovations primarily in the technological field.

However, NSE in its present shape is still far from offering an integral theory of economic development. Most of the research in NSE of the last decades has primarily concentrated on the real sphere of an economy (Hanusch and Pyka 2007b). Technological innovations propelling industry dynamics and economic growth obviously are a major source of economic development. But, technological innovations are not the only driving force, nor can industry development occur in a vacuum. Instead, development is accompanied and influenced by novelty and change shaping also the monetary realms of an economy as well as the public sector.

In such an institutional setting "Comprehensive Neo-Schumpeterian Economics" (CNSE) (Hanusch and Pyka 2007a) gains its special importance and relevance as a future-oriented theoretical concept. CNSE is based on the traditional Schumpeterian model and also on the Neo-Schumpeterian one. The most important feature of CNSE, however, is the idea of institutional relevance in the process of development, stressing besides the real sector also the financial and the public sphere of a socio-economic system. These are the decisive pillars of future-oriented dynamics causing in a co-evolutionary manner quantitative growth and qualitative transformations of economies. Novelties then occur in various and multifaceted forms, which embrace technological, institutional and organizational as well as ecological and social dimensions.

Conceptual Frame of the Study: Comprehensive Neo-Schumpeterian Economics (CNSE)

The central aim of our study is to gain new insights and findings concerning the "future preparedness" of OECD countries. In which way and to what degree are the different OECD countries prepared to master their economic future? Does there exist a certain pattern of future-orientation? Can specific similarities or dissimilarities between single countries be observed?

To answer these questions we will use a conceptual frame which is based on Schumpeterian thinking in the sense of CNSE. Future in this analytical context has a historical time dimension, it is open to "creative destruction", to permanent changes and unexpected events. It thus incorporates true uncertainty as a central element of development. This is the case for all three pillars of an economy, the real sector as well as the financial and public sphere. The development process of an economy is not limited to one of these sectors, but it takes place in a comprehensive, co-evolutionary manner in all of them. This is made possible by creating and disseminating an enduring flow of novelties in each of the three institutional entities of an economy. This kind of an "innovation fabric", however, needs preparatory elements, i.e. certain activities in each of the sectors and specific institutional relationships between them to keep the co-evolutionary development alive and strengthen it.

For instance, to be prepared for an uncertain future the real sector needs a "format of resilience" which will foster at all times the knowledge-oriented progress and the resulting wealth of an economy. This is attained primarily through innovation and parallel investments.

The financial sector, on the other hand, can do its best for the future of an economy if it strengthens this "resilience" of the real economy by engaging in a close almost symbiotic relationship. That means, its foremost task would be to establish a sound financial basis in order to accompany successfully individuals and companies in their future-oriented activities and to encourage their innovative projects and activities. This could even be done out of speculative motivations.

The governmental and political responsibilities in a co-evolutionary development lie, above all, in monitoring and controlling the future-oriented, long term relationship between the real and financial sector and, if necessary, to support the co-evolutionary process through specific budgetary and institutional means. On the expenditure side of the budget these are above all investments in education, health, and infrastructure as well as in science and research. All in all, the public sector has to fulfill, more or less, the role of an "entrepreneurial state" (Mazzucato 2013).

What consequences have to be drawn from these considerations for our indicator analysis?

We will have to find the right indicators which mirror empirically, on the one side, the evolutionary "innovation fabric" of a country and which picture, on the other side, the related co-evolutionary processes. That means, our primary task is to find indicators expressing the forces and elements of a CNSE-driven development. This challenge has to be met for each of the three pillars of the socio-economic system. Then, using cluster analysis, the pattern of similarities or dissimilarities, i.e. the variety of being prepared for the future, can be detected in the case of OECD countries. To point it out clearly, it isn't the primary goal of our study to create a ranking system with respect to future orientation of different countries.

Indicator Analysis Based on the Concept of CNSE

4.1. Data Set

Our study is based on a comprehensive set of indicators which corresponds with the CNSE concept. That means the data we draw upon are supposed to reflect activities entailing future oriented characteristics for the real, the financial and the public sector.

In total 45 indicators have been calculated for the 34 OECD countries listed in the appendix. The indicators used originate from various sources, the most important one being the World Bank's Open database, especially Main Science and Technology Statistics and its Educational database. From these three data samples, for instance patent statistics, R&D expenditure data as well as several indicators of national education systems and of qualification structures of national work forces have been extracted. Further main data sources used are the Global Competitive Report published by the World Economic Forum and the Market Line Data Base. We also used the OECD data base for demographic, internet and education related figures. And, the set of indicators for each pillars was checked statistically by significance analysis.

4.2. Indicator Sets for the Three Institutional Pillars: Real, Financial, Public Sector

The crucial feature of the **real sector** in a CNSE concept is its orientation towards the future, based on innovation and change. In order to comprise these dimensions structurally as well as from a process perspective the indicators used encompass three categories of characteristics:

"Structural characteristics", like "ease of doing business", "foreign direct investment" or "brain drain"

"Technological characteristics", like "high technology exports" or "availability of newest technology"

Characteristics concerning "research and development" as a prerequisite of innovation, like "business spending on R&D" or "researchers in R&D"

Under the category "technological characteristics" we subsumed also indicators dealing with digitalization (internet users). This new revolutionary technology will influence all spheres of human life in the near future. In the eyes of some economists it is even comparable with the first industrial revolution more than two hundred years ago (Brynjolfson and Mc Afee 2014).

For the **financial sector** we only have two categories, one for the "general finance situation", having in mind the soundness of the financial system, and the other for the "relationship between the real and the financial sector". Here we subsumed indicators like "availability of financial services" or "venture capital availability". These categories are of fundamental importance in the co-evolutionary process of an economy driven by innovations.

Unfortunately we were not able to find data for all OECD countries concerning digitalization in the financial sector. In this sector processes of using IT-technology have already revolutionized the system and they will continue to do so in the future (Dapp 2014).

The indicator set for the **public sector** consists of five categories:

The first one comprises "general characteristics" which may illustrate the political atmosphere in a country, either in favor or against innovativeness and future orientation. These indicators focus on institutional and legal as well as demographic conditions.

Categories 2, 3, 4, and 5 concentrate on the expenditure side of the budget and stress four government activities which are crucial for a future oriented development:

Education,
Science, Research and Development,
Health and
Infrastructure.

In the literature on innovation economics the "education system" is considered as a fundamental basis for preparing individuals to cope with the future and its unforeseen events. Cognitive skills can account for growth differences in various OECD countries (Hanushek and Woessmann 2010). So we tried to find as many data as possible to encompass the education sector of the OECD countries from a quantitative as well as qualitative perspective.

Not far less important for a future oriented governing of an economy is "science, research and development" financed and augmented by the public sector. Here, the main programs of technology policy find their expression in quantitative indicators like "research and development expenditures" or in qualitative indicators like "quality of scientific research institutions".

Concerning the category "health" some economists see in this field even the new upcoming 6th Kondratieff cycle (Nefiodow 2014).

In modern growth theory either of Neo Classical or Schumpeterian origin the physical infrastructure always plays a relevant role for explaining the development processes of an economy (Romp and De Haan 2007). Without a well-established infrastructure (Streets, railroads, ports, internet) an economy can't compete in the global economic contest. That is why we used indicators for infrastructure also to characterize a countries "preparedness for the future". In addition, we also found some data concerning "digital government" for all OECD countries.

Cluster Analysis to Detect Similarities

The indicator approach will be used in combination with the cluster analysis (see e.g. Jobson 1952). Target of the cluster analysis is to detect cross-national (dis-) similarities in the structure and composition of a socio-economic system, focusing on future-orientation.

The general rationale behind the cluster analysis as an analytical tool is to test a sample of variables for the degree of structural commonalities between the units of analysis. Its outcome is a categorization of the analyzed units so that the coherence of each group (or cluster) as well as the heterogeneity across different clusters is maximized. To determine the coherence of a certain cluster and to calculate the existing diversity of different clusters, distance values between the units of analysis need to be determined on the basis of the characteristics of each entity. In other words, "cluster analysis is a set of tools for building groups (clusters) from multivariate data objects. The aim is to construct groups with homogeneous properties out of heterogeneous large samples. The group should be as homogeneous as possible and the differences among various groups as large as possible" (Härdle and Simar 2007).

A simple outline of a cluster analysis could be the following: At the beginning, each country is treated as an individual cluster, and a so called "distance-matrix" is created according to the used attributes. Subsequently, those clusters of countries which display the least distance to each other are assigned to a new cluster. Again, the distance between the countries is measured and a new "distance-matrix" is created. This sequence is repeated until only one cluster remains.

To identify clusters, statistical standardization has been applied for every indicator as follows: (1) equalize and standardize (convert to [−1 to 1] score) for each indicator, (2) execute cluster analysis under the Wald-method for each pillar and (3) use the elbow-method to identify the step where the distance makes a bigger jump and in this way determine the ideal or most effective number of clusters.

Empirical Results

Real Pillar

The real pillar consists of five clusters:

Cluster 1
Australia, Canada, New Zealand, and Norway
Cluster 2
Austria, Denmark, Finland, Iceland, Israel, Luxembourg, Netherlands, Sweden, and Switzerland
Cluster 3
Belgium, France, Ireland, Korea, and United Kingdom
Cluster 4
Chile, Czech Republic, Estonia, Greece, Hungary, Italy, Mexico, Poland, Portugal, Slovak Republic, Slovenia, Spain, and Turkey
Cluster 5
Germany, Japan, and United States

Financial Pillar

The financial pillar consists of four clusters:

Cluster 1
Australia, Austria, Belgium, Canada, Chile, Denmark, Estonia, Finland, Israel, Luxembourg, Netherlands, New Zealand, Norway, Slovak Republic, Sweden, and Switzerland
Cluster 2
Czech Republic, Greece, Hungary, Iceland, Ireland, Italy, Korea, Mexico, Poland, Portugal, Slovenia, Spain, and Turkey
Cluster 3
France, Germany, Japan, and United Kingdom
Cluster 4
United States

Public Sector Pillar

The public sector pillar comprises five clusters:

Cluster 1
Australia, Austria, Belgium, Canada, Denmark, Finland, France, Germany, Iceland, Israel, Japan, Korea, Luxembourg, Netherlands, New Zealand, Norway, Spain, Sweden, Switzerland, and United Kingdom
Cluster 2
Chile, Mexico, and Turkey
Cluster 3
Czech Republic, Estonia, Ireland, Portugal, and Slovenia
Cluster 4
Greece, Hungary, Italy, Poland, and Slovak Republic
Cluster 5
United States

A first general result states that looking at the three constitutional pillars of an economy the OECD countries are quite diversified. The real and the public pillar encompass five clusters followed by the financial sector with four groupings. In a worldwide perspective there exists quite a dissimilarity concerning the different sectors with respect to its "preparedness for the future".

However, this diversity has to be seen as a relative phenomenon. The real sector, for instance, consists of two large clusters 2 and 4 containing nine and thirteen member states, and three small clusters 1, 3, 5 which embrace not more than five OECD countries.

Cluster 1 includes the advanced countries, Australia, Canada, Norway and New Zealand. If there is a common feature which may characterize their economies, it is the dependency on winning and exporting natural resources.

The larger Cluster 2 is formed mainly by smaller industrial economies from Europe supplemented by Israel. The size of the country as well its status of development seems to play a crucial role in the configuration of its "future preparedness".

Cluster 3 comprises the two English-speaking (Ireland, United Kingdom) or French-speaking (France or Belgium) countries from Europe added by South Korea.

The large cluster 4 shows a mixture of emerging countries from Europe, which in former times belonged to the COMMECON, as well as developing economies from South America (Chile, Mexico). Turkey is also part of this cluster. Surprisingly, the advanced economies of the Mediterranean region (Greece, Italy, Portugal, Spain) join this cluster of emerging countries. As older member states of the European Union and the Eurozone one wouldn't expect them in a cluster together with catching up economies.

Of certain interest is also cluster 5 which embraces Germany, Japan and the United States. These countries are the largest, internationally oriented economies in the OECD sample and apparently they are choosing similar strategies in the real sector to be prepared for the future.

A similar picture as the one for the real sector shows up in the financial pillar where cluster 1 encloses sixteen and cluster 2 thirteen member states. Cluster 3, in contrast, is limited to four countries and cluster 4 consists only of one economy, namely the United States. This configuration of clusters may confirm the conjecture that, on the one hand, large geographical parts of the global financial system have a similar pattern with regard to future orientation and the augmenting co-evolutionary processes between the real and the financial sector based on them.

On the other hand, a small number of countries is quite different compared to the large two clusters. There is the mighty United States which dominates the world of finance with its center New York and its global hub of risk capital, the Silicon Valley, where the two sides of an innovation-oriented co-evolutionary process are brought together, the technological and the financial sphere of an economy. Besides, the United Kingdom with London as a worldwide operating financial center, Japan with Tokyo, Germany with Frankfurt and France with Paris are the other global financial players. These four countries form an own future oriented cluster in the OECD sample.

A comparable picture shows up for the public sector. Here, even twenty countries form a joint Cluster 1 comprising countries across the globe, from the Pacific region (Australia, New Zealand) to all parts of Europe ranging from Austria and Switzerland to Iceland. Israel in the Near East is as well included as Japan and Korea in Asia. All over the world many economies rely on a similar institutional setting which might be called the traditional one giving the public sector a certain influence and role to shape an economy's "preparedness for the future".

Of some interest is also the fact that Mexico and Chile constitute an own South American Cluster 2 which is joined by Turkey. These three emerging countries seem to look out for an own way in solving future oriented problems, different from the traditional public sector approach.

Clusters 3 and 4 are mixed ones where countries from Central East Europe are together with economies from the Mediterranean region, Portugal in Cluster 3 and Italy and Greece in Cluster 4. This situation mirrors the one in the real sector: Italy, Greece and Portugal, three established member states of the European Union, participate in clusters which are formed by countries still struggling to leave behind the political boundaries and economic impediments of the former UDSSR.

The US builds an own cluster. This is not surprising because many of those future oriented activities which our study is assigning to the public sector are part of the private market sector in the United States. The public sector there doesn´t play such an important role as in other countries in Europe or Asia. That means, the co-evolutionary process in preparing for the future induced and controlled by the public sector exhibits its own specific character in the US.

Another interesting result illustrates that there exist groups of countries which depict a high degree of similarity in all three sectors. Their "National Innovation Systems" conduct more or less the same components and characteristics. These country groups are:

Austria, Finland, Denmark, Israel, Luxembourg, Netherlands, Sweden, Switzerland
Australia, Canada, New Zealand, Norway
Greece, Italy, Hungary, Poland
Mexico, Turkey
France, United Kingdom,
Germany, Japan.

The first group is a large one containing smaller advanced countries from Europe together with Israel. A simple explanation why these countries are staying so close together might be the size of their economies as well as their special quest to keep up with larger competitors in the global economic contest.

The second group is the one which we already know from the real sector. Perhaps, it's their dependency on national resources which shapes not only the real sector but their whole institutional setting in preparing for the future.

The third group is a mixed one consisting of countries from Central East and Southern Europe. Evidently, the new EU member states Hungary and Poland succeeded already in building up a "National Innovation System" which is similar to that of the older members Greece and Italy.

Mexico and Turkey also form a similar institutional configuration with respect to their sectors' ability to form future events. Both are very dynamic emerging countries which act as a kind of connecting bridge between the Protestant North and the Catholic South America, in the first case, and between Christian Europe and the Islamic Near and Middle East in the second case.

France and the United Kingdom are two major well established countries in the EU. In the time period under study they exhibit similar characteristics for all three sectors. This illustrates a closeness which might be derived from their specific role both countries played in the history of the 20th century.

Of special interest is also the result with respect to Germany and Japan. Both are in similar clusters in the real, the financial as well as the public sector. Both experienced a comparable economic history after World War II. They had to build up their economies from scratch and were able to ascend into front positions of the world economy. In the time period of our study their preparedness for future developments reveals more or less the same pattern.

Conclusion

The study has shown that CNSE can serve as an analytical frame for investigating empirically the "preparedness for future" of OECD countries. In the last ten years or so statistical sources were published which allow an international comparison based on indicators of innovativeness or future orientation. Such studies, however, can be exercised only for a time span of the last eight years. If we wanted to include more time periods in order to get a dynamic analysis picturing the process of future orientation over time we would have to wait for the coming years and the statistics offered then. At the moment, because of the data situation, a study of future orientation of countries (FCA) can show only a kind of snapshot for the OECD member states.

But, even this snapshot may deliver a number of insights and findings. For instance, an interesting result is the outstanding role of the US in the OECD sample. With respect to the financial and the public pillar it forms an own cluster.

Another interesting result is that Germany and Japan belong to the same cluster for all institutional pillars. Or, none of the countries entering the EU in 2004 or later belongs to clusters where the majority of established EU members are situated. A remarkable exception in that respect are the Mediterranean countries—Greece, Italy, Portugal and Spain—which seem to have more in common with emerging countries from Central Eastern Europe or other parts of the world concerning their "preparedness for future" than with the established industrial nations.

Besides the date of the EU-membership accession and the former socialist status of countries, also the size of an economy seems to play a crucial role, forming a relatively large homogenous country grouping with respect to future orientation.

If cohesion or catching up are relevant objectives for the future development of the world economy from where and in which way should processes start and be established to reach such global ends? Which role may the different institutional pillars play in a process of harmonization based on innovativeness and its consequences for improving economically? Should a country concentrate, first of all, on the real or better on the financial or preferably on the public sector as the primary institutional or structural candidates for its economic development? Is it still or again the real sector with its industrial production processes or is it the financial sector integrated in a globalized digital world which creates the dynamic impulses for progress and wealth? How does an "entrepreneurial state" fit into a future oriented co-evolutionary development process? Should he become a main player or should he stay back and allow the other sectors to work out the initiatives and actions oriented to the future?

There don't exist easy answers for questions like these. And, as it seems, there exists no general pattern of a useful masterplan in the membership states of the OECD. On the contrary diversity to a high degree pictures the reality shown in our data set.

Appendix

Indicator set for the real pillar

Sub categories	Indicator	Sample length	Data source
Structural characteristics	Ease of doing business index	2011 and 2012	Global competitiveness report
Structural characteristics	Value chain breadth	2006–2012	Global competitiveness report
Structural characteristics	Cooperation in labor-employer relations	2006–2012	Global competitiveness report
Structural characteristics	Brain drain (aka attract talent)	2009–2013	Global competitiveness report
Structural characteristics	Foreign direct investment, outward	2007–2011	Marketline database
Structural characteristics	Start-up procedures to register a business	2007–2011	World Bank database
Research and development	Technicians in R&D (per million people)	2007–2011	World Bank database
Research and development	Patent applications, residents	2005–2010	World Bank database
Research and development	Efficacy of corporate boards, 1–7 (best)	2006–2012	Global competitiveness report
Research and development	Capacity for innovation, 1–7 (best)	2006–2012	Global competitiveness report
Research and development	Company spending on R&D, 1–7 (best)	2006–2012	Global competitiveness report
Research and development	PCT patents applications/million pop.	2006–2012	World bank database
Research and development	Researchers in R&D (per million people)	2004–2009	World bank database
Technological characteristics	Availability of latest technologies 1–7	2006–2012	Global competitiveness report
Technological characteristics	Internet users (absolute number)	2008–2012	World bank database
Technological characteristics	High technology exports (US Dollar)	2008–2012	World bank database

Indicator set for the financial pillar

Sub categories	Indicator	Sample length	Data source
General finance situation	Bank capital to asset ratio (absolute)	2007–2011	Marketline database
General finance situation	Central bank, assets (absolute)	2007–2011	Marketline database
General Finance situation	Monetary gold reserves (absolute)	2007–2011	Marketline database
General Finance situation	Stocks traded, total value (current US$)	2008–2012	World bank database
Relationship between real and financial sectors	Availability of financial services 1–7 (best)	2006–2012	Global competitiveness report
Relationship between real and financial sectors	Net domestic credit (absolute)	2007–2011	Marketline database
Relationship between real and financial sectors	Venture capital availability	2009–2013	Global competitiveness report
Relationship between real and financial sectors	Ease of access to loans	2009–2013	Global competitiveness report

Indicator set for the public pillar

	Indicator	Sample length	Data source
General characteristics	Urban population (% of total)	2007–2011	World bank database
General characteristics	Strength of auditing and reporting standards, 1–7	2006–2012	Global competitiveness report
General characteristics	Population age structure	2010–2014	OECD Database
Education	Quality of management schools, 1–7	2006–2012	Global competitiveness report
Education	Public spending on education, total (% of government expenditure)	2005–2010	World bank database
Education	Number of students in primary education	2007–2011	Marketline database
Education	Number of students in secondary education	2007–2011	Marketline database
Education	Number of students in tertiary education	2007–2011	Marketline database
Science, research and development	Quality of scientific research institutions 1–7 (best)	2006–2012	Global competitiveness report

(continued)

(continued)

	Indicator	Sample length	Data source
Science, research and development	University-industry collaboration in R&D 1–7 (best)	2006–2012	Global competitiveness report
Science, research and development	Gov't procurement of advanced tech products 1–7 (best)	2006–2012	Global competitiveness report
Science, research and development	Number of scientific and technical journal articles	2005–2009	World bank database
Health	Public healthcare expenditure	2007–2011	Marketline database
Health	Life expectancy	2010–2014	OECD Database
Health	Total public and primary private health insurance (% of total population covered)	2010–2014	OECD Database
Infrastructure	Quality of railroad infrastructure, 1–7 (best)	2006–2012	Global competitiveness report
Infrastructure	Quality of port infrastructure, 1–7 (best)	2006–2012	Global competitiveness report
Infrastructure	Quality of air transport infrastructure, 1–7 (best)	2006–2012	Global competitiveness report
Digital government	E-government readiness index	2010–	OECD Database
Digital government	Businesses using the internet to interact with public authorities, sending filled forms	2010–	OECD Database
Public finances	Government 10-year bond rate (absolute)	2007–2011	Marketline database

References

Brynjolfson, E., & Mc Afee, A. (2014). *The second machine age*. New York: W.W. Norton & Company Inc.

Castellacci. (2014). A neo-schumpeterian approach to why growth rates differ. *Revue Economique, 55*(6), 1145–1170.

Dapp, T. (2014). *Fintech–The digital (R)evolution of the financial sector: algorithm-based banking with the human touch*. Frankfurt am Main: Deutsche Bank Research.

Härdle, W., & Simar, L. (2007). *Applied multivariate statistical analysis*. New York, Berlin, Heidelberg: Springer.

Hanusch, H., & Pyka, A. (2007a). The principles of neo-schumpeterian economics. *Cambridge Journal of Economics, 31*(2), 275–289.
Hanusch, H., Pyka, A. (eds.) (2007b). Elgar companion to neo-schumpeterian economics. Cheltenham UK: Edward Elgar.
Hanushek, E. A., Woessmann, L. (2010). How much do educational outcomes matter in OECD countries? NBER Working Paper No. 16515, November 2010.
Jobson, J. D. (1952). Applied multivariate data analysis: Volume II: Categorical and multivariate methods. New York, Berlin, Heidelberg: Springer.
Mazzucato, M. (2013). The entrepreneurial state, debunking private vs. public sector myths in risk and innovation. London, New York: Anthem Press.
Nefiodow, L. (2014). *The sixth Kondratieff: A new long wave in the global economy* (Translation of the 7th German Edition). Sankt Augustin: Rhein-Sieg Verlag.
Romp, W., & De Haan, J. (2007). Public capital and economic growth. *A Critical Survey, Perspektiven der Wirtschaftspolitik, 8*(1), 6–52.
Saviotti, P. P., Pyka, A. (2008). Product variety, competition and economic growth. *Journal of Evolutionary Economics, 18*(3–4), 323–347.
Schumpeter, J. A. (1912). *Theorie der wirtschaftlichen Entwicklung*. Leipzig: Duncker & Humblot.
Wallace, R. (2013). A new formal approach to evolutionary processes in socioeconomic systems. *Journal of Evolutionary Economics, 23*(1), 1–15.

Chapter 3
Comparing the National Innovation Systems in East Asia and Latin America: Fast Versus Slow

Keun Lee and Yee Kyoung Kim

Abstract Lee and Kim analyze the NIS of East Asia and Latin America, and to show the sources of the divergent economic performance in these groups of countries. This divergence between East Asia and Latin America reflects that these two regions selected different policy priority in knowledge development; the priority was given to technology in East Asia whereas it was given to science in Latin America. The main characteristic of R&D expenditure in Latin America is that universities and public labs are taking up most of the R&D but they are decoupled from the demands from the private sector. The role of Latin America's private sectors remains weak, and the difference in corporate R&D among the East Asian countries and Latin American countries are substantial. East Asia and Latin America initially imported foreign technologies, but only East Asia has been able to build up its indigenous technological capabilities. One of the reasons for this difference is that in East Asia, the domestic corporate sectors were the main agents of technology imports, whereas the trans-national corporations were the main agents for production in Latin America. R&D investment by TNCs in Latin America was mainly carried out in their home countries, and the TNCs sought to protect their technologies by confining it within the boundary of the TNCs [Hanson (Economic Development, Education and Transnational Corporations, Routledge, p. 54, 2008)]. Emerging new technologies in short cycle fields present better growth prospects, and the possibility of higher profitability associated with less collision with the technologies of advanced countries and the presence of first-mover advantages. This divergence in technological specialization can be considered as one explanation how the Asian countries went beyond the middle income trap situation in the mid-1980s, whereas Latin American countries failed to overcome the trap. The view of Lee and Kim based on short or long cycle times also differs from the traditional recommendation to focus on trade-based specialization, which is more suitable for low-income countries, because it argues that middle-income countries

K. Lee (✉)
Department of Economics, Seoul National University, Seoul, Korea (Republic of)
e-mail: kenneth@snu.ac.kr

Y.K. Kim
KISTEP, Seoul, Korea (Republic of)

T. Clarke and K. Lee (eds.), *Innovation in the Asia Pacific*,
https://doi.org/10.1007/978-981-10-5895-0_3

need to specialize in technological sectors that rely less on existing technologies, and look at the greater opportunities associated with new technologies. It is also complementary to the growth identification and facilitation framework of Justin Lin (New Structural Economics: A framework for Rethinking Development and Policy, Washington, DC, The World Bank 2012).

Keywords Innovation · East Asia · Latin America · Short cycle technologies · National innovation systems · Patents · Articles

Introduction

Divergent economic performance of East Asia versus Latin America has been one of the key issues in the development literature. The question is why such 'Asian style' catch-up is not happening in Latin America (Lee 2013). In the 1950s, Latin American countries were much better 'endowed' than East Asian countries, and Korea and Taiwan were less developed than Brazil and Mexico during the 1960s and the earlier 1970s (Lee and Kim 2009; Table 3.1). Korea and Taiwan began their catch-up processes as backward countries since the 1960s, overtook Brazil and Mexico by the 1980s, and finally reached the level of the high income country by the late 1990s. In contrast, many Latin American countries failed to sustain growth despite (maybe due to) the implementation of policy prescriptions along the so-called Washington Consensus emphasizing economic liberalization than promotion of domestic industry. So, Rodrik (2006) declared that Washington Consensus is dead, and now the issue is what to replace it.

Rodrik (1996, 2006) observed that the performance difference between East Asia and Latin American can be explained in terms of simultaneous adoption of 10 policy suggestions in the so-called Washington Consensus in Latin America versus sequential or gradual adoption of 10 policies in East Asia. In comparison, Lee and Kim (2009) argue that it is not only the difference sequencing but also the difference in emphasis on R&D and innovation that made the difference between Asia and Latin America. Now, there exist an increasing volume of researches that acknowledge technological innovation as one of the most serious bottlenecks in the middle-income countries in Latin America (Pack 2001; Alcorta and Peres 1998; Katz 2001; Velho 2004).

To analyze the source of differences in innovation achievement, many have consulted the concept of the national innovation system (NIS) developed by the Schumpeterian school of thought. Lunvall (1992) defines NIS as "elements and relationships which interact in the production, diffusion and use of new, and economically useful knowledge." That is, NIS is a concept relating to the efficiency of the production, diffusion and use of knowledge. Scholars from the Schumpeterian school such as Lundvall and Nelson have advocated the NIS concept, arguing that differences in NIS among countries gives birth to differences in innovation performance and thus countries' economic performance.

Table 3.1 Comparison of knowledge variables in Latin America and East Asia

		Korea		Taiwan		East Asia	
	Year	Mean	S.D.	Mean	S.D.	Mean	S.D.
GDP per capita	1960–1974	1609.76	441.57	2035.03	715.20	1278.29	358.05
	1975–1984	3182.50	426.52	4272.15	667.99	2489.58	356.40
	1985–1994	6413.92	1370.13	8552.89	1605.64	4719.90	935.72
	1995–2005	10967.30	1420.60	13402.88	1124.41	7594.36	750.95
Corporate patents	1960–1974	1.50	0.84	3.50	2.12	1.73	1.27
	1975–1984	7.17	6.77	5.22	2.39	5.26	4.62
	1985–1994	503.50	473.44	236.70	223.89	218.74	345.41
	1995–2005	2267.50	1302.43	1789.63	1058.15	1050.48	1319.83
SCI Journal articles	1975–1984	305.67	69.50	595.67	63.12	403.31	158.07
	1985–1994	1728.40	1095.43	2831.90	1625.18	1344.75	1394.82
	1995–2005	13199.82	5710.90	10202.73	2716.964	6413.77	2333.26
Corporate R&D	1975–1984	0.25	0.16	0.062	0.031	0.167	0.152
	1985–1994	1.702	0.411	0.333	0.199	0.64	0.716
	1995–2005	2.457	0.13	1.161	0.259	1.185	0.977
		Brazil		Argentina		Latin America	
		Mean	S.D.	Mean	S.D.	Mean	S.D.
GDP per capita	1960–1974	1878.25	435.39	6058.36	727.22	3326.05	450.87
	1975–1984	3216.07	186.61	7012.56	321.13	4299.72	308.81
	1985–1994	3453.89	115.71	6484.48	585.75	4507.98	361.85
	1995–2005	3718.13	111.23	7515.28	536.68	5463.80	365.14
Corporate patents	1960–1974	3.70	2.00	3.36	2.50	4.98	4.62
	1975–1984	9.22	2.49	3.56	2.24	7.14	5.44
	1985–1994	29.80	11.36	4.60	2.80	13.39	12.53
	1995–2005	39.43	15.09	9.14	3.63	20.15	16.45
SCI Journal articles	1975–1984	2127.67	186.78	1164.00	95.44	1267.06	581.28
	1985–1994	3480.20	938.50	1894.80	242.11	2009.8	1052.52
	1995–2005	9916.00	3286.35	4039.55	779.53	4909.45	3132.81
Corporate R&D	1975–1984	0.267	0.148	0.125	0.05	0.2	0.118
	1985–1994	0.248	0.048	0.105	0.057	0.206	0.114
	1995–2005	0.634	0.169	0.114	0.033	0.275	0.2002

Source GDP per capita: World Development Indicator, Corporate Patent: USPTO, SCI Journal Article: Web of Science (GDP per capita: Taiwan: Statistical yearbook of the Republic of China, various years)

Thus, this paper aims to analyze the NIS of East Asia and Latin America, and thereby to show the sources of the divergent economic performance in these groups of countries. Further along this line of Schumpeterian tradition, Lee (2013) conducted a patent-citation data based analysis of the NIS, showing that Asian tiger succeeded by continuously moving into short-cycle time based sectors, whereas Latin American countries remained with traditional long cycle-time based sectors, failing to upgrade into new or higher-valued added short-cycle or long-cycle sectors. This paper will also touch upon this issue.

Another aspect of comparison is scientific versus technological knowledge. Bernardes and Albuquerque (2003) argued that Latin American failure to uplift its scientific capacity has also resulted in failure in technology capacity, and that a threshold level may exist in scientific production, beyond which the efficiency in the use of the scientific output by the technological sector increases. However, we will show that reaching such a threshold is not enough to bring about an interaction between the scientific and technological sectors unless the industrial sector is getting strong and advanced enough. Since the industrial sector is a consumer of scientific knowledge, the underdevelopment of industrial sector implies that the scientific sector may function in an ineffective way. The scientific sector often lacks the ability to identify the technologies needed by the industrial sector. Since the demand from the industrial sector is little, the scientific sector tends to focus on academic basic research irrelevant to industrial sectors. Thus, putting an emphasis on the scientific sector without the developed industrial sector would run into a problem. The Latin American NIS is such a case. Thus, the prevalence of the industrial technology sectors over the science sector in East Asia can be said as the key factor to explain the difference between East Asia and Latin America.

In what follows, the first Sect. "Comparing the Basic Profile of East Asia and Latin America" compares the basic profile of East Asia and Latin America. Then, Section "Science & Technology Policy in East Asia and Latin America" delves into differences in science and technology policy in East Asian and Latin American countries. Section "Analyzing the NIS of East Asia and Latin America: Patent Citation Data" is about the comparative analysis of the NIS of countries using the variables made up by the patent citation data. Section "Concluding Remarks" concludes the paper with a summary.

Comparing the Basic Profile of East Asia and Latin America

This section is to map out the reversal of trends of GDP, science and technology in East Asia and Latin America. Figure 3.1 and Table 3.1[1] show the trend of the GDP per capita, corporate patents, SCI journal articles and R&D intensity in Korea, Taiwan, Brazil, Mexico and Argentina. The GDP per capita used to be higher in Latin America, but by the mid 1980s it was found to be reversed between East Asia and Latin America. Also, East Asian countries, such as South Korea and Taiwan, have achieved remarkable increases in innovations on average. Over the last

[1]Latin countries include Brazil, Argentina, Chile and Mexico, East Asia countries include Korea, Taiwan, Malaysia and Thailand.

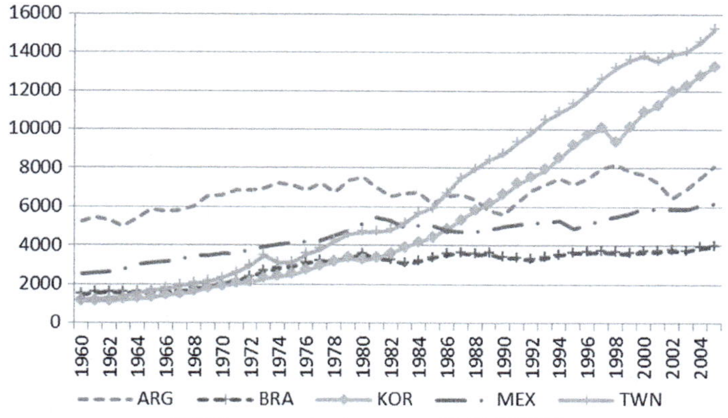

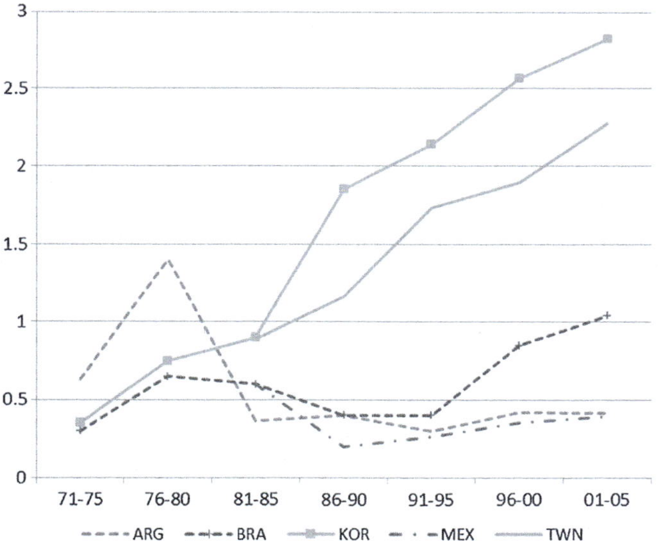

Fig. 3.1 Comparison of selected countries in Latin America and East Asia. *Source* GDP per capita: World Development Indicator (Taiwan: Statistical yearbook of the Republic of China, various years), Corporate Patent: USPTO, SCI Journal Article: Web of Science, R&D: UNESCO Yearbook (Taiwan: Statistical yearbook of the Republic of China, various years)

decades those countries that had been primarily imitators have been transformed into innovators. On the contrary, Latin American countries such as Argentina, Brazil, Chile and Mexico with similar initial economic conditions and similarly low initial levels of new-to-the-world innovation in the 60s and the early 70s have not improved substantially their capacities for innovation. As illustrated in Table 3.1 and Fig. 3.1, a sample of emerging Latin American and Asian countries registered similar number of USPTO patents between 1960 and 1984; by the mid 1990s, however, patents in the Asian economics dwarfed Latin American countries. Since the late 90s, Taiwan and South Korea have been highly ranked as the very active foreign inventors in the US (Velho 2004).

However, it is important to note that the science sector in Latin America used to be more productive than that in East Asia. This is supported by data for the period of 1985–1994; the average number of SCI journal articles in Latin America exceeded that of East Asia (2009 vs. 1344 in the 1985–1994 period). However, over the same period, patents in East Asia had rapidly risen and became twenty times as large as those in Latin America. East Asia had an average of about 219 patents in 1985–1994 whereas Latin America had no more than 15 patents over the same period. This suggests a possible reasoning that the early superiority in science by Latin America did not contribute to economic growth, whereas rapid increase of patents in East Asia may have been linked to its economic growth. Now, over the next period covering 1995–2005 the pattern was reversed; the average number of SCI journal articles in East Asia finally exceeded that of Latin America (6413 vs. 4909), which then implies a possible linkage from patents to articles.

This deviant pattern between East Asia and Latin America seems to reflect that these two regions had chosen the different policy priority in knowledge development; the priority was relatively given to technology in East Asia whereas that was given to science in Latin America. The most noteworthy characteristic of R&D expenditures in Latin America is that the government played a crucial role funding about two thirds of R&D mostly in public sector in 1990 and the fund has been decreasing and stabilizing around 57% from 1995 onwards (Velho 2004). Nevertheless, the role of Latin America's private sectors remains weak. In particular, the difference in corporate R&D among the East Asian countries and Latin American countries are substantial. None of selected Latin American countries have more than 1% of R&D expenditure to GDP. Thus, the absolute number of patents in each country which reflects the corporate R&D activities varies. In consequence, the difference in the absolute number of corporate patents, which are mainly the outcomes of corporate R&D, is indeed enormous. In the last decade of 1995–2005, the average number of corporate patents filed in the US by Koreans was 2267 whereas that of Brazil was no more than 40. However, during the 1960–1974, the average numbers of corporate patents of both Brazil and Mexico, i.e., 3.7 and 3.36 respectively were higher than that of Korea, i.e., 1.5. This was overturned since the mid 80s when the R&D ratio exceeded 2% of GDP in Korea.

To sum up, the pieces of evidence elaborated so far support the argument that technology rather than science determines the economic growth, and that the reversal of fortune between East Asia and Latin America during the 20th century is more or less the outcome of such a different choice of S&T policy (Fig. 3.2).

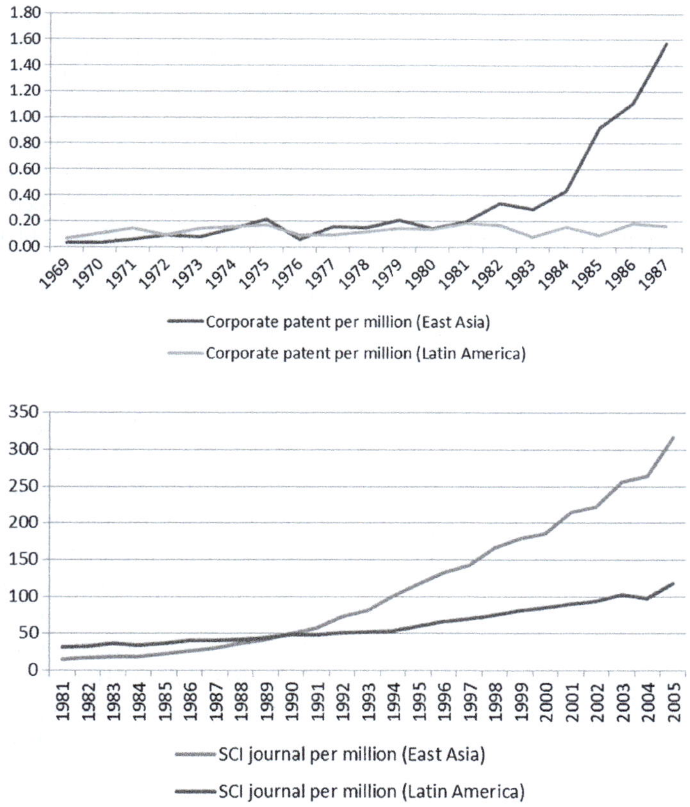

Fig. 3.2 Reversal of corporate patent intensity and SCI article intensity in Latin America and East Asia

Science & Technology Policy in East Asia and Latin America

As a latecomer, East Asia imported initially mature technology from the advanced countries, then assimilated them and increased the local R&D effort by establishing in-house R&D centers, and was finally able to acquire its own technological capabilities. Initially countries in East Asia chose follower strategies, and then succeeded in overcoming technological bottlenecks in the upgrading stage by increasing their effort and the share of private R&D (Lee 2005). In Korea, the share of R&D in sales in private firms was around 0.5% in 1982, it soon reached 1% by the mid 1980s and surpassed 2% by the early 1990s (OECD 1996). While incomparable to public R&D in the 1970s, the size of private R&D soon matched the size of public R&D by the mid 1980s and has come to account for more than 80% of total R&D in Korea since the early 1990s.

In contrast to East Asia, international technology transfer has been much less intensively linked into indigenous technological accumulation in Latin America (Bell and Pavitt 1993). There was not much demand for local R&D, given that transnational corporations (TNCs) innovate on the basis of R&D conducted in advanced countries (Katz 2001; Velho 2004; Cimoli 2000). Following trade liberalization, Katz (2001) noted that many firms no longer need 'in-house' design capabilities as they can now proceed on the basis of imported parts and components as well as employing 'on line' foreign engineering services (Katz 2001, p. 10). Domestic private industrial sectors have been substituted by imported technologies with little effort to adapt or assimilate them. TNCs' R&D activities were carried out in their home countries, whereas Latin American countries were only responsible for assembly. The policy of the Mexican government was rather focused on generation of scientific knowledge. There was an absence of incentive schemes for the diffusion of technology (Lopez et al. 2000, Chap. 8), and there were neither the policy mechanisms nor the means for Mexico to acquire manufacturing knowledge (specifically technology) from foreign owned industries. For example, Mexico provided no financial incentives for foreign companies to participate in joint ventures or even collaborative research where knowledge can be shared and transferred (Hanson 2008, Chap. 3. p. 46). There is some empirical research which argues that the lagging economic performance in Latin America was expected given the small investment in technologies. Matesco (1994) studied the technological effort of Brazilian firms to find that in a sample of 2117 firms only 3.5% of firms had any R&D expenditure. Dahlman and Frischtak (1993) reached similar conclusions for Brazil. A series of similar studies conducted for Venezuela concluded that there was no technological culture among Venezuelan firms (Alcorta and Peres 1998).

In summary, both East Asia and Latin America initially imported foreign technologies, but only East Asia has been able to build up its indigenous technological capabilities. One of the reasons for this difference is that in East Asia, the domestic corporate sectors were the main agents of technology imports, whereas the TNCs were the main agents for production in Latin America. R&D investment by TNCs in Latin America was mainly carried out in their home countries, and the TNCs rather sought to protect their technologies by confining it within the boundary of the TNCs (Hanson 2008, p. 54). This resulted in the divergence in the development of indigenous technological capabilities between the two regions. East Asia built up its technological capabilities by investing in its own R&D activities, whereas the Latin American countries were trapped in productive capabilities with few in-house R&D activities.

Science and technology in East Asia were rather co-developed and interlinked. More specifically, applied science which is needed in the industrial sector has been more emphasized and developed. Accordingly, scientific production is highly concentrated in disciplines with large impacts on industrial technology, like several engineering fields, computing, applied physics, materials science and chemistry

(Albuquerque 2001). Arnold (1988) reviewed Korea's science policy.[2] The institutional foundation of Korea's basic R&D infrastructure was strengthened in February 1966 when the government established the Korean Institute of Science and Technology (KIST). In the early 1970s, Korea's science strategy was primarily designed to "deepen" Korea's industrial structure, that is, to expand into heavy and chemical industries. Manpower policies stressed the strengthening of technical training and engineering education in fields related to these industries. Organizational and administrative efforts were made to link private and public R&D activities (Arnold 1988). The major contribution of Government Research Institutes (GRIs) during the growth period was to provide the science and technology (S&T) knowledge to be utilized for the absorption and assimilation of foreign technology and to carry out contract research for the private sector.

In contrast, Latin America's efforts were concentrated on the scientific end assuming a linear model of innovation (Velho 2004; Cimoli 2000). The science policy with a high quality crucial mass of researchers, well equipped labs and strong universities would result in "good science" which, sooner or later, would find its application in technological development. There was only a "supply-side oriented" S&T policy, meaning a policy which takes care of the supply side only (Velho 2004). According to this logic, by supporting scientific research and strengthening research-training capabilities in universities, governments were, indirectly, contributing to technological development of firms. Thus, in Latin America, identifying research priorities has traditionally been a task left to the research community and not negotiated with potential users. As such, research themes tend to be selected more on the basis of their scientific importance, taking the lead from international science, rather than on the basis of local needs. The scientific sector lacked the ability to identify the technologies needed in the industrial sector.

Further, since the demand from industrial sector itself was small, the scientific sector tended to focus on basic research that was irrelevant to the industrial sectors. Universities and public research institutes, which together perform almost 70% of R&D, have not created mechanisms to identify user needs. Instead their research agenda were selected based on the scientific criteria of international mainstream science (Arocena and Sutz 2001; Velho 2004; Cimoli 2000). Thus, the gap between the industrial sectors and the scientific sectors is expected, and both sectors could not take advantage of mutual interactions in the process of economic development. Rather, most of the successful exporting firms develop their linkages with firms and institutions in the advanced economies (Cimoli 2000, p. 123).

The government developed agencies responsible for science and technology policy created various R&D laboratories, mainly in the university sphere. In the case of Mexico,[3] the Mexican National Science and Technology Council (CONACYT, El Consejo Nacional de Ciencia y Tecnología,) has the mission of

[2]The following is based mostly on Arnold (1988).

[3]Information on the Mexican case is derived mainly from Hanson (2008).

funding, promoting and coordinating science and technology activities that lead toward national development. CONACYT's objectives include, among other things, providing scholarships for scientific training at national or international universities, funding and conducting scientific research projects, organizing groups of researchers and research centers, and coordinating R&D activities between national and international institutions of higher education. However, there are no systematic linkages pursuing knowledge acquisition between CONACYT and industry, in particular, maquiladora, which are foreign-owned manufacturing plants. Of the 15 principal projects supported in 2003, only one involved technological learning in maquiladoras. This reflects two things: (1) transnational firms in maquiladoras have no incentives for conducting R&D in or engaging in technology transfer to Mexico; and (2) Mexico possesses a weak domestic production platform. As a result, economic growth and industrial modernization followed a path that was independent of scientific and technological development. In most cases, domestic R&D activities consisted mainly of basic research and not research aimed at innovation.

With no demand made by the industrial productive sector, scientific institutions were themselves alienated from production activities. The reward system for R&D activities is related to scientific advances over technological achievements (Hanson 2008). Given that the industrial sector is a consumer of scientific knowledge, the underdevelopment of the industrial sector implies that the scientific sector may function in an ineffective way, lacking the ability to identify the technologies needed by the industrial sector. Further, since the demand from the industrial sector itself is small, the scientific sector tends to focus on academic basic research that is irrelevant to industrial sectors. Latin America is such a case.

In sum, the emphasis on scientific knowledge in LA versus technological knowledge in EA had been one of the most important sources for divergence pattern of economic growth. It is so because it is not scientific knowledge (academic articles) but technological knowledge (patents) that matters directly for economic growth in the latecomer countries where the NIS is not mature enough to facilitate mutual transformation of these two types of knowledge. As a matter of fact, Kim and Lee (2015) have conducted country-panel econometric analysis to prove such reasoning. They find that just generating scientific knowledge does not automatically lead to economic growth.

Some of the existing literature and policy discussion has placed emphasis on basic science; however, Kim and Lee (2015) empirically prove there is no significant impact of science on either technology generation or economic growth. Instead, they find corporate patents are more likely to contribute to generating scientific knowledge and promoting economic growth. The empirical findings suggest that the linear model of innovation emphasizing the role of scientific knowledge as an input for industrial innovation is not supported, especially when the NIS of countries is not effective or mature enough to facilitate such transformation of knowledge. They find that technological knowledge is primarily generated not by scientific knowledge but by corporate R&D efforts, which used to be more lacking in Latin American countries, compared to East Asia. An important policy implication emerges: without a technology policy emphasizing corporate R&D to invigorate industrial sector first, a policy that only emphasizes science may not bring about tangible economic benefits.

Analyzing the NIS of East Asia and Latin America: Patent Citation Data

Empirical analysis of innovation and knowledge is challenging because of the difficulty in measuring innovation and knowledge and the lack of data. However, patent data have increasingly become available and used for this purpose because they, especially patent citation data, can be considered as a proxy for the paper trail of knowledge flows. Like academic articles citing each other, patent citations are about which patents cite which other patents, and are presumed to be informative links between patented inventions. In other words, knowledge flows among inventors leave a paper trail in the form of citations in patents (Jaffe et al. 1993).

A methodology has been developed for quantifying NIS by using patent citation data extracted from the US patents database, and here we will briefly introduce it to use it to explain economic performance of EA and LA.[4] Citation data of patents represent how existing knowledge is used for subsequent inventions, and thus contains valuable information for the flow of knowledge (acquisition and usage). For this reason, patent citation data is useful for innovation system studies trying to capture efficiency in the creation and usage of knowledge. Jaffe and Trajtenberg (2002) provide extensive US patent data for researchers conveniently in the form of a CD. Their book also contains a description for the data and methodologies for econometric analysis using patents data. In comparing the NIS of countries, it would be problematic to use patent data from different patent office because they use different standards. Thus it is important to use patent data collected by a particular country to which the largest number of other countries apply for patents. The US Patents and Trademark Office has been collecting citation data for a long time, and thus US patents data is a perfect choice. In our international comparison, we use patents filed in the US by East Asia, Latin America, and other countries. Now let us introduce the main variables describing NIS.

The first NIS variable is related to the source in the acquisition of knowledge and the degree of localization in the production of knowledge. That is, it regards how much knowledge being created relies on foreign knowledge bases or domestic knowledge bases. In other words, it measures how much knowledge is created domestically by citing the patents owned by inventors of the same nationality. It can be referred to as a measure of the localization of knowledge creation and is a proxy for how often the patent filed by a country in the US cites patents filed in the US by its citizens.

[4]For further details on the methodology, please refer to Lee (2013).

To measure the degree of localization of knowledge creation or intra-national knowledge creation, this study uses the same methodology used by Lee and Yoon (2010), who adopted the methods used in the study by Jaffe et al. (1993). To compare the geographic localization of the citations made by the patents of different countries, Jaffe et al. (1993) suggest an approach to compare the probability of a patent matching the original patent by geographic area, conditional on its citing of the original patent, with the probability of a match not conditioned on the existence of a citation link. The non-citation-conditioned probability makes a baseline or reference value to compare the proportion of citation that matches. The basic insight of the approach by Jaffe et al. (1993) is that a probability (or degree) that country A's patents citing (or being cited by) country A's patents has to be compared with a similar probability defined with respect to a reasonably comparable reference patents. Borrowing this insight, this study can measure the degree of localization of knowledge creation and diffusion in a country as the difference between the probability of one country's patents citing that country's patents and the probability of the rest of the world's patents citing that country's patents.[5]

Using this method, calculations in Lee (2013, Chap. 3) investigates the degree of localization of knowledge creation and diffusion by several country groups, showing the differences among high- income countries, the group of Korea and Taiwan, and the group of Brazil and Argentina. It indicates that, whereas the averages for the high-income group range from 8 to 10%, the average for Korea and Taiwan indicates a steady and rapid catch-up since the mid-1980s to converge to the level of the old high-income average by the mid 1990s. By contrast, the two Latin American countries, Brazil and Argentina, do not show a similar catch-up in terms of localization of knowledge creation and diffusion. Given this contrast between the more and less successful catching-up countries or between EA and LA, there is a reason to suspect that localization of knowledge creation is one of the key variables that has differentiated economic performance in these two groups. Given that this degree measures the extent that patent citations are made within national boundaries, the fact that inventors in the high income countries tend to have a higher degree of localization of knowledge creation and diffusion is not surprising.

Beside the measure of knowledge localization, one of the most important variables representing the NIS is called the cycle time of technologies, which is about whether or not countries specialize in sectors with fast obsolescence of knowledge or slow obsolescence of knowledge (Lee 2013). This notion is expressed as the cycle time of technologies. It represents the length of the life expectancy of the particular knowledge being used. A short cycle time of technology means that the life span of the knowledge lasts only a few years and after that the usage declines dramatically as it soon becomes outdated or of less use. Cycle time of technology is

[5]This way of measuring the localization of knowledge creation is intended to control the size effects, such that a country cites more of its own nationality patents simply because of the size of the country and thus the size of patent pools. Technically, this formula may generate negative values, but it does not in the cases included in this study. An alternative is to use the ratios, not the difference.

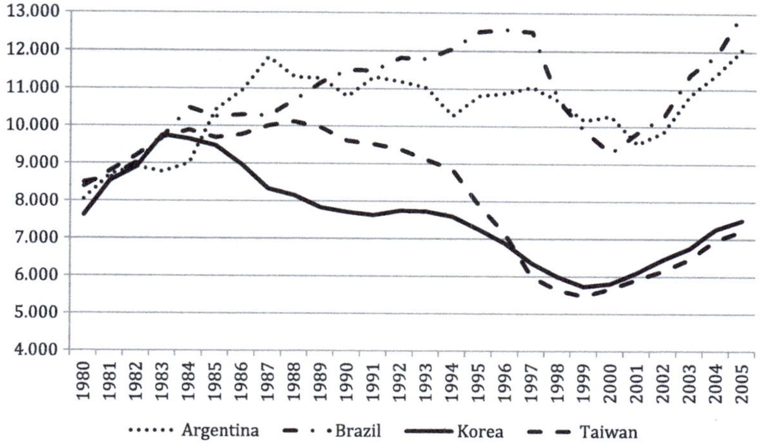

Fig. 3.3 Average cycle time of technologies in Korea, Taiwan, Argentina, and Brazil. *Source* Drawn using the statistical data from Lee (2013). *Note* The numbers in the vertical axis represent the average cycle time of US patents registered by each country, which is the average difference in application years between the citing patent and cited patents. A higher value of this indicator means the patent relies on older technology

calculated by measuring average time lags between the application (grant) years of the citing and cited patents. That is, it means how much on average a new patent relies on old technologies for invention of new knowledge.

Figure 3.3 shows the trend of average cycle time calculated by using the US patents filed by different country groups. An extremely interesting pattern is that of the Korea–Taiwan group, which shows values much lower than the averages for the high- to middle-income groups and the Brazil–Argentina group. A more important pattern is the sustained decline of this value since the mid-1980s, when these two countries started to catch up with the high-income ones. This contrast gives rise to the hypothesis that this variable must be one of those that generates the sustained catch-up of successful Asian countries. In general, Lee (2013, Chap. 3) proved that economic growth in these Asian economies was positively correlated with specialization in short cycle technologies, whereas growth in other economies, with specialization in long cycle technologies.

According to Lee (2013), short cycle time of technology means that the life span of the knowledge lasts only few years and after that the usage declines dramatically as it get soon outdated or become of less use. That is, it means how much old technologies on average a new patent relies on for invention of new knowledge. As shown by the eases of South Korea and Taiwan, specialization into short cycle sectors makes sense for latecomer countries because a short cycle time indicates less importance of old or existing knowledge which is dominated by the advanced countries and hence a lower entry barrier from the point of view of latecomers. Thus when a field of technologies is of such nature the disadvantages for the latecomer might not be that considerable. Also emerging new technologies in short cycle fields present higher growth prospects, as well as the possibility of higher profitability associated with less collision with the technologies of advanced countries and the presence of first-mover advantages. This divergence in technological specialization can be considered as one explanation how the Asian countries went beyond the middle income trap situation in the mid-1980s, whereas Latin American countries failed to overcome the trap.

Then, an intriguing question is whether the policy makers in these countries have the criterion of short cycle time in mind as they conducted industrial policy? While the answer to this question is no, they were in fact always asking themselves, 'What's next?'. They looked keenly at which industries and businesses were likely to emerge in the immediate future and thought carefully about how to enter the emerging ones. New or emerging industries or businesses are often the ones with short-cycle technologies because they rely less on existing technologies.

The advantage of specialization in short cycle technologies is consistent with the Schumpeterian concept of leapfrogging (Perez and Soete 1988), wherein emerging generations of technologies serve as a window of opportunity for the catching-up countries to leapfrog. Thus, these countries are able to grab new opportunities in emerging industries. A window of opportunity can be said to open at the time of emergence of a new generation of technologies. Overall, the emergence of digital technologies replacing analogue technologies seems to have served as a critical window of opportunity for some latecomers, especially Korea over Japan. Digitalization of many products has been undertaken for several decades since the mid-1980s, from the emergence of the digital calculator, followed by watches, fixed line telephones, mobile phones, cameras, and TVs. Digitalization of products and production processes implies lesser disadvantages for the latecomers because the functions and quality of products are determined more by electronic chips and less by skills of the engineers, which is more critical in analogue products. The view based on short or long cycle times also differs from the traditional recommendation to focus on trade-based specialization, which is more suitable for low-income countries, because it argues that middle-income countries need to specialize in technological sectors that rely less on existing technologies, and look at the greater opportunities associated with new technologies. It is also complementary to the growth identification and facilitation framework of Justin Lin (2012).

In terms of public policy, policy makers may want to choose to target an industry that is new to a latecomer country but mature in the forerunning countries. This is the beginning of a process moving into shorter-cycle sectors. Then, after a certain amount of technological capability is built up in the latecomer economy, policy makers can target another industry that is new to both the latecomer and forerunning economies. This is indeed an effort at leapfrogging, and China is already doing this in various industries. In other words, we are suggesting a distinctive policy argument that claims that sustained industrial catch-up requires not only an entrance into mature industries, but also leapfrogging into emerging industries that are new to both the advanced and developing countries.

The impact of technology cycle time on catch up deserves further discussion in view of the following three seemingly conflicting empirical findings in Lee (2013, Chap. 3). First, in the cross-country regressions, (longer) cycle time is shown to be positively related to growth, both in high-and middle-income countries. Second, however, the patents by high income countries tend to be of shorter cycle time than those by the middle-income countries, and the patents held by Korea and Taiwan tend to be of shorter cycle time than those by high-income countries. Third, for the successful catching-up economies, shorter cycle time is positively related to growth.

These patterns seem to imply the existence of a high equilibrium (high-income countries), a low equilibrium (low or middle-income countries), and a transition path between these two (catching-up countries). Although (longer) cycle time of technologies tend to be correlated with stable income growth in both high- and middle-income groups, high-income countries tend to specialize in high value-added activities in relatively medium—to long-cycle sectors (high equilibrium). Middle-income countries, on the other hand, tend to specialize in low value-added activities in long cycle sectors (low equilibrium). Fast growing countries, like Korea and Taiwan, catch up by specializing in shorter cycle sectors over time. However, as their patents spread out and become balanced at a later or more mature stage, these countries would converge to a high equilibrium pattern, getting closer to the level of the existing high-income countries, but still with shorter cycle time technologies. This concept of high versus low equilibrium is consistent with the idea by Hidalgo et al. (2007) of product spaces divided into a core versus peripheries in terms of the degree of sophistication of products. They argue that most countries can reach the core only by traversing empirically infrequent (or long) distances, which may help explain why poor countries have trouble developing more competitive exports and fail to converge to the income levels of rich countries. While their study does not discuss how to traverse the space, this chapter suggests a transition strategy from a low to high equilibrium, moving into shorter-cycle technologies (which is exemplified by the precedents of several Asian economies). This move into shorter cycle technologies can be gradual at the initial stage but at some point may involve leapfrogging, which is then consistent with the concept of 'long jump's mentioned in Hidalgo et al. (2007) which is required to make a shift to products far away from the current position in the space and to generate subsequent structural transformation.

The above discussion indicates the possibility of three alternative strategies for catching-up: high, low, and middle road. The "low road" refers to the situation of typical low—or lower middle-income countries specializing in low-value added activities or low-end goods in longer technological cycle fields. This condition can be regarded as a choice that depends on their comparative advantage dictated by initial resource endowments. Thus, along this road, countries tend to achieve a certain degree of economic growth, which may be the phenomenon called growth spurt named by Jones and Olken (2008) and Hausman et al. (2005). This phenomenon was evident in Korea and Taiwan in the 1960s and 1970s, in China in the early 1980s, and today's lower income economies, such as Bangladesh or Sri Lanka. However, these countries would find it difficult to move beyond the middle income unless they are able to initiate upgrading and establish a different specialization. The "high road" is a strategy trying to replicate directly the knowledge base of high-income countries by specializing in high-quality and highly original technologies. Several relatively advanced Latin American countries, such as Brazil and Argentina, seem to have been close to this road as they boasted a somewhat advanced level of academic research in science. However, specialization in high originality technology is not significantly related to economic growth. There may also be a low chance of localizing knowledge creation and diffusion because high originality technologies tend to be dominated by the advanced countries and thus those on this trajectory have to keep relying on those patents held by the advanced economies. Consequently, countries on the high road were not catching-up in the 1980s and 1990s.

Last, we can consider another variable for NIS which is about technological diversification. This regards whether countries or firms produce patents in a wide variety of fields or in a few limited areas. Lee (2013, Chap. 9) shows that advanced countries have a higher degree of technological diversification than developing countries, measured by in how many classes each country tend to file patents, specifically by dividing the number of patent classes registered by each country by the total number of patent classes (417) in three digit classification in the US PTO. High income countries have generally registered patents in about 40% of the 417 classes in the US patent system. In the case of South Korea and Taiwan, the degree of technological diversification has increased since the mid-80s, and the gains made by Korea and Taiwan are impressive, especially when compared to Latin American countries which started at the same level. By the early 1990s, Korea and Taiwan had effectively surpassed the level of average high income countries and had reached the 60% level that is more akin to that of the top G5 countries.

Concluding Remarks

This paper has analyzed and compared the different NIS and economic performance of countries in EA and LA, following the Neo-Schumpeterian approach. The main arguments may be summarized as follows.

During the '60s and '70s, Latin American economies were more advanced than East Asian, but this pattern was reversed later. This reversal of fortune may be explained by the Science and Technology policy choice that Latin America and East Asia have emphasized. In East Asia, policymakers preferred technology policy to science policy by putting emphasis on technological development in private industrial sectors. In contrast, based on the belief that science is an important input for industrial technology and leads to innovation, Latin America placed an emphasis on science rather than on technology. Such a policy choice isolated the science sector from the technology sector. The science sector was not able to reflect the industrial needs and was oriented toward more academic research. Therefore, the co-evolution was not achieved and finally both sectors began to lag behind. In contrast, domestic firms in East Asia have invested in their own R&D activities after adapting and assimilating the foreign technologies. In turn, the increasing demand for research on applied science from the industrial sectors enabled the co-evolution of the science sector. In other words, the divergence of economic growth in East Asia and Latin America can be explained by a policy order between technology policy and science policy.

The paper also compares the specific National Innovation Systems of East Asia and Latin America. It finds that East Asia has shown the rapid increase of the degree of knowledge localization, the rapid specialization into short cycle technologies, and increasing technological diversification since the mid 1980s or their catching-up period, which can be contrasted with the opposite case in Latin America. For latecomers, such as South Korea and Taiwan, specialization into short cycle sectors made sense because emerging new technologies in short cycle fields present higher growth prospects, as well as lower entry barriers associated with less collision with the existing technologies of advanced countries. This divergence in technological specialization can be considered as another explanation how the Asian countries went beyond the middle income trap situation in the mid-1980s, whereas Latin American countries failed to overcome the trap.

Appendix 1: Data Sources

GDP per capita (constant 2000 US $): Per capita GDP in constant 2000 US dollars. Source: World Bank, *World Development Indicators*, CD-Rom, 2007.

Population: Total population. Source: World Bank, *World Development Indicators*, CD-Rom, 2007, except for the population data of Taiwan which is from the *Statistical Yearbook of the Republic of China* (various years) published by the Government (Executive Yuan) of Taiwan.

Capital formation: Gross capital formation (% of GDP). Source: World Bank, *World Development Indicators*, CD-Rom, 2007.

Secondary school enrollment: School enrollment, secondary (% of gross). The gross secondary school enrollment ratio is the ratio of total enrollment, regardless of age, to the population of the age group that officially corresponds to the level of secondary education. Source: Herrera and Pang (2005), Barro and Lee (2000) and their Database.

Corporate patents: The number of US granted corporate patents. Source: NBER USPTO patent database by Hall.

SCI journal articles: The number of SCI journal articles, Source: ISI Web of Knowledge, Thomson.

Appendix 2

Table 3.2 Variance inflation factor of growth Equation (1)

Growth equation	VIF	1/VIF
(Log of GDP per capita)$_t$	6.43	0.155496
(Log of SCI journal per million)$_{t-1}$	5.89	0.169642
(Log of corporate R&D intensity)$_t$	5.84	0.171229
(Log of secondary education enrollment)$_t$	2.86	0.350215
(Log of population growth)$_t$	1.63	0.612763
(Log of physical investment)$_t$	1.11	0.89773
Mean	3.14	

Note Models also include time dummy but their VIFs are not reported to conserve the space. No indication of multicollinearity was found

Table 3.4 Variance inflation factor of technological knowledge production Equation (3)

Innovation equation	VIF	1/VIF
(Log of no of corporate patent intensity)$_{t-1}$	5.48	0.182566
(Log of R&D intensity)$_t$	2.76	0.362715
(Log of SCI journal intensity)$_{t-1}$	4.140	0.241
(Log of export ratio)$_t$	1.29	0.774542
(Log of US Ph.D. holders per million)$_t$	1.16	0.863982
Mean	2.420	

Note Models also include time dummy but their VIFs are not reported to conserve the space. No indication of multicollinearity was found

References

Albuquerque, E. (2001). Scientific infrastructure and catching up process. *Revista Brasileira de Economia, 55*(4), 545–566.

Albuquerque, E. (2003). *Immature systems of innovation: Introductory notes about a comparison between South Africa, India, Mexico and Brazil based on Science and Technology Statistics. Textos para DiscussÃ£o Cedeplar-UFMG td221*. Cedeplar: Universidade Federal de Minas Gerais.

Alcorta, L., & Peres, W. (1998). Innovation systems and technological specialization in Latin America and the Caribbean. *Research Policy, 26,* 857–881.

Arocena, R., & Sutz, J. (2001). Changing knowledge production and Latin American Universities. *Research Policy, 30*(8), 1221–1234.

Arnold, W. (1988). Science and Technology development in Taiwan and South Korea. *Asian Survey, 8*(4), 437–450.

Barro, R. J.,& Lee, J. (2000). International data on educational attainment: Updates and implications. *CID Working Paper, 42.*

Bell, R. M., & Pavitt, K. (1993). Technological accumulation and industrial growth: Contrasts between developed and developing countries. *Industrial and Corporate Change, 2*(2), 157–210.

Bernardes, A., & Albuquerque, E. (2003). Cross-over, thresholds, and interactions between Science and Technology: Lessons for less-developed countries. *Research Policy, 32,* 865–885.

Cimoli, M. (Eds.) (2000). *Developing innovation systems: Mexico in a global context.* New York: Continuum.

Dahlman, C. J., & Frischtak, C. R. (1993). National systems supporting technical advance in industry: The Brazilian experience. In R. R. Nelson (Eds.), *National innovation systems. A comparative analysis* (pp. 414–450). New York, Oxford: Oxford University Press.

Hanson, M. (2008). *Economic development, education and transnational corporations.* UK: Routledge.

Herrera, S., & Pang, G. (2005). Efficiency of public spending in developing countries: An efficiency frontier approach. *Policy Research Working Paper Series* 3645, The World Bank.

Hidalgo, C.A., Klinge, B., Barabási, A.L., & Hausmann, R. (2007). The Product Space Conditions the Development of Nations. *Science 317*(5837), 482–487.

Hausmann, R., Pritchett L., & D. Rodrik 2005. Growth accelerations. *Journal of Economic Growth, 10*(4), 303–329.

Jaffe, A. B., Trajtenberg, M. & Henderson, R. (1993). Geographic localization of knowledge spillovers as evidenced by patent citations. *Quarterly Journal of Economics 108*(3), 577–598.

Jaffe, A. B., & Trajtenberg, M. 2002. Patents, Citations, and Innovations: A Window on the Knowledge Economy. US: MIT Press.

Jones, B. F., & Benjamin A. Olken 2005. The Anatomy of Start-Stop Growth. *NBER Working Papers, 11528.*

Justin Lin, Y. (2012). New Structural Economics: A framework for Rethinking Development and Policy. Washington, DC: The World Bank.

Katz, J. (2001). Structural reforms and technological behavior: The sources and nature of technological change in Latin America in the 1990s. *Research Policy, 30,* 1–19.

Kim, Y. K., & Lee, K. (2015). Different impacts of scientific and technological knowledge on economic growth: Contrasting science and technology policy in East Asia and Latin America, *Asian Economic Policy Review, 10*(1), 43–66.

Lee, K. (2013). *Schumpeterian analysis of economic catch-up: Knowledge, path-creation, and the middle-income trap.* Cambridge Univ. Press.

Lee, K., & Kim, B.-Y. (2009). Both institutions and policies matter but differently for different income groups of countries: Determinant of long run economic growth revisited. *World Development, 37*(3), 533–549.

Lee, K. (2005). Making a technological catch-up: Barriers and opportunities. *Asia Journal of Technology Innovation, 13*(2), 97–131.

Lee, K., & Yoon, M. (2010). International, intra-national, and inter-firm knowledge diffusion and technological catch-up: The US, Japan, Korea, and Taiwan in the memory chip industry. *Technology Analysis and Strategic Management, 22*(5), 553–570.

Lopez-Martinez, E., & Piccaluga, A. (2000). *Knowledge flows in national systems of innovation.* Edward Publisher.

Lundvall, B. A. (1992). *National systems of innovation: Towards a theory of innovation and interactive learning.* London: Printer Publishers.

Matesco, V. (1994). *Technology strengths of Brazilian businesses.* IPEA, Brazil: Discussion Paper.

OECD. (1996). *Reviews of national Science and Technology Policy: Republic of Korea.* Paris: OECD.

Pack, H. (2001). Technological change and growth in East Asia: Macro and micro perspectives. In J. Stiglitz & S. Yusuf (Eds.), *The Asian miracle revisited.* Oxford: Oxford University Press.

Perez, C., & Soete, L. (1988). Catching up in technology: Entry barriers and window of opportunity. In G. Dosi et al. (Eds.), *Technical change and economic theory.* London: Pinter Publishers.

Rodrik, D. (1996). Understanding economic policy reforms. *The Journal of Economic Literature, 34*(1), 9–41.
Rodrik, D. (2006). Goodbye Washington Consensus Hello Washington Confusion? A review of the World Bank's. Economic Growth in the 1990s: Learning from a decade of reform (2005). *Journal of Economic Literature, 44* (Dec.), 973–987.
Velho, L. (2004). Science and Technology in Latin America and the Caribbean: An overview. *UNU-INTECH Discussion Paper* 2004-4. UN University-INTECH, 1–73.

Websites

The National Science and Technology Information Service: sts.ntis.go.kr USPTO, "Patent Statistics Reports: 2009": www.uspto.gov/web/offices/ac/ido/oeip/taf/tafp.html

Chapter 4
Catching up and Innovation in the Asia-Pacific: An Evolutionary Approach

Keiichiro Suenaga

Abstract In an analysis of an evolutionary approach to innovation Suenaga examines how several countries and firms in the Asia Pacific move from imitating developed countries to generating innovation? Neo-classical economics often assumes that only one production curve exists for the whole economy of a country, when actually there are various production curves depending on the industry, product, and process, and the introduction of a new production curve involves high risk. Innovative, risk-taking entrepreneurs are required for the introduction of a new production curve, even in developing countries. With reference to the production capability required to improve productivity, i.e., to shift the production curve upwards, when workers and technicians accumulate production experience, they develop increased expertise, resulting in improved productivity. Economies and firms in the Asia Pacific have realized technological changes by engaging not only in simple imitation but also in 'creative imitation' (Kim and Nelson 2000). An example involves adapting technologies to their environments and applying them to other industries. What is the relationship between innovation and the division of labour? Smith (1776: 9) points out the following three effects of the division of labour: (1) an increase in productivity, (2) saving time, and (3) the invention of machines. Smith's discussion specifically concerns the division of labour in a workshop, however the division of labour between factories or industries also stimulates an increase in productivity and the invention of machines. The ideas of Smith and Schumpeter appear to contradict one another at first glance: Smith's 'division of labour' and the 'new combinations' which Schumpeter regards as a key factor in economic development. Suenaga inquires whether the main factor involved in economic development is a 'dividing' or a 'combining' one? The views of Smith and Schumpeter are not contradictory he argues but complementary. Specialization in particular processes is made possible by the division of labour, yet the possibility of a new combination is also born during these processes, and this encourages a further

K. Suenaga (✉)
Meiji University, Tokyo, Japan
e-mail: od03008@yahoo.co.jp

K. Suenaga
Josai University, Sakado, Japan

T. Clarke and K. Lee (eds.), *Innovation in the Asia Pacific*,
https://doi.org/10.1007/978-981-10-5895-0_4

division of labour by extending the market. Suenaga (2015a) refers to this pattern of economic development as 'Smithian = Schumpeterian development.'

Keywords Evolutionary approach · Catching-up · Flying-geese theory · Division of labour · Creative immitation · Capability · Innovation diagram · Open innovation

Introduction

The aim of this chapter is to discuss a number of theories on ways in which the Asia Pacific have caught up with developed countries and realized innovation. The discussion will also consider factors associated with the failure of some countries in the region to catch up and innovate.

Developed countries acquire technological and other forms of knowledge. Developing countries learn these, adjust them to their environments, and gradually create their own unique knowledge. To acquire and improve upon these types of knowledge, various capabilities, including technological capabilities, are required. Developing countries cultivate these capabilities and gradually raise their technological and economic levels.

In the Asia Pacific, although some countries caught up to a certain economic level, they then remained stagnant in what is known as the 'middle-income trap.'[1] Whether or not a country becomes caught in this trap depends largely on its accumulation of technological capabilities. For example, a country had succeeded in catching up to a certain extent as a result of its affiliation with foreign firms, but when those firms left the country before it had established its own technological capabilities, the subsequent process of catching up might stagnate.[2]

In addition, over the course of the above-mentioned development, the division of labour has greatly affected the technologies and economies of developing countries. Developing countries have not attempted to develop all sectors simultaneously, but have entered processes, products, and industries with low levels of technology and then expanded gradually into sophisticated sectors. Nor have developed countries realized technological innovation in all processes, products, and industries simultaneously. Instead, they have gradually developed sophisticated technological innovations alongside technological capabilities. In recent years, which have been referred to as the age of the 'vanishing hand' (Langlois 2003), the division of labour has increased, and it has become possible to leapfrog into specific sectors that require high levels of technology. When technological capabilities which specialize

[1]See Lee (2013) on the middle-income trap.

[2]Therefore, catching up economically (where income levels catch up) is not the same as catching up technologically (where firms catch up in terms of technological capabilities).

in certain processes, products, or industries are accumulated, it becomes possible to leapfrog into the corresponding sector.

These processes are evolutionary rather than pertaining to the equilibrium assumed by orthodox economics. This paper takes an evolutionary economics perspective to discuss how countries and firms in the Asian Pacific have caught up and created new technological knowledge. It pays attention to concepts such as technological knowledge and capability, and the role of government and the division of labour in the processes of catching up and innovation.

Catching up in the Asia Pacific

Macro Theory of Catching up

How developed countries catch up has been examined from various perspectives. For example, Gerschenkron (1962), Abramovitz (1986) analyzed this phenomenon at country (macro) level, discussing the possibility that developing countries could achieve higher growth rates than those of developed countries by making full use of the advantages of backwardness. However, catching up involves removing systematic barriers and fostering social capabilities.[3]

What are social capabilities? According to Abramovitz (1989: 45), they are 'a country's ability to exploit the potential of science and best-practice technology,' and include a wide range of issues, ranging from those involving each worker or firm to those shared by an entire society, such as systems and a sense of values. This paper refers to the former as technological capabilities, and the latter as social capabilities. For developing countries to imitate the technologies of developed countries, both technological and social capabilities are essential.[4]

The mechanisms underlying how developing countries catch up can be classified under the headings 'capital accumulation type' and 'technology imitation type.'[5] In the mechanism underlying the capital accumulation type, based on the Solow model, the level of capital accumulation is lower in developing than in developed countries, so marginal productivity of capital is higher in the former, which results in higher economic growth in developing countries. In the technology imitation type, the technological level is lower in developing than in developed countries,

[3]The advantages of backwardness are closely related to issues of independence. How much a country attaches weight to independence depends on the country's history, culture, and circumstances, and differs greatly according to the era. For developing countries, how to foster their own industries is important. When a country's goal involves rapid industrial development, it may not consider independence important. Following the progress of globalization, the importance of the country as a framework is reduced. For the relationship between 'economic independence' and 'priority on economic growth,' refer to Nakamura (1999).

[4]For social capabilities, see also Abramovitz (1995), Suenaga (1997).

[5]See also Romer (1993), Krugman (1994), Suenaga (2002).

so the former can imitate the technologies of developed countries, leading to higher economic growth.

However, in order for developing countries to reach the economic and technological levels of developed countries, a number of conditions are required, which is why this is often referred to as conditional catching up. For example, in the mechanism underlying the capital accumulation type of catching up, parameters such as savings ratio and population growth rate play an important role. In the mechanism underlying the technology imitation type of catching up, social capabilities are indispensable. A number of quantitative analyses have been undertaken to elucidate the factors required for a country to catch up, and education, capital investment, economic openness, and political stability are considered important for the process.[6]

The 'Flying-Geese' Theory of Catching up[7]

Akamatsu, who proposed the 'flying-geese' theory (1945, 1961, 1965), studied how developing countries catch up. Within this theoretical framework, Kemanai (1998: 196–198) defined the process of import, production, and export of a certain manufacturing product as the basic 'flying-geese' pattern of industrialization, and the succession from consumer goods to capital goods, or from crude products to refined products, a deformation type of 'flying-geese' pattern. In addition, he defined a series of countries, from the most advanced to those in various developmental stages, as those that exhibit the general type of 'flying-geese' pattern.

Figure 4.1a shows a schematic diagram of the three types of 'flying-geese' pattern in industrialization. In this figure, a developing country 1, which began the 'flying-geese' pattern of industrialization earlier than the others, exports primary products and imports consumer goods in phase I, produces consumer goods domestically and imports capital goods in phase II, imports primary products, exports consumer goods, and produces capital goods domestically in Phase III, and imports consumer goods and exports capital goods in phase IV. Subsequently, developing countries 2 and 3 advance following a pattern similar to that of country 1. In this figure, the horizontal axis in the two-dimensional plane represents the basic type, the vertical axis in the two-dimensional plane represents the deformation type, and the vertical axis perpendicular to the two-dimensional plane represents the general type of 'flying-geese' pattern of industrialization.

Akamatsu (1945, Chap. 3) examined the process involved in the stages of production in Japan's cotton industry, from cotton yarns (intermediate goods) to cotton cloth (final goods) and finally spinning and weaving machines (capital goods). He also examined the process of development from coarse yarns (low-quality products)

---

[6]See also Baumol (1986), Fagerberg (1987), Fagerberg and Godinho (2006).

[7]See Suenaga (2012a) for clarification of this and the next subsection.

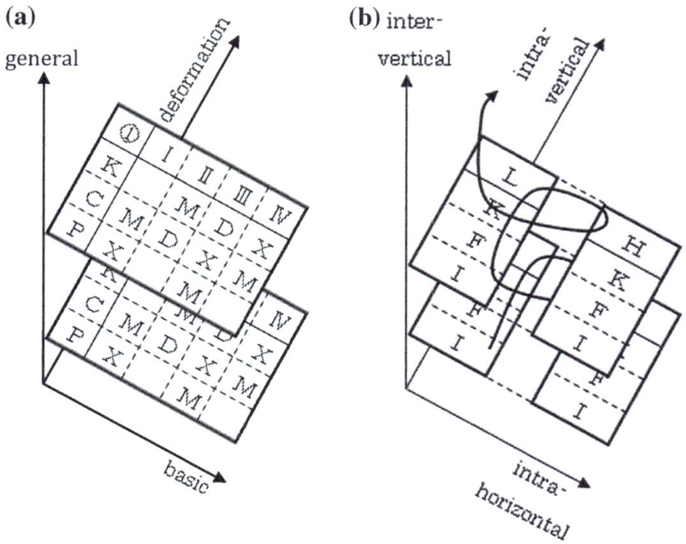

Fig. 4.1 Three-dimensional schematic diagram of 'flying geese' **a** basic, deformation, and general **b** deformation (intra-vertical, intra-horizontal and inter-vertical). *Source* Suenaga (2012a: 468 and 471). Key K capital goods; *C* consumer goods; *P* primary products; *M* importation; *D* domestic production; *X* exportation; *L* low quality; *H* high quality; *F* final goods; *I* intermediate goods

to fine yarns (high-quality products) and from light to heavy industry. According to Akamatsu's classification of the division of labour, the deformation type in the 'flying-geese' theory can be classified as an intra-industry vertical type when the process moves from intermediate goods → final goods → capital goods, an intra-industry horizontal type when it moves from low quality → high quality, and an inter-industry vertical type when it moves from light industries → heavy industries.[8]

Figure 4.1b shows a three-dimensional schematic diagram of these three deformation types in the 'flying-geese' theory. Figure 4.1b was obtained by examining in detail the vertical axis in the two-dimensional plane shown in Fig. 4.1a. In Fig. 4.1b, the vertical axis in the two-dimensional plane represents the intra-industry vertical type, the horizontal axis in the two-dimensional plane represents the intra-industry horizontal type, and the vertical axis perpendicular to the two-dimensional plane represents the inter-industry vertical type. Figure 4.1b also shows 'spiral pattern development' in the 'flying-geese' pattern of industrialization (deformation type). Thus, the development from crude to refined products occurs through the intra-industry horizontal type of 'flying geese' pattern in industrialization, while the development of intermediate goods → final goods → capital goods occurs through the intra-industry vertical type. Thereafter, the development

[8]See Akamatsu (1965: 129-130) for his concepts of the division of labour.

to high-technology industries occurs through the inter-industry vertical type of 'flying geese' pattern.[9]

As mentioned above, the 'flying-geese' theory analyzes the process of catching up from various perspectives. Although it has been quoted often in analyses of economic development in the Asia Pacific, some problems have been identified with the theory. This paper classifies these problems according to the three types of flying-geese pattern (basic, deformation, and general). First, regarding problems with the basic type, there have been an increasing number of cases in which a pattern of import → production → export (→ import) has not always been observed. In particular, the number of cases in which the import stage is unnecessary has increased as the amount of direct foreign investment has increased. Second, regarding problems with the deformation type, it has been pointed out that, because the 'flying-geese' theory analyzes the industry as a unit, it cannot cope sufficiently with international specialization that uses process as a unit, and process has become more important than ever. Third, with regard to problems with the general type, the 'flying geese' pattern of industrialization has been particularly disrupted as a result of China's economic growth.

The Division of Labour and Catching up

The 'flying-geese' theory examined in the previous subsection indicates a close relationship between catching up and the division of labour. This subsection re-examines this relationship. For example, although developments in the British cotton industry did not always lead to a division of labour, various types of the division of labour took place, such as those between low-quality and high-quality yarns, spinning and weaving processes, and the machinery industry and machine tools (Suenaga, forthcoming). Japan entered the spinning industry and expanded its sector of activity, while importing spinning machines from Britain and specializing in certain processes, e.g., spinning and products such as low-quality yarns.

The above relationship between the process of catching up and the division of labour can also be seen in the semiconductor industry, the development of which has taken place primarily in the United States. During the process of development, silicon wafers, manufacturing equipment, assembly and testing processes, electronic design automation (EDA), design, and wafer processing were undertaken by different firms, resulting in vertical disintegration. Under such circumstances, developing countries (Japan, South Korea, Taiwan, and China) entered the semiconductor industry and attempted to catch up with the United States by specializing in certain processes and expanding their active sectors (Suenaga 2010).

[9]The order of the intra-industry vertical type and the intra-industry horizontal type is sometimes reversed, and both types are sometimes in progress simultaneously.

A trend similar to that observed in the semiconductor industry can be seen in the computer industry. The International Business Machines Corporation (IBM) in the United States has played the most important role in the history of this industry; the IBM System/360 and the IBM Personal Computer led to modularization of the computer industry. Thus, a firm specializing in a certain module was able to sell a product cheaply if it was compatible with a component manufactured by IBM, and a firm was able to sell a computer that was compatible with one manufactured by IBM by combining modules produced by other firms. Consequently, a structure was generated for the division of labour which called for a huge cluster of modules. Firms in developing countries could enter the production of a certain module by making use of their comparative advantage, and these firms then launched production of other modules, gradually improving their technological capabilities at the same time.[10]

Thus, specialization became extremely important if developing countries were to catch up to a significant level, and it played an essential role in the global structure of the division of labour.[11] It may be said that developing countries can catch up more easily as the division of labour advances.

Studies have examined the relationship between the division of labour and catching up in the context of a number of different theories.[12] For example, the dual economy theory proposed by Lewis (1954), Ranis and Fei (1961) may be germane to the inter-industry vertical type in the 'flying geese' theory. As the progress of the manufacturing sector in a developing country expands, labour must shift from the agricultural to the manufacturing sector, and when there is surplus labour, it can be shifted without decreasing production in the agricultural sector. This argument plays an important role in examining the inter-industry vertical type of catching up.

Recently, following the increase in the division of labour, the concept of catching up at a micro level has attracted the attention of a number of researchers. For example, Hobday (1995) examined the process by which a firm in a developing country moves from original equipment manufacturer (OEM) for a firm in a developed country, accumulates technological capabilities, begins original design manufacturing (ODM), and finally manufactures its own brand (OBM). This process can be defined as the intra-industry vertical type of catching up. Shi (1996) considered a strategy by which a firm in a developing country could catch up based on a 'smile curve' in the supply chain of personal computers. In particular, Shi examined how a firm in a developing country would need to start manufacturing or processing components with high added values without continuing to manufacture components with low added values. This is an example of the intra-industry vertical

[10]See also Baldwin and Clark (2000) on this point.

[11]The importance of the division of labour varies according to the industry and the era.

[12]Although a number of people have recently emphasized aspects of the division of labour such as fragmentation, outsourcing, off-shoring, unbundling, spin-offs, module clusters, open innovation, open source, intra-industry trade, vertical disintegration, selection and concentration, commodity chains, and OEM (Original Equipment Manufacturing), these concepts have a close relationship with the division of labour.

Table 4.1 The relationship between the 'flying-geese' theory and other theories of catching up

'Flying geese' type		Other theories of catching up
General		Gerschenkron (1962), Abramovitz (1986)
Deformation	Inter-industry vertical	Lewis (1954), Ranis and Fei (1961)
	Intra-industry vertical	Hobday (1995), Shi (1996), Jones and Kierzkowski (1990)
	Intra-industry horizontal	Selection and concentration
Basic		Import substitution and export-oriented industrialization

Source Suenaga (2012a: 474)

type of catching up. Further, the fragmentation theory (e.g., Jones and Kierzkowski 1990) may also be applicable to the intra-industry vertical type of catching up.

A strategy for catching up in developing countries can be examined from the perspective of 'selection and concentration.' This strategy is proposed for a firm that concentrates its management resources on a certain product within a wide range of product lines, while considering its comparative advantage. After succeeding in manufacturing the product, the firm may expand its manufacturing range to other products. This case is similar to the one examined for the intra-industry horizontal type in the 'flying-geese' theory.

The basic type in the 'flying-geese' theory was originally examined with respect to the way in which the productivity of certain processes, such as spinning and weaving, could be improved. The mechanism underlying this basic type is important in examining the import-substituting and export-oriented industrialization.

Table 4.1 summarizes the relationship between the various types involved in the 'flying-geese' theory and those in other theories of catching up. Although many studies have used these theories to examine a few aspects of the relationship between catching up and the division of labour, the relationship has been summarized systematically in Table 4.1 in terms of the 'flying-geese' theoretical framework.

The Role of Government in Catching up

The role of government in economic development has been discussed from different perspectives, and it is impossible to examine all these discussions. In this subsection, the role of government will therefore be considered in the context of the discussions which specifically relate to catching up.

Many researchers have recognized that governments in a variety of Asian countries have been significantly involved in their economy. Opinions differ along two lines about the ways in which an Asian country can improve its economic performance and development: one where government intervention is needed and one where it is not. Neo-classical researchers believe that improvements in basic conditions, such as education and the macro economy, have led to successful economic growth. They have suggested that, in many instances, government intervention in an individual industry has failed.[13] In contrast, revisionist researchers, including Amsden (1989), Wade (1990), have emphasized that the governments of these countries have played an important role in their economic growth.

The World Bank (1993) noted that governments of East-Asian countries had improved their fundamental conditions and selectively pursued policies such as export promotion programs, which had led to successful economic growth. However, the World Bank scarcely acknowledges the effectiveness of industrial policy and guidance policy finance. They insisted that the former generally fails, and is not an effective measure for promoting the economy of a developing country, and that the latter succeeds under certain circumstances but entails high risk.

With respect to the above-mentioned arguments on the role of market and government, Aoki et al. (1996) proposed a market-enhancing view. Instead of a dichotomy between market and government, the market-enhancing view states that government plays a role in facilitating private-sector coordination. Aoki et al. also addressed failures in coordination and examined measures for overcoming these issues. These measures included providing contingent rents, in which remuneration is offered for successful coordination.

There has been a vigorous discussion on the role of government in economic development in terms of 'the East-Asian Miracle,' or the rapidity with which East-Asian countries have caught up. However, in the wake of the Asian financial crisis in 1997, government intervention in terms of rent seeking has once again been considered. In many Asian countries, although rent seeking existed in a wide range of public and private sectors, their economic development was attained. Khan and Jomo (2000) attempted to summarize the concepts of rent and examined the reasons for successful economic development in some Southeast-Asian countries despite the fact that rent seeking had been a common practice. Ross (2001) defined the action of a government that acquired the right to allocate rents as 'rent-seizing', and conducted an empirical analysis of institutional breakdown as a result of rent-seizing in Southeast-Asian countries.[14]

Innovation in the Asia Pacific

From Imitation to Innovation

How did several countries and firms in the Asia Pacific move from imitating developed countries to generating innovation? The process by which developing countries caught up while imitating developed countries was examined in the

---

[13]See the 'market-friendly' approach of the World Bank (1991).

[14]See also Chang (2011) for a discussion of industrial policy.

previous section. However, the process by which developing countries generates innovation was not elucidated clearly.

This subsection examines technological changes and capabilities in the context of a production function (curve) in orthodox economics (neo-classical economics). In neo-classical economics (e.g., the Solow model of economic growth), improvement in productivity is expressed as an upward shift of this curve, and the change in the factor ratio is expressed as a move on the curve. The technology imitation type of catching up in a developing country is a process by which the production curve shifts upward and productivity approaches that of developed countries. The capital accumulation type of catching up, on the other hand, is a process by which a country's capital stock per capita increases (moves to the upper right of the curve) to approach that of developed countries.

However, even if developing countries can imitate their developed counterparts, their productivity will not improve naturally. When technologies from developed countries are introduced into developing countries, it is extremely rare that they lead instantly to high productivity. Instead, a number of improvements and adaptations are required. In many cases, those required for developing countries differ from the requirements of developed countries, and these improvements may result in innovations (e.g., process innovation).

With respect to the change in the factor ratio, neo-classical economics assumes that each economic unit can select a technology freely and instantaneously (or in an extremely short period of time) from a wide range of available technologies. However, if this involves a technology that has not been used previously, it is difficult to implement. As Nelson and Winter (1982) pointed out, the use of a new technology essentially constitutes an innovation.

In many cases, neo-classical economics assumes that only one production curve exists for the whole economy of a country. Actually, there are various production curves depending on the industry, product, and process, and the introduction of a new production curve involves high risk. Innovative, risk-taking entrepreneurs are required for the introduction of a new production curve, even in developing countries.[15]

Up to this point, technological changes have been examined from the perspective of production curves in neo-classical economics. However, contrary to the assumption of neo-classical economics, there are several types of technological change. Here, the *shift in* the production curve is defined as an improvement in productivity, the *shift on* the curve is defined as the change in the factor ratio, and the *change in* the curve is defined as the change in the production function. The technological capability required to improve productivity is defined as production capability, that required to change the factor ratio is defined as switching capability,

[15]The new production curve may coexist with the old one ('co-evolution'), or may take the place of the old one ('creative destruction').

and that required to change the production function is defined as innovative capability.[16] Each capability is discussed further below.

With regard to the production capability required to improve productivity, i.e., to shift the production curve upwards, efforts in fields of production are important. When workers and technicians accumulate production experience, they develop increased expertise, resulting in improved productivity. In fields of production, 'learning to learn' (Stiglitz 1987), i.e., understanding the importance of learning, is important. In developing countries, it is essential to acquire the capabilities required to pursue improvements, as these are different from those in developed countries.

Second, with respect to the switching capability required to change the factor ratio, the accumulation of experience is important in order to change a production technology effectively. A firm must obtain the information about the production technology required to realize a new factor ratio, and must examine whether the production technology can be adopted. Even if this is possible, the technological capability necessary to realize the production technology is required. In the process of adopting the production technology, production facilities may be changed considerably, and the technological capability required to cope with the change is also necessary.

Finally, developing the innovative capability required to introduce a new production function is closely related to the accumulation of production and switching capabilities. The ability to improve productivity and change the factor ratio also improves the capability to introduce a new, sophisticated production function. The risk involved in using a new production function is higher because the function is more innovative. Therefore, it is also important to develop an ability to predict the potential of a new technology, as well as a mechanism for hedging against the risk of using such a technology.

Among the above-mentioned technological capabilities, many are tacit and cannot be codified. Therefore, it is important to transmit experience and knowledge effectively. As mentioned above, although some technological capabilities differ from each other qualitatively, some are related. For example, when a production technology is examined thoroughly in order to improve productivity, the knowledge obtained may be useful in modifying the factor ratio. To introduce a new production function, a number of related technologies are required. Therefore, the accumulation of innovative capabilities may also stimulate the accumulation of switching capabilities.

Countries and firms in the Asia Pacific have realized technological changes by engaging not only in simple imitation but also in 'creative imitation' (Kim and Nelson 2000). An example involves adapting technologies to their environments and applying them to other industries. These technological changes can be considered innovations. Improvements in productivity and changes in the factor ratio

[16]Westphal et al. (1985), Dahlman et al. (1987) classify technological capabilities into three categories: production, investment, and innovation capability. See also their books and Suenaga (2002) for the arguments in this subsection.

can also be described as innovation, and the introduction of a new production function requires innovative capability. Innovation brought about by the above-mentioned imitation can improve the capability to create a new production function.[17]

The Division of Labour and Innovation

What is innovation? Schumpeter (1934: 66) suggests that there are five new combinations of factors involved in economic development, but we discuss technological innovation that is most important in economic development. Freeman and Soete (1997: 201) define technological innovation as 'the first commercial application or production of a new process or product'. The increased productivity by process innovation, the introduction of production technology based on a new ratio of production factors, and creativity and application of a new production function can also be considered technological innovation. They are also new combinations of existing knowledge (whether it is explicit or tacit knowledge). As Nelson and Winter (1982: 130) state, 'innovation in the economic system—and indeed the creation of any sort of novelty in art, science, or practical life—consists to a substantial extent of a recombination of conceptual and physical materials that were previously in existence'.

How is the relationship between innovation and the division of labour? Smith (1776: 9) points out the following three effects of the division of labour: (1) an increase in productivity, (2) saving time, and (3) the invention of machines. Although his discussion specifically concerns the division of labour in a workshop, the division of labour between factories or industries also stimulates an increase in productivity and the invention of machines.[18]

It is interesting that their ideas appear to contradict one another at first glance: Smith's 'division of labour' and the 'new combinations' which Schumpeter regards as a factor in economic development. In simple terms, is the factor involved in economic development a 'dividing' or a 'combining' one? The views of Smith and Schumpeter are not contradictory but complementary. Specialization in particular processes is made possible by the division of labour. However, the possibility of a new combination is also born (or promoted) during these processes, and it encourages a further division of labour by extending the market. Suenaga (2015a) calls this type of pattern of economic development 'Smithian = Schumpeterian development'.

---

[17]Many skills and activities required in reverse engineering have easily been transformed into activities called R&D as some countries have approached the technological frontier (Kim and Nelson 2000: 5).

[18]However, when the division of labour takes place in distinct places, the effects of saving time vanish. On the other hand, time is saved by the invention of new transportation machines and the development of communications technology.

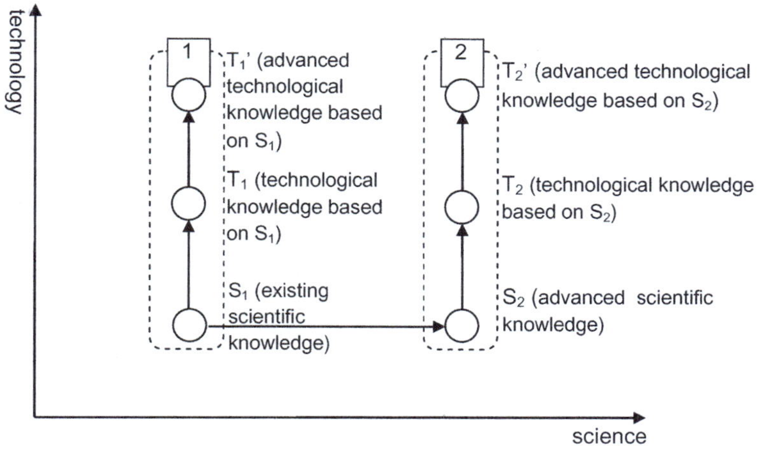

Fig. 4.2 Technological paradigms and trajectories, based on Yamaguchi's innovation diagram. *Note* This figure illustrates Dosi's (1982) view, based on Yamaguchi's innovation diagram (2006). See Suenaga (2015b)

As discussed in Sect. "Catching up in the Asia Pacific", countries and firms in the Asia Pacific have specialized in particular processes by entering into certain sectors of the global division of labour, and have realized new combinations in specific processes. In other words, the division of labour plays a significant role not only in the process of catching up, but also in innovation or new combinations in follower countries.[19]

Science and Innovation[20]

This subsection discusses new combinations of scientific and technological knowledge. Kuznets (1966) indicates that the application of science to economic production is the main characteristic of modern economic growth, and the so-called 'new economics of science' also draws attention to the role of science in economic development.[21] We focus on Dosi's (1982) 'technological paradigms' and Yamaguchi's (2006) 'innovation diagram'.

Figure 4.2 illustrates Dosi's 'technological paradigms' and 'technological trajectories', based on Yamaguchi's innovation diagram. In Yamaguchi's diagram, existing scientific knowledge (S) advances through scientific research etc., and

[19]See, for instance, Suenaga (2010) on the relationship between the division of labour in the global semiconductor industry, and catching up and innovation in the East-Asian semiconductor industry.

[20]See Suenaga (2015b) for clarification of this subsection.

[21]For example, see Dasgupta and David (1994).

advances in scientific knowledge are indicated by a rightward arrow ($S_1 \rightarrow S_2$). Existing technological knowledge (T) advances through technological development etc., and this is illustrated by an upward arrow ($T_1 \rightarrow T_1'$).

Using Dosi's (1982) definitions as a basis, if we define 'technological paradigms' as 'a "model" and a "pattern" for a solution to *selected* technological problems, based on *selected* scientific knowledge', and define 'technological trajectories' as 'the progressive process of technological knowledge, based on a technological paradigm', technological paradigms are expressed as a dotted line, and technological trajectories are illustrated as upward arrows within technological paradigms. Given the stock of scientific knowledge, Dosi discusses the process by which technology is selected from existing scientific knowledge. However, scientific progress such as progress from S_1 to S_2 is illustrated in this figure. Advanced scientific knowledge, S_2, may induce new technological knowledge, T_2, or may be triggered by existing technological knowledge, T_2. Therefore, Fig. 4.2 includes both cases.[22] Improvement along a technological trajectory can be called 'paradigm-sustaining innovation', and a shift in paradigm, with new technological trajectories emerging, can be called 'paradigm-disruptive innovation'.[23]

While accumulating technological capability, some countries and firms in the Asia Pacific have imitated leader countries and become giving rise to innovation. However, there is relatively little paradigm-disruptive innovation in the Asia Pacific. In the future, how to increase this type of innovation will become important.

The Role of Government in Innovation

While the role of government in follower countries has been actively discussed, how government should play a role in innovation is argued from a number of viewpoints. In recent years, many firms have reduced their central research laboratories and promoted industry-university cooperation (Rosenbloom and Spencer 1996). It is changing from an era of closed innovation in which research and development take place within a firm, to an era of open innovation in which there is also collaboration with universities and other firms (Chesbrough 2003). In particular, joint research is becoming widespread because the expense involved in cutting-edge R&D is enormous.

[22]Whether these advances are improvements along a technological trajectory, or a shift in paradigm, with new technological trajectories emerging, depends on whether the 'selected scientific knowledge', which is the basis of the technological trajectory, is new (even if scientific knowledge precedes technological knowledge, or technological knowledge precedes scientific knowledge).

[23]For clarification of 'paradigm-sustaining innovation' and 'paradigm-disruptive innovation', see Yamaguchi (2006).

Research and development can face a number of issues, including inappropriability and overlapping investment. Private incentive to invest in research and development can decrease because it can be difficult to appropriate the benefits of outputs. On the other hand, incentive can become excessive when investments overlap (Itoh et al. 1991). A research and development consortium has the advantage of being able to avoid overlapping investments and internalize inappropriability. However, since it is difficult for private firms to resolve these issues, governments often intervene.

Although neo-Schumpeterian researchers have been investigating national systems of innovation (Lundvall 1992; Nelson 1993), local government has been playing an increasingly important role in recent years. For example, a consortium involving the New York State government and the State University of New York at Albany, and a consortium involving the Flemish government, IMEC, have been very successful.[24] On the other hand, central government plays an important role in the Japanese semiconductor industry which has been on the decline for a few decades. This has a number of effects on the level of globalization, which influences R&D significantly; foreign firms and organizations are excluded from consortia in Japan, because central government takes the initiative. On the other hand, in the Albany and IMEC consortia, because local governments maintain external effects on their district's industry and education as the purpose of policies, it is easy to get organizations from other districts and countries to participate and to build global organization (Suenaga 2012b).

Conclusion

This chapter has taken an evolutionary approach in terms of discussing catching up and innovation in the Asia Pacific. A number of conditions apply if follower countries are to catch up with leader countries by utilizing the advantage of backwardness. In Akamatsu's 'flying geese' theory, not only macro theory of catching up but also various theories of catching-up are developed. A number of theories examine the relationship between catching up and the division of labour, and these are classified in Table 4.1. The chapter has also discussed controversies over the role of government in how countries have caught up in the Asia Pacific.

Although these countries and firms have built their capability by imitating others, their capability has evolved into a capability to innovate in their own right. This capability has a relationship with the division of labour. Follower countries and firms have specialized in particular processes by entering into certain sectors within the global structure of the division of labour, and new combinations have developed in the specific processes. In addition, these countries have climbed the

[24]On consortia between industry, academia, and government, see the 'Triple Helix' model of Etzkowitz and Leydesdorff (2000).

ladder of process, production, and industry, and some firms have leapfrogged stages.

Although innovation involves new combinations, the combination of scientific and technological knowledge plays a significant role in the emergence of new industries and technological paradigms. When follower countries catch up with the leader's technological level, paradigm-disruptive innovation becomes more significant. In particular, in an era of open innovation, how we realize innovation like this is a crucial problem, and the role of government in this process should be studied further in future.

References

Abramovitz, M. (1986). Catching up, forging ahead, and falling behind. *The Journal of Economic History, 46,* 385–406.

Abramovitz, M. (1989). *Thinking about growth: And other essays on economic growth and welfare*. Cambridge: Cambridge University Press.

Abramovitz, M. (1995). The elements of social capability. In B. H Koo & D. H. Perkins (Eds.), *Social capability and long-term economic growth* (Ch. 3, pp. 19–47). St. Martin's Press.

Akamatsu, K. (1945). *Keizai Shin Titsuzyo no Keisei Genri*. Risosya (in Japanese).

Akamatsu, K. (1961). A theory of unbalanced growth in the world economy. *Weltwirtschaftliches Archiv, 86,* 196–217.

Akamatsu, K. (1965) *Sekai Keizai Ron*. Kunimoto Shobo (in Japanese).

Amsden, A. H. (1989). *Asia's next giant: South Korea and late industrialization*. New York: Oxford University Press.

Aoki, M., et al. (Eds.). (1996). *The role of government in East Asian economic development: Comparative institutional analysis*. New York: Oxford University Press.

Baldwin, C. Y., & Kim B. C. (2000). *Design Rules, vol.1: The Power ofModularity*. MIT Press.

Baumol, W. (1986). Productivity growth, convergence, and welfare: What the long-run data show. *American Economic Review, 76,* 1072–1085.

Chang, H.-J. (2011). Industrial policy: Can we go beyond an unproductive confrontation? *Annual World Bank Conference on Development Economics 2010, Global* (pp. 83–109). The World Bank.

Chesbrough, H. (2003). *Open innovation: A new imperative for creating and profiting from technology*. Harvard Business School Corporation.

Dahlman, C. J., et al. (1987). Managing technological development: Lessons from the newly industrializing countries. *World Development, 15,* 759–775.

Dasgupta, P., & David, P. A.. (1994). Toward a new economics of science. *Research Policy, 23,* 487–521.

Dosi, G. (1982). Technological paradigms and technological trajectories. *Research Policy, 11,* 147–162.

Etzkowitz, H., & Leydesdorff, L. (2000). The dynamics of innovation: From National systems and "Mode 2" to a triple helix of university—industry—government relations. *Research Policy, 29,* 109–123.

Fagerberg, J. (1987). A technology gap approach to why growth rates differ. *Research Policy, 16,* 87–99.

Fagerberg, J., & Godinho, M. M. (2006). Innovation and catching-up. In J. Fagerberg, D. C. Mowery, & R. R. Nelson (Eds.), *The oxford handbook of innovation.* Oxford University Press.

Freeman, C., & Soete, L. (1997). *The economics of industrial innovation* (3rd ed). Routledge.

Gerschenkron, A. (1962). *Economic backwardness in historical perspective*. Berkeley and Los Angeles: Harvard University Press.

Hobday, M. (1995). *Innovation in East Asia: The challenge to Japan*. Edward Elgar.

Itoh, M., et al. (1991). *Economic analysis of industrial policy*. Academic Press.

Jones, R. W., & Kierzkowski, H. (1990). The role of service in production and international trade: A theoretical framework. In Jones, R. & Krueger, A. (Eds.), *The political economy of international trade* (Ch. 3, pp. 31–48).Oxford: Basil Blackwell.

Kemanai, Y. (1998). Keizai Seisaku no Kihon Mondai to Akamatsu Keizai Seisaku ron. *The Review of Economics and Political Science, 66,* 127–162. (in Japanese).

Kim, L., & Nelson, R. R. (2000). Introduction. In L. Kim & R. R. Nelson (Eds.), *Technology, learning, and innovation* (Ch. 1, pp. 1–9). Cambridge University Press.

Khan, M. H., & Jomo, K. S. (2000). Rents, rent-seeking and economic development: Theory and evidence in Asia. Cambridge University Press.

Krugman, P. (1994). The fall and rise of development economics. In L. Rodwin & D. A. Schon (Eds.), *Rethinking the development experience*. Washington, D.C.: The Brookings Institution.

Kuznets, S. (1966). *Modern economic growth: Rate, structure and spread.* : New Haven and London, Yale University Press.

Langlois, Richard N. (2003). The vanishing hand: The changing dynamics of industrial capitalism. *Industrial and Corporate Change, 12,* 351–385.

Lee, K., (2013). *Schumpeterian analysis of economic catch-up: knowledge, path-creation, and the middle-income trap*. Cambridge University Press.

Lewis, A. W. (1954). Economic development with unlimited supplies of labour. *Manchester School of Economic and Social Studies, 22,* 139–191.

Lundvall, B.-A. (Ed.). (1992). *National systems of innovation: Towards a theory of innovation and interactive learning*. London: Pinter.

Nakamura, F. (1999). Higashi Asia Keizai no Kiseki to Pakkege gata Gaikoku Tyokusetsu Toshi. *The Review of Economics and Political Science, 67*(5–6), 23–41. (in Japanese).

Nelson, R. R., & Winter, S. G. (1982). *An evolutionary theory of economic change*. The Belknap Press of Harvard University Press.

Nelson, R. R. (Ed.). (1993). *National innovation systems: A comparative analysis*. New York: Oxford University Press.

Ranis, G., & Fei, J. C. (1961). A theory of economic development. *American Economic Review, 51,* 533–558.

Romer, P. M. (1993). Idea gaps and object gaps in economic development. *Journal of Monetary Economics, 32,* 543–573.

Rosenbloom, R. S., & Spencer W. J. (Eds.) (1996). *Engines of innovation: U.S. industrial research at the end of an era*. Harvard Business Press.

Ross, M. L. (2001). *Timber booms and institutional breakdown in Southeast Asia*. Cambridge University Press.

Schumpeter, J. A. (1934). *The theory of economic development*. Oxford University Press.

Shi, Z. (1996). *Reengineering acer*. Tai bei: Tian xia wen hua chu ban gong si. (in Chinese).

Smith, A. (1920). *[1776]. An inquiry into the nature and causes of the wealth of nations*. Ltd: Methuen & Co.

Stiglitz, J. E. (1987). Learning to learn, localized learning and technological progress. In P. Dasgupta & P. Stoneman (Eds.), *Economic policy and technological performance* (Ch. 5, pp. 125–153). New York: Cambridge University Press.

Suenaga, K. (1997). An analysis of catch-up in abramovitz model. *Journal of Economics, 7,* 201–216. (in Japanese).

Suenaga, K. (2002). *Economic development and government: toward a theory of economic structural change* (Ph. D. thesis). Meiji University (in Japanese).

Suenaga, K. (2010). Vertical disintegration and catch-up in the semiconductor industry. *Informatics, 3*(2), 5–20.

Suenaga, K. (2012a). The flying-geese theory, division of labor, and catching-up. *The Review of Economics and Political Science, 80,* 303–322. (in Japanese).

Suenaga, K. (2012b). The role of local government in an era of open innovation: An analysis based on the example of a flemish government-funded NPO. *Journal of Urban Management and Local Government Research, 27*, 1–10.

Suenaga, K. (2015a). The division of labour and economic development: An evolutionary approach. *Research Paper of Japan academy for international trade and business, 4,* 1–20.

Suenaga, K., (2015b). The emergence of technological paradigms: The evolutionary process of science and technology in economic development. In A. Pyka & J. Foster (Eds.), *The evolution of economic and innovation systems* (pp. 211–227). Springer.

Suenaga, K. (forthcoming). The division of labour and economic development: The evolution of the division of labour between the cotton and machine industry in Great Britain in the era of the 'Invisible Hand'.

Wade, R. (1990). *Governing the market: Economic theory and the role of government in East Asian industrialization*. Princeton University Press.

Westphal, L. E., et al. (1985). Reflections on the republic of Korea's acquisition of technological capability. In N. Rosenberg & C. Frischtak (Eds.), *International technology transfer: Concepts, measures, and comparisons* (Ch. 6, pp. 167–221). Praeger, New York.

World Bank. (1991). *World development report 1991*. New York: Oxford University Press.

World Bank. (1993). *The East Asian miracle: Economic growth and public policy*. New York: Oxford University Press.

Yamaguchi, E. (2006). *Innovation: Paradigm disruptions and fields of resonance*. NTT publishing (in Japanese).

Chapter 5
A Tale of Two Cities: Innovation in Singapore and Hong Kong

Jue Wang

Abstract Singapore and Hong Kong are two small highly successful economies in Asia that illustrate very divergent paths of catching up and innovation as Jue Wang reveals. Singapore and Hong Kong have a similar history: both developed from British colonies and experienced an upgrade of industrial structure from labor intensive industries such as textile and clothing to high tech industries such as electronics and to banking and financial services (Young in NBER Macroeconomics Annual 7:13–51, 1992). The two city states have comparable economic performance and competitiveness and are often placed close to each other in various rankings such as Global Competitiveness Report (WEF 2016), World Competitiveness Yearbook (IMD 2016), Global Innovation Index (GII 2016). The GDP per capita in these two economies was almost identical until the 2000s. Singapore's economic growth slowed down in the late 1990s but quickly recovered and surpassed Hong Kong in 2004 and even overtook the US in 2011. With its recent success in finance and other sectors, Singapore is presently ahead of Hong Kong on many indicators. Although there are many similarities, the differences in the development trajectory of these two cities are clear, the most important distinction is the role of the government. Singapore is noted as government-made city-state for the high level of government intervention in various aspects of the society (Mok in Res Policy, 34, 537–554, 2005). By contrast, Hong Kong adopts a "positive non-intervention" policy that favors the free economy and minimizes the power of government in influencing the market. The difference is reflected in the innovation policy in these two economies. The Singapore government has actively implemented a series of strategies and allocated substantial funds to promote innovation and entrepreneurship. While a similar set of policies and programs are in place to drive research and innovation in Hong Kong, the scale is much smaller.

This chapter is a revised version of the journal article Wang (2018) Innovation and government intervention: A comparison of Singapore and Hong Kong

---

J. Wang (✉)
Nanyang Technological University, Singapore, Singapore
e-mail: WangJue@ntu.edu.sg

T. Clarke and K. Lee (eds.), *Innovation in the Asia Pacific*,
https://doi.org/10.1007/978-981-10-5895-0_5

Keywords Innovation strategy · Innovation activities · Patents · Singapore · Hong Kong

Introduction

Singapore and Hong Kong are two small economies in Asia, with 5.4 million and 7.2 million respectively for population and 716 and 1104 km^2 for land size. They are often placed to compare with each other due to many similarities. They are both limited by natural resources and comprised primarily of Chinese population. They have similar history, both developed from British colonies and experienced an upgrade of industrial structure from labor intensive industries such as textile and clothing to high tech industries such as electronics and to banking and financial services (Young 1992). Their economic performance and competitiveness are rather comparable, which often places them next to each other in various rankings such as Global Competitiveness Report (WEF 2016), World Competitiveness Yearbook (IMD 2016), Global Innovation Index (GII 2016) etc. GDP per capita in these two regions was almost identical until the 2000s. Singapore's economic growth slowed down in the late 1990s but quickly recovered and surpassed Hong Kong in 2004 and even overtook the US in 2011 (Fig. 5.1).

Despite of the many similarities, the differences in the development trajectory of these two cities are also noticeable, one of which is the role of the government. Singapore is known as government-made city-state for the high level of government intervention in various aspects of the society (Mok 2005). By contrast, Hong Kong adopts a "positive non-intervention" policy that favors free economy and minimizes the power of government in influencing the market. The difference is reflected in the innovation policy in these two regions. Singapore government has been actively

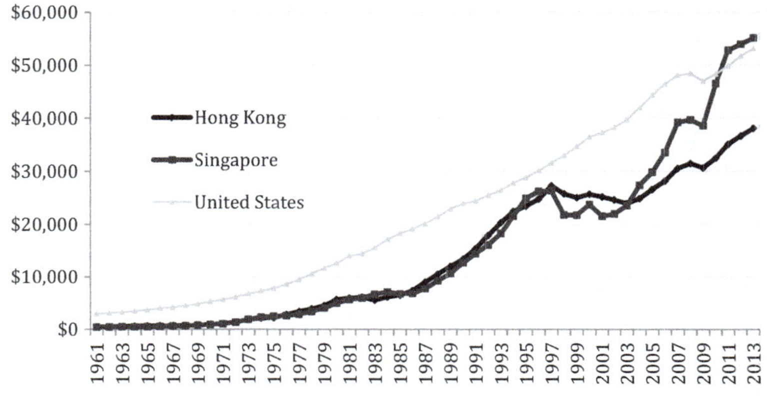

Fig. 5.1 GDP per capita for Singapore and Hong Kong (in current US$). *Source* World Bank (2016)

implementing a series of strategies and allocated substantial fund to promote innovation and entrepreneurship. While a similar set of policies and programs are in place to drive research and innovation in Hong Kong, the scale is much smaller.

Given the similarities and differences, Singapore and Hong Kong comprise interesting cases for comparison. In this chapter, we will analyze innovation activities in these two regions and explore the different innovation dynamics in the context of contrasting government policies. The comparison could shed light on the implication of government involvement in innovation.

The Case of Singapore

The Singapore government has been actively involved in the economic development of the nation. Since independence in 1965, the state has planned and implemented several economic development strategies, promoting labor-intensive export-oriented manufacturing in the 1960s–1970s, foreign invested high-tech industries in the 1980s, R&D and value-added activities in the 1990s (Wong 2001; Yeung 2000). Through the regulated labor market, taxation and financial incentives, and state-owned enterprises, the state successfully led industrial restructuring (Huff 1995). The strong state and active intervention is regarded as a distinctive feature of the national competitiveness of Singapore (Yeung 2000).

In the 1980s and 1990s, foreign investment was a top priority on government agenda and great efforts were made to attract the multinational companies (MNCs) to locate their R&D centers to Singapore. By 1992, 75% of manufacturing output and 85% of direct export were contributed by wholly foreign-owned firms or joint ventures (Huff 1995). During that period government support for science and technology was focused on technology absorption—facilitating technology transfer and diffusion from MNCs—rather than technology development (Wong 2001). The National Automation Master Plan formulated in 1988 and National IT Plan issued in 1985 were such examples. The availability of funding for indigenous innovation was very limited with only two venture capital firms in Singapore. Government initiatives to promote science and technology R&D were not evident until the late 1990s, when the government realized the vulnerability of over-reliance on foreign capital and the lack of indigenous entrepreneurship and innovation (Yeung 2000). The five-year national plan on science and technology started in 1991 with US$1.25 billion (S$2 billion), and increased to US$2.9 billion (S$4 billion) in 1996 and US $3.2 billion (S$6 billion) in 2001.[1] In 1999, the National Science and Technology

[1]The currency Singapore Dollar was converted to US Dollar based on the Foreign Exchange Rates in the respective years published by the Monetary Authority of Singapore (http://www.federalreserve.gov/releases/h10/hist/). The currency Hong Kong Dollar was converted to US Dollar based on the fixed exchange rate of US$1 = HK$7.8 as published by the Hong Kong Monetary Authority (http://www.hkma.gov.hk/eng/key-functions/monetary-stability/history-hong-kongs-exchange-rate-system.shtml).

Fig. 5.2 Government R&D funding in 2012. *Source* ASTAR (2013; Table 1.6); C&SD (2013)

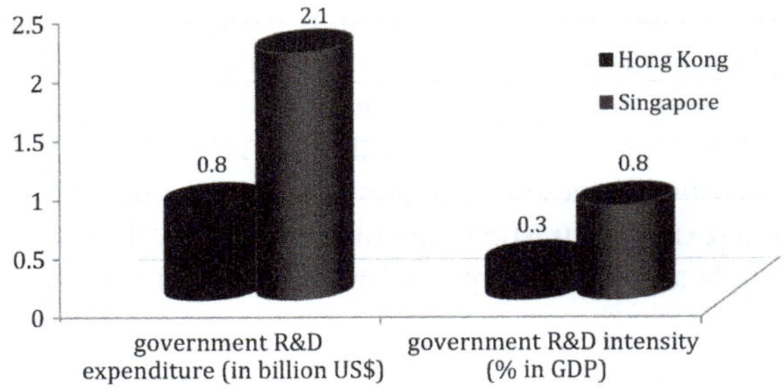

Board set up a Technopreneurship Innovation Fund with US$1 billion to promote high tech entrepreneurship by co-investing in new businesses with venture capitalists (NRF 2015). The year 2006 was a milestone and witnessed the active involvement of the Singapore government in R&D and innovation. A cabinet level organization Research, Innovation and Enterprise Council (RIEC) was launched to advise Singapore's R&D strategies and policies. The National Research Foundation (NRF) was founded to support RIEC and encourage greater innovation. The Science and Technology 2010 Plan budgeted US$9 billion (S$13.55 billion) for R&D in 2006–2010 and aimed to strengthen the foundation for R&D. The commitment in R&D was then continued by another five-year plan RIE 2015 with US $12.4 billion (S$16.1 billion). Strategic Direction for S&T Policy 2006–2010 identified two new strategic areas for R&D: environmental and water technologies (clean water and clean energy), and interactive and digital media. In 2008, the NRF launched the National Framework for Research, Innovation and Enterprise to encourage technology commercialization. In 2012, the Singapore government provided US$2.1 billion (S$2.7 billion) for R&D, accounting for 0.8% of GDP (Fig. 5.2). Higher education institutes (including universities and polytechnics) and public research institutes under Agency for Science Technology and Research (ASTAR) are the major recipients (36% and 33% respectively), followed by government organizations (21%), and the private business sector (10%) (Fig. 5.3).

Similar as the government expenditure on innovation, the size of R&D activities in Singapore is growing over the years. R&D personnel in 2011 were 44855 for Singapore, 0.87% of the total population. The R&D expenditure in 2012 was US $5.8 billion (S$7.2 billion),[2] accounting for 2.1% of GDP (ASTAR 2013). 61% of R&D expenditure was contributed by the industry, followed by universities and research institutes (29%) and government institutions (10%). Manufacturing industry is the backbone, comprising 47% of R&D performing enterprises and accounting for 60% of business R&D in 2013 (Table 5.1).

[2]The currency was converted based on the Foreign Exchange Rate 2012 published by the Board of Governors of the Federal Reserve System. USD: SGD was 1:1.22 (30th December 2012). http://www.federalreserve.gov/releases/h10/hist/.

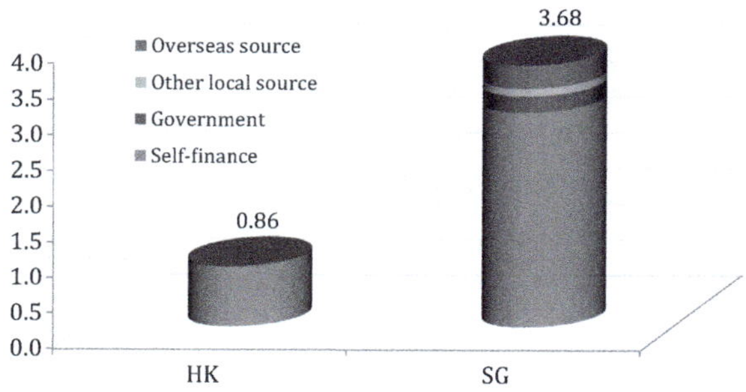

Fig. 5.3 Sources funds for Business R&D in 2012 (in Billion US$). *Source* Data are compiled by the author (ASTAR 2013; C&SD 2013)

Table 5.1 Business sector R&D activities in Singapore in 2012

Industry	GDP	R&D expenditure	No. of firms with R&D
Primary industries[a]	5.7%	0.2%	1.0%
Manufacturing	19.4%	60.2%	46.8%
Service[b]	68.8%	39.5%	52.2%
Total	US$284 B (100%)	US$3,679 M (100%)	699 (100)%

Source ASTAR (2013), DOS (2013); computed by author
[a]Comprise construction, utilities, agriculture, fishing and quarrying
[b]Includes ownership of dwellings

Together with the increase in R&D expenditure, the innovation output reflected in patents grew rapidly over time. Here we use patents granted by the United States Patent and Trademark Office (USPTO) as a measure of innovation output. As both Singapore and Hong Kong are small economies with limited domestic markets, the US is the major targeted overseas market and USPTO is the largest patent filing office. The USPTO patent data was retrieved from PATSTAT database in July 2015 for both Singapore and Hong Kong by searching the inventor country field. Patents filed by Singaporean inventors were predominantly utility patents (94%). Utility patents are granted to new product, machine and process, while design patents are meant for protecting new ornamental design that is related only to the appearance (USPTO 2015). Given that utility patents have a higher standard for innovation, the analysis below refers to utility patents only. Starting with less than 20 counts before 1989, patents with at least one inventor based in Singapore reached its peak of 806 in 2006, and then declined to 432 in 2012 (Fig. 5.4). The annual growth rate was 17% on average during 1990–2012.

Eighty-three percent of USPTO patents with Singaporean inventors were from industry, 7% from universities and 7% from research institutes (Fig. 5.5). Five percent of patents were contributed by individuals (not co-filed with institutional partners). The sum of the shares is slightly over 100%, due to double counting of inventor sector for those associated with multiple inventors from different sectors. Inventor sectoral composition is rather stable in the recent two decades. About 12%

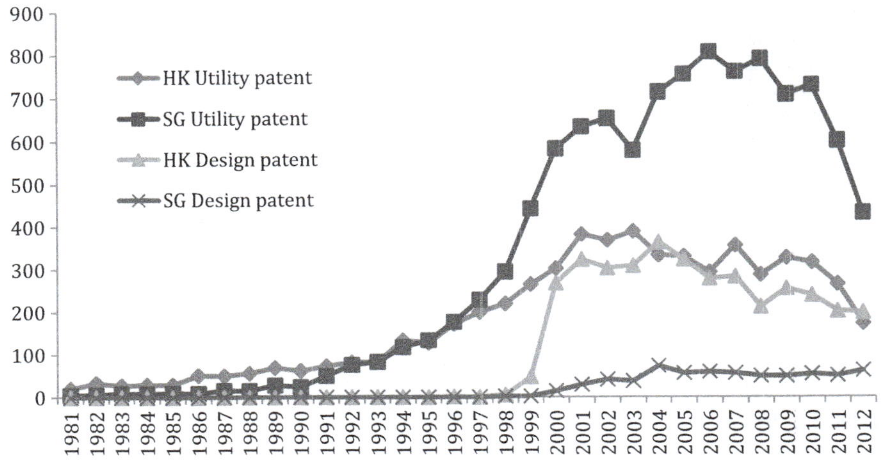

Fig. 5.4 USPTO patents in Singapore and Hong Kong

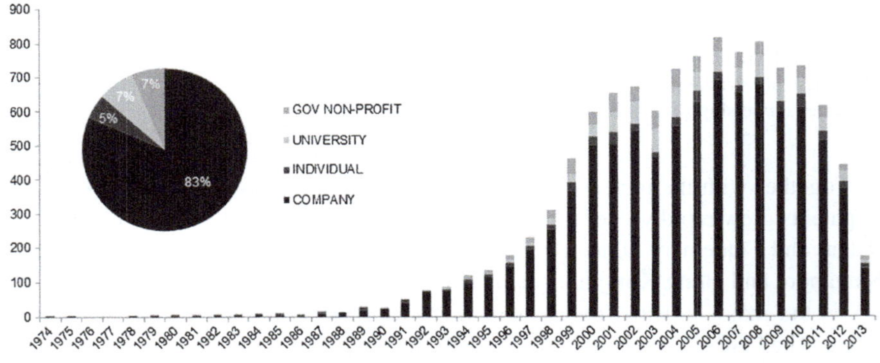

Fig. 5.5 Innovation performers in Singapore

of patents in universities and 10% of patents in government institutes are co-filed with industry partners (Fig. 5.6).

The role of multinational companies is quite notable in the innovation system of Singapore. About 69% of industry patents in Singapore are contributed by MNCs.[3] Six out of ten top patent holders are MNCs, with only two local firms (Table 5.2). The other top players are two public research institutions—ASTAR and National University of Singapore. Even Chartered Semiconductor Manufacturing, the top patent contributor, was later acquired by a US company Globalfoundries in 2009 (#10 on the top list). The US is the major R&D collaborating country for Singapore.

[3]A patent is classified under MNCs if the parent firm or headquarter of the applicant firm is located in other countries, despite the fact that the applicant firm might be based in Singapore.

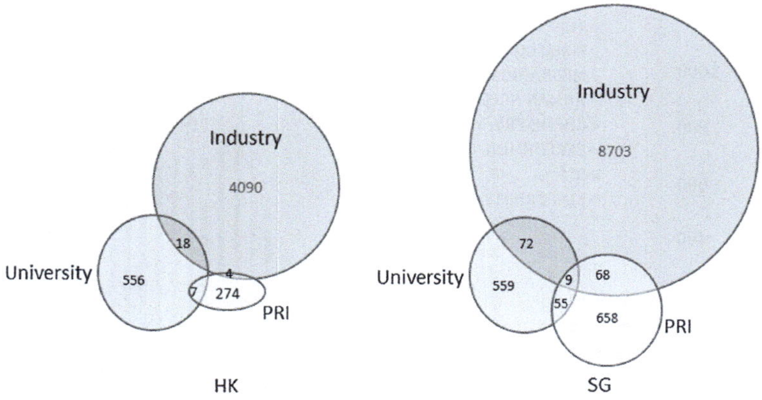

Fig. 5.6 Cross-sectional co-patenting in Singapore and Hong Kong

Table 5.2 Top patent assignees and top local industry patent assignees in Singapore

	Patent assignees	#	%	Local industry patent assignees	#	%
1.	Chartered Semiconductor Manufacturing (SG)	968	9	Chartered Semiconductor Manufacturing	968	35
2.	STATS ChipPAC (SG)	796	7	STATS ChipPAC	796	29
3.	ASTAR (SG)	729	7	Creative Technology	110	4
4.	Micron Technology (US)	377	4	TriTech Microelectronics	56	2
5.	Seagate Technology (US)	358	3	United Test & Assembly Center	43	2
6.	National University of Singapore (SG)	355	3	Trek 2000 International	30	1
7.	Hewlett-Packard (US)	301	3	ST Engineering (ST)	21	1
8.	STMicroelectronics (Switzerland)	294	3	Systems on Silicon Manufacturing Company	21	1
9.	Panasonic Corporation (Japan)	287	3	Advanpack Solutions	20	1
10.	Globalfoundries (US)	240	2	E-Book Systems	19	1
	Sum of top ten	*4619*	*43*	*Sum of top ten*	*2084*	*75*
	Total patent counts	*10685*	*100*	*Total local industry patents*	*2784*	*100*

Twenty percent of the patents were co-invented with inventors who reside in the US, followed by Japan (4%), Taiwan (3%) and Malaysia (2%).

While MNCs are still the major player in Singapore's industrial innovation system, innovation output from local industry started to pick up in mid-1990s. In early 1990s, only 10–20% of patents came from local firms, and the share increased to around 30% in the 2000s. A total of 540 local companies have been granted with USPTO patents, but a small number of innovators are playing a dominating role,

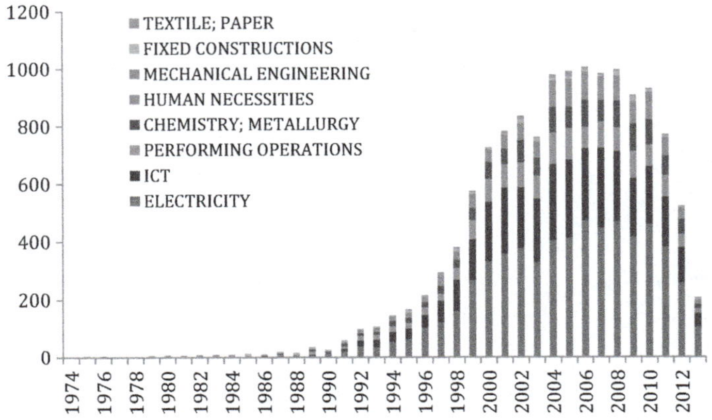

Fig. 5.7 Technical fields of patents in Singapore

with top ten companies account for 75% of patents filed by local industry (Table 5.2).

Patents in Singapore are predominately focused on the categories of electronics and ICT, accounting for 57 and 32% of total patents respectively (Fig. 5.7). The other popular categories include machinery (13%) and chemistry (11%). The dominant role of electronics and ICT was not established until 1990. Before then, there was no significant difference in areas of the patenting activities. Starting from 1990, patents in electronics and ICT have grown rapidly and far surpassed other fields. It is also evident in the top patent applicant list, where all the top industry patent performers are rooted in the semiconductor and electronics industry (Table 5.2). As reflected in the technical fields, innovation in Singapore is highly responding to the government initiatives, with the patenting activities being rather coordinated and concentrated in the strategic areas.

The Case of Hong Kong

While the outstanding economic performance of Singapore and other Newly Industrialized Countries (NICs) in East Asia in the 1980s and 1990s can be attributed to the strong state and active interventionist industrial policy by the governed market theory (Wade 1990), Hong Kong is an exception, with equally successful economic growth but less active industrial policy. State invention in Hong Kong varies in different period of time. In the 1960s and 1970s, due to the limited financial resources and conservative nature of the state, Hong Kong was regarded as laissez-faire capitalism with non-interventionist economic philosophy and low public expenditure. It features free trade, no restrictions on import or currency, low taxes, small government, little state borrowing, regular budget surpluses, no long-term state planning and market intervention (Goodstadt 2005; Sharif 2012). Starting from the 1980s, the Hong Kong government adopted a new state intervention strategy that could be described as positive non-interventionism—no resource allocation but responding to industries' with regulations. Public expenditure still remained low. After sovereignty change in 1997, the government was under pressure to perform and became more interventionist oriented (Cheung 2000). Hong Kong was perceived to be less successful in technology development than Taiwan and Singapore, and there was a call for greater government involvement in areas such as science parks, government R&D subsidy and expansion of university engineering research activities (Davies 1996). Several state initiatives to promote industrial development and the economy were announced in this period, although the scope and scale were rather limited compared with other NICs. In 1997, Hong Kong government revisited its technology policy and became more proactive in promoting innovation and technology commercialization (Yam et al. 2011). In 2000, the Innovation and Technology Commission (ITC) was set up to encourage innovation and technology development. In 2006, ITC set up five R&D centers in selected areas to drive industry-oriented R&D and facilitate commercialization: automotive parts and accessory systems; information and communications technologies; logistics and supply chain management enabling technologies; nanotechnology and advanced materials; and textiles and clothing. A similar cabinet level organization—the Steering Committee on Innovation and Technology was founded in 2004 to coordinate innovation policies and activities. Financial support for innovation comes from the Innovation and Technology Fund (ITF) that was set up in 1999 with US$0.6 billion (HK$5 billion) and is managed by ITC (2015). The bulk of the funding goes to various competitive schemes under the fund, with a certain portion earmarked for the Hong Kong Applied Science and Technology Research Institute. In addition, it also funds several research institutes such as the Nano and Advanced Materials Institute, the Hong Kong Research Institute of Textiles and Apparel, the Automotive Parts and Accessory Systems Research and Development Centre and the Research and Development Centre for Logistics and Supply Chain Management Enabling Technologies. In May 2001 the Hong Kong Science and Technology Parks Corporation (HKSTPC) was established to provide infrastructural support to high technology businesses and activities. The Hong Kong Science Park opened in 2002 is one of the key venues. However, these initial efforts were not further supplemented by other initiatives and resources. Government investment in R&D remains modest and does not keep up with the publicized commitment to step-up innovation (Shih and Chen 2010). Small government and big market still features Hong Kong's current economic and innovation policymaking apparatus (Sharif 2012). In 2012, the Hong Kong government financed US$0.8 billion (HK$ 6.8 billion) for R&D, only 0.3% of GDP (C&SD 2013) (Fig. 5.2). The lion share of the funding went to the universities and research institutes. The private business sector only received 1% of the government funding and is largely left to itself for the financing of R&D (Fig. 5.3). Close to 86% of R&D expenses are self-financed and 12% are from affiliates or parent companies. Little public policy support was there to grow high technology sectors such as the IC design industry (Fuller 2010) (Table 5.3).

Table 5.3 Business sector R&D activities in Hong Kong in 2012

Industry	GDP	No. of Establish ments	R&D expenditure	No. of firms with R&D	No. R&D personnel
Manufacturing	1.5%	3.0%	5.1%	11.7%	7.8%
Import/export, wholesale and retail trades, and accommodation and food services	29%	50%	37.7%	44.2%	34%
Information and communications	3.5%	3.2%	31.1%	24.3%	39.6%
Financing, insurance, real estate, professional and business services	27.4%	25.6%	19.9%	*12.4%*	*14.4%*
Other service	33.1%	18.3%	6.2%	7.4%	4.2%
Total	US $261 B (100%)	300,241 (100%)	US$852M (100%)	4499 (100%)	11,385 (100%)

Source C&SD (2014, 2015a, b); computed by author

The size of R&D activities in Hong Kong is much smaller than that in Singapore. R&D personnel in 2011 were 24,460 for Hong Kong, 0.35% of the total population. The R&D expenditure in 2012 was US$1.9 billion (HK$14.8 billion), only 0.73% of GDP (C&SD 2013). Universities and research institutes outperformed industry, accounting for 51% of R&D expenditure. Industry and the government sector (mainly public technology support organization[4]) performed 45% and 4% respectively. Trade, accommodation and food service, and finance dominated Hong Kong's industry sector, accounting for 79% of the firms in 2012. They also employed 88% of R&D personnel and contributed to 89% of business R&D activities. The role of manufacturing industry in innovation is quite minimal with 7.8% of R&D personnel and 5.1% of R&D expenditures (C&SD 2014).

Together with the increase in R&D expenditure, the innovation output reflected in grew rapidly until the 2000s, when patenting activities started to stagnate (Fig. 5.4). One notable difference can be found between patent statistics in Hong Kong and Singapore: while patents filed by Singaporean inventors were predominantly utility patents, Hong Kong inventors were equally interested in utility patents and design patents. Starting from 2001, half of USPTO patents in Hong Kong were

[4]Includes Hong Kong Productivity Council, Hong Kong Applied Science and Technology Research Institutes, Hong Kong R&D Center for Logistics and Supply Chain Management Enabling Technologies, Hong Kong Institute of Textiles and Apparel, and Nano and Advanced Materials Institute.

Fig. 5.8 Innovation performers in Hong Kong

design patents. To be consistent with the Singapore case, we refer to utility patents only for the analysis below. The number of utility patents (patents thereafter) in Hong Kong is slightly higher than Singapore before the mid-1990s, and grew steadily yet slower until the early 2000s when reaching the peak of 389 in 2003. Since then it has been declining gradually. The gap between the patent counts in Hong Kong and Singapore has been enlarged and reached its maximum in 2008, when Singapore had 2.75 times of the patents in Hong Kong.

The patent applicant profile shows some difference between Singapore and Hong Kong. In Hong Kong, public research institutions are quite active in R&D, with universities producing 9% of patents and research institutes 4% (Fig. 5.8). They also accounted for six of the top ten patent assignees (Table 5.4). The industry sector filed 4108 patents, accounting for 67% of total patents. Surprisingly individuals in Hong Kong are quite enthusiastic in filing patents. The share of patents filed by individuals with no institutional partners was as high as 20% and the proportion was still increasing in most recent years.

The local industry doesn't lag too much to that in Singapore with a total patent count of 2056 (Table 5.4). Half of industrial patents were contributed by local firms while the other half came from MNCs, mainly US (21%) followed by mainland China (5%) and UK (2%). Three local firms and one US firm appear on the top assignee list. Innovation activities are much spread out in Hong Kong, with 1348 local companies being granted with patents and the top ten companies accounting only 26% of the local industry patents (compared with 75% in Singapore). Cross sectional collaboration is even less in Hong Kong, with only about 3% of patents in universities and 1% patents in government institutes are co-filed with industry partners (Fig. 5.6).

The fields of patents are more dispersed in Hong Kong than that in Singapore. The leading category of patenting is human necessities (31%), particularly in the fields of domestic appliances (8%), medical science (8%) and sports/games (8%) (Fig. 5.9). Electronics (30%) and ICT (27%) are the other two active categories, which is similar to Singapore. Starting at close to 50% in the 1970s and 1980s, the share of human necessities declined in the 1990s and went below 20% in 2000. It was overtaken by electronics and ICT in the mid-2000s.

Table 5.4 Top patent assignees and top local industry patent assignees in Hong Kong

	Patent assignees	#	%	Local industry patent assignees	#	%
1.	Hong Kong Applied Science and Technology Research Institute (HK)	189	3	SAE Magnetics	148	7
2.	Hong Kong Polytechnic University (HK)	159	3	ASM Assembly Automation	82	4
3.	Hong Kong University of Science and technology (HK)	151	2	Johnson Electric	69	3
4.	SAE Magnetics (HK)	148	2	ASAT	53	3
5.	City University of Hong Kong (HK)	93	2	Wonderland Nurserygoods	48	2
6.	Asm Assembly Automation (HK)	82	1	Defond Manufacturing	36	2
7.	Astec International (US)	77	1	Silverlit Toys Manufactory	34	2
8.	Chinese University of Hong Kong (HK)	69	1	The Sun Lock Company	25	1
9.	Johnson Electric (HK)	69	1	VTECH Electronics	25	1
10.	University of Hong Kong (HK)	64	1	World Wide Stationery Manufacturing	24	1
	Sum of top ten	*1099*	*18*	*Sum of top ten*	*544*	*26*
	Total patent counts	*6147*	*100*	*Total local industry patents*	*2056*	*100*

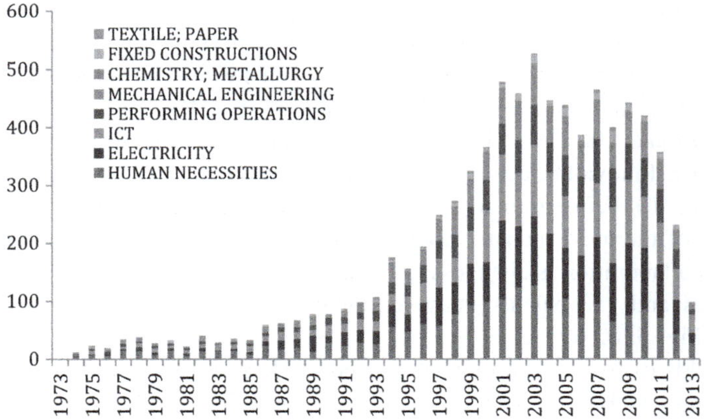

Fig. 5.9 Technical fields of patents in Hong Kong

Discussion

This study intends to portray innovation characteristics in two economies that are similar but with contrasting government roles. Singapore is well known for its strong government and long history of government intervention in economy. The government has directed the economic upgrade from labor intensive industry to technology intensive industry. In the recent decade, the government is actively promoting R&D and innovation activities and tries to transform Singapore into an innovation-led economy. The large amount of R&D budget, a series of S&T and innovation plans, and set-up of R&D coordination and funding agencies can be seen as evidence. By contrast, Hong Kong is known for the laissez-faire capitalism with the characteristics of non-interventionism and later positive non-interventionism. The government keeps a low public budget and has a limited role in the market. While Hong Kong also intends to stimulate innovation by setting up innovation fund, the effort is rather small in both scope and scale.

The overall counts of patents granted by USPTO to Singapore and Hong Kong are similar. However, a big portion of innovation in Hong Kong is in design, which is regarded as less innovative compared with utility patents that are meant for invention. In terms of utility patents only, the number of patents produced in Singapore is 1.78 times of that produced in Hong Kong, and the gap is increasing over the years, reaching 2.5 in 2012. Industry innovation capacity appears to be lagged in Hong Kong, contributing to only 67% of utility patents, while in Singapore, the share of industry is 83%. The limited role of Hong Kong industry is also reflected in the R&D expenditure, accounting for 45% of the R&D expenditure in 2012, with only 4.8% from manufacturing industry. Manufacturing industry in Singapore accounted for 58% of R&D expenditure in 2012, more than ten times of that in Hong Kong. The comparison shows the manufacturing industry in Hong Kong is not very active in innovation. It is partly due to the negligible government support for industrial innovation. Only 1% of government R&D budget was allocated to the industry sector in 2012, which was less than one-tenth of the proportion for Singapore. But the primary reason is the small share of manufacturing sector in the industrial structure. In 2012, manufacturing in Hong Kong accounted for only 1.5% of GDP, while the service industry acted as the backbone of the economy with a contribution of 93% of GDP (C&SD 2015a). In the same period in Singapore, the shares were 19.4% and 68.8% respectively (DOS 2013). The high cost in labor and land in the 1980s posed threats to the development of manufacturing industry in Hong Kong. A big portion of the industry was relocated to mainland China especially the Pearl River Delta area that is adjacent to Hong Kong due to lower costs (Yam et al. 2011). Together with that, R&D activities were also substantially transferred to mainland China (Huang and Sharif 2009). For businesses with external R&D collaboration in 2013, 72.7% of them were collaborating with organizations in the Pearl River Delta area (C&SD 2014). The extent of R&D activities based in Hong Kong is inevitably affected by the relocation and appeared to have stagnated since then.

On the other hand, while the industry sector in Singapore performs much better in R&D, a big credit would be taken by MNCs. Over 70% of private sector R&D expenditure came from MNCs (ASTAR 2013). A similar share of industry patents was also contributed by MNCs. The domination of MNCs brings opportunities for Singapore's economy, but also poses challenges for the development of indigenous firms. Overall the pool of local industrial innovation performers in Singapore is much smaller than that in Hong Kong. The number of local industry patent holders is 540 for Singapore and 1348 for Hong Kong. Since the 2000s, with the policy emphasis moving from foreign investment to local innovation and the subsequent large amount R&D investment, the local industry became more involved in R&D activities and its share in patent counts has been slowly but steadily climbing. The progress is largely driven by the government. The only two local innovators on the top patent assignees list (Table 5.2), Chartered Semiconductor and STATS ChipPAC, have obvious connections with the Singapore government. Chartered Semiconductor was established as a joint venture between a state-owned defense company ST Engineering and two US companies Sierra Semiconductor and National Semiconductor. It was then fully acquired by ST Engineering, before taking over by Globalfoundries. STATS ChipPAC started as a result of acquisition of ChipPAC, a US-based chip packaging company, by ST Assembly Technology Service (STATS), a Singapore government linked company (GLC). The merger is one of the attempts that the Singapore government has made to grow the chip sector.

In addition to more innovation output, the high government intervention in Singapore also led to more coordinated R&D activities. Around 80% of patents are in the category of electronics and ICT, which is the area that Singapore has been promoting since the 1980s. It is now one of the leading industries, accounting for 27% of total output in the manufacturing sector. The high concentration of innovation activities in a few selected fields shows that innovation in Singapore is largely directed and spurred by government policy. Large amount of R&D expenditure in priority areas together with high standard infrastructure and platform contributed to the innovation. Likewise, in areas that are not favored by the government, patents are quite minimal. It again shows that innovation in Singapore is more top-down, pushed by the government. Private sector-led cluster development is still limited. By contrast, while Hong Kong government also cherry-picked several priority areas for development, the efforts are not reflected in the innovation activities. Patents are more spread across fields. The mismatch between public R&D and private R&D implies that areas set by the funding agencies are not responding to industrial needs (Shih and Chen 2010). In addition, small local firms and individuals are the main innovation performers in Hong Kong, who are less influenced by government policy.

Both regions are now planning for the next step development of innovation and technology, which implies that stronger government is perceived to be desirable. Singapore has been working on the next five-year RIE2020 plan. They will continue to selectively support some priority areas for national needs, including biomedical science, digital technology, and water/energy technologies (Teo 2015).

Particular attention will be given to challenges faced by local firms in R&D. Various funding schemes are set up to address the financial needs at different stages. Local firms are also encouraged to collaborate with public research institutions for technological needs. Hong Kong is also in the process of strengthening the role of government in the innovation system. The Academy of Sciences of Hong Kong was inaugurated on 5th December 2015 to promote the development of science and technology. It also launched a new Innovation and Technology Bureau on 20th November 2015, encompassing the existing Innovation and Technology Commission and the Office of Government Information Chief Officer. With a starting budget of US$9 million, the new initiative aims to work with the Hong Kong Science Park, Cyberport and the Productivity Council and boost the development of the IT sector in Hong Kong (Li 2015). It is also proposed to inject another HK$5 billion to the Innovation and Technology Fund and add a few new schemes to support university technology commercialization and private sector R&D activities (CEDB 2015).

Conclusion

Innovation dynamics in both Singapore and Hong Kong are rather unique. Singapore has a strong government that tries to direct innovation activities by providing a large amount R&D investment in selected research areas. It appeared to be quite effective with a rapid growth in patents, particularly in those selected areas. While small and medium enterprises (SMEs) are generally the main innovation players in many countries, it is not the case in Singapore. Singapore's economy and innovation activities are dominated by MNCs and GLCs, which together accounted for more than half of firms performing R&D in 2012 (ASTAR 2013). The share would be much bigger if we look at the number of R&D personnel or R&D expenditure. Motivating more local companies to perform R&D and facilitating the knowledge spillover from MNCs and GLCs will be the key challenge for Singapore.

The innovation characteristics in Hong Kong appear to be just the opposite: relatively small amount of government investment with little contribution to the industry, more spontaneous research and more diversified research fields. The lagging performance in innovation has been in a great part attributed to the neglect of the government and insufficient policy support. The technology industry appears to be shrinking and the manufacturing sector is almost negligible. Top patent holders are mostly public sector universities and research institutes, who are the main recipients of the limited government R&D funding. On the other hand, industry R&D, despite low figures in R&D expenditure and patent statistics, was mainly contributed by local firms with their own funds. Innovation is not dominated by big players and there is no significant role of MNCs. The number of local firms involved in R&D is even bigger than Singapore, which forms a good base for Hong Kong to draw on for the development of innovation economy.

References

ASTAR. (2013). *National survey of R&D in Singapore 2012*. Singapore: Agency for Science, Technology and Research.

C&SD. (2013). Hong Kong innovation activities statistics 2012. Hong Kong: Census and Statistics Department.

C&SD. (2014). Hong Kong innovation activities statistics 2013. Hong Kong: Census and Statistics Department.

C&SD. (2015a). Hong Kong Statistics, http://www.censtatd.gov.hk/hkstat/sub/sp250.jsp?tableID=036&ID=0&productType=8. Accessed November 6th 2015.

C&SD. (2015b). 2014 Gross Domestic Product. Hong Kong: Census and Statistics Department.

CEDB. (2015). 2015 Policy Address—CEDB Major Policy Initiatives: Innovation and Technology, http://www.cedb.gov.hk/about/policy3.htm. Accessed 15th November 2015.

Cheung, A. B. L. (2000). New interventionism in the making: Interpreting state interventions in Hong Kong after the change of sovereignty. *Journal of Contemporary China, 9*(24), 291–308.

Davies, H. (1996). High IQ and low technology: Hong Kong's key to success. *Long Range Planning, 29*(5), 684–690.

DOS. (2013). Yearbook of Statistics Singapore 2013. In Department of Statistics Singapore (ed.), Singapore.

Fuller, D. B. (2010). Government neglect and the decline of Hong Kong's integrated circuit design industry. In D. B. Fuller (Ed.), *Innovation policy and the limits of Laissez-fair: Hong Kong's policy in comparative perspective* (pp. 242–266). New York, NY: Palgrave Macmillan.

GII. (2016). *The global innovation index 2016 report*. Geneva, Switzerland: World Intellectual Property Organization.

Goodstadt, L. F. (2005). *Uneasy partners: The conflict between public interest and private profit in Hong Kong*. Hong Kong: Hong Kong University Press.

Huang, C., & Sharif, N. (2009). Manufacturing dynamics and spillvers: The case of Guangdong Province and Hong Kong, Macau and Taiwan (HKMT). *Research Policy, 38*(5), 813–828.

Huff, W. Gregg. (1995). The developmental State, Government, and Singapore's economic development since 1960. *World Development, 23*(8), 1421–1438.

IMD. (2016). *IMD world competitiveness yearbook 2016*. Lausanne, Switzerland: IMD World Competitiveness Center.

ITC. (2015). *Innovation and technology fund: Memorandum note*. Hong Kong: Innovation and Technology Commission.

Li, J. (2015). Hong Kong to Foster IT Industry with New Bureau Established, *CRIEnglish* http://english.cri.cn/12394/2015/11/21/4203s905183.htm. Accessed 24th November 2015.

Mok, K. H. (2005). Fostering entrepreneurship: Changing role of government and higher education governance in Hong Kong. *Research Policy, 34,* 537–554.

NRF. (2015). Innovation and Enterprise Milestones, http://www.nrf.gov.sg/innovation-enterprise/innovation-enterprise-milestones. Accessed 5 June 2015.

Sharif, N. (2012). Facilitating and promoting innovative entrepreneurship in Hong Kong: Theory and practice. *Canadian Journal of Administrative Sciences, 29,* 139–153.

Shih, C., & Chen, S.-H. (2010). On reform of Hong Kong's Public Research Funding System. In D. B. Fuller (Ed.), *Innovation policy and the limits of Laissez-faire: Hong Kong's policy in comparative perspective* (pp. 114–144). New York, NY: Palgrave Macmillan.

Teo, C. H. (2015). Opening of the Singapore Scientific Conference 2015, https://www.mha.gov.sg/Newsroom/speeches/other-speeches/Pages/The-Opening-of-the-Singapore-Scientific-Conference-2015-Speech-by-Mr-Teo-Chee-Hean,-Deputy-Prime-Minister.aspx. Accessed 15 November 2015.

USPTO. (2015). Types of patents, http://www.uspto.gov/web/offices/ac/ido/oeip/taf/patdesc.htm. Accessed 16 November 2015.

Wade, R. (1990). *Governing the market: Economic theory and the role of Government in East Asian Industrialization*. Princeton, NJ: Princeton University Press.

WEF. (2016). *The global competitiveness report 2016–2017*. Geneva, Switzerland: World Economic Forum.

Wong, P.-K. (2001). The role of State in Singapore's industrial development. In P.-K. Wong & C.-Y. Ng (Eds.), *Industrial policy, innovation and economic growth: The experience of Japan and the East Asian NIEs* (pp. 503–569). Singapore: Singapore University Press.

World Bank. (2016). GDP per capita (current US$), http://data.worldbank.org/indicator/NY.GDP.PCAP.CD?page=6. Accessed January 15 2016.

Yam, R. C. M., et al. (2011). Analysis of sources of innovation, technological innovation capabilities, and performance: An empirical study of Hong Kong manufacturing industries. *Research Policy, 40,* 391–402.

Yeung, H. W.-C. (2000). State intervention and neoliberalism in the globalizing world economy: Lessons from Singapore's regionalization programme. *The Pacific Review, 13*(1), 133–162.

Young, A. (1992). A tale of two cities: Factor accumulation and technical change in Hong Kong and Singapore. *NBER Macroeconomics Annual, 7,* 13–51.

Chapter 6
National Innovation Systems in the Asia Pacific: A Comparative Analysis

Thomas Clarke, John Chelliah and Elizabeth Pattinson

Abstract In the final Chapter of Part One Clarke, Chelliah and Pattinson offer a comparative survey of the contrasting innovation systems of the Asia Pacific. While Asian economies have achieved rapid industrial progress, as they reach the global technological frontier they need to develop new institutional capabilities for sustaining international competitiveness. Foundational institutions including education, research, law and finance require coordination around coherent national innovation systems to sustain commitment to innovative products and processes. Technological innovation is more likely to succeed "when the elements of the broader environment surrounding firm's activities are well articulated into a system, than in situations where each element works largely isolation… The overall innovation performance of an economy depends not so much on how specific formal institutions (firms, research institutes, universities) perform, but on how they interact with each other as elements of a collective system of knowledge creation and use, and on their interplay with social institutions (such as value, norms and legal frameworks)" (Dodgson in Elgar companion to neo-Schumpeterian economics. Edward Elgar Publishing, Cheltenham, U.K, pp. 193–200, 2007: 592). The national innovation system essentially facilitates how knowledge is generated and accumulated in the economy to serve as the catalyst and fuel for innovation (Yim and Nath in Science Technology Society 10, 2005).

Keywords Innovation systems · Industry policy · Green growth

Introduction

Innovation is now widely recognized as the basis of new jobs, growth productivity and competitiveness, and there is a race to achieve higher levels of innovation among both the advanced and developing economies (Chandra et al. 2009; OECD

T. Clarke (✉) · E. Pattinson
University of Technology Sydney, Sydney, Australia
e-mail: t.clarke@uts.edu.au

J. Chelliah
University of Fiji, Lautoka, Fiji

T. Clarke and K. Lee (eds.), *Innovation in the Asia Pacific*,
https://doi.org/10.1007/978-981-10-5895-0_6

2010, 2015). Governments internationally have become committed to advancing innovation, and as earlier chapters in this book have demonstrated innovation is at the centre of industrial policy in the Asia Pacific where the national innovation systems have proved robust (UNESCO 2016). Historically international competition is moving from a factor driven economy based largely on the costs of labour and raw materials, through an investment driven economy based on the efficiency gains of increased investment in productive processes, to an innovation economy based on competition in new ideas, products and processes in an increasingly digital international economy as Fig. 6.1 illustrates (Porter et al. 2007; UNCTAD 2017).

This chapter aims to examine what is meant by the concept of innovation, to analyze the characteristics of competing innovation systems, to review the evolution of economic theories of growth and development, to analyze the elements of competing innovation systems to investigate problems relating to the present structure of manufacturing industry, and to examine the nature of the emerging knowledge-based economies. The characteristics of different national innovation systems are highlighted, and the different modes of technological progress examined. The limits of innovation systems are explored, and the challenges facing Asia Pacific innovation strategies are investigated.

Green (2015) offers a contemporary view of the expansive nature and scope of the concept of innovation. "The innovation 'system' comprises the relationships between knowledge creating organisations (principally research and education bodies), knowledge adopters (industry and the businesses that constitute it) and government (in its policy, funding, market creation and regulatory roles). Financial institutions, including venture capital investors, innovation intermediaries, professional advisers and consultants all play an important financing, enabling and integrating role. In essence, innovation is ideas applied successfully."

This broad view of the scope of innovation covers new products, services and methodologies, scientific insights and technological breakthroughs, new perceptions in design, market behaviours, consumer preferences, business models, corporate finance, and international relations. From this perspective innovation is an 'open' system with local, national and international dimensions, reflecting the growing linkages in science, research, product development, and the globalisation of businesses—including businesses—as they participate in global markets and value chains (Green 2015).

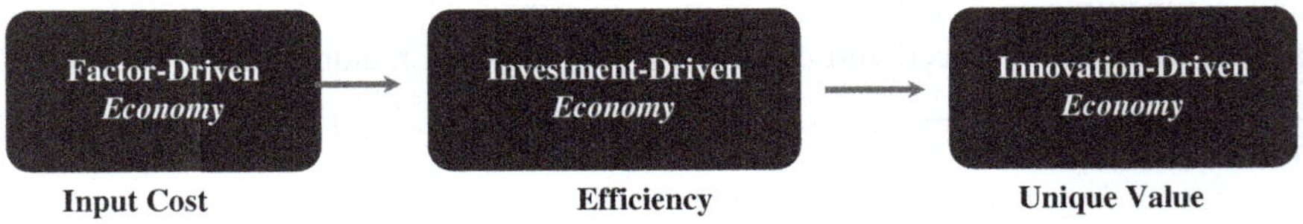

Fig. 6.1 Stages of competitive development. *Source* Adapted from Porter et al. (2007)

A great deal of the investment in innovation by industry is in 'non-technology' innovation. Therefore Green argues, innovation policy must focus not only on the potential to apply ideas developed through research in science, technology, engineering and mathematics (STEM), but must also give attention to research in the humanities, arts and social sciences (HASS). "Innovation policy is concerned with how ideas are diffused and consumed, as well as how (and where) they are generated. The ability to sustain and grow start-up businesses and encourage established businesses to absorb ideas and capitalize on market opportunities critically shapes business success and the transformation of entire industries and economies" (Green 2015).

A taxonomy of innovation from a largely technological perspective is offered by Freeman (1987, 1992, 1997, 2002, 2004, 2008) which summarizes the patterns of the different trajectories of innovation that have occurred historically into four types:

1. ***Incremental Innovation***

Incremental innovation occurs almost continuously in any industry or service activity, though at different rates in different industries and economies, depending on the impact of demand, socio-cultural context, technological opportunities and innovation trajectories. They are associated with scaling up of plant, quality improvements to products, and increasing efficiency.

2. ***Radical Innovations***

Radical innovations are discontinuous changes the results of research and development within businesses or universities and government research. Discontinuous innovations lead to the growth of new products and markets, surges in investment, and sometimes economic booms. They bring about structural changes in aggregate demand if they are related to the rise of new industries or services, such as synthetic fibres, or semi-conductors.

3. ***Change of Technology System***

Change of technology systems involve far reaching transformations of technology involving several branches of the economy, and giving rise to new economic sectors. They combine incremental and radical innovation with significant organizational and managerial innovation. These can be conceived in Schumpetarian terms as 'constellations of innovation' for example the cluster of petro-chemical innovations, and machinery innovations in moulding and extrusion introduced in the 20th century.

4. ***Changes in Techno-Economic Paradigms***

Changes in techno-economic paradigms amount to technological revolutions, with such profound effects that they have a major influence on the entire economy. A change of this nature carries with it many clusters of radical and incremental innovation, disruptive change of existing products and services, and the development of new technology and services. The pervasive effects throughout convey the sense that 'everything has changed.' This can amount to a new techno-economic paradigm (Perez 1983), as the changes go beyond technology, and impact cost-structures, and conditions of production and distribution—amounting to Schumpeter's long cycles of "creative gales of destruction" as a succession of techno-economic paradigms leads to a changing institutional framework and structural changes (Freeman 2008: 48; Clarke and Clegg 2000). Such long waves the early mechanization produced by the steam engine; the successive innovations associated with railways, steel and the arrival of electricity; the development of electrical engineering with automobiles, aircraft and telecommunications; the development of computers, pharmaceuticals and micro-electronics; and the information and communication revolution of the Internet, robotics, and broad band technology (Freeman 2008: 50–55).

The development of thinking regarding innovation, is a result of the deep concern of political economy with the sources of economic growth and development that have existed since the origins of industrialism but become compounded with the increasing global competitiveness of the contemporary economy. At times of limited economic growth, attention has turned to innovation as the source of ideas and technologies that may stimulate new gains in growth and prosperity.

The Evolution of Theories of Growth and Development

The emphasis of classical economic theory commencing with Smith's (1776) concern for absolute advantage derived from unique factors of production, and Ricardo's recognition of the comparative advantage specialization may bring, was reinterpreted in the Heckscher, Ohlin, Samuelson (HES) theory asserting that perfectly competitive markets, alongside free comparative-advantage-based trade, optimizes national and global resource allocation and competitiveness. These theoretical presuppositions unthinkingly applied in the contemporary global context of dominant advanced industrial countries competing with economically weaker developing countries, has often consigned many economies of Africa, South Asia and South America to lives of endless struggle with asymmetric terms of trade. As Pitelis (2009: 5) states, "The macroeconomic policy prescriptions deriving from the analytical foundations of the neoclassical perspective have been encapsulated in the various versions of the Washington and post-Washington-type policy advice to developing and transition economies (Shapiro and Taylor 1990). Their record has been at least questionable (Stiglitz 2001; Rodrik 2004; Dunning 2006)."

Confirming how a more interventionist stance has facilitated the more rapid growth of different regions in the world, Krugman (1989, 1992) highlights how in the context of imperfect competition, increasing returns, spill-over effects and first mover advantages, that strategic trade policies to support particular sectors and firms may leverage advantage. Markets are less effective at identifying new possibilities for development and innovation, than in signaling the profitability of activities that already exist (Scott-Kemmis 2008: 63). Endogenous growth or new growth theory transcends the logic of development strategies based simply on the accumulation of physical capital, emphasizing the increasing returns to ideas as the key to growth (Sen 1994; Romer 1994; Easterly 2001). Rates of return for investment in new knowledge are consistently higher than rates of return to physical capital, and investment in human capital is equally powerful (Helpman 2004). New growth theory is complemented by institutional approaches that emphasize the importance of institutional development to long run economic growth (Hoff and Stiglitz 2001; Rodrik 2004; Acemoglu and Robinson 2005).

Illustrative of a distinctive endogenous growth approach was the success of the Japanese economy in the period from the 1960s–1980s with an emphasis on achieving market share through all forms of innovation including managerial, organizational, and human resources (Romer 1986; Lucas 1988), together with a focus on targeting strategic sectors (Krugman 1987; Shapiro and Taylor 1990). Finally of significance was the Japanese emphasis on maintaining domestic competition, as in Porter's (1990) analysis of the importance of clusters of competing and collaborating producers. Porter (1990) is associated with the stress on the importance of the coexistence of important factor conditions, demand conditions, firm and sector strategy and rivalry, and related and supporting industries.

A development of this is the systems of innovation approach with the belief that innovation is promoted best not by competitive markets alone, but by systems wide linkages involving markets, firms, governments, and social capital promoting institutions (Pitelis 2009: 12; Freeman 1995). This constitutes a more holistic conception of the innovative process relative to the linear model of neo-classical theory (Table 6.1).

In relation to the systems perspective on innovation as a basis for policy "the argument is that government has a role to play in two areas. The first is provision of capabilities in areas where firms and markets may not be able to provide accessible support, such as basic R&D, marketing infrastructures, and training. The second lies in institutions and organisations that support the operations of the innovation system as a whole—education at all levels, intellectual property rights institutions, the finance system (especially with respect to venture capital), regulatory frameworks, and so on. The considerations suggest that the public support apparatus of the innovation system cannot consist of a single set of activities. Just as innovation is a complex process, so is the support apparatus likely to be characterized by complexity: by a range of organisations, with different functions, objectives, and modes of operation" (Georghiou et al. 2003: 38).

In this context the work of Schumpeter on the role of radical innovation in driving growth has become increasingly influential. As Howitt (2009: 16) elucidates "Schumpeterian theory starts from the same premise as almost every other growth theory, namely that long-run growth is driven by productivity growth, which in turn is driven by technological progress. It differs from neoclassical theory by treating technological progress as an economic phenomenon. And it differs from other

Table 6.1 Neo-classical and systems of innovation growth theories

	Neo classical	Systems innovation
Underlying assumptions	• Equilibrium • Perfect information	• Non equilibrium asymmetric information
Focus	• Allocation of resources for invention	• Interactions innovation processes
Main policy Main rationale Government intervenes to (examples)	• Science policy (research) • Market failure • Provide public goods • Mitigate externalities • Reduce barriers to entry • Eliminate inefficient market structures	• Innovation policy/systematic problems • Solve problems in the system or to facilitate the creation of new systems • Induce changes in the supporting structure for innovation: support the creation and development of institutions and organizations and support networking • Facilitate transition and avoid lock-in
Main strengths of innovation policies designed under each paradigm	• Clarity and simplicity • Long time series of science based indicators	• Context specific • Involvement of all policies related to innovation • Holistic conception of the innovation process
Main weaknesses of innovation policies designed under each paradigm	• Linear model of innovation • Framework conditions are not explicitly considered in the model (for example institutional framework) • General policies	• Difficult to implement in practice • Lack of indicators for the analysis of the IS and evaluation of IS policies

Source Adapted from Chaminade and Edquist (2006)

endogenous growth theories in emphasising that the main force driving technological progress is industrial innovation, the same force that is central to the competitive process of any market economy."

Schumpeter also emphasized that successful technology strategies vary from country to country, depending on such factors as the state of development of institutions, geography, educational levels, environmental conditions, and particularly how close the country is to the world technology frontier. Countries that are nearer the frontier of technology tend to produce leading-edge innovations, whereas countries that are further from the frontier tend to implement technologies that have been developed elsewhere. It thus produces a context-dependent theory of what has been called "appropriate growth policy" (Aghion and Howitt 2009). In the context of the current limits to growth Schumpetarian approaches offer the dynamic alternative of open innovative economic systems (Yun 2015).

National Systems of Innovation

The diverse origins and different institutional forms of national systems of innovation are outlined in Table 6.2. Whether initiated as prestigious national research institutions, university based research laboratories, or practical industry based research workshops, these institutions possessed a common aspiration: to advance the body of knowledge that might lead to innovative change in industry, the economy and society. According to Texeira (2014) from the late 1980s onwards a new approach emerged to promoting innovation, based on the concept of National Systems of Innovation (NSI) (Lundvall 1992; Nelson 1993; Kim and Nelson 2000). Instead of focusing on various aspects of innovation in isolation, this approach involves a more holistic perspective, emphasizing the role of interaction between different actors and how this interaction is influenced by broader social, institutional and political factors (Fagerberg and Verspagen 2009).

Texeira (2014) highlights how this approach has broad applications in policy contexts including by regional authorities and national governments, as well as by international organisations such as the OECD, the European Union, United Nations Conference and Trade and Development (UNCTAD) and United Nations Industrial Development Organization (UNIDO) (Edquist 2005; Sharif 2006). According to Lundvall (2007), the diffusion of the national systems of innovation approach is impressive taking into account that 20 years ago only a few academics had discussed the concept. From this perspective national systems of innovation can be seen as an analytical framework (Sun and Liu 2010), which serves as both model and tool, focusing upon the systemic characteristics of innovation, rapid technological change and globalisation. The nationals systems of innovation approach is in this way useful as a general framework to study the differences between the productive and research systems of countries, making it possible to analyse absorptive capacities and the learning capability of individuals and organisations that take part in innovation processes and contribute to its advance (Álvarez and Marín 2010; Texeira 2014).

Table 6.2 National Systems: institutional sources of innovation

17th century	Academies of Science, Royal Society 1662, Proceedings and Journals, Internationalism of Science, Science Education
18th century	Industrial Revolution—factory innovation, Technical Education, Nationalism of Technology, Consulting Engineers
19th century	Growth of Universities, Ph.D. and Science Faculties, Technische Hochschulen, Institutes of Technology, Government Laboratories, Industrial R&D in house, Standards Institutes
20th century	Industrial in-house R&D in all industries; Big Science and Technology; Research Councils, National Science Foundation, Ministries of Science and Technology, Services industries, R&D Networks

Source Adapted from Freeman (2008: 111)

Dahlman (2009) illustrates a generic innovation system for developing economies (Fig. 6.2). The ideas for innovations may be acquired from overseas, or be acquired from other institutions in the same country. At a more advanced stage increasingly knowledge is developed within the country in research institutes, universities and within firms. There are a range of modes of knowledge acquisition and transfer internationally including purchase of technology and capital goods, securing technical assistance or education and training overseas, immigration of highly skilled people, or international knowledge networks. Locally there are similar processes for the transfer of knowledge, including incubators and spin-off firms with new technology, movement of people from universities, and local knowledge networks. Dissemination and use of knowledge occurs through firms, government departments, public institutions, and social organisations.

The dissemination and application of knowledge leads to the growth of more advanced firms, technology and people networks. However all of this innovation activity is supported and facilitated by a broader economic and institutional regime which includes macroeconomic conditions (particularly inflation, interest rates, exchange rates), the business environment (the rule of law, and effectiveness of government and regulation), and the quality of information and communication

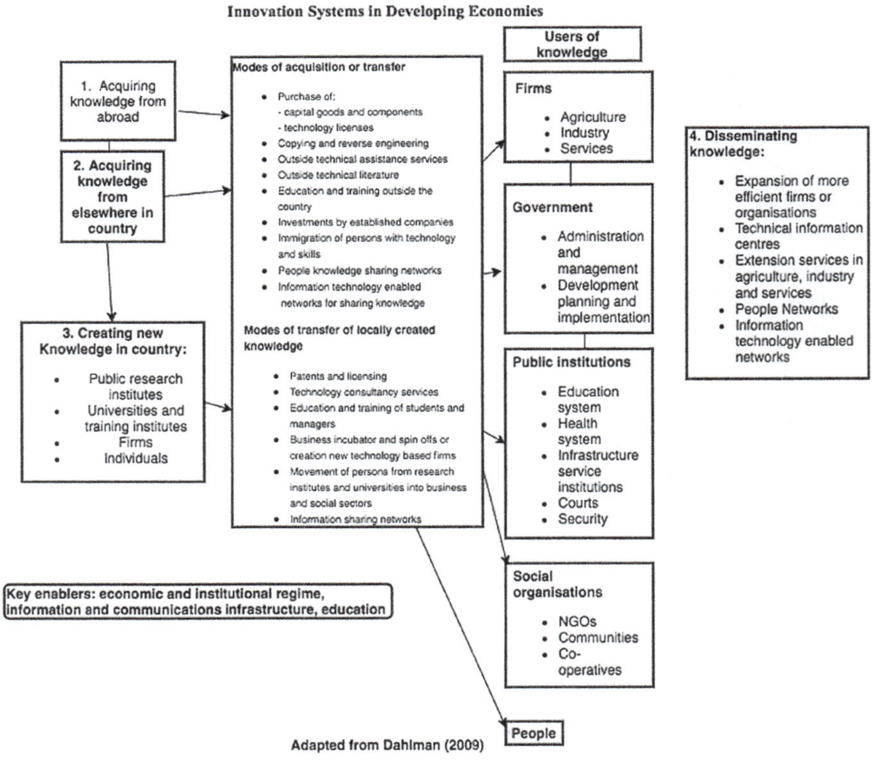

Fig. 6.2 The innovations systems in developing economies

infrastructure. Above all the education and skills of the people are critical, and the support offered by technology and institutions, particularly universities and government research laboratories, and technical and management service industries. All of these institutions and relationships encompass the innovation system and strategies of different economies.

Although advances in technology are not the exclusive source of innovation, technology transfer and absorption features importantly in many processes of innovation, and in the activity of national innovation systems. Figure 6.3 illustrates the modes of technology transfer in developing economies (Burns 2009). At the first stage the economy and its scientists are exposed to developments at the technology frontier internationally. This occurs at a personal level through education and other interactions among scientists, and at a business and economic level though direct contact with higher-technology business processes, products, and services. This can occur through foreign trade, foreign direct investment, the activities of a national diaspora, and through other forms of communication. "The larger these flows, the greater the exposure of the economy to the global technological frontier" (Burns 2009: 173). The technological sophistication of economies varies with the extent to which scientists in an economy absorb and exploit the ideas flowing from more advanced economies (Goldberg et al. 2008).

However exposure to new ideas and techniques is not sufficient to ensure progress on the ground. The technological absorptive capacity of the economy and

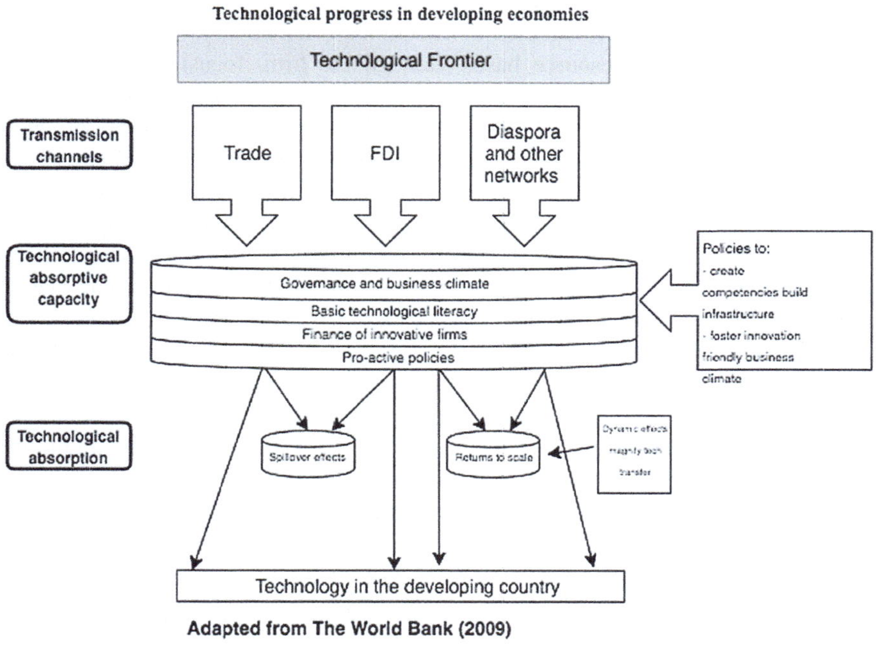

Fig. 6.3 Technological progress in developing economies

quality of the incentives for the scientific community will be critical to successful application, and in turn this depends on the quality of macroeconomic and government management, and the willingness of entrepreneurs to take risks with new to market technologies. The availability of finance for innovative companies, and the contribution of government to the provision of information and communications infrastructure, and for creating a facilitative business environment.

> Technological flows, technological absorptive capacity and technology creation influence each other, and the extent to which technology diffuses depends on various market imperfections, including increasing returns to scale and technological spillovers. Here the existence of a financial sector that intermediates between savers and innovators may be necessary to overcome the initial cost of some new technologies. In particular, access to finance may be essential if innovative firms are to reach the scale necessary to unleash a potential virtuous circle, such that the additional income garnered by the successful exploitation of one new technology permits the acquisition of another, resulting in further gains (Burns 2009: 173).

Scott-Kemmis (2008) captures the increasing sense of the complexity and interdependence of successful economic systems: "The evolution of firms and industries involves systemic interdependence between technologies and organisations and institutions, interaction involving market and non-market relationships and the key drivers from increasing returns. Just as firms increasingly outsource elements of their production system, so they also increasingly outsource elements of their innovation systems. Just as there are many more options for business models so there are many more options for firms to develop their innovation systems, and again we see a great deal of exploration with knowledge-related relationships, (for example, through open innovation) the use of intermediaries, alliances, and collaboration."

Finally there is the resource based view of the firm, focusing on the firm's capabilities, and suggesting in a more dynamic market economy firms position themselves in terms of their resources and capabilities, rather than on the products and services currently derived from their capabilities (Barney 1991; Grant 1996). The resource-based theory of the firm leads on logically to an emerging knowledge-based theory of the firm, which emphasises the role of knowledge as the critical resource in organisations. Grant (1996) reviews the essential characteristics of knowledge based business resulting from the acceleration in the accumulation and availability of knowledge in recent decades.

As David Teece argues, "The decreased cost of information flow, increases in the number of markets (e.g. for intermediate products, and for various types of risk), the liberalization of product and labour markets in many parts of the world, and the deregulation of international financial flows is stripping away many traditional sources of competitive advantage and exposing a new fundamental core as the basis for wealth creation. That fundamental core is the development and astute deployment and utilization of intangible assets, of which knowledge, competence, and intellectual property are the most significant" (2000: 3). Teece (2000) demonstrates how the flow of information, the expansion of markets, and the proliferation of alliances to access complementary assets is eroding away the traditional sources of competitive advantage. The special access to natural resources and skilled labour is

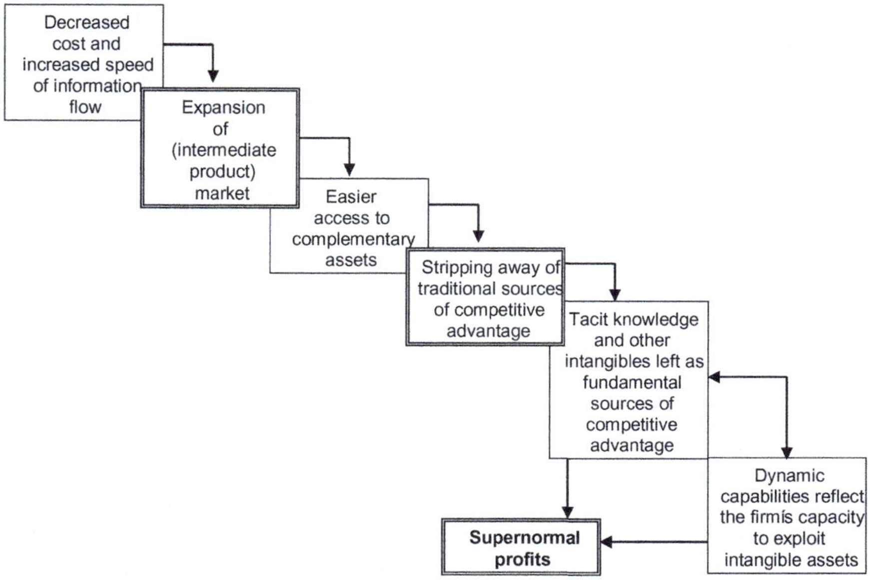

Fig. 6.4 Development of knowledge and competitive advantage. *Source* Adapted from Teece (2000: 4)

gone; scale and scope is of questionable value once you can rent physical assets or capacity on favourable terms. This leaves knowledge and competence, coupled with dynamic capabilities (the firm's entrepreneurial and strategic asset orchestration capabilities) as the foundation of competitive advantage (Fig. 6.4).

The Evolution of Industry Policy

The current concern for fostering national innovation systems, relates to the earlier strategic interventions into the economy of many governments in the 20th century, known as industry policy. The evolution of thinking about the rationale for industrial policy interventions, Warwick (2013) suggests has moved from:

- a traditional position based largely on product market interventions (production subsidies, state ownership, tariff protection),
- through the attempt at market failure-correcting taxes and subsidies operating mainly on factor markets (R&D incentives, training subsidies, investment allowances, help with access to finance),
- to a new focus on interventions that help build systems, create networks, develop institutions and align strategic and innovation priorities (Warwick 2013).

There is some evidence of a renaissance of interest in new industrial policy Warwick (2013) notes in recent literature, research programs, popular commentary and government initiatives. The World Bank has been researching in this area for some time, as in Rodrik's (2008) work for the World Bank on industrial policy and Yusuf's (2012) consideration of the experience of East Asia and its applicability elsewhere. Policy lessons from Asia have also been studied by the Washington-based Petersen Institute's Noland and Pack (2003, 2005). In Japan RIETI (2011) have launched a programme of basic research for a new industrial policy. In Brussels, Aghion et al. (2011) have been rethinking industrial policy, as has UNCTAD in Geneva (Ul Haque 2007). Elsewhere in the UN system, WIDER has been researching new challenges for industrial policy (Naudé 2010). The *Economist* (2010) ran a headline "Industrial Policy is Back in Fashion" and Ciuriak (2011) titled his recent survey the "Return of Industrial Policy" (Warwick 2013: 6).

Examples of new national industry policies in Asia Pacific highlighted by Warwick 2013: 7) include:

- Japan's industrial policy plan (METI 2010) targeting a deliberate movement away from a 'monopole' structure based on automobiles and electronics to a structure based on five strategic areas: infrastructure-related and infrastructure system exports; environmental/energy problem-solving industries (including green vehicles); culture (fashion, food and tourism); medical and healthcare; and advanced areas traditional to Japan (robotics, space, aerospace).
- Korea, a traditional proponent of active industrial policy, designated sector-specific strategies for those sectors it considers to be its flagship industries: automobiles, shipbuilding, semiconductors, steel, general machines, textiles and parts and materials. In addition Korea set out a number of priority growth engines for the future. Based on an analysis of where it believes its comparative advantage lies, Korea identifies 17 such sectors under three headings: green tech, high-tech convergence technology and value-added services (Ministry of Knowledge Economy 2011).
- The 12th Five-Year Plan of China, *The Plan for Science and Technology Development*, launched in July 2011, targeted 11 essential sectors including ICT equipment, energy technology, genetically modified foods, pollution technology, pharmaceuticals and civilian aerospace. In July 2012 the *Plan for National Strategic Emerging Industries* was published, identifying seven strategic emerging industries and 20 key projects, together with policy measures to facilitate the development of the relevant industries. Under this plan the GDP share of the strategic emerging industries was targeted to rise by 8 percentage points by 2015 and by 15 percentage points by 2020.
- In India, the Department of Industrial Policy and Promotion (DIPP) published a *National Manufacturing Policy* in November 2011, targeting an increase in the share of manufacturing value added in GDP from the current 16–25% by 2022. At its core was the planned creation of national investment and manufacturing zones (NIMZs), which enjoy planning exemptions and fiscal incentives and are developed as autonomous self-governing townships in partnership with the

private sector. The DIPP also aimed to make India a location of choice for foreign direct investment and to increase India's share of global inward FDI from 1.3% in 2007 to 5% by 2017 (Warwick 2013: 8–10).

Innovation policies have become more central as traditional industry policies have failed to stimulate growth. The development of manufacturing industry was the mainstay of the advance of Asian economies for the last fifty years, however this can no longer be relied on in the same way in future. Globally manufacturing industry has gone through a series of transformations that have made it more complex and competitive for all businesses. These transformations have included the disaggregation of value chains, and their distribution throughout the developing economies, though heavily concentrated in Asia; the introduction of automation and advanced robotics; the increased competiveness between suppliers; and the saturation of world markets. In this context manufacturing's share in GDP and employment in OECD countries has been declining for several decades, due to a number of factors (Pilat et al. 2006), including:

- Saturated demand for manufacturing products, in particular in the OECD area.
- Rapid productivity growth in the manufacturing sector, implying that despite growth in real manufacturing output and value added, less employment is needed to produce more value.
- A blurring of manufacturing with services, where manufacturing firms increasingly capture value in the associated services they provide rather than in manufacturing production itself. This also implies that certain firms initially classified as manufacturing firms are now classified as services firms.
- A growing internationalization and competitiveness of manufacturing production (Warwick 2013).

The increasing importance of services to manufacturing firms, together with growing internationalization of production, has made firms consider the position they presently occupy and seek to occupy in future in global value chains. For example as Fig. 6.5 indicates, in many industries, much of the value added in a value chain is created in the downstream or upstream stages of the value chain, where activities tend to have a strong service component (Warwick 2013: 11).

The developing disaggregation of the global value chain isolates the high value added controlling functions of finance, R&D and commercialization in the advanced industrial countries, where companies can accumulate vast fortunes by outsourcing the manufacturing of components and assembly of products to developing countries where workers are employed often on low wages and poor conditions. The fashionable products such as iphones, laptop computers, high-tech flat screen televisions, and luxury cars are then expensively marketed to the affluent customers of the richer countries. In the earlier stages of the transition to industrialism this low-value added labour intensive manufacturing was sought after in many Asian economies, but now having realized the much greater rewards available to those who control the finance, design and marketing of products, it is these higher reaches of the value chain that Asian manufacturers are increasingly reaching for.

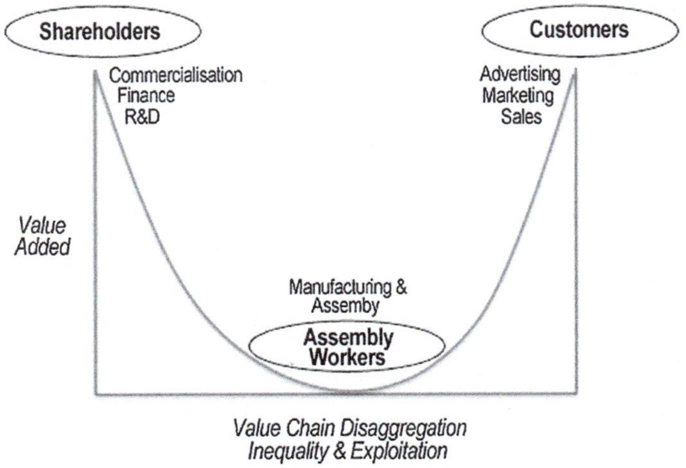

Fig. 6.5 The disaggregation of global value chains. *Source* Adapted from Mudambi (2007)

The historical progression of the location of production for lap top computers illustrates the transitions in the global value chain gradually taking place with many other electronic and manufactured products (Fig. 6.6). Early in the 2000s while the US retained control of the concept (including finance, design and marketing) and production planning, US manufacturers increasingly had disaggregated all production to developing economies. Japan initially retained control of prototype production, but soon exported this to Taiwan. Taiwan itself initially focused on mass production of manufactured goods, but by later in the 2000s had adopted a focus on design and prototype production, exporting mass production to China and the rest of East Asia. China was early in the 2000s confined to mass production but later in the 2000s had achieved a position higher in the value chain in design and prototype production, with aspirations for own brand design and production.

By 2017 Korea had led the way up to the top of the international market value chain with the remarkable success Samsung in smart phones in competition with Apple, and in televisions in competition with Japanese manufacturers, while Hyundai matched the competition in both the US and Europe in quality automobiles. Meanwhile China is looking for the same opportunities, and has enjoyed initial success with Huawei in telecoms equipment, in the auto industry with international investment in overseas production, and in the finance sector with the overseas growth of its three main banks.

Questions have been posed regarding the contribution of the different national innovation systems in the Asia Pacific to the success of industry policy and to continuing competitiveness and growth. National innovation systems literature continues to focus in terms of concepts, policy and practice on the advanced industrial economies, and less on developing economies (Lorentzen 2009;

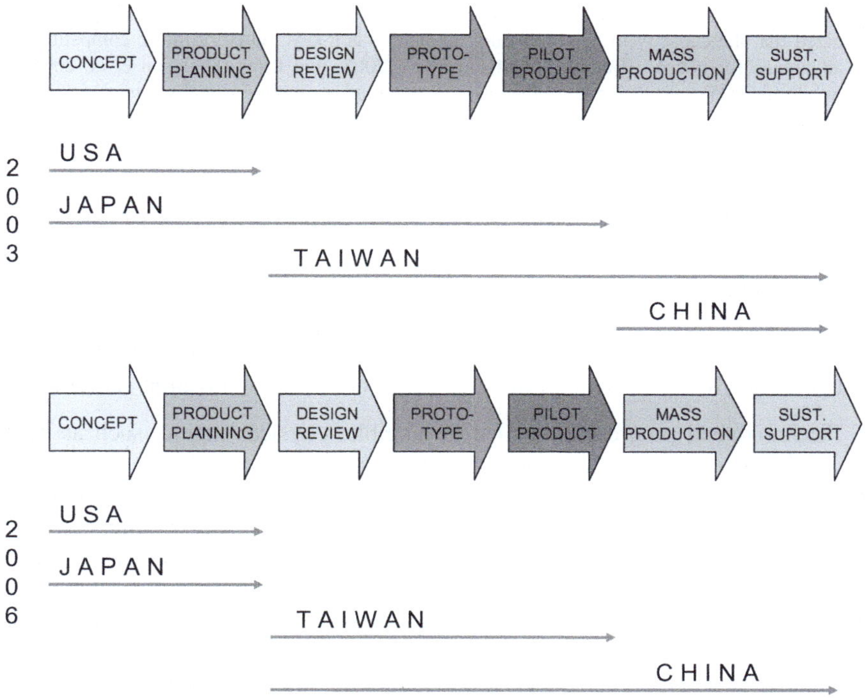

Fig. 6.6 Transition of location of product development for laptop computers. *Source* Adapted From Market Intelligence Center, Institute for the Information Industry, Taiwan

Fagerberg and Srholec 2008; Lundvall 2007; Albuquerque 2007; Lorentzen 2009). Concerns regarding the operational value and implementation of national innovation systems continue (OECD 2002; Texeira 2014). Measuring the application of innovation systems remains problematic, and performance indicators devised to reflect the effectiveness of national innovation systems remain underdeveloped (Lundvall 2002). Surveys of national innovation systems include Lundvall (2007), Godin (2009), Fagerberg and Sapprasert (2011), Texeira (2014), Carlsson (2006).

On a more positive note, Dodgson (2009: 591) analyzing the promising characteristics of Asian national innovation systems suggests, "The developing innovative capacity of some Asian nations raises numbers of questions for those concerned with understanding the relationships between business and the political economy. Firms operate in contexts shaped by national characteristics and distinctive institutions and regulations supporting innovation." Dodgson continues:

> There has been much discussion of the challenges confronting the more technological advanced Asian economies as they become global innovation leaders (Kim 1997; Dodgson 2000; UNCTAD 2000, 2017; Chen and Lee 2004; Gu and Lundvall 2006). Countries such as Korea, Taiwan, Singapore and China are developing, through increased investments in research and new institutional forms such as venture capital, more coherent national innovation systems providing the capacity to be important international sources of

innovative products and processes (McKinsey 2005; Sigurdson 2005). It is widely recognized that the capacity to be continually innovative is a key source of future competitive advantage for nations (Baumol 2002; Fagerberg 2005) and firms (Dodgson et al. 2008; Schilling 2005), and Asian countries and corporations are enthusiastically pursuing innovation as a key objective (Dodgson 2009: 590).

Strategies for Future Innovation and Growth

Looking to the future, the question is what strategies for innovation and growth in the economies of the Asia Pacific should be pursued as increasingly they compete directly with the advanced industrial economies(Dodgson et al. 2005; UNCTAD 2017) ? The OECD recognizes the multiple benefits that innovation can bring:

- Technological progress embodied in tangible, physical capital, such as better machinery, smarter equipment or greener buildings.
- Intangible, knowledge-based, capital, such as software, data, research and development (R&D), design, intellectual property, and firm-specific skills.
- Smarter, more efficient use of labour and capital to generate so-called multi-factor productivity growth (also referred to as total factor productivity).
- Strengthening the dynamics in the economy, with new innovative firms entering the market, replacing other slower, less innovative ones in a process known as creative destruction. Together, these four dimensions account for as much as half of GDP growth (Wyckoff 2016).

However there are other impacts of innovation critical to the well-being of the economy and society "Innovation is not just about supporting growth; it is also vital for addressing deep social and global challenges, like ageing, resource scarcity, disease and climate change. Innovation spurs education, skills and wellbeing throughout life too. At the same time, innovation can contribute to inequality, which is why it needs to be accompanied by appropriate labour and social policies" (Wyckoff 2016).

A long-term commitment to innovation is recommend by Wyckoff (2016), who concentrates his prognosis for the future around the impact of the digital economy, setting the following priorities:

- ***Strengthen investment in innovation and foster business dynamism***. In many OECD countries, firms now invest as much in knowledge-based assets as they do in physical capital, but these should be seen as a bundle, not separate investments. Young firms drive renewal and creative destruction in the economy. The problem is that policies too often favour incumbents, shoring up the status quo and stifling the experimentation with new ideas, technologies and business models that underpin the success of young firms and limit innovation potential.
- ***Invest in and shape an efficient system of knowledge creation and diffusion***. Public funding is needed to address the inherent underinvestment in basic

research of private firms, as this drives long-run productivity growth and facilitates the adoption of innovations across the economy.

- ***Seize the opportunities of the digital economy***. An open and accessible internet, where creativity, sharing, entrepreneurship and experimentation can flourish, is essential for innovation in the 21st century. Big data and data analytics have become a driving force in science, product innovation, processes, organisational methods and services, including healthcare. Policies are needed to promote skills in data analytics, and to foster investments in appropriate infrastructure, including data itself. At the same time, striking the right balance between the free flow of data and safeguarding personal privacy and confidence will require constant attention among policymakers.
- ***Foster talent and skills***. only one-third of workers have the required skills for a technology-rich environment, which raises a major challenge for innovation. Funding for lifelong learning and policies to encourage training are needed to address this (Clarke 1999). Women in particular should be given every opportunity to participate in science and entrepreneurship and contribute more fully to innovation. Policies should also enable international mobility among highly skilled workers as knowledge flows back and forth between countries and regions, enabling many countries to benefit.
- ***Improve the governance and implementation of policies for innovation***. A wide range of government policies affect innovation, which implies that they have to be well-aligned, not only at the level of central government, but also between the central government and regional and local authorities. There is also a need to cooperate with other countries and global institutions, including to help address common global challenges and share the costs of investment in basic research. Monitoring and evaluation of approaches and outcomes will help governments learn from experience and bolster policy performance and adaptability over time. Not every country can become an innovation leader, but every country can do better at tapping into, and developing, its knowledge-based capital and improving its position along global value chains (Wyckoff 2016).

Another approach suggests constructing advantage embracing the new dynamics of innovation and the capacity to exploit them which are essential to growth. This 'new competitive advantage' (Best 2001) highlights regional development economics, the dynamic of which draws upon constructed advantage. Cooke and Leydesdorff (2006: 7) maintain this knowledge-based construction of advantage requires interfacing developments in various directions:

- ***Economy***—the regionalization of economic development; the adoption of 'open systems' inter-firm interactions; the integration of knowledge generation and commercialization; investing in smart infrastructures; and strong local and global business networks.
- ***Governance***—the multi-level governance of associational and stakeholder interests; with strong policy-support for innovators; enhanced budgets for research; vision-led policy leadership; and global positioning of local assets.

- ***Knowledge Infrastructure***—the universities, public sector research, mediating agencies, professional consultancies, and other agencies have to be actively involved as structural puzzle-solving capacities.
- ***Community and culture***—the encouragement of cosmopolitanism; sustainability; talented human capital; creative cultural environments; and social tolerance. This public factor provides a background for the innovative dynamics in a Triple Helix of university-industry-government relations (Leydesdorff and Etzkowitz 2003).

A further strategic recipe for reviving the innovation process is offered by Criscuolo (2015), who argues future growth will involve releasing the forces of knowledge diffusion to enable businesses to adopt technological and organizational innovations. In order to achieve this what is required is:

- ***Global connections*** need to be extended and deepened, so that firms can learn from successful counterparts across the world. This requires trade, foreign direct investment, participation in global value chains, and the international mobility of skilled labour.
- ***New firms*** need to be able to enter markets and experiment with new technologies and business models. The productivity slowdown coincided with a near-collapse of overall business investment and a slowdown in business dynamism, reflected in a decline in business start-ups. These trends need to be reversed.
- ***Better 'matchmaking'*** is needed across the economy, to ensure that the most productive firms have the resources—labour, skills, and capital—to grow. The larger the frontier firms become, the greater the extent to which their performance gets reflected in overall economic growth. The most productive and dynamic firms do not always grow to optimal scale. In some economies, the most advanced firms have productivity levels close to the global frontier, but they are under-sized relative to their peers in other countries. Inefficient resource reallocation keeps frontier firms from growing. It also slows the diffusion of best practices to other firms.
- ***Investment in innovation*** should extend beyond technology to include skills, software, organisational know-how (i.e. managerial quality). Innovation depends on the bundling of these investments, and policy initiatives (Criscuolo 2015).

Finally Mazzucato (2016) offers a new framework for innovation policy—moving from market fixing to market creating. Policies based on building systems of innovation focus on the need for nations to build a "network of institutions in the public and private sectors whose activities and interactions initiate, import, modify and diffuse new technologies" (Freeman 1995). As Mazzucato (2016) states "The emphasis here is not on the stock of research and development, but on the circulation of knowledge and its diffusion throughout the economy (Lundvall 1992). Institutional change is not assessed through criteria based on static allocative efficiency, but rather on how such change promotes technological and structural change. This perspective is neither macro nor micro, but more meso, where individual firms are seen as part of broader network of firms with which they cooperate and compete. The systems of innovation approach have been crucial for highlighting deficiencies in the market failure perspective, as it regards innovation policy (Freeman 1995; Lundvall 1992). It has emphasized the inability of the market failure perspective to tackle lock-in effects and to specific types of institutional failures that arise from feedback processes along the entire innovation chain (Verspagen 2006)."

That is key innovation institutions, such as universities, will only allow the innovation system to achieve its potential if they are lined up synergistically with other institutions in the entrepreneurial ecosystem. Mason and Brown (2014) suggest "Policy intervention needs to take a holistic approach, focusing on the following: the entrepreneurial actors within the ecosystem; the resource providers within the ecosystem; entrepreneurial connectors within the ecosystem and the entrepreneurial environment of the ecosystem."

Such innovation eco-systems and networks can be national, international or global in terms of geographical span, involve multiple actors for many purposes including training, technology development, product design, marketing. These networks and eco-systems can be formal or informal, may be along a production chain, or university led. Among the conditions contributing to shaping networks and eco-systems are intellectual property rights protecting partners during collaboration; open innovation allowing partners to tap into external responses to develop modern strengths; and the globalization/fragmentation of production, which together with enhanced specialization have increased the need for cooperation to integrate different components of products, and access complementary skills. The availability of shared assets is an attraction of networks and eco-systems, but all partners will need to have valuable assets to share. Finally effective information and communication technologies are the basis of the eco-system or network sharing information and knowledge (OECD 2015, 2017; UNCTAD 2017).

Innovation for Green Growth in the Asia Pacific

The greatest innovation challenge the Asia Pacific faces, is the same challenge that is threatening the rest of the world—the imminent dangers of climate change, and the search for a sustainable economy (Clarke 2016). However much business success and economic growth has been celebrated as the means of escaping poverty and creating opportunities for the people of Asia, inevitably in recent decades, the expansion of economic activity has been accompanied by growing global environmental concerns, such as climate change, energy security and increasing scarcity of resources. Economic growth as an end in itself, without attention to the environmental consequences is no longer a viable industrial policy or business model.

In response to this impending threat, manufacturing industries have recently shown more interest in sustainable production and have adopted corporate social responsibility initiatives.

Nevertheless, as the OECD (2009a) accepts such efforts fall far short of meeting these pressing challenges. Moreover, improved efficiency in some regions has been offset by increases in consumption and growth in others. Something much more radical and effective is required if climate change is to be halted, and the environment recovered. What is required is to apply the genius of innovation to the goal of sustainability. This is now happening around the world, indeed innovation and sustainability are becoming the most powerful combined force in industrial change, providing the most promising opportunities in almost every business sector. As the OECD (2009a) insists;

"In this context, sustainable manufacturing and eco-innovation are very much at the heart of this century's policy and industry practices. These concepts have become popular with policy makers and business leaders in recent years, and they encourage business solutions and entrepreneurial ideas for tackling environmental challenges" (OECD 2009a: 8). Considerable initiatives are being launched across all industries to achieve sustainable solutions to these environmental dilemmas for example the huge commitment of Toyota motors to the development of hydrogen engines (the only emission of which is clean water). As the OECD comments:

> In recent years, the efforts of manufacturing industries to achieve sustainable production have shifted from end-of-pipe solutions to a focus on product lifecycles and integrated environmental strategies and management systems. Furthermore, efforts are increasingly made to create closed loop, circular production systems and adopt new business models… Sustainable manufacturing involves changes that are facilitated by eco-innovation. Integrated initiatives such as closed-loop production can potentially yield higher environmental improvements but require appropriately combining a wide range of innovation targets and mechanisms. While current eco-innovations in manufacturing tend to focus primarily on technological advances, organisational or institutional changes have often driven their development and complemented the necessary technological changes. Some advanced players started adopting new business models or alternative modes of provision. (OECD 2009a: 5–6).

Eco-innovation can be defined as innovation that results in a reduction of environmental impact. Various eco-innovation activities can be analysed along three dimensions:

- targets (the focus areas of eco-innovation: products, processes, marketing methods, organisations and institutions);
- mechanisms (the ways in which changes are made in the targets: modification, redesign, alternatives and creation); and
- impacts (effects of eco-innovation on the environment) (OECD 2009b).

Greening growth (GG) and moving towards a greener economy (GE) is complex and multidimensional. It entails

(i) pricing externalities and valuing natural assets for the long-run services they provide and pricing externalities;

(ii) innovation as a means of breaking with unsustainable growth paths;
(iii) the creation and dissemination of new, more environmentally sustainable technologies, goods, and services; and
(iv) sectoral shifts and changes in comparative advantage that inevitably imply winners and losers. If greening growth and a greener economy is to help move countries towards more sustainable development, the social consequences and local contexts of the transition to a greener economy must be central to managing change (GGKP 2013).

China's chief environmental objective (under its 12th Five-Year Plan 2011–15) is gradually to establish a carbon market, which represents a shift in policy attention to reducing dependency on fossil fuel and promoting higher-value added and more sustainable industries. Korea's green growth strategy takes a systemic approach to meeting sustainability goals combined with a new growth strategy. Many other OECD countries have strategies to support this transition through a dedicated green economy agenda or as part of energy and industrial regeneration strategies, and Japan's policy is (*Japan is Back, Low Carbon Technology Plan*). These policies and other commitments to innovate towards a sustainable green economy will provide the framework and systems for the growth and success of Asia Pacific economies in the 21st century.

References

Acemoglu, D., Johnson, S., & Robinson, J. (2005). Institutions as the fundamental cause of long-run growth. In P. Aghion & S. Durlauf (Eds.), *A(eds)*. Handbook of Economic Growth, Amsterdam: Elsevier.

Aghion, P., & Howitt, P. (2006). Appropriate growth policy: An integrating framework. *Journal of the European Economic Association, 4,* 69–314.

Aghion, P., & Howitt, P. (2009). *The economics of growth.* Cambridge, MA: MIT Press.

Aghion, P., Boulanger, J., & Cohen, E. (2011, June). *Rethinking industrial policy.* Bruegel Policy Brief, 2011/4.

Albuquerque, E. M. (2007). Inadequacy of technology and innovation systems at the periphery. *Cambridge Journal of Economics, 31,* 669–690.

Álvarez, I., & Marín, R. (2010). Entry modes and national systems of innovation. *Journal of International Management, 16,* 340–353.

Barney, J. (1991). Firm resources and sustained competitive advantage. *Journal of Management, 17,* 109–122.

Baumol, W. (2002). *The free-market innovation machine: Analyzing the growth miracle of capitalism.* Princeton: Princeton University Press.

Best, M. (2001). *The new competitive advantage.* Oxford: Oxford University Press.

Burns, A. (2009). Technology diffusion in the developing world. In Chandra et al. (Eds.), pp. 169–201.

Carlsson, B. (2006). Internationalization of innovation systems: A survey of the literature. *Research Policy, 35,* 56–67.

Chaminade, C., & Edquist, C. (2006). *Rationales for public policy intervention from a systems of innovation approach: The case of VINNOVA.* CIRCLE Electronic Working Paper Series Paper no. 2006/04.

Chen, T.-J., & Lee, J. (2004). *The New knowledge economy of Taiwan*. Cheltenham: Elgar.
Clarke, T. (1999). The development of management education in China. *Education and Training, 41*, 6/7, 273–276.
Clarke, T. (2016). The Widening scope of directors duties: The impact of social and environmental responsibility. *Seattle University Law Review, 39,* 531–578.
Clarke, T., & Clegg, S. (2000). *Changing paradigms: The transformation of management knowledge for the 21st century*. London: HarperCollins.
Cooke, P., & Leydesdorff, L. (2006). Regional development in the knowledge-based economy: The construction of advantage. *The Journal of Technology Transfer, 31*(1), 5–15.
Chandra, V., Eröcal, D., Padoan, P., & Braga, C. (2009). *Innovation and growth: Chasing a moving frontier*. OECD/World Bank.
Ciuriak, D. (2011). The Return of Industrial Policy, http://ssrn.com/abstract=1929564.
Criscuolo, C. (2015). Productivity Is Soaring at Top Firms and Sluggish Everywhere Else, Harvard Business Review, 24 August, 2015 https://hbr.org/2015/08/productivity-is-soaring-at-top-firms-and-sluggish-everywhere-else.
Dahlman, C. (2009). Different innovation strategies, different results: Brazil, Russia, India, China and Korea (the BRICKs). In Chandra et al. (Eds.), pp. 131–168.
Dodgson, M. (2000). Policies for science, technology and innovation in Asian Newly industrializing economies. In R. R. Nelson & L. Kim (Eds.), *Technology, learning and innovation* (pp. 229–268). Cambridge: Cambridge University Press.
Dodgson, M. (2007). Technological collaboration. In H. Hanusch & A. Pyka (Eds.), *Elgar companion to neo-Schumpeterian economics* (pp. 193–200) Cheltenham, U.K.: Edward Elgar Publishing.
Dodgson, M. (2009). Asia's national innovation systems: Institutional adaptability and rigidity in the face of global innovation challenges. *Asia Pacific Journal of Management, 26*, 589–609.
Dodgson, M., Gann, D., & Salter, A. (2005). *Think, play, do: Technology, innovation and organization*. Oxford: Oxford University Press.
Dodgson, M., Gann, D., & Salter, A. (2008). *The management of technological innovation: Strategy and practice* (2nd ed.). Oxford, United Kingdom: Oxford University Press.
Dunning, J. H. (2006). Towards a new paradigm of development: Implications for the determinants of international business activity. *Transnational Corporations, 15*(1), 173–228.
Edquist, C. (2005). Systems of innovation—perspectives and challenges. In J. Fagerberg, D. C. Mowery, & R. Nelson, (Eds.), *Oxford handbook of innovation*. Oxford: Oxford University Press.
Easterly, W. (2001). *The elusive quest for growth: Economists' adventures and misadventures in the tropics*. Cambridge, MA: MIT Press.
Fagerberg, J. (2005). Innovation: A guide to the literature. In J. Fagerberg, D. Mowery, & R. Nelson (Eds.), *The oxford handbook of innovation*. Oxford: Oxford University Press.
Fagerberg, J., & Srholec, M. (2008). National innovation systems, capabilities and economic development. *Research Policy, 37*, 1417–35.
Fagerberg, J., & Verspagen, B. (2009). Innovation studies—the emerging structure of a new scientific field. *Research Policy, 38,* 218–233.
Fagerberg, J., & Sapprasert, K. (2011). National innovation systems: The emergence of a New approach. *Science and Public Policy, 38*(9), 669–679.
Freeman, C. (1987). *Technology policy and economic performance: Lessons from Japan*. London: Pinter.
Freeman, C. (1992). *The economics of hope: Essays on technical change and economic growth*. London: Pinter.
Freeman, C. (1995). The 'national system of innovation' in historical perspective. *Cambridge Journal of Economics, 19*, 5–24.
Freeman, C. (1997). The diversity of national research systems. In R. Barre, M. Gibbons, J. Maddox, B. Martin, & P. Papon (Eds.), *Science in tomorrow's Europe*. Paris: Economica International.

Freeman, C. (2002). Continental, national and sub-national innovation systems—complementarity and economic growth. *Research Policy, 31*, 191–211.

Freeman, C. (2004). Technological infrastructure and international competitiveness. *Industrial and Corporate Change, 13*(3), 541–69.

Freeman, C. (2008). *Systems of innovation: Selected essays in evolutionary economics*. Cheltenham: Edward Elgar.

Georghiou, L., Smith, K., Toivanen, O., & Ylä-Anttila, P. (2003). *Evaluation of the finnish innovation support system* (38 pp). Finland: Ministry of Trade and Industry Publications 5/2003.

Green Growth Knowledge Platform (GGKP). (2013). *Moving towards a common approach to green growth indicators*. Switzerland: Green Growth Knowledge Platform.

Godin, B. (2009). National innovation system: The system approach in historical perspective. *Science Technology Human Values, 34*(4), 476–501.

Goldberg, I., Branstetter, L., Goddard, J., & Kuriakose, S. (2008). *Globalization and technology absorption in Europe and Central Asia: The role of trade, FDI, and cross-border Knowledge flows, world bank working paper 150, world bank.*

Grant, R. (1991). The resource-based theory of competitive advantage: Implications for strategy formulation. *California Management Review, 33*(1991), 114–135.

Grant, R. (1996). Toward a knowledge-based theory of the firm. *Strategic Management Journal, 17,* 109–122.

Green, R. (2015). *Australia's INNOVATION future: A Report on the Structure and Performance of Australia's National Innovation System.* Committee Expert Consultant Report, Economics Reference Committee, Australian Parliament.

Gu, S., & Lundvall, B. A. (2006). China's innovation system and the move toward harmonious growth and endogneous innovation. *Innovation: Management, Policy and Practice, 8*(1–2), 1–26.

Helpman, E. (2004). *The mystery of economic growth*. Cambridge, MA: Harvard University Press.

Hoff, K., & Stiglitz, J. (2001). Modern economic theory and development. In G. Meier, J. Stiglitz, & N. York (Eds.), *Frontiers of development economics*. NY: Oxford University Press.

Howitt, P. (2009). Competition, innovation and growth: Theory, evidence, and policy challenges. In V. Chandra, D. Evocal, P. Padoan, & C. Bragg (Eds.), *Innovation and growth: Chasing a moving frontier* (pp. 15–24). OECD/World Bank.

Kim, L. (1997). *Imitation to innovation: The dynamic of Korea's technological learning*. Boston: Harvard Business School Press.

Kim, L., & Nelson, R. R. (2000). *Technology, learning and innovation: Experiences of newly industrializing economies*. Cambridge: Cambridge University Press.

Krugman, P. R. (1987). Is free trade passe? *Journal of Economic Perspective, 1*(2), 131–44.

Krugman, P. R. (1989). *Exchange rate instability.* Cambridge: MIT Press.

Krugman, P. R. (1992). Does the new trade theory require a new trade policy? *The World Economy, 15*(4), 423–442.

Leydesdorff, L., & Etzkowitz, H. (2003). Can "the public" be considered as a fourth helix in university-industry-government relations? Report of the fourth triple helix conference. *Science and Public Policy, 30*(1), 55–61.

Lorentzen, J. (2009). Learning by firms: The black box of South Africa's innovation system. *Science and Public Policy, 36*(1), 33–45.

Lucas, R. E. (1988). On the mechanics of economic development. *Journal of Monetary Economics, 22*(1), 3–42.

Lundvall, B.-Å. (1992). *National systems of innovation: Towards a theory of innovation and interactive learning*. London: Pinter Publishers.

Lundvall, B.-Å. (2002). *Innovation, growth and social cohesion: The Danish Model.* Cheltenham: Edward Elgar.

Lundvall, B.-Å. (2007). National innovation systems—analytical concept and development tool. *Industry and Innovation, 14*(1), 95–119.

Mason, C., & Brown, R. (2014). Entrepreneurial ecosystems and growth oriented entrepreneurship. OECD.

Mazzucato, M. (2016). From Market fixing to market-creating: A new framework for innovation policy. *Industry and Innovation, 23*(2), 140–156.

McKinsey. (2005). Asia's next export: Innovation. New York: *McKinsey Quarterly*.

METI. (2010). *The Industrial Structure Vision 2010*, Japanese Ministry for Economy, Trade and Industry http://www.meti.go.jp/english/policy/economy/pdf/Vision_Outline.pdf.

Ministry of Knowledge Economy. (2011). *Industry Policies*, www.mke.go.kr.

Naudé, W. (2010, September). *New challenges for industrial policy*. Working Paper No. 2010/107, United Nations University, World Institute for Development Economics Research.

Nelson, R. (1993). *National innovation systems: A comparative analysis*. OUP.

Noland, M., & Pack, H. (2003). *Industrial policy in an era of globalization: Lessons from Asia*. Washington DC: Peterson Institute for International Economics.

OECD. (2002). *Dynamising national innovation systems*. Paris: OECD.

OECD. (2009a). *Sustainable manufacturing and eco-innovation. Framework, practices and measurement*. Paris, France: OECD.

OECD. (2009b). *Sustainable manufacturing and eco-innovation: Towards a green economy*. Paris, France: OECD.

OECD. (2010). *The OECD innovation strategy: Getting a head start on tomorrow*. Paris: OECD.

OECD. (2015). *Innovation strategy 2015: An agenda for policy action*. Paris: OECD.

OECD. (2017). *Innovation networks and clusters*. Innovation Policy Platform: OECD.

Perez, C. (1983, October). Structural Changes and the assimilation of new technologies in the economic and social system. *Futures, 15*(5), 357–75.

Pilat, D., Cimper, A., Olsen, K., & Webb, C. (2006). *The Changing Nature of Manufacturing in OECD Economies, OECDScience, Technology and Industry Working Papers, 2006/09*. Paris: OECD Publishing.

Pitelis, C. (2009). The sustainable competitive advantage and catching-up of nations: FDI, clusters, and the liability (Asset) of smallness? *Management International Review, 49*(1), 95–120.

Porter, M. E. (1990). *The competitive advantage of nations*. Basingstoke: Macmillan.

Porter, M., Ketels, C., & Delgado, M. (2007). The microeconomic foundations of prosperity: Findings from the business competitiveness index. In A. Lopez-Claros, M. E. Porter, X. Sali-i-Martin, & K.Schwab (Eds.), *The global competitiveness report* 2006–2007. World Economic Forum.

RIETI. (2011). *Basic Research for a New Industrial Policy*, August 22, 2011–July 31, 2013, Research Institute of Economy, Trade and Industry, IAA, Tokyo http://www.rieti.go.jp/en/projects/program/pg-06/index.html#.

Rodrik, D. (2004). *Growth strategies*. Working Paper, Kennedy School of Government, Harvard University.

Rodrik, D. (2008). *Normalizing industrial policy*. Commission on Growth and Development Working Paper No. 3, Washington DC.

Romer, P. M. (1994). The origins of endogenous growth. *Journal of Economic Perspectives, 8*(1), 3–22.

Romer, P. M. (1986). Increasing returns and long-run growth. *Journal of Political Economy, 94* (5), 1002–1037.

Schilling, M. A. (2005). *Strategic management of technological innovation*. New York: McGraw-Hill.

Scott-Kemmis, D. (2008). *Industry policy frameworks for a knowledge economy, Review of the Australian Textile, clothing and footwear industry* (Vol. 2). Canberra: Commonwealth of Australia.

Sen, A. (1994). Well-being, capability and public policy. *Gionale degli Economist e Annali di Economia, 53*, 333–347.

Shapiro, H., & Taylor, L. (1990). The state and industrial strategy. *World Development, 18*(6), 861–878.

Sharif, N. (2006). Emergence and development of the national innovation systems concept. *Research Policy, 35*, 745–66.
Sigurdson, J. (2005). *Technological superpower China*. Cheltenham: Elgar.
Smith, A. (1776). *An inquiry into the nature and causes of the wealth of nations*. London: W. Strahan and T. Cadell.
Stiglitz, J. F., & Polanyi, K. (2001). *The great transformation, the political and economic origins of our time*. Boston: Beacon Press.
Sun, Y., & Liu, F. (2010). A regional perspective on the structural transformation of China's national innovation system since 1999. *Technological Forecasting and Social Change, 77*, 1311–1321.
Teece, D. (2000). *Managing intellectual capital*. Oxford: Oxford University Press.
Texeira, A. (2014). Evolution, roots and influence of the literature on national systems of innovation: A bibliometric account. *Cambridge Journal of Economics*, *38*(1), 181–214.
Texeira, A., & Silva, J. (2013). The intellectual and scientific basis of science, technology and innovation research. *Innovation: European Journal of Social Science Research, 26*(4).
Ul Haque, I. (2007). *Rethinking industrial policy*, UNCTAD Discussion Paper No. 183, United Nations Conference on Trade and Development.
UNCTAD. (2000). *Trade and Development Report 2000, United Nations Trade and Development Report*.
UNCTAD. (2017). *World Investment Report—Investment and the Digital Economy, UNCTAD*.
UNESCO. (2016). *UNESCO Science Report—Towards 2030*, UNESCO Publishing http://en.unesco.org/unesco_science_report.
Verspagen, B. (2006). Innovation and economic growth. In J. Fagerberg, D. C. Mowery, & R. R. Nelson (Eds.), *The Oxford handbook of innovation* (pp. 487–513). New York: Oxford University Press.
Warwick, K. (2013). Beyond Industrial Policy: Emerging Issues and New Trends, OECD Science, Technology and Industry Policy Papers, No. 2, OECD Publishing. http://dx.doi.org/10.1787/5k4869clw0xp-en.
Wyckoff, A. (2016). *Better Innovation for better lives*. OECD Yearbook: OECD.
Yim, D. S., & Nath, P. (2005). National innovation systems in Asian context. *Science Technology Society, 10*(1).
Yun, J. (2015). How do we conquer the growth limits of capitalism? Schumpeterian Dynamics of Open Innovation, *Journal of Open Innovation: Technology, Market, and Complexity, 1*, 17.
Yusuf, S. (2012). *East Asian experience with industrial policy and its implications for South Africa: Towards an urban-industrial growth strategy*. Washington DC: The World Bank.

Part II
Modes of Innovation

Chapter 7
Governance and Performance of Publicly Funded R&D Consortia

Hiroyuki Okamuro and Junichi Nishimura

Abstract R&D consortia have been regarded as an effective means of promoting innovation, and several R&D consortia obtain public financial support, which may affect its governance structure and performance. This study investigates the governance mechanisms of publicly funded R&D consortia and their effects on innovation. Regarding R&D consortia, few studies have empirically addressed the effect of project monitoring by the government. Moreover, the role of project leadership in R&D consortia remains poorly explored. Focusing on a major support program for R&D consortia in Japan and using a sample of 315 firms that participated in publicly funded R&D consortia from 2004 to 2009, we empirically confirm that project leadership by a private firm, especially its coordination capability, significantly increases the probability of project success (early commercialization of innovation outcomes). We also find that project performance is positively affected by the strictness of project monitoring and evaluation by the government, but negatively affected by interventions in application procedures. Finally, we find neither complementarity nor substitution between project leadership and government monitoring with regard to the effects on project performance.

Keywords R&D consortia · Public subsidy · Leadership · Monitoring · Commercialization

---

H. Okamuro (✉)
Graduate School of Economics, Hitotsubashi University, Tokyo, Japan
e-mail: okamuro@econ.hit-u.ac.jp

J. Nishimura
Faculty of Economics, Gakushuin University, Tokyo, Japan
e-mail: junichi.nishimura@gakushuin.ac.jp

T. Clarke and K. Lee (eds.), *Innovation in the Asia Pacific*,
https://doi.org/10.1007/978-981-10-5895-0_7

Introduction

R&D consortia (collaborative R&D projects among private firms, universities, and public research institutes) have been attracting increasing attention in several countries as an effective means of promoting innovation (Hemmert et al. 2014). Especially for SMEs, such collaboration provides important opportunities to access and obtain advanced scientific knowledge generated at universities and public research institutes (Motohashi 2005). However, efficient governance of R&D consortia is a difficult task because they include both academic and business partners that have different interests and incentives. Free-riding and opportunistic behavior may also occur. Therefore, the governance of R&D consortia matters for innovation performance (Mora-Valentin et al. 2004). Moreover, government often provides financial support to R&D consortia in order to promote innovation by involving SMEs. Such public support may affect project performance directly by increasing R&D expenditures, but also indirectly through project monitoring and evaluation.

We focus on a major support program for R&D consortia in Japan, the "Consortium R&D Project for Regional Revitalization" (CRDP) by the Ministry of Economy, Trade and Industry (METI). This program aims at commercializing scientific seeds of universities and public research institutes. Therefore, each consortium to be supported has to include at least a private firm and a university. Regarding the project governance, the government (METI) concludes a commissioned research contract with the project management organization, which in turn is expected to coordinate the consortia partly by concluding joint research contracts with all project members. METI selects R&D consortia to be financially supported based on project proposals and evaluates the performance of subsidized projects after the first year (midterm evaluation) and the second year (final evaluation). Various follow-up supports may be offered to several projects even after the funding period. Thus, both project leadership and public monitoring may be important for project performance, as internal and external disciplines.

However, regarding R&D consortia, few studies have empirically addressed the effect of project governance. Specifically, the effect of project monitoring by the government has scarcely been investigated. Moreover, the literature of innovation management has long recognized the role of innovation champions in private R&D (e.g. Chakrabarti 1974), but the role of project leadership in R&D consortia remains poorly explored. Therefore, focusing on the effects of project leadership and public monitoring, this chapter empirically examines the determinants of project performance of publicly funded R&D consortia in Japan using original survey data. In this way, we will investigate the contribution of project leadership and public monitoring to generating innovation.

The remainder of this chapter is organized as follows. In the next section, we provide a brief review of previous literature. In section "Conceptual Framework and Hypotheses", we present conceptual framework and some hypotheses for empirical estimation. In section "Empirical Analyses", we explain the data, sample and estimation models, and show and discuss the results of empirical estimations. Section "Concluding Remarks" concludes the chapter with contributions and limitations of this chapter and some future research agenda.

Previous Literature

Several studies have investigated the effect of R&D consortia (Zucker and Darby 2001; George et al. 2002; Motohashi 2005; Eom and Lee 2010) and public support for R&D (Klette et al. 2000; Czarnitzki et al. 2007) on innovation outcomes. However, to the best of our knowledge, few studies have empirically addressed the effect of project organization on the performance of R&D consortia, although it has often been argued that organization of R&D cooperation matter for innovation (e.g. Mora-Valentin et al. 2004; Morandi 2013; Casper and Miozzo 2013). For example, Okamuro (2007) examined how project characteristics affect the technological and commercial success of inter-firm cooperative R&D projects, but not that of R&D consortia including both private firms and universities. Okamuro and Nishimura (2013) explored the impact of university's intellectual property right policy on the performance of R&D consortia. Hemmert et al. (2014) provided an international comparison, comprising the US, Japan, and South Korea, on the effects of project characteristics on trust formation in the university-industry research collaboration, but not on project performance.

Especially the literature of innovation management has long recognized the role of innovation champions in private R&D (e.g. Chakrabarti 1974; Hemmert et al. 2014), but the role of project leadership in R&D consortia remains poorly explored, regarding econometric studies, due to data constraints. Some studies in the management literature have addressed the effects of project leadership, but they are mostly based on case studies or very small samples.

Moreover, the effect of project monitoring by the government has scarcely been investigated, although we could expect that project monitoring would have a significant impact on project management and performance. Regarding inter-firm R&D cooperation, both theoretical and empirical studies have been conducted on the contractual modes and its backgrounds (Hagedoorn and Hesen 2007, 2009; Van de Vrande et al. 2006), but scientific research on the governance of publicly funded R&D consortia, especially focusing on external monitoring, has been scarce. Some empirical studies argue that public subsidy for R&D consortia reduces opportunistic behavior of participants (Tripsas et al. 1995) or promotes trust among participants and thus increases project performance (Okamuro and Nishimura 2015), but they do not explicitly consider the role of government monitoring and evaluation. Thus, this study bridges these gaps and examines whether and how the type of project leader and project leadership as well as the project monitoring by the government improve innovation performance of R&D consortia.

Conceptual Framework and Hypotheses

Publicly funded R&D consortia have two important contractual aspects. The first one is the relationship among the participants including both private firms and research institutes with different interests and incentives. Another aspect is the relationship between the provider and the recipient of public funding, namely the government and the project leader. Therefore, an efficient governance mechanism of publicly funded R&D consortia should consider both contractual relationships.

R&D consortia comprise players with different incentives for R&D: Private firms seek for profits by patenting and commercializing R&D outcomes, while universities and public research institutes aim at creation and dissemination of new findings and ideas by presenting and publishing research outcomes. Hence, it is fundamentally important for the project success to efficiently coordinate different interests of different members. In this regard, the role of project leaders is essential. As mentioned above, METI's support program aims at commercialization of innovation outcomes, which is in line with the incentives of private firms. Therefore, project leadership by a private firm and her coordination ability are the keys for the performance of R&D consortia supported by METI.

Especially in the case of METI's CRDP, government can be regarded as the principal and project leader the agent, because both parties conclude a commissioned R&D contract. Under information asymmetry, the agent knows his or her ability and efforts (and those of the other members to some extent), while the principal has no or little information about the agent. In such circumstances, moral hazard of the agent may occur and lower project performance. A first-best solution of this problem would be an incentive contract, in which the payment to the agent is set to depend on his performance. However, this solution is difficult to apply to public funding of R&D projects because usually a public subsidy does not depend on the achieved performance (ex post measures), but is fixed ex ante based on some selection criteria.

Thus, instead of incentive contract, monitoring and evaluation by the government should play an important role in the governance of publicly funded projects. The government may check the progress of cooperative R&D and possibly intervene after midterm evaluation with advices and requests. The consortia with lower performance may be excluded from supplemental support and new public subsidy in the next round. In this sense, government monitoring involves an ex post incentive mechanism.

Thus, we can discuss the governance of publicly funded R&D consortia from the viewpoints of internal and external disciplines. The former refers to the role of the project leader and the relationship among consortium members. The latter comprises project evaluation and monitoring by the government. Main questions regarding project leadership are (1) whether the project leader is a manager of a private firm or a university professor and (2) what roles the project leader plays (project design, progress control, coordination, etc.). Regarding government monitoring, key questions include how strict it is with regard to (1) application procedure, (2) budget control, (3) progress control, and (4) evaluation.

Based on the above discussion, we present the following hypotheses for the empirical analysis in the next section:

H1: Project leadership matters for project performance: Project leadership by a private firm, as compared to a university or a public research institute, increases the probability of project success.
H2: Specifically, project leader's coordination capability positively affects the probability of project success.
H3: Project monitoring and evaluation by the government also matters for project performance: The probability of project success is positively affected by the strictness of evaluation.

Moreover, we may expect that project leadership and monitoring be complementary or substitutive, rather than affecting the project performance independently. Complementarity means that the combination of strong leadership and strong monitoring increases project performance. Substitution means that such combination lowers project performance. We will empirically check whether complementary or substitution effect dominates between leadership and monitoring, or there is no such relationship between them.

Empirical Analyses

Data and Sample

We focus on a major support program for R&D consortia in Japan, the "Consortium R&D Project for Regional Revitalization" by the Ministry of Economy, Trade and Industry (METI), which aims at commercializing scientific seeds of universities and public research institutes. We conducted a questionnaire survey in 2011 for 1550 firms that obtained public subsidy by this program during the period from 2004 to 2009. Our final sample comprises 315 respondents to this survey (response ratio: 20%). Among them, 80% are SMEs with less than 300 employees. The ratio of R&D expenditures to sales of the sample firms amounts to 7.3% on average, so that our sample comprises R&D-intensive firms.

The consortia in which the sample firms participated are distributed in all regions in Japan and in various high-tech areas such as manufacturing technology (27%), biotechnology (22%), nanotechnology (14%), environmental technology (13%), and information/communication technology (10%). Only 8% of these consortia can be classified to basic research projects, 32% to applied research projects, and 60% to development. They comprise 7 members on average: 3 private firms and 4 universities, public research institutes, etc. All subsidized consortia have project leaders, of whom 46% belong to private firms and 50% to universities or public research institutes. 75% of the consortia concluded formal internal contracts with consortia members regarding task assignment, treatment of R&D outcomes (intellectual property rights), project budget, and schedule.

These consortia obtained on average 60 million yen in the first year and 35 million yen in the second and last year as public funds. After the funding period, 25% of the consortia obtained follow-up support from METI including additional subsidy, and invitations to research seminars and business matching. By March 2010, 22% of the R&D consortia of the sample firms have achieved the commercialization of their innovation outcomes, which lies below the target of this support program (30%). 18% reported project failure (no prospect for commercialization) and 57% have not yet achieved commercialization, expecting it in the near future.

Models and Variables

We hypothesize that both project leadership that generates internal discipline and government monitoring as external discipline affect the incentive and efficiency of project members to achieve the purposes of the consortia, thus project performance. We measure it as the probability of commercialization of project outcomes, which is the aim of this support program. Thus, we use the commercialization dummy (*d_commercial*), which takes the value 1 if project outcomes have already been commercialized, and 0 otherwise, as the dependent variable. Because this is a dummy variable, we employ a binary probit model for the empirical analysis.

The independent variables include those for project leadership and public monitoring. An important variable for project leadership is the type of project leader (*business*), which takes the value 1 if a private firm is the project leader and 0 otherwise (university or public research institute). According to Hypothesis 1, we expect that the coefficient of this variable be positive and significant. Other variables for project leadership represent subjective evaluations by the respondents on the following characteristics of project leadership: (1) project planning (*leader_planning*), (2) checking progress (*leader_progress*), (3) coordination among project members (*leader_coordination*), and (4) encouraging to achieve the goal (*leader_goal*). These variables are measured with a 4-point Likert scale (from 1: weak to 4: strong). Moreover, considering positive correlation across these variables, we construct an integrated variable *leader* as the first principal component by the principal component analysis of the leadership variables (Cronbach's alpha: 0.836). According to Hypothesis 2, we expect that the coefficients of these leadership variables be positive and significant.

Further, we measure the strictness of government monitoring as subjective evaluations by the respondents on the following monitoring: (1) application procedure (*monitor_application*), (2) budget (*monitor_budget*), (3) checking progress (*monitor_progress*), and (4) midterm project evaluation (*monitor_midterm*). These variables are measured also with a 4-point Likert scale (from 1: weak to 4: strong). Also in this regard, we construct an integrated variable *monitor* as the first principal component by the principal component analysis of the monitoring variables (Cronbach's alpha: 0.783). According to Hypothesis 3, we expect that the coefficients of these variables be positive and significant.

We will check the relationship between project leadership and government monitoring, complementarity or substitution, by using the interactive term of *leader* and *monitor*. Both factors can be complementary if government monitoring strengths the effect of leadership on project performance (and vice versa) or substitutive if the former weakens the latter's effect (and vice versa). For this interactive term, we expect a positive coefficient if leadership and monitoring are complementary and a negative coefficient if they are substitutive.

We also control for some basic characteristics of R&D consortia including the number of participants (*project size*), whether the joint research was conducted at the location of a partner (*location*), research orientation (basic or applied research: *basic*, *applied*), technology field (dummy variables for IT, biotechnology, manufacturing, environment, energy, and others), and the starting year of the subsidized consortia (dummy variables for the fiscal years 2005, 2006, 2007, and 2008). We expect that the consortia that include a few members and conduct basic research be less likely to commercialize project outcomes than those including many members and focusing on development stage.

We have to control for technology fields and starting years of the projects, because the probability of early commercialization of project outcomes may differ across technology fields. Moreover, we face a truncation problem because we collected information including the commercialization of project outcomes using a questionnaire survey in 2011. Public funding for selected R&D consortia were provided for two years, so that the first cohort in our sample starting in 2004 ended in 2005, while the last cohort starting in 2008 ended in 2009. It means that the first cohort had more than 7 years for commercializing project outcomes, whereas the last cohort had only 3 years for this purpose: The older the project, the more likely is the commercialization.

Table 7.1 presents the basic statistics (mean and standard deviation) of the variables explained above. As mentioned before, 22% of the respondents report that their project has already achieved commercialization of project outcomes. Regarding leadership variables, 43% of the respondents point out that the project leader belonged to a private firm in their projects. Moreover, they provide relatively high average scores (around 3 in the four-point scale) for the evaluation of project leadership. Also the strictness of government monitoring is relatively highly evaluated with mean scores around 3 in the four-point scales).

Table 7.1 Basic statistics of the variables

	Variables	Obs.	Mean	S.D.
Performance	*d_commercial*	306	0.222	0.416
Project leadership	*business*	315	0.432	0.496
	leader_planning	302	3.215	0.763
	leader_progress	302	2.980	0.760
	leader_coordination	302	3.007	0.765
	leader_goal	302	3.255	0.763
	leader	302	0.000	1.641
Government monitoring	*monitor_application*	299	3.130	0.660
	monitor_budget	298	3.450	0.705
	monitor_progress	299	2.819	0.705
	monitor_midterm	299	2.973	0.660
	monitor	298	0.000	1.560
Other project characteristics	*location*	307	0.381	0.486
	project size	315	7.384	3.601
	basic	308	0.081	0.274
	applied	308	0.318	0.467

Estimation Results and Discussion

Table 7.2 provides the estimation results. After excluding several responses with missing values, the empirical analyses are based on 292 observations. The estimation includes dummy variables for starting years and technology fields of the projects, which are not shown in the table to save space. The marginal effects and robust standard errors of the variables are presented here.

The empirical estimation of the propensity of commercialization (*d_commercial*) using a probit model shows that, as expected, project leadership by a private firm (as compared to a university or a public research institute) (*business*), and specifically project leader's coordination capability (*leader_coordination*), significantly increases the probability of commercialization of project outcomes. The consortium whose leader belongs to a private firm is 14% more likely to achieve commercialization than that whose leader belongs to a university or a public research institute. We also confirm that, regarding government monitoring, project performance is positively affected by the strictness of progress monitoring and midterm evaluation, but negatively affected by strict application procedures. These results support all hypotheses presented before.

The aggregated leadership variable (*leader*) has a highly significant effect, while the aggregated monitoring variable (*monitor*) has a negative but weakly significant effect, on project performance. The coefficient of the interactive term of *leader* and *monitor* is not significant, suggesting that leadership and monitoring are neither complementary nor substitutive.

Table 7.2 Estimation results on the commercialization of project outcomes (probit estimation)

	Variables	*d_commercial*		*d_commercial*	
		Marginal effect	Robust S.E.	Marginal effect	Robust S.E.
Leadership	*business*	0.145**	0.058	0.139**	0.059
	leader_planning	0.002	0.039		
	leader_progress	−0.002	0.049		
	leader_coordination	0.045*	0.024		
	leader_goal	0.034	0.044		
	leader			0.038***	0.014
Monitoring	*monitor_application*	−0.085**	0.042		
	monitor_budget	0.032	0.044		
	monitor_progress	0.099**	0.047		
	monitor_midterm	0.125***	0.047		
	monitor			−0.027*	0.016
Cross term	*leader * monitor*			0.002	0.008
Other Characteristics	*location*	0.001	0.049	0.015	0.050
	project size	0.011*	0.006	0.008	0.008
	basic	−0.162**	0.046	−0.158**	0.053
	applied	−0.015	0.050	−0.007	0.051
	starting year dummies	yes		yes	
	technology fields dummies	yes		yes	
	Pseudo R square	0.114		0.083	
	Log pseudo likelihood	−138.260		−143.047	
	Observations	292		292	

Note *, **, and *** denote statistical significance at the 10%, 5%, and 1% levels, respectively

Regarding the control variables, we find that the dummy variable for basic research shows a significant and negative effect, suggesting that, as expected, R&D consortia focusing on basic research are less likely to achieve commercialization than those focusing on development stage.

Robustness Checks

We conducted some additional estimation for robustness checks. First, we used leadership and monitoring variables separately (interchangeably) in the estimations and confirmed that the estimation results did not significantly differ from those presented in Table 7.2. Second, we added some variables for respondents' characteristics such as size, age, and R&D intensity, but they did not show any direct significant effects on project performance.

Third, we conducted an ordered probit estimation using another performance variable *commercial*. This variable can take 3 values: 1 if a consortium failed in commercializing project outcomes, 2 if it has not yet commercialized the outcomes but has it in prospect, and 3 if it has already commercialized the outcome. In this way, we alternatively estimate the determinants of the extent of commercialization of project outcomes. The results are very similar to those of probit estimation, except that the effects of *leader_goal* and *location* are significant in ordered probit estimation results.

Concluding Remarks

R&D consortia are often funded by the government for the purpose of promoting innovation. Several empirical studies have been carried out on R&D consortia and its performance, but few studies have focused on the roles of project leadership and public monitoring, although such internal and external disciplines should be important in the governance of organizations. Therefore, we empirically addressed these issues by using original survey data on publicly funded R&D consortia in Japan.

Based on our empirical results, we may conclude that, for the performance of publicly supported R&D consortia, project governance matters. Specifically, project leadership by a private firm seems to be more effective in commercializing project outcomes than that by a university or a public research institute. Strong leadership especially in coordinating among project members increases the probability of commercialization. Moreover, government monitoring, especially strict progress check and midterm evaluation, is important for project performance. Thus, major contributions of this chapter are that we empirically investigated and confirmed the roles of internal discipline (project leadership) and external discipline (public monitoring) for the innovation performance of R&D consortia. We find neither complementary nor substitution effect between internal and external discipline, suggesting that both are important.

We can derive following policy implications from these results. First, project leader's type (affiliation) may be related to the incentive mechanism in the consortia and thus to project outcomes. Therefore, in order to promote the commercialization of R&D outcomes, project leadership by a private firm may be more appropriate than that by a university or a public research institute. Second, project monitoring and evaluation by the government also matters for project performance. Public support of R&D consortia should be combined with a strict project evaluation, but not with strict application procedures or budget control.

Despite these contributions and implications, our analyses have still some limitations. First, we do not directly compare between R&D consortia with and without public funding. We only compare the effects of public monitoring within the sample of publicly funded consortia with regard to the strictness of public monitoring. Hence, we cannot directly evaluate the effect of public funding or public monitoring as compared to the consortia that did not obtain public funds.

Second, we conducted project-level analyses based on the data that are obtained from individual participants of R&D consortia. Regarding subjective evaluation, especially on project leadership and monitoring, the responses may differ among project members. It is not sure whether the response we obtained may be representative for the consortia members, at least for private firms. Thus, it is difficult to strictly identify the real differences in the project leadership and government monitoring across consortia from those across individual respondents.

Third, our investigation is based on micro data from a retrospective one-shot survey, although R&D consortia involve a dynamic process. Therefore, we should also take the dynamics of the whole project explicitly into consideration: for example, project leadership may change during the project, especially after the midterm evaluation based on the comments or demands by the evaluators. Therefore, future research should more appropriately consider dynamic changes in some variables. For example, we may focus on the effects of project leadership and government monitoring on the engagement of participants in joint R&D processes, such as commitment and free-riding, which in turn may affect project performance.

Appendix 1: Overview of the "Consortium R&D Project for Regional Revitalization" (CRDP) by METI

This program is carried out as R&D projects contracted by METI to competitively selected research consortia, so that the R&D expenditures of the supported projects are fully covered by the subsidy. The subsidy is paid for the contracted work; thus, payment is received after a project is finished. Each consortium has a management organization that can be a private firm, university, public research institute or a public agency and that prepares for and submits applications (project proposals). These proposals include detailed information on research and commercialization plans, project schedules, budget plans, management organization, project leaders, sub-leaders, and each of the members (e.g., firms, university professors, etc.), and each member's role in the project.

Upon acceptance, the management organizations of selected consortia must enter into a formal contract with a regional department of METI to conduct the projects. Then, management organizations usually enter into subcontracting agreements with project members. Project members are also asked to provide collective confirmation for the commercialization of research outcomes.

After finishing the project (typically within two years), each management organization submits a project report to METI, which then reimburses the R&D expenditures for the project. Project evaluation is conducted by METI based on the final report provided by the management organization. In the final report and evaluation, not only the technological achievements of the project, but also the efficiency of project coordination and any efforts to improve it are taken into consideration. METI publishes information on the selected consortia, including membership and the final reports of these projects. Moreover, METI follows up on further research and the commercialization of project outcomes by the supported consortia for five years after the end of the projects.

In this way, METI and its regional departments monitor and evaluate UIC projects, enforce clear mutual agreements among members, and publicize project information. We expect such an institutional background to encourage trust formation in UIC projects.

Appendix 2: Questionnaire Items for the Leadership and Monitoring Variables

(translated from Japanese original into English by the authors)

2–4. Please evaluate the strength of leadership by the project leader of the entire consortium for each of the following items by the four-point scale:

1: weak, 2: rather weak, 3: rather strong, 4: strong.

(1) Designing the research plan of the project
(2) Progress control of the project
(3) Coordination among the participants during the project
(4) Efforts to achieve the goal of the project.

2–5. Please evaluate the strictness of project monitoring by the government for each of the following items by the four-point scale:

1: weak, 2: rather weak, 3: rather strong, 4: strong.

(1) Reminders in project application procedures
(2) Budget (expenditures) control
(3) Progress check in R&D
(4) Midterm evaluation
(5) Final evaluation.

References

Casper, S., Miozzo, M. (2013). Open innovation and governance: Innovation partnerships between industry and university in science-based sectors. Paper presented at the 35th DRUID Celebration Conference 2013, Barcelona, Spain, June 17–19, 2013.

Chakrabarti, A. K. (1974). The role of champion in product innovation. *California Management Review, 17,* 58–62.

Czarnitzki, D., Ebersberger, B., & Fier, A. (2007). The relationship between R&D collaboration, subsidies, and R&D performance: Empirical evidence from Finland and Germany. *Journal of Applied Econometrics, 22,* 1347–1366.

Eom, B. Y., & Lee, K. (2010). Determinants of industry-academy linkages and their impact on firm performance. The case of Korea as a latecomer in knowledge industrialization. *Research Policy, 39,* 625–639.

George, G., Zahra, S. A., & Wood, D. R. (2002). The effects of business-university alliances on innovative output and financial performance: A study of publicly traded biotechnology companies. *Journal of Business Venturing, 17,* 577–609.

Hagedoorn, J., & Hesen, G. (2007). Contract law and the governance of inter-firm technology partnerships. An analysis of different modes of partnering and their contractual implications. *Journal of Management Studies, 44,* 342–366.

Hagedoorn, J., & Hesen, G. (2009). Contractual complexity and the cognitive load of R&D alliance contracts. *Journal of Empirical Legal Studies, 6,* 818–847.

Hemmert, M., Bstieler, L., & Okamuro, H. (2014). Bridging the cultural divide: Trust formation in university-industry research collaborations in the US, Japan, and South Korea. *Technovation, 34,* 605–616.

Klette, T. J., Moen, J., & Griliches, Z. (2000). Do subsidies to commercial R&D reduce market failures? Microeconometric evaluation studies. *Research Policy, 29,* 471–495.

Mora-Valentin, E. M., Montoro-Sanchez, A., & Guerras-Martin, L. A. (2004). Determining factors in the success of R&D cooperative agreements between firms and research organizations. *Research Policy, 33,* 17–40.

Morandi, V. (2013). The management of industry-university joint research projects: How do partners coordinate and control R&D activities? *Journal of Technology Transfer, 38,* 69–92.

Motohashi, K. (2005). University-industry collaborations in Japan: The role of new technology-based firms in transforming the national innovation system. *Research Policy, 34,* 583–594.

Okamuro, H. (2007). Determinants of successful R&D cooperation in Japanese small businesses: The impact of organizational and contractual characteristics. *Research Policy, 36,* 1529–1544.

Okamuro, H., & Nishimura, J. (2013). Impact of university intellectual property policy on the performance of university-industry research collaboration. *Journal of Technology Transfer, 38,* 273–301.

Okamuro, H., Nishimura, J. (2015). Not just financial support? Another role of public subsidy in university-industry research collaborations. *Economics of Innovation and New Technology, 24,* 633-659.

Tripsas, M., Schrader, S., & Sobrero, M. (1995). Discouraging opportunistic behavior in collaborative R&D: A new role for government. *Research Policy, 24,* 367–389.

Van de Vrande, V., Lemmens, C., & Vanhaverbeke, W. (2006). Choosing governance modes for external technology sourcing. *R&D Management, 36,* 347–363.

Zucker, L. G., & Darby, M. R. (2001). Capturing technological opportunity via Japan's star scientists: Evidence from Japanese firms' biotech patents and products. *Journal of Technology Transfer, 26,* 37–58.

Chapter 8
Patents and Innovation in China

Albert G. Hu, Peng Zhang and Lijing Zhao

Abstract In the following chapter Hu, Zhang and Zhao examine the relationship of patents to technology innovation. The development of patents is conventionally regarded widely as a significant part of the innovation process in many modes of innovation. Patents are often used as an indicator of technology innovation, and China's patenting surge raises the question whether China has become as innovative as her patent numbers suggest? If patents measure innovation output, a measure of inputs to the innovation process is R&D expenditures. China's R&D spending has more than kept pace with the rapid growth of GDP in China. R&D as a share of GDP increased from 1.4 in 2007 to 1.8% in 2011, which was not far from the OECD average. However, patent numbers have been growing even faster than the increase in R&D expenditure. The number of invention patents granted to resident, non-individual applicants per 10 million dollars of R&D expenditure (in 2011 purchasing power parity prices) was 3 for China and 2 for the U.S. in 2007. In four years, the ratio for China rose to 6.3, and that for the U.S. increased more modestly to 2.4. While not impossible, it would seem unlikely that this large and widening disparity in patents to R&D ratio can be explained by the difference in the productivity of R&D of the two countries. The objective of this chapter is to explore both innovation and non-innovation-related explanations of China's patenting surge and to discuss their policy implications. "The conventional role of patents lies in preventing copying and pre-empting unauthorized entry, the need for which rises when new technologies are created, thus implying a tight connection between technology innovation and patenting." Recent experience in developed countries,

---

This chapter is adapted from Hu, Zhang and Zhao (2017).

A.G. Hu (✉)
National University of Singapore, Singapore, Singapore
e-mail: ecshua@nus.edu.sg

P. Zhang · L. Zhao
National Bureau of Statistics of China, Beijing, China

T. Clarke and K. Lee (eds.), *Innovation in the Asia Pacific*,
https://doi.org/10.1007/978-981-10-5895-0_8

particularly the U.S., indicates that applying for patents has also been driven by firms' concerns that an unfavorable court ruling over the ownership of intellectual property could inflict significant financial damages on them. This has led firms to build up a war chest of patents that might increase their bargaining power in anticipation of such intellectual property disputes. The propensity to apply for patents can increase, when the underlying rate of technology innovation has not significantly, but when developments in legal institutions and public policy change the firms' perception of the need for such strategic maneuvers.

Keywords Patents · Technology innovation · Intellectual property rights · Economic development · China

Introduction

China's State Intellectual Property Office (SIPO) became the busiest patent office in the world in 2011, having seen its resident patent applications growing at 30% in the preceding decade. In comparison, the growth rate had been −2.8, 6.5 and 3.4% respectively for Japan, South Korea and the U.S. during the same time. To the extent that patents are often used as an indicator of technology innovation, China's patenting surge raises the question whether China has become as innovative as her patent numbers suggest.

If patents measure innovation output, a measure of inputs to the innovation process is R&D expenditures. China's R&D spending had more than kept pace with her rapid growth of GDP—R&D as a share of GDP increased from 1.4 in 2007 to 1.8% in 2011, which was not far from the OECD average.[1] However, patents had been growing even faster. The number of invention patents granted to resident, non-individual applicants per 10 million dollars of R&D expenditure (in 2011 purchasing power parity prices) was 3 for China and 2 for the U.S. in 2007. In four years, the ratio for China rose to 6.3, and that for the U.S. increased more modestly to 2.4. While not impossible, it would seem unlikely that this large and widening disparity in patents to R&D ratio can be explained by the difference in the productivity of R&D of the two countries.[2]

[1]Even this acceleration of R&D intensity at the aggregate level may belie the even more rapid growth in R&D in certain sectors of the Chinese economy, such as telecommunication equipment.

[2]We use the number of patents granted to non-individual applicants in 2011 as the numerator and R&D expenditures incurred in 2008 as the denominator. The R&D expenditures are measured in 2011 prices that have been adjusted for purchasing power parity—we obtained the figures by multiplying GDP in 2011 PPP prices by the R&D to GDP ratio. We build in a three-year lag between patent grant and R&D spending. The GDP and R&D to GDP ratio data are obtained from World Development Indicators (http://data.worldbank.org/indicator/all).

The objective of this chapter is to explore both innovation and non-innovation-related explanations of China's patenting surge and to discuss their policy implications. The conventional role of patents lies in preventing copying and pre-empting unauthorized entry, the need for which rises when new technologies are created, thus implying a tight connection between technology innovation and patenting. However, recent experience in developed countries, particularly the U.S., indicate that applying for patents has also been driven by firms' concerns that an unfavorable court ruling over the ownership of intellectual property could inflict significant damages on them and by their intention to build up a war chest of patents that would increase their bargaining power in anticipation of such disputes. The propensity to apply for patents can increase, when the underlying rate of technology innovation has not, when developments in legal institutions and public policy change the firms' perception of the need for such strategic maneuvers.

An important non-innovation-related driving force of the patenting surge in China has been the Chinese government's encouragement of the acquisition of intellectual property as part of its push for raising the level of technology innovation in the Chinese economy. For instance, the 12th Five-Year Plan of Science and Technology Development, which covers the five-year period from 2011 to 2015, set an explicit target for patents: it aimed to increase the number of SIPO invention patents in force per 10,000 people from 1.7 in 2010 to 3.3 in 2015. To execute plans such as this, Chinese government at various levels has introduced incentives to promote patent applications.

We present evidence based on a novel data set to ascertain the contributions of both innovation and non-innovation-related forces to China's patenting surge. In our data set SIPO patents have been matched to Chinese industrial firms at the firm level. This database spans the population of China's large and medium size industrial enterprises, which account for the majority of R&D conducted in Chinese industry.

A key finding of our analysis is that the association between patents and R&D and between patents and labor productivity had weakened in China's large and medium size enterprises from 2007 to 2011. This trend is particularly conspicuous for utility models, which require no substantive examination at the patent office for them to be granted, and for firms and regions that had patented relatively less in the past, i.e., the extensive margin of growth. These results lend credence to the role of non-innovation related forces in driving the patenting surge.

Understanding what has been behind China's patenting surge is important for assessing technological progress in China. While it is beyond the scope of the current paper to analyze the consequences of patenting motivated by non-innovation related forces, they are unlikely to be innocuous. For example, the rapid increase in patent applications has increased the workload at SIPO, potentially reducing the amount of time examiners spend on each application, which in turn may lead to undeserving patents to be granted. The policy incentives may create distortionary effect on technology innovation by shifting too much resources to activities that would lead to patents.

China's Great Leap Forward in Patenting: An International Comparison

Patent applications at SIPO have experienced exponential growth. In Fig. 8.1 we plot the number of resident patent applications (in logarithm) filed at four national patent offices: Japan Patent Office, Korea Patent Office, SIPO and US Patent and Trademark Office. From 1985 to 2012, resident patent applications at USPTO had been increasing at an annual rate of 5.5%—inviting much commentary and analysis of what is called the U.S. patent explosion (Kortum and Lerner 1999; Jaffe and Lerner 2004; Hall 2004). In contrast, resident patent applications at SIPO registered an annual growth rate of 20%, with significant acceleration in recent years.

Resident patent applications at the Japan Patent Office had been rising from the mid 1980s to the late 1990s (Sakakibara and Branstetter 2001; Nagaoda 2009), but started declining after that, with the number of applications filed in 2012 similar to that for 1985. South Korea, a country that has made the transition from imitation to innovation (Kim 1997), started in the mid 1980s with a similar number of resident patent applications as China, but only grew its patent applications at a lower rate of 16 per cent per annum. If resident patent applications at SIPO had followed similar growth patterns as those at the USPTO and South Korea's patent office up until 2005, they clearly embarked on a much faster growth trajectory after that.

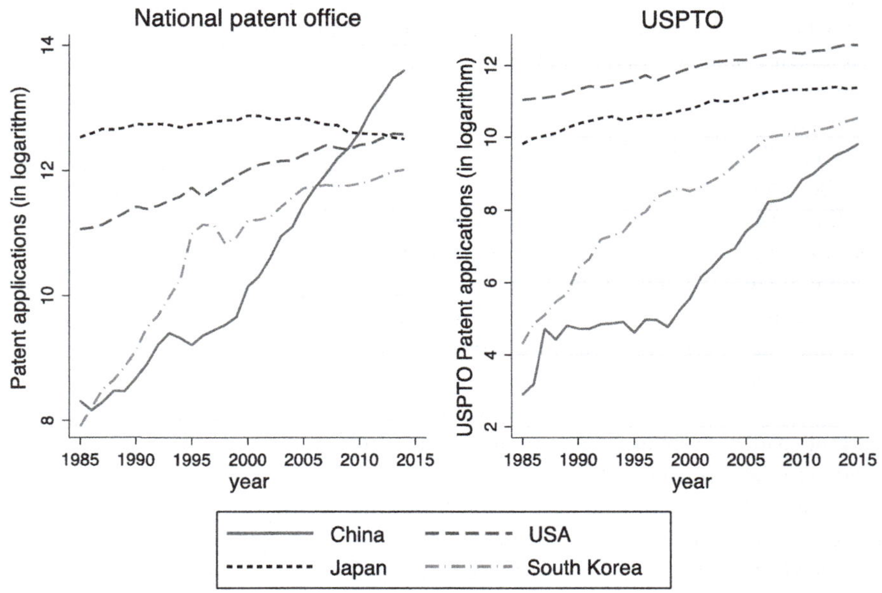

Source: World Development Indicators 2016, U.S. Patent and Trademark Office

Fig. 8.1 Patent applications at national patent offices and the USPTO

Comparison of resident patent applications filed at national patent offices is subject to a home bias. For large countries, the domestic market represents the largest opportunity for inventors to realize the returns to their inventions, and thus the inventors tend to seek out patents in their home country first. The cost of obtaining a foreign patent is also higher than that for a domestic one, contributing to the home bias in resident patent applications. Thus we plot in the right panel of Fig. 8.1 the numbers of applications from the four countries at a single national patent office, the USPTO, to try to account for the home bias. Given the home "advantage" of U.S. applicants at the USPTO, we focus on the comparison between China, Japan and South Korea. China's USPTO patent applications, although growing at a faster rate, are still outnumbered by those of Japan and South Korea.

One potential explanation of the underperformance of Chinese applicants at the USPTO could be that many of the Chinese high-tech companies have not turned the U.S. into a major market for their products. Nevertheless the incongruence between the two figures raises questions about the technological significance of China's patenting surge.

The Literature

Hu and Jefferson (2009) provided the first economic analysis of China's patenting surge when it was still at an early stage and the driving forces behind it appeared to be somewhat different from those of today. They estimated a patent production function using a dataset of Chinese large and medium size manufacturing enterprises from 1995 to 2001. The results showed that increasing R&D expenditure could only explain a fraction of the patent explosion. A novel feature of the Chinese patent explosion that is absent in other episodes of rapid patent growth is the role of foreign direct investment, which they found to have prompted Chinese firms to file for more patent applications. They also found that both the strengthening of the Chinese patent law and ownership reform that has clarified the assignment of property rights have increased Chinese firms' propensity to patent.

Hu (2010) focused on the rapid growth of foreign (non-resident) applications at SIPO. He investigated two hypotheses in explaining the foreign patenting surge in China: market covering and competitive threat. With foreign companies more deeply engaged with the Chinese economy, returns from protecting their intellectual property in China have increased. As domestic Chinese firms' ability to imitate foreign technology gains strength and competition between foreign firms intensifies in the Chinese market, such competitive threat heightens the urgency to protect intellectual property. Using a database that comprises SIPO and USPTO patents, he found support for the competitive threat hypothesis.

Li (2012) investigated the impact of Chinese government's patent subsidy programs on China's patenting surge, using province-level aggregate data for the period from the mid 1990s to 2007. His results showed that patent applications increased after a province launched a patent application fees subsidy program.

Investigating the rapid growth of Chinese patent applications at the USPTO, Branstetter et al. (2015) found that much of the surge of Chinese patenting in the U.S. has been driven by multinational corporations' R&D activity in China, rather than indigenous Chinese firms' inventions.

The Data

The NBS-SIPO Firm-Level Patent Database

National Bureau of Statistics of China and SIPO started a collaboration in 2007 to match SIPO patents that have been granted to large and medium size Chinese industrial firms with these firms' financial and technology indicators that are part of the large and medium size industrial enterprises (LME) census database. The resulting database is what we use for the current analysis, which covers the period of 2007 to 2011. For each LME, we know the numbers of their patent applications and grants by year. The patent counts are available for three types of patents: invention patents, utility models and designs.[3] In addition, the database also includes information on the number of patents that are "in force" for the three types of patents. These are patents that have been granted and have not lapsed because the firms have paid renewal fees to maintain their legal status. Since designs are usually considered a different and more rudimentary type of innovation from those protected by invention patents and utility models, for the current analysis we will concentrate on the latter two categories of patents.

There have been other efforts to match SIPO patents to the Chinese firms that own them. And all these researchers did the matching by comparing the name of a firm in a firm database with the name of a patent applicant in the SIPO database. For example, He et al. (2013) matched SIPO patents to publicly listed Chinese firms; Holmes et al. (2015) identified the SIPO patents for a sample of multinational corporations operating in China; and Xie and Zhang (2015) matched SIPO patent data with the widely diffused "above scale" Chinese industrial firm database.

Our database is unique in that it is constructed using the firm's legal person code, rather than name in the matching. Each Chinese enterprise is assigned a unique legal person code by the General Administration of Quality Supervision, Inspection and Quarantine of China. And SIPO and NBS have used that code to link the SIPO patent database with the NBS large and medium size enterprise database. This approach has the advantage of eliminating the ambiguity and error created by the different ways a firm's name is recorded in various databases.

The number of industrial LMEs, as reported in Table 8.1, ranged from 36,251 in 2007 to 60,391 in 2011. In 2011 NBS changed the criteria by which an enterprise

[3]SIPO refers to all three as patents with the respective qualifiers of invention, utility model and design.

Table 8.1 The LME sample

	2007	2008	2009	2010	2011
All LME	36,251	40,314	40,764	45,531	60,391
All manufacturing	32,621	36,102	36,552	41,000	54,490
Balanced	19,546	19,546	19,546	19,546	19,546

qualifies as a large or medium size enterprise for the industrial census. This explains the large jump in the number of LMEs from 2010 to 2011. Manufacturing consistently accounted for around 90% of all LMEs. Among manufacturing LMEs, 19,546 enterprises appeared in all five years in the database. These firms constitute the balanced sample that our statistical analysis is based on.

How Representative Is the LME Sample in Accounting for Patenting at SIPO?

In its statistical reporting system, SIPO categorizes patents into domestic and foreign patents, based on the country of origin of the applicant of a patent. Within each category, patents are further classified into "service" and "non-service" patents, which are SIPO's terms for non-individual and individual patents respectively, depending on the identity of the applicant of a patent. Within the domestic service patents category, patents are further classified into four categories based on the nature of business of the applicants: universities, research institutions, government and non-profit organizations, and enterprises.

The top panel of Table 8.2 tabulates the total numbers of patent applications and grants for inventions and utility models for all domestic enterprises.[4] From 2007 to 2011, invention patent applications have more than tripled and utility model applications have more than quintupled, while the grants of these two types of patents have more than quadrupled.[5] The second panel of the table reports LMEs' share of all enterprise patents. By and large, the LMEs have maintained their shares of various patent counts at between 30 and 45%.

[4]We obtained these numbers from SIPO's Patent Statistics Annual Report (www.sipo.gov.cn/tjxx/). The enterprise patents consistently accounted the bulk of all domestic service, or non-individual patents, e.g., they were consistently responsible for around 70% of all domestic, service applications for invention patents from 2007 to 2011.

[5]Invention patent applications include both successful and unsuccessful applications. The ratio of contemporaneous patent grants to applications does not correspond to the likelihood of a patent application being granted given the time it takes to process the application. Also since applications have been growing very rapidly in China, the contemporaneous ratio is particularly uninformative. Assuming an application-grant lag of three years, the grant to application ratio works out to be close to 60%.

Table 8.2 Shares of patenting activities: various samples

	Invention	Utility model	Invention	Utility model
All enterprises				
2007	73,893	63,371	12,851	53,451
2008	95,619	91,374	22,493	70,242
2009	118,257	147,618	32,160	95,407
2010	154,581	212,081	40,049	183,289
2011	231,551	336,298	58,364	236,959
LMEs' shares of all enterprise patents				
2007	0.39	0.34	0.35	0.34
2008	0.36	0.36	0.41	0.37
2009	0.35	0.31	0.44	0.36
2010	0.33	0.31	0.45	0.33
2011	0.31	0.3	0.42	0.33
Manufacturing LMEs' shares of all enterprise patents				
2007	0.3	0.32	0.25	0.32
2008	0.31	0.34	0.28	0.35
2009	0.34	0.3	0.43	0.34
2010	0.32	0.3	0.44	0.32
2011	0.29	0.29	0.4	0.31
Balanced manufacturing's share of all enterprise patents				
2007	0.26	0.26	0.19	0.26
2008	0.24	0.25	0.21	0.27
2009	0.23	0.21	0.26	0.25
2010	0.21	0.19	0.29	0.21
2011	0.18	0.16	0.26	0.18

Source Authors' own calculation using the firm-level Database and SIPO's annual reports

The manufacturing LMEs' shares of all enterprise patents reported in the next panel indicate that manufacturing accounts for the vast majority of LME patenting, around 95% of all four counts in 2011. One notable trend is that the LMEs' share of invention patent grants has increased over the years, while their share of invention patent applications has declined or maintained at the same level.

Finally, at the bottom of Table 8.2, we report the shares of total enterprise patents for firms in the balanced manufacturing sample, which had been declining, except for invention patent grants. We can compute the shares of the firms in the balanced manufacturing sample in total LME manufacturing patents by comparing the bottom two panels. For example, the balanced sample's share of all manufacturing LMEs' invention patent applications declined from 84% in 2007 to 60% in 2011. Similarly for utility models, the balanced sample's share went down from 81 to 56% in five years. This has to do with the fact that the LME sample has been growing in size over time as more Chinese firms qualify for the LME status.

In sum, the LME sample captures a significant portion of SIPO domestic, non-individual patents. Moreover, if the average technological significance of patents increases with firm size, then the share of LMEs in the total number of technologically significant patents should be even higher than suggested here.

The "Democratization" of Patenting from 2007 to 2011

An important feature of the patenting surge from 2007 to 2011 is that many firms that were previously not patenting or only occasionally patenting account for the bulk of the patenting increase. That is, the extensive, rather than intensive, margin of growth of patenting has been a major contributor to the surge. We observe this both along the industry and geographical dimensions.

Extensive Versus Intensive Margin of Patenting Growth

We first examine the incidence of patenting and conducting R&D, measured as the share of firms engaging in the respective activity. As Table 8.3 shows, the incidences of filing invention patent and utility model applications more than doubled to 21 and 26% respectively during the period 2007 to 2011, while the incidence of receiving invention patent grants quadrupled from 3 to 13%. Although the share of LMEs conducting R&D also increased, from 30 to 41%, the increase is much more modest compared with that of patenting, suggesting that more LMEs were patenting without R&D activity than before.

We compute and report in Table 8.4 the average number of patents per firm and average R&D expenditures per firm for three samples: the full balanced sample, the invention sub-sample—comprising firms that had filed invention patent applications each year, and the utility model sub-sample—consisting of firms that had filed utility model applications each year. For the full balanced sample, from 2007 to 2011, average invention patent applications per firm more than doubled from 0.97

Table 8.3 Incidence of patenting and R&D performance

	2007	2008	2009	2010	2011
Invention applications	0.09	0.12	0.16	0.18	0.21
Invention grants	0.03	0.04	0.07	0.1	0.13
Utility model applications	0.12	0.15	0.2	0.23	0.26
Utility model grants	0.1	0.13	0.17	0.23	0.25
R&D	0.3	0.33	0.39	0.38	0.41

Table 8.4 Average patent counts and R&D expenditures: balanced sample

	2007	2008	2009	2010	2011	2011/
Full sample		N = 19,546/year				
Invention patents	0.97	1.17	1.39	1.7	2.09	2.16
Utility models	0.85	1.19	1.6	2.09	2.77	3.24
R&D expenditures	7.37	8.36	9.88	11.3	12.93	1.75
Invention sub-sample		N = 631/year				
Applications	24.97	28.15	30.77	35.02	38.09	1.53
R&D expenditures	74.88	81.52	86.54	101.58	119.42	1.59
Utility model sub-sample		N = 1014/year				
Applications	12.16	15.19	17.02	21.1	24.36	2
R&D expenditures	54.52	58.49	63.45	72.49	84.5	1.55

Note R&D expenditures are in million yuan. The invention sub-sample comprises firms that had filed invention patent applications each year; the utility model sub-sample consists of firms that had filed utility model applications each year
Source Authors' own calculation using the firm-level database

to 2.09, whereas average utility model applications more than tripled, from 0.85 to 2.77. On the other hand, R&D expenditures had only registered a 75% increase in four years. Thus the growth of patent applications had far outpaced the growth of R&D expenditures.

The serial innovators that populate the invention sub-sample filed significantly more invention patent applications than the rest, but unlike the case of the balanced sample, the 53% increase from 24.97 to 38.09 applications a year is slightly smaller than the 59% increase of these innovators' R&D expenditures.

The numbers for the utility model sub-sample exhibit different patterns. Although these firms also filed many more utility model applications than the average firm, unlike the serial innovators in the invention sub-sample, the growth of these firms' utility models outstripped that of their R&D expenditures.

To measure the extensive versus intensive margin of growth, we define intensive margin of growth as that of the growth of the patents of the serial innovators discussed earlier. Using the numbers reported in Table 8.4, our calculation shows that 38% of the increase of 21,892 invention patent counts from 2007 to 2011 for the sample had come from the serial innovators. In other words, the extensive margin of growth had contributed 62% of the invention patenting growth. Similar calculation reveals that two thirds of the utility model application growth had resulted from the extensive margin of growth.

Taken together, these statistics indicate that (1) invention patent applications had been growing in proportion to R&D expenditures for the innovators—firms that had been consistently applying for such patents, but they had far outpaced the growth of R&D for those firms that were new to patenting or had only occasionally patented; (2) compared with invention patent applications, utility model applications had been growing faster than R&D expenditures; (3) the extensive margin of growth was responsible for the bulk of the recent patenting surge.

Industry Dimension

Both technology opportunity and the propensity to patent vary by industry (Levin et al. 1987; Cohen et al. 2000). The U.S. patent explosion, for example, was largely concentrated in the computing and electronics sectors (Hall 2004), which was partly explained by the predisposition of firms in these sectors to the strategic motive of seeking patents. We plot the industry distributions of invention patent and utility model applications for our balanced sample in Figs. 8.2 and 8.3. In each figure we compare the distribution of the beginning year with that of the ending year.

There are sharp differences in the propensity to patent across industries. The telecommunications equipment and computers industry dwarfs the other industries, accounting for over half of all manufacturing invention patents in 2007. The utility model applications are less concentrated, but the top five industries, general equipment, special equipment, transport equipment, electric, and telecommunication equipment and computers, accounted for three quarters of the total in 2007.

The distributions flattened somewhat from 2007 to 2011: the telecommunication equipment and computers industry's share of invention patent applications fell to 39% in 2011. The top five industries based on invention patent applications in 2007 saw their share of the total fall from 77 to 69% in four years. Similarly the top five industries' share of utility model applications fell from 74 to 68%, with the telecommunication equipment and computers industry losing its top position to the electric industry.

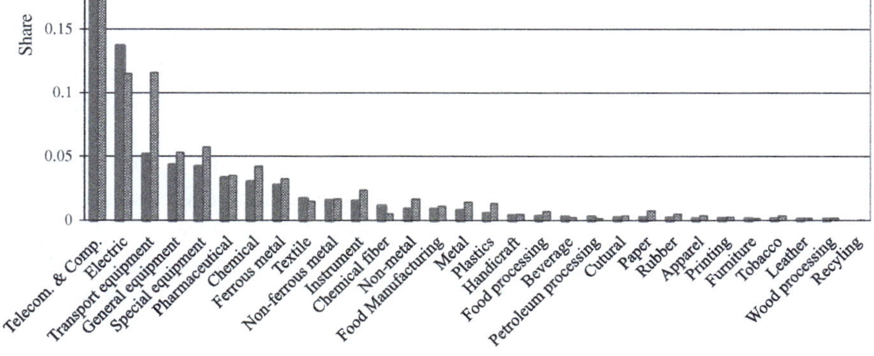

Fig. 8.2 Industry distribution of invention patent applications

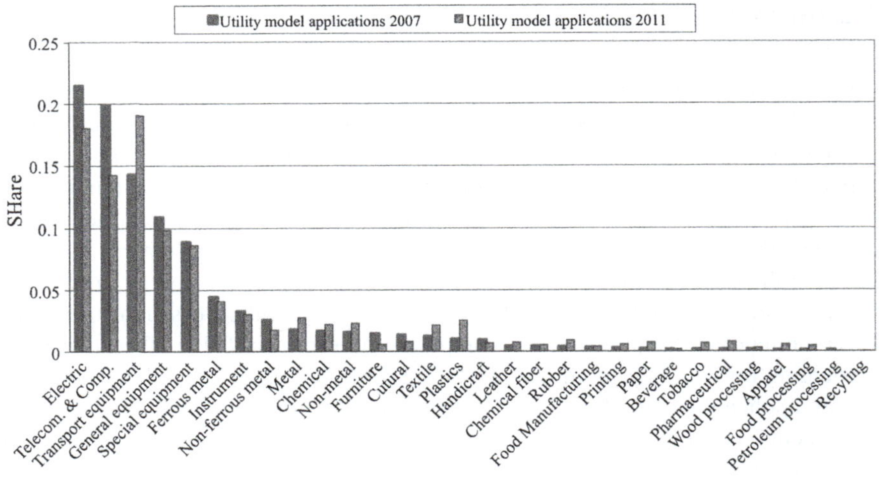

Fig. 8.3 Industry distribution of utility model applications

That patenting has been growing faster in sectors that have not traditionally been the most active in seeking patent rights is in line with our earlier observation that the extensive margin of growth explained the bulk of the patenting surge. It is notable that telecommunication equipment and computers, which is more prone to strategic patenting, has seen their patenting growth outpaced by that of sectors not usually associated with patenting for strategic gains. This raises questions about strategic patenting as an explanation of the patenting surge.

Geographical Dimension

As innovation figures more prominently in the evaluation of the performance of local government officials at various levels, patents have become an important performance indicator. The urge to boost their patent counts is likely to be greater in regions that had lagged in innovation and patenting. The plot of the geographical distribution of the invention patent applications in Fig. 8.4 shows that Guangdong dominates, accounting for over half of all manufacturing patents in 2007. But Guangdong saw its dominant position decline to 36% of the total in 2011. In figures not shown here where we excluded the telecommunications equipment and computers industry from the distribution, Guangdong's dominance was much less salient. This is not surprising as Guangdong hosts some of the top manufacturers from the telecommunication equipment and computers industry (e.g., Huawei and

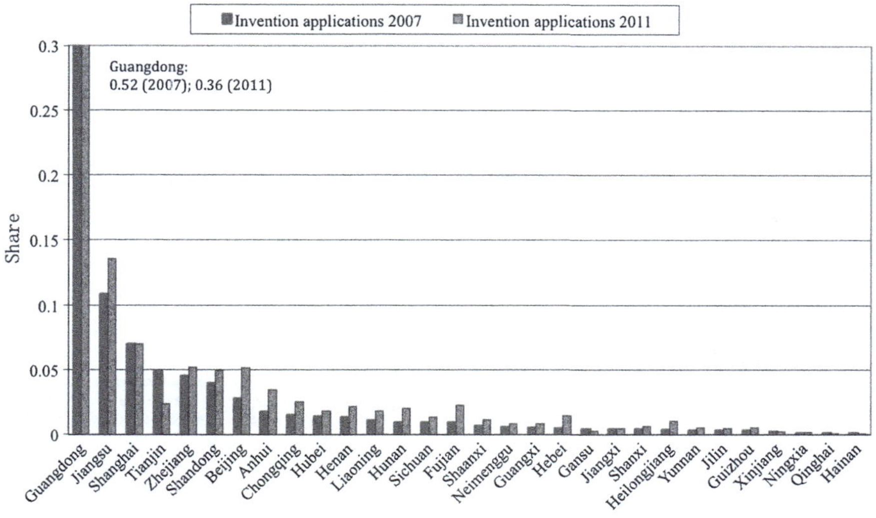

Fig. 8.4 Provincial distribution of invention patent applications

Foxconn) and given that this industry was responsible for over half of the invention patent applications filed by Chinese manufacturing firms. Thus the erosion of Guangdong's dominance in patent applications tracks the decline in the share of telecommunications equipment and computers in all patents.

For the rest of the provinces, all but three, i.e., Gansu, Qinghai, and Tianjin, gained shares from 2007 to 2011. This catch-up by the lagging provinces in patenting is another manifestation of the extensive margin of growth dominating the intensive one. Notwithstanding the catch-up, by 2011, Beijing, Guangdong, Jiangsu, Shandong and Shanghai remained as the top invention patent filing provinces/municipalities, although their share of the total declined from 77 to 67% in four years.

Similar patterns across provinces and over time emerge in Fig. 8.5, where the geographical distributions of utility models are plotted, except that they are less concentrated than are the invention patents. The top five regions filed 51% of all the applications in 2011, down from 62% in 2007.[6]

[6]The top five regions for utility model applications in 2011 were Guangdong, Jiangsu, Zhejiang, Shanghai, Shandong, and Chongqing.

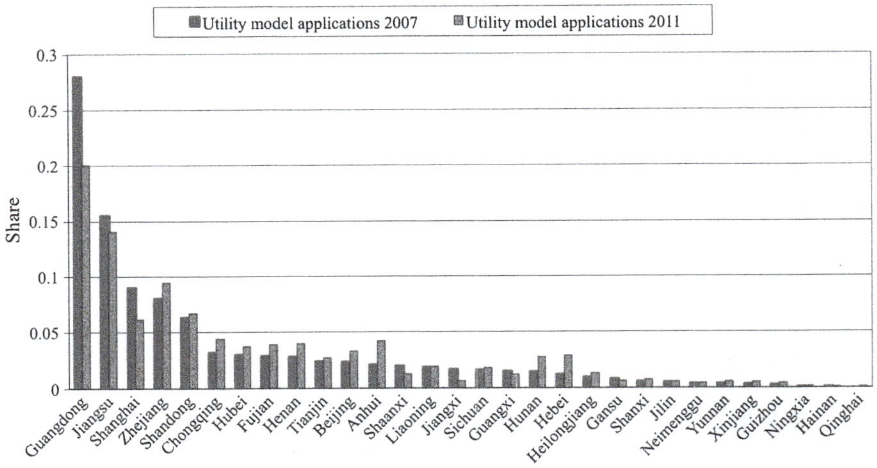

Fig. 8.5 Provincial distribution of utility model applications

Summary of Statistical Analysis

We further investigate the contributions of the extensive versus intensive margin of growth to China's patenting surge by estimating a knowledge production function:

$$E(\text{patents}_{it}) = \exp\left(\sum_{t=2007}^{2011} \alpha_{it} D_{it} * \log(\text{R\&D stock})_{it} + \sum_{t=2007}^{2011} \beta_t D_t + X_{it}\theta\right) \quad (8.1)$$

That is, we assume that the mean of patents produced by firm i in year t is proportional to the firm's knowledge stock accumulated up to that year, which we approximate using a measure of R&D stock constructed using the firm's historical R&D expenditures and the perpetual inventory model. In Eq. (8.1), we allow the R&D elasticity of patents to vary by year, while separately estimating year fixed effects, Dt. The vector of variables X collects the rest of the controls including firm size and firm fixed effects. For patents we use invention patent and utility model applications as two separate measures.

We estimate Eq. (8.1) using a conditional fixed effects Poisson estimator and correct for the inconsistency of the estimates of the standard errors by following Wooldridge (2002)'s suggestion of computing standard errors clustered by firm.

We will not reproduce the statistical estimates and the related discussion here. Interested readers can refer to Hu, Zhang and Zhao (forthcoming) for details. Instead we will just highlight the key results in summary form.

Our estimates of the patent production function show that (1) the patent—R&D association had become weaker from 2007 to 2011, particularly for utility models and for the sample of firms that exclude those from the telecommunication equipment and computers industry; and (2) there was a sharp increase in the propensity to patent in 2010 and 2011 for all but six industries that typically have greater propensity to patent, i.e., pharmaceutical, chemical fiber, electric and telecommunication equipment and computers.

Innovators Versus Non-innovators

A potential explanation of the declining patent elasticity of R&D is that it just reflects diminishing returns to R&D. As the firms increase their R&D efforts, they exhaust technology opportunities and R&D on the margin generates fewer patents. We subject the diminishing returns hypothesis to test by estimating the year-specific patent—R&D elasticities for two groups of firms: the innovators and the non-innovators. For the invention patent regressions, innovators are firms that filed for invention patent applications in each and every year from 2007 to 2011; for the utility model regressions, innovators are defined similarly using utility model applications.

Our definition of innovators versus non-innovators corresponds to the distinction we made earlier regarding the intensive versus extensive margin of growth of the patenting surge. There the intensive margin of growth was defined as growth of patenting by firms that are serial innovators, those that filed patent applications in each of the years from 2007 to 2011, whereas the extensive margin of growth was defined by what we now call non-innovators. Thus the current exercise will shed light on the nature of the patent-R&D correlation at the intensive and extensive margin of growth of China's recent patenting surge.

The statistical results show that it was the non-innovators, rather than the innovators, that had seen diminishing association between patents and R&D. This militates against the exhaustion of technology opportunity and thus diminishing returns hypothesis as an explanation for the declining patent-R&D elasticity. This also raises questions about the quality of the extensive margin of the patenting growth, which we have observed earlier accounts for nearly two thirds of the patenting surge.

Patent Poor Versus Patent Rich Regions

If what drives the recent patenting surge is Chinese firms responding to the government policy incentives for acquiring patents, then we should expect such policy-driven patenting to be more prevalent in regions where there was relatively little patenting to begin with. In those regions, the local governments were more likely to provide incentives that would promote the acquisition of patents. Numerous authors have discussed the importance of competition between sub-national Chinese governments in explaining China's economic success.[7] To examine this hypothesis, we separate the provinces into two groups, using the number of invention patents in force per 10,000 people in 2006, the year preceding the beginning year of our sample. Those provinces with their invention patents per 10,000 people above (and inclusive of) the median are classified as "patent rich", whereas those with below median patent counts are called "patent poor." In Table 8.5 we report the patent statistics for the 31 provinces/municipalities for 2006 and 2011. The last column contains the ratio of the 2011 figure to that of 2006. The entries in the table are sorted by the 2006 patent number in descending order.

Beijing, Shanghai, Tianjin, Guangdong, Liaoning, Zhejiang, and Jiangsu lead the country, with the first two municipalities already meeting the target set for 2015 in 2006. For 2006, the national median is Hunan's 0.26, significantly below the national average of 0.55. From 2006 to 2011, the typical provinces had seen their invention patents per 10,000 people at least quadruple, with Guangdong, Chongqing, Anhui, Jiangsu and Zhejiang leading the race. Firms from the patent rich regions had on average increased their invention patents in force by 320%, whereas those from the patent poor regions had achieved growth of 324%.

We have estimated Eq. (8.1) separately for the two regions. The results are quite different: for the patent rich regions, invention patents show greater correlation with R&D than do utility models, and the correlation declines significantly for the latter but not for the former, but for the patent poor regions, R&D is as correlated with utility models as it is with invention patents, and the patent-R&D elasticity declines over time for both utility models and invention patent applications. We also find that for the patent rich region, patents are highly correlated with firm size, measured by sales revenue, but there is no such correlation for the patent poor region. One potential explanation to rationalize the patent poor region's patenting—rapidly growing and yet tenuously related to technology innovation—would be that it has been the consequence of the local governments in those regions rolling out policy incentives that have changed the firms' motive for applying for patents.

Patents and Labor Productivity

Our data does not allow us to estimate total factor productivity; instead we investigate the link between patents and labor productivity, which we define as sales revenue per worker. For the patent measure, we use the number of patents that are legally active, or in force. This is the number of a firm's patents that have been granted and that which the firm has chosen to pay the renewal fees for in order to keep them legally active. The advantages of using this measure are that (1) it is a

[7]For example, Xu (2011) characterized China's fundamental economic institution as a regionally decentralized authoritarian regime that combines political centralization with economic decentralization. This system fosters inter-regional competition among the Chinese subnational governments and incentivizes policy making that promotes regional economic development and growth.

Table 8.5 Invention patents in force per 10,000 people

Province	2006	2011	2011/2006
Beijing	8.42	26.02	3.09
Shanghai	3.9	13.26	3.4
Tianjin	2.01	6.02	3
Guangdong	0.77	5.58	7.26
Liaoning	0.77	2.38	3.11
Zhejiang	0.72	4.71	6.56
Jiangsu	0.56	3.72	6.6
Jilin	0.51	1.37	2.68
Shaanxi	0.43	2.19	5.07
Hubei	0.41	1.54	3.72
Heilongjiang	0.37	1.51	4.04
Shandong	0.32	1.63	5.02
Shanxi	0.32	0.93	2.95
Ningxia	0.3	0.5	1.68
Sichuan	0.27	1.15	4.32
Hunan	0.26	1.28	4.88
Yunnan	0.24	0.66	2.8
Fujian	0.23	1.35	5.93
Chongqing	0.22	1.63	7.33
Hebei	0.18	0.6	3.33
Xinjiang	0.17	0.41	2.34
Gansu	0.17	0.61	3.65
Guizhou	0.16	0.61	3.82
Hainan	0.16	0.78	4.85
Qinghai	0.16	0.36	2.28
Neimenggu	0.15	0.45	3
Henan	0.13	0.65	5.05
Anhui	0.12	0.8	6.72
Guangxi	0.1	0.4	3.8
Jiangxi	0.1	0.41	4.2
Tibet	0.07	0.27	3.84
National average	0.55	2.61	4.7
National Median	0.26	1.15	4.38

Source Authors' calculation using SIPO Annual Reports and China Statistical Yearbooks

stock measure, representing a firm's cumulative patenting and innovation effort and (2) it is the number of patents that a firm chooses to maintain after they are granted by paying renewal fees, so that they are economically relevant. Therefore it is more desirable than stock measures constructed using patent applications or grants. The only shortcoming of using this measure is that in our database we only have data for this measure for the last three years, 2009–2011.

The labor productivity regression results follow similar patterns as those obtained by estimating the patent production function. That is, both the R&D-innovation connection and the innovation-productivity link have weakened over the years when the patenting surge took place. It would be interesting to see whether and how the results would change if we have a longer duration of the panel.

Concluding Remarks

China's extraordinary patenting ascent in recent years has taken place against a backdrop of increasing technological sophistication of Chinese firms and Chinese government proactively promoting the acquisition of intellectual property. Chinese firms have been aggressively applying for patents as a result of their newly acquired capability to invent new technologies and their response to the government incentives and other strategic considerations. While the former is most likely to be a result of conscious R&D effort, the latter would have increased the propensity to patent independent of technology innovation.

We investigated the extent to which this most recent episode of patenting surge was driven by technology innovation by estimating a patent production function and by using a unique Chinese firm-level data set where the SIPO patent records have been matched to the large and medium size industrial firms. The data set covers the period of 2007–2011, which saw the most dramatic surge in Chinese patent applications. Our main findings include: (1) the extensive margin of growth, patenting by firms that were not actively patenting in the past, was responsible for nearly two thirds of the patenting surge; and (2) the association between patents and R&D had been weakening.

Another key insight of our research is that the increasing disjointedness between patents and R&D does not apply to all segments of the patenting surge. It is more conspicuous for utility models than for invention patents; it is less prominent for the telecommunication equipment and computers industry than for the other industries; it is most evident with firms that were not actively patenting in the past, or the extensive margin of the patenting growth; and it is far more striking for regions that had been lagging in patenting. These findings are reaffirmed by the results from regressing a firm's labor productivity on its stock of patents in force.

We caution against potential misinterpretation of the findings reported here. While we have shown that a significant portion of the recent patenting surge may have less to do with technology innovation than meets the eye, it would be a mistake to think that China's patent boom is just a mirage. As we have emphasized, the result mostly applies to the extensive margin of the patenting surge.

We have discussed two potential explanations for non-innovation related patenting: strategic considerations and government policy incentives. The evidence we have presented favors the government policy incentive hypothesis. But there could be other motivations that played a part in driving the patenting surge. For example, Chinese firms may have developed greater appreciation of the value of patents as an instrument to facilitate technology licensing, cooperation and venture financing, and as performance measures for R&D personnel. A full investigation of all these potential motives for applying for patents is beyond the scope of the paper.

The Chinese patenting surge adds to the on-going debate and discussion of the role of the patent system in technology innovation, and in economic development in general. What kind of patent system can best serve the development needs of China deserves greater attention of academics and policy makers than it currently receives. In particular, a greater appreciation of the less innocuous effect of rapidly growing patent right claims, especially those that could erect barriers for future technology innovation, is needed.

References

Branstetter, L., Li, G., & Veloso, F. (2015). The rise of international convention. In A.B. Jaffe & B. Jones (Eds.), *The changing frontier: Rethinking science and innovation policy* (pp. 135–168). University of Chicago Press.

Cohen, W. M., Nelson, R. R., & Walsh, J. P. (2000). *Protecting their intellectual assets: Appropriability conditions and why US manufacturing firms patent (or not)*. NBER Working Paper No. 7552.

Hall, B. H. (2004). *Exploring the patent explosion*. NBER Working Paper No. 10605.

He, Z.-L., Tong, T. W., He, W., Zhang, Y., & Lu, J. (2013). *Chinese patent database user documentation: Matching SIPO Patents to Chinese publicly-listed companies and subsidiaries.*

Holmes, T. J., McGrattan, E. R., & Prescott, E. C. (2015). Quid pro quo: Technology capital transfers for market access in China. *Review of Economic Studies* (forthcoming).

Hu, A. G. (2010). Propensity to patent, competition and China's foreign patenting surge. *Research Policy, 39*(7), 985–993.

Hu, A. G., & Jefferson, G. H. (2009, September). A great wall of patents: What is behind China's recent patent explosion? *Journal of Development Economics, 90*(1), 57–68.

Hu, A. G., Zhang, P., & Zhao, L. (2017). China as number one? Evidence from China's most recent patenting surge. *Journal of Development Economics, 124,* 109–119.

Jaffe, A. B., & Lerner, J. (2004). *Innovation and its discontents: How our broken patent system is endangering innovation and progress, and what to do about it*. Princeton: Princeton University Press.

Kim, L. (1997). *Imitation to innovation: The dynamics of Korea's technological learning*. Boston: Harvard Business School Press.

Kortum, S., & Lerner, J. (1999). What is behind the recent surge in patenting? *Research Policy, 28* (1), 1–22.

Levin, R. C., Klevorick, A. K., Nelson, R. R., & Winter, S. G. (1987). Appropriating the returns from industrial research and development. *Brookings Papers on Economic Activity, 1987,* 783–820.

Li, X. (2012). Behind the recent surge of Chinese patenting: An institutional view. *Research Policy, 41*(1), 236–249.

Nagaoda, S. (2009). Reform of patent system in Japan and challenges. In National Research Council (Ed.), *21st Century Innovation Systems for Japan and the United States: Lessons from a Decade of Change: Report of a Symposium*. The National Academies Press.

Sakakibara, M., & Branstetter, L. (2001, Spring). Do stronger patents induce more innovation? Evidence from the 1988 Japanese patent law reforms. *Rand Journal of Economics, 32*(1), 77–100.

Wooldridge, J. M. (2002). *Econometric analysis of cross section and panel data*. Cambridge, MA: MIT Press.

Xie, Z., & Zhang, X. (2015). The patterns of patents in China. *China Economic Journal, 8*(2), 122–142.

Xu, C. (2011). The fundamental institutions of China's reforms and development. *Journal of Economic Literature, 49*(4), 1076–1151.

Chapter 9
Network Capitalism and the Role of Strategy, Contracts and Performance Expectations for Asia-Pacific Innovation Partnerships

Jochen Schweitzer

Abstract With the growth of emerging economies in Asia-Pacific over the last three decades collaboration with the aim of innovation between firms within and with partners outside the region have developed substantially. Not always have such partnerships fulfilled their anticipated strategic objectives. The literature suggests that the nature of market arrangements and the role of government within that system play a role, but also innate contracting practices and governance of innovation partnerships are related. Yet, our understanding about the specific relationships between these factors and the emerging partnership innovation culture that facilitates joint business activities in an Asia-Pacific context remains vague. In this conceptual chapter we suggest how characteristics of so called network capitalism in conjunction with the nature of contractual agreements between partners, the alignment of their innovation objectives and the ambiguity inherent in their mutual contributions to the partnership can be interpreted as indicators of joint innovation culture. However, while innovation partnerships generally may result to be bureaucratic, market, clan, or adhocracy, we discuss how in an Asia Pacific context, innovation partnerships are limited by the extent of codification and diffusion of information and the social embeddedness of economic transactions.

Keywords Innovation partnerships · Contracting · Innovation culture · Network capital

---

Research for this paper was aided by support from the Management Discipline Group and the Centre for Management and Organization Studies at the University of Technology Sydney.

J. Schweitzer (✉)
Centre for Business and Social Innovation, University of Technology Sydney, Sydney, Australia
e-mail: Jochen.Schweitzer@uts.edu.au

T. Clarke and K. Lee (eds.), *Innovation in the Asia Pacific*,
https://doi.org/10.1007/978-981-10-5895-0_9

Introduction

In the last decade the Asia-Pacific region has become ever more central to the long-term strength and prosperity of the global economy. While the most significant development continues to be the rise of China, the entire region is becoming more economically integrated. The past years saw substantial progress on a number of major trade deals that will further strengthen the region's status as the engine of global economic growth. Not only has foreign direct investment (FDI) in the region grown over the years, also outbound foreign direct investment (ODI) by, for example, non-state-owned Chinese companies increased by 35% in only ten years (MofCom 2013). According to the Ministry of Commerce of the People's Republic of China, the countries ODI may have exceeded FDI for the first time in 2014 (MofCom 2015).

A number of previously regional players have grown to become global players by attracting foreign investment and by forging partnerships within and outside the region, which has helped reinforcing their foothold in the global business community.

Numerous studies have investigated the development strategies of these firms (Bartlett and Ghoshal 2000; Ibeh et al. 2004; Rialp et al. 2005), however little is known about their capacity for further growth based on their capacity to innovate. Yet, innovation is the central strategy for many companies in the region to endure and develop in what are increasingly competitive and dynamic business settings. Co-operation is a vital way for companies to achieve innovation objectives. Regardless of the term 'innovation' being notoriously ambiguous and often lacking a specific definition or measure (Adams et al. 2006) commercial, non-commercial and government organizations alike view innovation as an essential way of improving managerial efficacy, profitability and overall economic performance (Clegg et al. 2017). In this chapter, we understand innovation in Schumpeter's (1934) terms, who incorporates five types of activity; new production methods, new sources of supply, the creation of new products, the capitalization of new markets, and organizing business in new ways. The latter especially contains new methods of creating value through collaboration.

Many enablers of innovation strategies have been explored. Examples include strategic vision, culture, governance, and sense of urgency of the organization. Firms that successfully balance exploitative and explorative ways of innovation do so by aligning infrastructure, resources and organizational strategy to create dynamic innovation capabilities (Clegg et al. 2011; Leung et al. 2016). However, the concept of developing unique competences within the boundaries of one company as an exclusive source of strategic advantage is particularly insufficient in contemporary markets in Asia Pacific. Closed innovation based on self-reliance of R&D is often too slow and also expensive (Edwards et al. 2015). Thus, during the past three decades innovation has gone through evolutionary steps to collaborative innovation and more recently to open-innovation and co-innovation (Lee et al. 2010).

We focus on collaborative innovation, which includes partnerships, strategic alliances, joint ventures, and technology/patent relationships that allow firms combining own competencies with those of other firms (Gudergan and Schweitzer 2008). Examples in Asia Pacific include firms such as Nissan, Samsung or the Dongfeng Motor Group and outside the region companies like SEEK, Apple, Cisco, HP, Dell, Procter & Gamble and many others that have successfully collaborated (Tapscott and Williams 2008).

Specific alliances are often described very broadly, so that it is nearly impossible to differentiate them from other types of inter-firm relationships and economic transactions like e.g. supplier relationships. As "hybrid" organizational forms they are a way to manage exchanges or relationships that are more complex than a standard market exchange since they involve purposive linkages (Kale et al. 2000), exchange, sharing or co-development (Gulati 1995b)—yet they do not merit full integration (Gulati 1998; Williamson 1991; Zenger and Hesterly 1997). Hence, we see innovation alliances as a unique form of organization, which in its simplest form can be defined as a group of stakeholders intentionally organized to accomplish an overall, common innovation goal, which is explicit or implicit, carefully considered and established through a strategic planning process.

An example is the recently established Asia Pacific Innovation Center by Johnson & Johnson in Shanghai with satellites in Singapore, Australia and Japan, thereby extending the existing network of Johnson & Johnson's strategic innovation initiatives in life sciences hotspots. The centre aims at identifying and developing early-stage opportunities across the company's key strategic focus areas including pharmaceuticals, medical devices and diagnostics and consumer healthcare products. At the heart of this innovation strategy is to collaborate with the best minds in the region to advance new technologies and deliver transformative solutions for the people of China and Asia Pacific at large.

Generally, alliances like the above mentioned have been shown to be effective mechanisms for transferring knowledge (Doz 1996), spreading risk (Hennart 1988), learning (Inkpen and Crossan 1995; Schweitzer and Gudergan 2010) and innovation capability development (Schweitzer 2014). Research studies have examined a host of factors that relate to how alliances are set up and what their role is in realizing strategic objectives. This growing body of research has also dealt with several aspects of innovation alliances and found, for example, that the ability to successfully set up and manage alliances is affected by the contracting and governance arrangements that are put in place (Schweitzer 2016). Similarly, research suggests a positive and significant role of organizational culture or climate on innovation (Ahmed 1998; Isaksen et al. 2001; Lee et al. 2008) and that innovation within alliances can be achieved by creating a learning culture (Linnarsson and Werr 2004). The specific aspects of alliance contracting, governance and culture are inter-related, but no yet well understood. Such interrelations are particularly important to understand in growing economic environments like the Asia Pacific region, since collaboration for innovation is taking up an increasing part of all innovation activity here (IBM 2012).

Our focus here is on examining the alliance contractual nature and culture as key aspects for effectively managing innovation partnerships in the Asia Pacific context. We develop a conceptual framework that is embedded in economic perspectives of network capitalism (Boisot and Child 1996; Tung and Worm 2001), organizational control theory (Ouchi 1980) and theoretical developments on organizational culture (Cameron and Quinn 2011) and alliance contracts and contractual complexity (Ariño and Reuer 2006a; Reuer and Ariño 2007). Our objective is to add to the academic dialogue about contractual aspects and culture within Asia Pacific innovation alliances.

Theoretical Background

Network Capitalism

Boisot and Child (1996) coined the term 'network capitalism' to describe a distinctive institutional form that had evolved in China due to it's continuing transformation and decentralization of a state controlled bureaucracy. Network capitalism occurred following a combination of limited information codification in China combined with communal property rights and organization of economic transaction. It is largely about the localization of transactions where economic subjects act locally instead of being involved in transactions in a depersonalized market with a potentially unlimited number of participants. In that way, China's path via network capitalism to economic renewal and evidently substantial growth over the last three decades juxtaposes the Western way of market expansion, which is typically based on intensive information codification (Boisot and Child 1996; Boisot et al. 2011).

Yet, the most relevant feature of network capitalism in the context of understanding its role for innovation partnerships is the depth and nature of its social embeddedness and closeness of its actors, which both have deep historical roots in Chinese cultural tradition. The Chinese system of network capitalism had grown under conditions of very considerable uncertainty and until today works through the implicit and fluid dynamic of trust-based relationships, where trust is heavily based on familial or community membership that is normally difficult for outsiders to gain. Network capitalism is suited to handling complexity and uncertainty since networks offer greater capacity for generating and transmitting new information. If networks are enabled through trust-based relationships they even offer protection against the possibility of failure - the familiar associate of uncertainty.

Boisot and Child's describe closeness in network capitalism by borrowing the concept of 'clans' from Ouchi (1980), expressing how market transactions under network capitalism are embedded in ties of kinship, in other words: friendly relations. Clan structures appreciate the entrepreneurial potential of situations where, for example, government policies provide entry barriers the market. They indeed create a structure for economic activities in informal sectors of the economy and are consequently very flexible and adaptable (Child and Ihrig 2013). Not only the thriving economic activities in mainland China but also in Malaysia, Indonesia, Hong Kong, and Singapore are attributed to the fact that economic activities here are largely embedded in Chinese communities and their extended clan-type structures (Fukuyama 1996). The Chinese approach based on clan-like networks also has an advantage in handling and responding to cognitive complexity (Snell and Tseng 2002). Hence, with a distinctive Chinese path to growth and modernization suggested, the widespread legitimacy of conventional Western assumptions is truly questioned (Boisot and Child 1996).

Further analysis of the difference between modernization in China and Western economies exposed the culture space or C-space (Boisot 1986, 1987), a conceptual framework that relates the extent to which transactionally relevant information can be diffused, and hence shared, within a target population to how far it has been codified. Without effective codification and given traditional Chinese social organization and embeddedness, decentralization leads not to markets or hierarchies but to clans that permits a much more local and personalized social order of network capitalism. With now extended institutional possibilities it is possible to explain growth and innovation in China. Boisot and Child (2007), Boisot et al. (2011) further suggest that modern information and communication technologies facilitate network capitalism by lowering the cost of transacting to less codified clan-like structures within populations that are larger and located across great distances.

We note that social embeddedness, information diffusion and information codification are three central features of network capitalism and associate clan-like structures, which are likely to determine the development, governance, and management of innovation partnerships within the region and with partners from outside the Chinese and larger Asia-Pacific context.

Governance

Governance of innovation partnerships is about establishing mechanisms that influence and control partners and managers so that their decisions and actions aid common goals. The alliance literature distinguishes relational and formal governance mechanisms (Hoetker and Mellewigt 2009) and also defines alliance governance structure by distinguishing non-equity and equity alliances. Formal governance mechanisms are policies, instruments, processes, and practices, which in innovation alliances can involve a performance based pay scheme, use of a board of directors, appointment of local partnership managers, or mutual agreement on formal provisions in a partnership contract. Relational governance relates to social mechanisms that promote open communication and the sharing of information, trust, cooperation and other informal encouragement of a specific work ethic. The alliance partners' choices and combination of governance mechanisms results in a distinct governance form (or structure), which represents the joint organizational context in which the alliance takes place (Ariño and Reuer 2006a).

Both, formal and relational governance have been studied widely and are influenced by aspects like co-ordination costs and appropriation concerns (e.g. Gulati and Singh 1998; Oxley 1997); risks; partnership task-scope and transaction-level characteristics (e.g. Oxley 1999; Oxley and Sampson 2004); technological intensity (Osborn and Baughn 1990); strategic motivation (Nielsen 2003); division of labour (Reuer et al. 2002); task complexity and inter-partner diversity (White and Lui 2005); trust among partners (e.g. Gulati 1995a; Krishnan et al. 2006; Lui and Ngo 2004; Nooteboom et al. 1997; Zaheer et al. 1998); and inter-organizational structures (e.g. Gerwin and Ferris 2004; Ring and Van de Ven 1992, 1994). The management and control of these factors is reflected in the use of contractual provisions between partners (e.g. Reuer and Ariño 2003; Reuer et al. 2006; Sampson 2004), that is, partners use contracts to define mutual rights and obligations by specifying resource allocations, practices of interaction and problem solving, as well as expected outputs (e.g. Argyres et al. 2007; Ariño and Reuer 2006a; Lerner and Merges 1998; Luo 2002). These arrangements provide the basis for operating the partnership. In this way, governance mechanisms correspond not only with the structure of the alliance, but also the emerging partnership culture.

Culture

The organizational culture within innovation partnerships, while related to contracting and governance is also a function of the underlying values and beliefs of the people who are operating it and thereby define in a simple fashion the actor's view of themself and their environment (Schein 2010). These beliefs and expectations serve as a normative order that influences how people perceive, think, feel and behave (O'Reilly 1989). As such, culture may directly or indirectly influence alliance governance. While understanding the role of culture remains a difficult task due to its elusive nature (Duncan 1989), it certainly plays an integral part both as a reflection of and influence on characteristics of innovation partnerships including—for example—the general economic paradigm and by extension the formality and centrality of decision-making, the level to which actions are based on mutual understanding and trust or the degree to which information is codified.

Hence, while governance and culture of innovation partnerships are naturally related, they are also associated with contractual specifications and related complexity. Here, we focus on the emergent organizational culture of the partnership and follow organizational control theory to explain the occurrence of alternative types of partnership cultures. The organizational control perspective (Ouchi 1980) and later additions (Cameron and Ettington 1988; Mintzberg 1993) suggest that different organizational cultures can be classified in terms of archetypes, namely market, clan, bureaucracy, adhocracy or any hybrid form of these. These types reflect the goal incongruence and performance ambiguity among partners

(Cameron and Quinn 1999; Ouchi 1980). Goal incongruence refers to the fact that the goals of partners may not be entirely consistent, describing a state of diverging preferences or a lack of overlapping goals. Performance ambiguity, on the other hand, arises when the measurement of the partners' contributions within the partnership is subject to uncertainty.

Accordingly, antecedent factors to culture including levels of goal incongruence and performance ambiguity result in any one of four archetype cultures being the most efficient to mediate joint transactions: market culture is efficient when performance ambiguity is low and goal incongruence is high, bureaucracy is efficient when both goal incongruence and performance ambiguity are high, clans are efficient when goal incongruence is low and performance ambiguity is high (Ouchi 1980), and, finally, adhocracies are efficient when goal incongruence and performance ambiguity are low (Cameron and Ettington 1988; Mintzberg 1993). The market culture type values productivity and efficiency; information is assumed complete and partners are aware of an explicit competitive price for each task or exchange. With a focus on achievement, this culture emphasizes centralized decision making and more formal coordination and control systems. The partners' commitment to the joint organization's objectives is obtained by self-interest and based on the price mechanism.

Bureaucracies involve close personal surveillance and direction of subordinates by superiors with the information that is necessary for task completion being contained in rules. The cost of administration in bureaucracies is typically high. This culture values stability and control and emphasizes formal coordination, centralized decision-making and vertical communications where team members' roles are defined and enforced through formal rules and regulations.

The clan culture adds a social dimension in assuming that in situations of great uncertainty and complexity, managerial control is established through the group's system of beliefs and perceptions rather than through its behaviour or output. Accordingly, in clan culture it is assumes that individuals are acculturated into a system of controls and meanings. Structurally, there is less emphasis on formal coordination and control systems, and a greater emphasis on participation, decentralized decision-making, horizontal communications and teamwork.

Lastly, adhocracies represent a highly organic and unordered organizational culture. Members within an adhocracy generally perform complex work in small teams with substantial personal communication. Adhocracy is designed to be flexible and adaptable to rapidly changing environments; it emphasizes growth and adaptability. Similar to the clan culture, there is an emphasis on informal coordination, control systems and horizontal communications (Quinn et al. 1991; Zammuto and Krakower 1991).

The four cultural orientations are also confirmed by research that examined the relationship between organizational culture and effectiveness (Quinn and Rohrbaugh 1981) where it was shown that changes in effectiveness could be explained by an organization's attention inward (toward internal dynamics) versus outward (toward external environment) and its preference for governance to depict flexibility versus control (Goodman et al. 2001).

Contracting

We now consider the role and importance of contracting in innovation partnerships—specifically the contractual complexity of partnership agreements between innovation partners. A generally much observed heterogeneity of partnership agreements is due to variations in contractual complexity, which in turn reflects the often very different relational and situational characteristics of the partnership. Indeed, previous studies have suggested that complexity of agreements is the central concept of contracting (Reuer and Ariño 2003). Following this work we understand contractual complexity as a design feature of the partnering firms' agreements that reflects the number and stringency of the provisions that are being employed. Important aspects and antecedents of contractual complexity include asset specificity of the partnership, existence of prior ties among partnering organizations, time boundedness of the agreement, strategic importance of the partnership, and partner search costs (Reuer and Ariño 2003).[1] Although this work captures important aspects of contractual complexity, there are possibly additional factors like types of relational or environmental uncertainty, or the frequency of transactions between partners, or the underlying economic paradigm and organization of economic transaction as well as the degree to which information is codified that can affect the complexity of partnership agreements. Recognizing the early stage of research in understanding antecedents of contractual complexity we focus on the not yet systematically studied link between contractual complexity and partnership culture.

While the different archetypes featured by the organizational control perspective address and explain social, cultural, and relational aspects of the partnership culture, the theory does not explicitly take into account the complexity of contractual provisions between parties; complexity that is heterogeneous across different types of partnerships. Yet, the conceptualization of contractual complexity (Ariño and Reuer 2006a) and organizational culture (Ouchi 1980) share theoretical foundation in transaction cost economics. Both perspectives assume environmental uncertainty, asset specificity, bounded rationality, and behavioural uncertainty to result in transaction costs that mediate the characteristics of the relationship between partnering organizations as well as their joint transactions. Hence, we consider the organizational control perspective as a suitable theoretical basis to address the role of contractual complexity in innovation partnerships because both goal incongruence and performance ambiguity share antecedents with contractual complexity.

Goal incongruence, for example, is linked to asset specificity through related levels of decision-making uncertainty and trust among alliance members; it relates

[1]Asset specificity is the extent of the partners' transaction-specific investments for the partnership; prior ties captures the role of previous partnerships; time boundedness is about the duration to operate the initiative; strategic importance is about the significance that partners give to their collaborative venture; and, finally, partner search concerns the costs that are associated with finding, evaluating, and negotiating with potential partners.

to partner search costs through associated efforts of strategic goal alignment in the process of finding innovation partners; it is associated with prior ties through the degree of behavioural uncertainty and trust among partners; and it relates to the time boundedness of the partnership through the partners' ability to better predict environmental uncertainties when the duration of the partnership is predetermined.

Performance ambiguity too, is linked to prior ties through existing experience and trust among partners, and it relates to time boundedness through potentially opportunistic partner behaviour in fixed term partnerships. In addition to the common set of antecedents, recent research has shown that variation in partnership governance can also be attributed to contractual complexity (e.g. Reuer and Ariño 2007), a concept distinctively different to both goal incongruence and performance ambiguity.

In sum, to better understand the role and potential of innovation partnerships in the Asia-Pacific region, we need to further discuss the theoretical relationships between social embeddedness of actors, diffusion and codification of information (as features of network capitalism) and contractual complexity, performance ambiguity and goal incongruence (as key aspects of partnership governance, contracting and culture). We suppose that the here presented perspectives of network capitalism, organizational control and contracting provide not only a comprehensive explanation for emerging innovation cultures but also a suitable theoretical foundation for our conceptual framework.

Towards a Model of Network Capitalism in Asia-Pacific Innovation Partnerships

Contractual Complexity and Partnership Culture

First, we argue that the culture of innovation partnerships may differ depending on the complexity of contractual provisions. That is, the various enforcing and coordinating aspects of contractual provisions that guide joint transactions provide control beyond safeguarding partners against unforeseen events or partner opportunism (Ariño and Reuer 2006a) since they, together with goal incongruence and performance ambiguity, influence the culture of the partnership. In what follows we discuss high, low, and moderate levels of contractual complexity and derive different effects for each of them.

Contractual complexity refers to the stringency of the provisions to control various aspects of the partnership. This can include, for example, enforcement provisions like a detailed account of property rights and knowledge sharing, or informational aspects like measures of performance for each partner organization. Poppo and Zenger (2002) assert that complex contracts are more detailed regarding the specification of promises, obligations, and processes for the resolution of disagreements. Complex contracts include details like roles and responsibilities to be performed or specific procedures for monitoring, consequences of non-compliance, and description of expected outcomes or output.

A bureaucratic culture emerges when the parties to a partnership seek to eliminate the potential for opportunistic behaviour by quantifying and monitoring joint activities and mutual performance. Hence, within bureaucracies, partners assume that the majority of contingencies can be dealt with by policies, standardized procedures, formal division of responsibility, and hierarchical structures (Mintzberg 1993), which are typically established within the contractual agreement for the partnership.

Low levels of contractual complexity, on the other hand, mean that there are few and lenient provisions agreed upon. Partners may deliberately choose to only agree on a few provisions and not control aspects of the partnership because of high information costs or because contract terms may not be enforceable or are assumed to evolve as the partnership unfolds. Partners may then find it necessary to renegotiate their contracts at some stage, either because they encounter situations in which the contract is silent or where the contract specifies inefficient terms. Yet, while a contractual agreement between collaborating organizations may only encompass a few agreements for a fraction of the partnership's scope, it can still enforce and entirely safeguard partners' interests for the given situation. A complex contract, in contrast, including less enforcement but more informational provisions, might fail to protect partners' interests because of a lack in stringency of the set provisions. Overall, less contractual complexity gives partners more flexibility to experiment with different ways to control and shape the innovation partnership, while at the same time exposing it to more risk involved with uncertain situations.

Within adhocracies formal and complex contractual agreements are rare because intensive informal interaction, spontaneity, casualness, and interpersonal familiarity act as their coordinating and integrating mechanisms (Jarillo 1988). Because of these characteristics, adhocracies rely more on relational contracts (e.g. Bryant and Colledge 2002; Goldberg 1976; Heide 1994; Macaulay 1963) than on explicit and formal contracts. That is, innovation partners demonstrate flexibility and solidarity while solving problems as they desire continuity in the relationship, so that increased co-operation, dependency, mutual trust, and commitment make it unnecessary to cover all contingencies in complex agreements (Anderson and Weitz 1992; Jeffries and Reed 2000). Low contractual complexity can therefore support the development of adhocracy cultures for innovation partnerships; it helps foster minimal formalization of procedures, a highly organic structure, and mutual long-term relationships (Achrol 1997; Daft 1995). It also allows partners to make decisions without the presence of hierarchical structures and policies (Cameron and Ettington 1988; Mintzberg 1979).

Hence, the interplay of contractual complexity, performance ambiguity, and goal incongruence is associated with different organizational cultures. While high levels of contractual complexity, performance ambiguity, and goal incongruence may lead to bureaucracies, low levels of contractual complexity, performance ambiguity, and goal incongruence may lead to adhocracy governance. We encapsulate the above by advancing the following two hypotheses:

Hypothesis 1: High contractual complexity, high goal incongruence, and high performance ambiguity in innovation partnerships is associated with bureaucracy culture.
Hypothesis 2: Low contractual complexity, low goal incongruence, and low performance ambiguity in innovation partnerships is associated with adhocracy culture.

Moderate contractual complexity represents the partners' intention to balance between too much and too little control through contractual provisions. We associate the clan and market cultures with moderate levels of contractual complexity and suppose that moderate contractual complexity in combination with high performance ambiguity and low goal incongruence results in clan culture, while moderate contractual complexity in combination with low performance ambiguity and high goal incongruence results in market culture.

This is supported by the characteristics and the information requirements of clan and market cultures. In a partnership that has the attributes of a clan, trust and mutual understanding among the members usually reduces the need for monitoring, both in the pre-contractual and post-contractual phases. Consequently, the formal contracts that bind partners would likely display greater levels of completeness when opportunistic behaviour is a possibility. On these grounds, Williamson and Ouchi distinguish between "hard" and "soft" contracting and argue that soft contracting represents the clan-type culture. Hence, clan culture presumes that the identity of interests between the parties is much closer and formal contracts among parties are incomplete (Williamson 1975). Further, clan culture is based on traditions where information is implicit; existing but mostly unstated (Ouchi 1979), it is embedded in established systems of shared values and beliefs, common goals, and mutual understanding that, once adopted, are only moderately explicit and complex. While clan members may share general orientations but not necessarily specific knowledge (Williamson 1975), they trust each other and trust the fact that know-how always stays within the clan, and that whatever action they take based on whatever knowledge they possess will ultimately be beneficial for all. Accordingly, there is less need to contractually formalize knowledge transfer, restrict knowledge sharing, and safeguard against knowledge spill over effects, since a common vision, shared objectives, and relational bonds among members of the clan predict those risks sufficiently.

The market culture, on the other hand, represents an open structure in which highly autonomous partners establish contractual relationships that are characterized by discrete, often short-term, agreements that aim to facilitate an economically efficient exchange. Partner performance is unambiguous because the conditions and agreements of the collaboration are specific, complete, and monetized. Hence, information requirements within market cultures are explicit, fully accessible, and easy to understand (Ouchi 1979) so that a market culture is based on simple mechanisms following simple contracts. Moreover, within market culture, exchange objects tend to be non-specific, that is, the resources, products, services or knowledge that a partner contributes can also be found with other partners (Macneil 1978;

Williamson 1985). Therefore, highly complex contractual agreements are not necessary since the competitive marketplace and standard contract regulations and corresponding laws provide efficient safeguards to the parties for mediating their transactions (Ring and Van de Ven 1992). Besides, in a market culture, partners are equal and free, so that social relations among them are limited since developing them could incur costs or be irrelevant (Williamson 1985). As a consequence, partners avoid the costs of agreeing on complex contracts that can influence and control their transactions. We encapsulate the above in the following two hypotheses.

Hypothesis 3: Moderate contractual complexity, high goal incongruence, and low performance ambiguity in innovation partnerships are associated with market culture.
Hypothesis 4: Moderate contractual complexity, low goal incongruence, and high performance ambiguity in innovation partnerships are associated with clan culture.

Innovation Partnership Culture and Network Capitalism

Organizational culture has been repeatedly and consistently shown to play an important role for innovation (Chang and Lee 2007; Higgins and McAllaster 2002; Lau and Ngo 2004; Lloréns Montes et al. 2004; Martins and Terblanche 2003; Mumford 2000; Obendhain and Johnson 2004; Ruigrok and Achtenhagen 1999). While not many studies have examined the role of culture in the Asia-Pacific context, some studies argue from a Western European perspective, that in order to innovate firms have to meet clear requirements in regards to the managerial behaviour within the organization and its management of external relationships (Tylecote 1996). Others (Siguaw et al. 2006) point out that organizational culture is a facet of operational competency shaped by the innovation orientation of the firm.

Overall, throughout the literature, culture plays a central part in achieving innovation objectives (Ahmed 1998; Higgins and McAllaster 2002; Jamrog et al. 2006; Jassawalla and Sashittal 2002; Lau and Ngo 2004; Martins and Terblanche 2003; Mumford 2000). It generally influences innovation in two ways: socialization and co-ordination (Tesluk et al. 1997). We suggest that innovation partnerships are no different than other organisations in their tendency to develop their own organisational culture. Through socialization, members of the partnership learn whether creative and innovative behaviours are part of what is valued within the partnership. In addition, via co-ordination through activities, policies and procedures the partnership engenders values, which can encourage creative behaviour and reward innovation. As a result the innovative capacity improves. Hence, the culture of innovation partnerships determines the extend to which innovative behaviour among its members is inspired and innovation is accepted as a basic value (Dulaimi and Hartmann 2006) so that members of the partnership can foster commitment to it.

We suggest that the core features of network capitalism including information diffusion, social embeddedness and information codification affect the ability for members of innovation partnerships to develop a culture that fosters innovation. The previous described theoretical relationships between contractual complexity, goal incongruence and performance ambiguity with partnership culture are controlled by the context in which they occur.

Information codification is the selection and compression of data into stable structures (Shannon 2001); it exists on a continuum and alongside information diffusion. Boisot and Child explain: "If Zen masters trade in the kind of tacit knowledge that is hard to codify and that can only be imparted slowly and face to face to a limited number of disciples, bond traders, by contrast, deal in well-codified prices that can be diffused worldwide in seconds by electronic means" (Boisot and Child 1996, p. 602). Hence, codification and diffusion of information make up the transactional environment and shape the conditions for institutional options of the participating actors. We suggest that low information diffusion under network capitalism confines the effect of goal incongruence but increases the effect of performance ambiguity on partnership culture, while low information codification under network capitalism reduces the effect of contractual complexity on partnership culture.

Similarly, social embeddedness, which is defined as a kind of strong social situatedness or the extent to which modelling the behaviour of an actor requires the inclusion of other actors as individuals rather than as an undifferentiated whole (Edmonds 1999), affect partnership culture. A high degree of social embeddedness reduces the effect of both goal incongruence and performance ambiguity on partnership culture. With typically uncodified information and limited or restricted information diffusion and high social embeddedness in China, we follow our logic and suggest that clan-like structures are the preferred institutional choice for partnerships in the region (Fig. 9.1).

We encapsulate the above in the following three additional hypotheses.

Hypothesis 5: Information diffusion moderates the effect of goal incongruence and performance ambiguity on partnership culture of innovation partnerships.
Hypothesis 6: Social embeddedness moderates the effect of goal incongruence and performance ambiguity on partnership culture of innovation partnerships.
Hypothesis 7: Information codification moderates the effect of contractual complexity on partnership culture of innovation partnerships.

Overall, network capitalism favours clan culture that stresses flexibility while focusing on internal organization. Characteristics of clan-type innovation partnerships include teamwork, involvement and the partnering organisation's commitment to members of the partnership. Autonomy and freedom based on social embeddedness, low information codification and diffusion encourage creativity, which is the key for developing innovations. This contrasts the existence of rules and regulations and excessive authority or poor participation of members that will limit the capacity of partnership members to assume the risks of innovation (Child 1973).

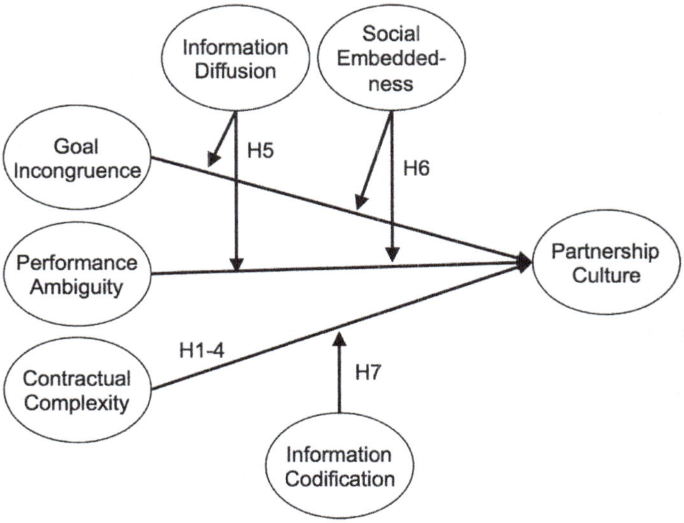

Fig. 9.1 Conceptual framework of innovation partnership cultures in Asia-Pacific

Conclusion

The present chapter is an initial theoretical investigation of the relationships between network capitalism and the contractual complexity of partnership agreements, the goal incongruence and performance ambiguity among innovation partners as well as the implications of these factors for the organisational culture of innovation partnerships. Our aim was to clarify the intricacies of certain facets of the Asia-Pacific region in conjunction with current thinking about how partnerships achieve the necessary conditions for achieving innovation outcomes. We discussed the roles of information codification and diffusion and social embeddedness as important elements of network capitalism and their relationship with contractual complexity, goal incongruence and performance ambiguity as important factors determining the organisational cultures present in contemporary innovation partnerships.

Bureaucracy, market, clan, and adhocracy cultures are different alternatives to safeguard opportunistic threats in innovation partnerships based on their associated levels of goal incongruence, performance ambiguity, and contractual complexity. Yet—in the Asia-Pacific context such choices might be limited given the effect of network capitalism. The primary objective of our framework is to discuss and integrate the related literature, thereby framing network capitalism as an important factor for the development of innovation partnerships in the region.

Our framework contributes to the study of innovation, contracting, and governance in various ways. While previous research regarding contractual complexity in innovation partnerships has focused on the role and importance of contributory influences (e.g. Ariño et al. 2006; Ariño and Reuer 2006a; Reuer and Ariño 2002, 2007; Reuer et al. 2006), our conceptualization further expands this research by discussing the implication of contractual complexity for partnership innovation culture. In the same way, we begin to fill an important gap in the partnership culture literature by examining a specific aspect, that is, network capitalism, and its implications for emerging partnership cultures and structures in Asia-Pacific.

From a managerial perspective our conceptual framework suggest how important it is for innovation partners to better understand what the roles of strategy, contracts and performance expectations are particularly when aiming for specific innovation outcomes with partners in Asia-Pacific. For example, the firm's ability to negotiate partnership contracts under of network capitalism is greatly influenced by a range of factors which, when explicit and better understood, can help the partners avoid futile complex agreements or, on the other hand, include critical agreements to safeguard against the unwanted actions of partners and innovation team members.

A limitation of our framework and this study is that it rests on restricted theoretical assumptions. Even though we focus on the perspectives of network capitalism and organizational control theory, there might be other aspects of partnership and alliance management that would be important to consider. For example, Ring and Van de Vens' (1994) process perspective of alliance contracting implies an influence of a psychological contract on the behavioural uncertainty that the contracting parties face once they are partners. Another theoretical perspective that we have not considered here and which has in general not been considered much in the field of partnership management and governance is the organizational behaviour perspective (Ariño and Reuer 2006b).

Future research could, for example, include further factors that determine the environment of economic transactions in Asia-Pacific, or take a specific look at the implications of the relationships proposed in this chapter and examine how they relate to other innovation management and collaboration phenomena. This may include various types of behavioural dynamics at the individual or group level, process dimensions of collaboration, and the organizational and managerial context of partnership formation and management including managerial capabilities, leadership behaviour, and the functioning of teams within and across organisations. Hence, expanding on the model presented here offers a plethora of additional research opportunities.

References

Achrol, R. S. (1997). Changes in the theory of interoganisational relations in marketing: Toward a network paradigm. *Journal of the Academy of Marketing Science, 25*(1), 56–71.

Adams, R., Bessant, J., & Phelps, R. (2006). Innovation management measurement: A review. *International Journal of Management Reviews, 8*(1), 21–47.

Ahmed, P. K. (1998). Culture and climate for innovation. *European Journal of Innovation Management, 1*(1), 30–43.

Anderson, E., & Weitz, B. A. (1992). The use of pledges to build and sustain commitment in distribution channels. *Journal of Marketing Research, 29,* 18–34.

Argyres, N. S., Bercovitz, J., & Mayer, K. J. (2007). Complementarity and evolution of contractual provisions: An empirical study of IT services contracts. *Organization Science, 18*(1), 3–19.

Ariño, A., Ragozzino, R., & Reuer, J. J. (2006). Contractual renegotiations in entrepreneurial alliances. In A. Ariño & J. J. Reuer (Eds.), *Strategic alliances: Governance and contracts.* London, UK: Palgrave.

Ariño, A., & Reuer, J. J. (2006a). Alliance contractual design. In O. Shenkar & J. J. Reuer (Eds.), *Handbook of strategic alliances* (pp. 149–167). Thousand Oaks: Sage Publications.

Ariño, A., & Reuer, J. J. (2006b). Introduction: Governance and contracts in strategic alliances. In A. Ariño & J. J. Reuer (Eds.), *Strategic alliances: Governance and contracts*. London, UK: Palgrave.

Bartlett, C., & Ghoshal, S. (2000). Going global. *Harvard Business Review, 78*(2), 132–141.

Boisot, M. H. (1986). Markets and hierarchies in a cultural perspective. *Organization Studies*, *7*(2), 135–158.

Boisot, M. H. (1987). *Information and organizations: The manager as anthropologist*. Fontana Press.

Boisot, M., & Child, J. (1996). From fiefs to clans and network capitalism: Explaining China's emerging economic order. *Administrative Science Quarterly, 41*(4), 600–628.

Boisot, M., & Child, J. (2007). 7. China and the new economy: A case of convergence? *The Digital Business Ecosystem*, 127.

Boisot, M., Child, J., & Redding, G. (2011). Working the system: Toward a theory of cultural and institutional competence. *International Studies of Management & Organization, 41*(1), 62–95.

Bryant, A., & Colledge, B. (2002). Trust in electronic commerce business relationships. *Journal of Electronic Commerce Research, 3*(2), 32–39.

Cameron, K. S., & Ettington, D. R. (1988). Conceptual foundations of organizational culture. In J.C. Smart (Ed.), *Higher education: Handbook of theory and research* (Vol. 4, pp. 356–396). New York: Agathon Press.

Cameron, K. S., & Quinn, R. E. (1999). *Diagnosing and changing organizational culture*. Upper Saddle River, NJ: Prentice-Hall.

Cameron, K. S., & Quinn, R. E. (2011). *Diagnosing and changing organizational culture: Based on the competing values framework*. Wiley.

Chang, S., & Lee, M. (2007). The effects of organizational culture and knowledge management mechanisms on organizational innovation: An empirical study in Taiwan. *The Business Review, 7*(1), 295–301.

Child, J. (1973). Predicting and understanding organization structure. *Administrative Science Quarterly*, 168–185.

Child, J., & Ihrig, M. (2013). *Knowledge, organization, and management: Building on the work of Max Boisot*. Oxford University Press.

Clegg, S., Carter, C., Kornberger, M., & Schweitzer, J. (2011). *Strategy: Theory and practice*. Sage Publications, Incorporated.

Clegg, S., Schweitzer, J., Whittle, A., & Pitelis, C. (2017). Strategy: Theory and Practice (2nd ed.): *SAGE Publications*.

Daft, R. L. (1995). *Organization theory and design* (5th ed.). Minneapolis, St. Paul: West Publishing Company.

Doz, Y. L. (1996). The evolution of cooperation in strategic alliances: Initial conditions or learning. *Strategic Management Journal, 17,* 55–83.

Dulaimi, M., & Hartmann, A. (2006). The role of organizational culture in motivating innovative behaviour in construction firms. *Construction Innovation, 6*(3), 159–172.

Duncan, W. J. (1989). Organizational culture: "Getting a fix" on an elusive concept. *The Academy of Management Executive, 3*(3), 229–236.

Edmonds, B. (1999). Capturing social embeddedness: A constructivist approach. *Adaptive Behavior, 7*(3–4), 323–347.

Edwards, M., Logue, D., & Schweitzer, J. (2015). Towards an understanding of open innovation in services: Beyond the firm and towards relational co-creation. In *The handbook of service innovation* (pp. 75–90). London: Springer.

Fukuyama, F. (1996). *Trust: The social virtues and the creation of prosperity*. New York: Free press.

Gerwin, D., & Ferris, J. S. (2004). Organizing new product development projects in strategic alliances. *Organization Science, 15*(1), 22–38.

Goldberg, V. (1976). Towards an expanded economic theory of contract. *Journal of Economic Issues, 10,* 45–61.

Goodman, E. A., Zammuto, R. F. & Gifford, B. D. (2001). The competing values framework: Understanding the impact of organizational culture on the quality of work life. *Organization Development Journal, 19*(3), p.58.

Gudergan, S. P., & Schweitzer, J. (2008). Alliances. In S. Clegg & J. R. Bailey (Eds.), *International encyclopedia of organization studies* (pp. 51–55). Thousand Oaks, CA: Sage Publications.

Gulati, R. (1995a). Does familiarity breed trust? The implications of repeated ties for contractual choice in alliances. *Academy of Management Journal, 38*(1), 85–112.

Gulati, R. (1995b). Social structure and alliance formation pattern: A longitudinal analysis. *Administrative Science Quarterly, 40,* 619–642.

Gulati, R. (1998). Alliances and networks. *Strategic Management Journal, 19,* 293–317.

Gulati, R., & Singh, H. (1998). The architecture of cooperation: Managing coordination costs and appropriation concerns in strategic alliances. *Administrative Science Quarterly, 43*(4), 781–815.

Heide, J. B. (1994). Interorganisational governance in marketing channels. *Journal of Marketing, 58,* 71–85.

Hennart, J.-F. (1988). A transaction cost theory of equity joint ventures. *Strategic Management Journal, 9*(4), 361–374.

Higgins, J. M., & McAllaster, C. (2002). Want innovation? Then use cultural artifacts that support it. *Organizational Dynamics, 31*(1), 74–84.

Hoetker, G., & Mellewigt, T. (2009). Choice and performance of governance mechanisms: Matching alliance governance to asset type. *Strategic Management Journal, 9999*(9999), n/a.

Ibeh, K., Johnson, J. E., Dimitratos, P., & Slow, J. (2004). Micromultinationals: Some preliminary evidence on an emergent 'star' of the international entrepreneurship field. *Journal of International Entrepreneurship, 2*(4), 289–303.

IBM. (2012). *Leading through connections: The global CEO study*. Somers, NY: IBM Institute for Business Value.

Inkpen, A. C., & Crossan, M. M. (1995). Believing is seeing: Joint ventures and organization learning*. *Journal of Management Studies, 32*(5), 595–618.

Isaksen, S. G., Lauer, K. J., Ekvall, G., & Britz, A. (2001). Perceptions of the best and worst climates for creativity: Preliminary validation evidence for the situational outlook. *Creativity Research Journal, 13,* 171–184.

Jamrog, J., Vickers, M., & Bear, D. (2006). Building and sustaining a culture that supports innovation. *People and Strategy, 29*(3), 9.

Jarillo, J. C. (1988). On strategic networks. *Strategic Management Journal, 9*(1), 31–41.

Jassawalla, A. R., & Sashittal, H. C. (2002). Cultures that support product-innovation processes. *The Academy of Management Executive, 16*(3), 42–54.

Jeffries, F. L., & Reed, R. (2000). Trust and adaptation in relational contracting. *Academy of Management Review, 25*(4), 873–883.

Kale, P., Singh, H., & Perlmutter, H. (2000). Learning and protection of proprietary assets in strategic alliances: Building relational capital. *Strategic Management Journal, 21*(3), 217–237.

Krishnan, R., Martin, X., & Noorderhaven, N. G. (2006). When does trust matter to alliance performance? *Academy of Management Journal, 49*(5), 894–917.

Lau, C. M., & Ngo, H. Y. (2004). The HR system, organizational culture, and product innovation. *International Business Review, 13*(6), 685–703.

Lee, C.-K., Tan, B., & Chiu, J.-Z. (2008). The impact of organisational culture and learning on innovation performance. *International Journal of Innovation and Learning, 5*(4), 413–428.
Lee, S. M., Olson, D. L., & Trimi, S. (2010). Strategic innovation in the convergence era. *International Journal of Management and Enterprise Development, 9*(1), 1–12.
Lerner, J., & Merges, R. P. (1998). The control of technology alliances: An empirical analysis of the biotechnology industry. *Journal of Industrial Economics, 46,* 125–156.
Leung, L., Nikolova, N., Schweitzer, J., Golsby-Smith, T., Whybrow, T., & Jurd, K. (2016). The View From The Top – 2016 Innovation Report: A conversation with Chairs & CEOs of 20+ major corporations on the state of innovation in Australia. Sydney, Australia: Second Road, Spencer Stuart, University of Technology Sydney.
Linnarsson, H., & Werr, A. (2004). Overcoming the innovation-alliance paradox: A case study of an explorative alliance. *European Journal of Innovation Management, 7*(1), 45–55.
Lloréns Montes, F. J., Ruiz Moreno, A., & Miguel Molina Fernández, L. (2004). Assessing the organizational climate and contractual relationship for perceptions of support for innovation. *International Journal of Manpower, 25*(2), 167–180.
Lui, S. S., & Ngo, H.-Y. (2004). The role of trust and contractual safeguards on cooperation in non-equity alliances. *Journal of Management, 30*(4), 471–485.
Luo, Y. (2002). Contract, cooperation, and performance in international joint ventures. *Strategic Management Journal, 23*(10), 903–919.
Macaulay, S. (1963). Non contractual relations in business: A preliminary study. *The American Economic Review, 28*(1), 55–69.
Macneil, I. R. (1978). Contracts: Adjustment of long-term economic relations under classical, neoclassical and relational contract law. *Northwestern University Law Review, 72,* 854–905.
Martins, E., & Terblanche, F. (2003). Building organisational culture that stimulates creativity and innovation. *European Journal of Innovation Management, 6*(1), 64–74.
Mintzberg, H. (1979). *The structuring of organizations*. Englewood Cliffs, NJ: Prentice-Hall.
Mintzberg, H. (1993). *Structure in fives. Designing effective organizations*. Englewood Cliffs, NJ: Prentice-Hall.
MofCom. (2013). *Import and Export Statistics: People's Republic of China Ministry of Commerce*.
MofCom. (2015). *Import and Export Indicators: People's Republic of China Ministry of Commerce*.
Mumford, M. D. (2000). Managing creative people: Strategies and tactics for innovation. *Human Resource Management Review, 10*(3), 313–351.
Nielsen, B. B. (2003). An empirical investigation of the drivers of international strategic alliance formation. *European Management Journal, 21*(3), 301–322.
Nooteboom, B., Berger, H., & Noorderhaven, N. G. (1997). Effects of trust and governance on relational risk. *Academy of Management Journal, 40*(2), 308–339.
Obendhain, A. M., & Johnson, W. C. (2004). Product and process innovation in service organizations: The influence of organizational culture in higher education institutions. *Journal of Applied Management and Entrepreneurship, 9*(3), 91.
O'Reilly, C. (1989). Corporations, culture, and commitment: Motivation and social control in organizations. *California Management Review, 31*(4), 9–25.
Osborn, R. N., & Baughn, C. C. (1990). Forms of interorganizational governance for multinational alliances. *Academy of Management Journal, 33*(3), 503–519.
Ouchi, W. G. (1979). A conceptual framework for the design of organizational control mechanisms. *Management Science, 25*(9), 833–848.
Ouchi, W. G. (1980). Markets, bureaucracies, and clans. *Administrative Science Quarterly, 25*(1), 129–141.
Oxley, J. E. (1997). Appropriability hazards and governance in strategic alliances: A transaction cost approach. *Journal of Law Economics and Organization, 13*(2), 387–409.
Oxley, J. E. (1999). Institutional environment and the mechanisms of governance: The impact of intellectual property protection on the structure of inter-firm alliances. *Journal of Economic Behavior & Organization, 38*(3), 283–309.

Oxley, J. E., & Sampson, T. C. (2004). The scope and governance of international R&D alliances. *Strategic Management Journal, 25*(8–9), 723–749.
Poppo, L., & Zenger, T. (2002). Do formal contracts and relational governance function as substitutes or complements? *Strategic Management Journal, 23*(8), 707–725.
Quinn, R. E., Hildebrandt, H. W., Rogers, P. S., & Thompson, M. P. (1991). A competing values framework for analyzing presentational communication in management contexts. *Journal of Business Communication, 28*(3), 213–232.
Quinn, R. E., & Rohrbaugh, J. (1981). A competing values approach to organizational effectiveness. *Public Productivity Review, 5*(2), 122–140.
Reuer, J. J., & Ariño, A. (2002). Contractual renegotiations in strategic alliances. *Journal of Management, 28*(1), 47–68.
Reuer, J. J., & Ariño, A. (2003). *Strategic alliances as contractual forms*. Paper presented at the Academy of Management (AoM), Seatle, USA.
Reuer, J. J., & Ariño, A. (2007). Strategic alliance contracts: Dimensions and determinants of contractual complexity. *Strategic Management Journal, 28*(3), 313–330.
Reuer, J. J., Ariño, A., & Mellewigt, T. (2006). Entrepreneurial alliances as contractual forms. *Journal of Business Venturing, 21*(3), 306–325.
Reuer, J. J., Zollo, M., & Singh, H. (2002). Post-formation dynamics in strategic alliances. *Strategic Management Journal, 23*(2), 135–151.
Rialp, A., Rialp, J., & Knight, G. A. (2005). The phenomenon of early internationalizing firms: What do we know after a decade (1993–2003) of scientific inquiry? *International Business Review, 14*(2), 147–166.
Ring, P., & Van de Ven, A. H. (1992). Structuring cooperative relationships between organizations. *Strategic Management Journal, 13*(7), 483–498.
Ring, P., & Van de Ven, A. H. (1994). Developmental processes of cooperative interorganizational relationships. *Academy of Management Review, 19*(1), 90–118.
Ruigrok, W., & Achtenhagen, L. (1999). Organizational culture and the transformation towards new forms of organizing. *European Journal of work and organizational psychology, 8*(4), 521–536.
Sampson, R. C. (2004). The cost of misaligned governance in R&D alliances. *Journal of Law Economics and Organization, 20*(2), 484–526.
Schein, E. H. (2010). *Organizational culture and leadership*. Wiley.
Schumpeter, J. A. (1934). *The theory of economic development: An enquiry into profits, capital, credit, interest and the business cycle*. Cambridge, Mass.: Harvard University Press.
Schweitzer, J. (2014). Leadership and innovation capability development in strategic alliances. *Leadership & Organization Development Journal, 35*(5), 442–469.
Schweitzer, J., & Gudergan, S. (2010). Leadership behaviours as ongoing negotiations and their effects on knowledge and innovation capabilities in alliances. *International Journal of Knowledge Management Studies, 4*(2), 176–197.
Schweitzer, J. (2016). How contracts and culture mediate joint transactions. of innovation partnerships. *International Journal of Innovation Management, 20*(1), 33.
Shannon, C. E. (2001). A mathematical theory of communication. *ACM SIGMOBILE Mobile Computing and Communications Review, 5*(1), 3–55.
Siguaw, J. A., Simpson, P. M., & Enz, C. A. (2006). Conceptualizing innovation orientation: A framework for study and integration of innovation research*. *Journal of Product Innovation Management, 23*(6), 556–574.
Snell, R., & Tseng, C. S. (2002). Moral atmosphere and moral influence under China's network capitalism. *Organization Studies, 23*(3), 449–478.
Tapscott, D., & Williams, A. D. (2008). *Wikinomics: How mass collaboration changes everything*. Penguin.com.
Tesluk, P. E., Farr, J. L., & Klein, S. R. (1997). Influences of organizational culture and climate on individual creativity. *The Journal of Creative Behavior, 31*(1), 27–41.
Tung, R. L., & Worm, V. (2001). Network capitalism: The role of human resources in penetrating the China market. *International Journal of Human Resource Management, 12*(4), 517–534.

Tylecote, A. (1996). Cultural differences affecting technological innovation in Western Europe. *European Journal of Work and Organizational Psychology, 5*(1), 137–147.

White, S., & Lui, S.-Y. S. (2005). Distinguishing costs of cooperation and control in alliances. *Strategic Management Journal, 26*(10), 913–932.

Williamson, O. E. (1975). *Market and hierarchies: Analysis and antitrust implications*. New York: Free Press.

Williamson, O. E. (1985). *The economic institution of capitalism*. New York: Free Press.

Williamson, O. E. (1991). Comparative economic organization: The analysis of discrete structural alternatives. *Administrative Science Quarterly*, 269–296.

Zaheer, A., McEvily, B., & Perrone, V. (1998). Does trust matter? Exploring the effects of interorganizational and interpersonal trust on performance. *Organization Science, 9*(2), 141–159.

Zammuto, R. F., & Krakower, J. Y. (1991). *Quantitative and qualitative studies of organizational culture*. Greenwich, CT: JAI Press Inc.

Zenger, T. R., & Hesterly, W. S. (1997). The disaggregation of corporations: Selective intervention, high-powered incentives, and molecular units. *Organization Science, 8*(3), 209–222.

Chapter 10
Industry Sustainability and Innovation System: A Comparative Case Study in China

Guanyu Liu and Ping Gao

Abstract Technological innovation systems (TIS) play significant roles in technology innovation. Apart from promoting technology innovations, some TIS can contribute to the sustainability of industry, while others cannot. However, existing innovation studies about understanding how TIS can impact industry sustainability have proven to be insufficient, especially in the industry of information technology (IT). By comparing two TISs of TD-SCDMA and TD-LTE in China' telecommunication industry, this work aims to answer the questions about how TIS may impact IT industry sustainability, and what kinds of TIS enhance sustainability? An innovation system functions based framework is applied to structure the data collection and result analysis. Extensive documentary research and semi-structured interviews are conducted in this research. The comparative case study suggests: a well-functioned TIS significantly contributes to sustainability of IT industry, by pushing forward the process of socio-technical transformation; TIS functions are determined by its configuration, and a well-configured TIS could be characterised as: constituted by stable and early enrolled core actors, who connect with diversified and early developed networks, and influenced by both regulative powers and normative influences. This work advances the understanding of how industry sustainability is impacted by TIS, and what a TIS should be for enhancing sustainability. In practice, this work also offers practical implications for other technology late-coming countries who want to catch up through technology innovation like China.

Keywords Technology innovation system · Technological change · Sustainability · Telecommunication · IT industry

G. Liu (✉) · P. Gao
Information School, Capital University of Economics and Business, Beijing, China
e-mail: liuguanyu@cueb.edu.cn

T. Clarke and K. Lee (eds.), *Innovation in the Asia Pacific*,
https://doi.org/10.1007/978-981-10-5895-0_10

Introduction

The IT industry worldwide has maintained a rapid growth trajectory in recent decades, as more and more technology late-coming countries take part in a globalized wave of technology innovation. Late-coming countries are transforming their development strategy from imitating the frontiers to catch up through promoting indigenous technology innovations (Choung et al. 2012; Xiao et al. 2013). Some of them have made a good progression in promoting indigenous technology innovations, like South Korea and China. In China, taking wireless mobile technology as example, since 2008 when the indigenous 3G mobile technology—TD-SCDMA was first adopted, the telecommunication industry has undergone a remarkable expansion, and currently has become one of the leading countries in the world. Benefiting from the sustained indigenous technology innovation, a group of domestic technology enterprises in China, like Huawei, ZTE, and MediaTek, have gradually grown into important vendors in global market. Along with indigenous technology innovations, the sustainability of telecommunication industry in China has been tremendously improved (Lee and Oh 2006; Tsai and Wang 2011; Gao et al. 2014).

Sustainability describes the capability to endure, and activities toward sustainability are labelled as processes of sustainable technological transitions, industrial transformation, and socio-technical change (Geels 2002). Socio-technical change is interchangeable with technological change, since technological change always co-evolves with changes in the social system. Innovation, especially technology innovation is a key process in sustainable social-technical change, which determines the sustainability of an industry (Hekkert and Negro 2009). Technological innovation system plays significant roles in technology innovation. Apart from promoting innovations, it has also been witnessed that, some TIS can contribute to the sustainability of industry, while others cannot (Chang and Shih 2004; Wang 2007). Innovation system studies have put great emphasis on exploring how systems can promote technology innovations (Chang and Shih 2004; Iyer et al. 2006; Zhang and Liang 2012), while the studies about understanding how TIS impact industry sustainability are still limited (Hekkert and Negro 2009).

Interrelationships between technology innovation, sustainable socio-technical change, and industry sustainability that are illustrated by scholars have provided a solid theoretical foundation for this work. Therefore, through comparing the TIS of TD-SCDMA and TD-LTE mobile system in China' telecommunication industry, this work aims to bridge the divide by answering the questions about how TIS impact IT industry sustainability (RQ1), and what a TIS should be if it aims to enhance sustainability (RQ2)? The innovation of TD-SCDMA and TD-LTE in China has provided a good empirical case study for us, to comparatively understand how TIS of TD-SCDMA and TD-LTE influence the sustainability of China's telecommunication industry.

This article is structured into seven sections. In sections "Industry Sustainability and Sustainable Socio-technical Change" and "Technology Innovation and

Technological Innovation System", we review related literature about technological change, technology innovation, and technological innovation systems. Then a conceptual framework is developed in section "Conceptual Framework". Section "Methodology" demonstrates the methodology, which includes research design and methods of data collection. In section "Empirical Case Studies", cases of China's TD-SCDMA and TD-LTE innovation, associated with TIS for each of them, are comparatively reviewed. Then the final section illustrates the analysis, findings, implications and conclusions of this research.

Industry Sustainability and Sustainable Socio-technical Change

Sustainability of industry strongly relates to the sustainability of socio-technical change (Geels 2002). Scholars describe the norm of sustainability as the capability to endure. Activities like processes of sustainable technological transitions, industrial transformation, and socio-technical change are viewed as the approaches that can impact the sustainability of an industry (Hekkert and Negro 2009). Within these three main components, socio-technical change, which is interchangeable with technological change, is recognized as the most significant process that can impact industry sustainability. The more sustainable the change is, the higher sustainability the industry maintains (Scott-Morton 1991; Geels and Schot 2007; Hekkert and Negro 2009).

In terms of analysing socio-technical changes, socio-theoretical frameworks like structuration theory (Orlikowski and Robey 1991) or social shaping of technologies (Howcroft et al. 2004) have been adopted based on linear process perspective. Geels (2002) defines socio-technical change as a fundamental change in the relationships between social and technological co-evolution, and suggests a multi-level perspective framework which analyse the change from levels of niches, regime and landscape. Furthermore, socio-technical change is also analysed from a system perspective by information system scholars, and the socio-technical model (S-T model) developed by Leavitt is most frequently applied (Lyytinen and Newman 2008). The model believes social-technical changes cannot by achieved by a single entity and must take place in an organizational field, thus it divides the field into different multivariate systems which are composed by four interacting and aligned components—task, structure, actor, and technology. For bridging the TIS and industry sustainability in this work, the perspective of socio-technical change is most appropriate (Klein and Hirschheim 1989; Orlikowski and Robey 1991; Crowston and Myers 2004; Crossan and Apaydin 2010).

Figure 10.1 shows the content of four components and their interactions suggested by Leavitt. In this model, technology stands for the technical environment for change, like development tools or technical platforms; structure presents the participate organizations and the institutional arrangements with them; people are

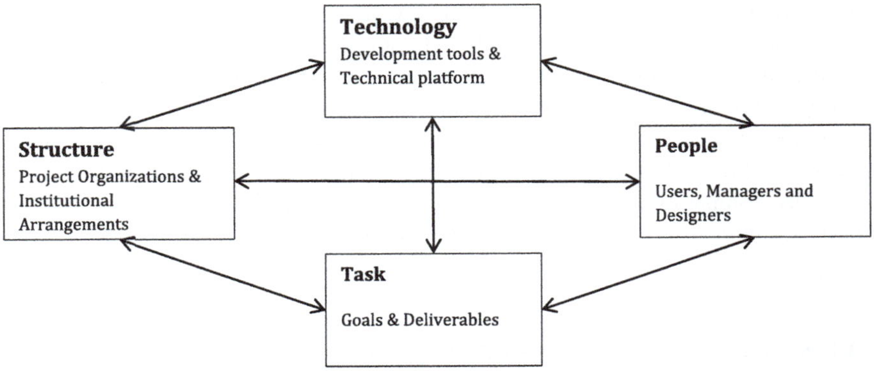

Fig. 10.1 Model of socio-technical change (adopted from Lyytinen and Newman 2008)

the group actors or individuals that inside or outside are involved in organizations who carry out the work or have influence on the change process; and task describes the targets or purposes of the change. Each two of them are interconnected, and the dynamic of each of them can be both incremental and punctuated. According to this model, sustainable socio-technical change then could be viewed as persistent technological change achievement (tasks) with sustained change of the dynamic social (people and structure) and technical environment (technology) (Lyytinen and Newman 2008). The model provides a measurable and operational frame for this work to understand how systems of technology innovation can impact the sustainability of socio-technical change hence the sustainability of industry.

Technology innovation is a key process in sustainable socio-technical change (Hekkert and Negro 2009). Scholars have conducted many empirical studies to explain the significance of technology innovation in sustainable transitions. For instance, by reviewing development history from the UK and US, and technology innovations in emerging economies, Freeman (2002) confirms the synchronized moving path of economic exploitation and the cluster of technology innovation, and points out that regional economic development is mainly driven by technologies exploration. Besides, Fagerberg and Srholec (2008) examine the role of capabilities in economic growth by using factor analysis on 25 indicators in 115 countries between 1992 and 2004. They identify four different types of capabilities and suggest technology innovation is the most significant one for national economic development. Vernon introduces the "product life-cycle theory" and suggests that technologies would be transformed from the innovator country to other developing places with large markets or low costs as normally observed. As the innovator countries normally just transform the part of processing and manufacturing of the product rather than the core technology, thus they hold a majority of profits through IPR and brand effect. The theory of product life-cycle also helps to understand how sustainable comparative advantages are achieved through technology innovation, and why countries are promoting indigenous innovation.

Technology Innovation and Technological Innovation System

Locating at the central of innovation studies, technology innovation is described as the innovation of a product or a producing process that relates to new technology (Fagerberg 2005). Studies have analysed practices of technology innovation from different perspectives, like organizational change (Teo et al. 2014), industrial reform (Tilson and Lyytinen 2006a; Kshetri et al. 2011), market restructure (Funk and Methe 2001; Siu et al. 2006), policies or regulations (Tilson and Lyytinen 2006b; Yu et al. 2012; Gao et al. 2014), and roles of stakeholders (Montealegre 1999; Damsgaard and Lyytinen 2001; Siu et al. 2006; Currie and Guah 2007; Tsai and Wang 2011). Moreover, technology innovation is normally understood from the system view of innovation, which named as technological innovation system (TIS) (Lundvall et al. 2002; Nelson and Nelson 2002; Carlsson 2006; Hekkert et al. 2007; Bergek et al. 2008). As defined by Carlsson et al. (2002, p. 236), a TIS is "a network of agents interacting in the economic or industrial area under a particular institutional infrastructure and involved in the generation, diffusion, and utilization of technology". Therefore, TIS itself, also maintains the function of analysing how technology is developed and diffused. For instance, Currie and Guah (2007) apply TIS to analyse a complex technological change in the health care sector in Sweden, composed of several technological systems that support technological artefacts applicable in the health care sector; Hekkert and Negro (2009) employ five empirical studies in renewable energy technologies, in order to test whether the functions of the TIS frame are valid or not on analysing processes of technological change, with a positive result; Chung (2013) summarizes how a different social and political environment can impact TIS through comparing different biotechnology TISs from Taiwan and South Korea.

According to Carlsson et al. (2002), a TIS is normally constituted by three components—actors, relationships and institutions. Actors include not only organizations along the value chain, universities and research institutions, but also public bodies, venture capitalists, and industrial alliances, etc. Relationships between these actors are also significant. Within TIS, both formal and informal networks exist, like problem-solving networks, buyer-supplier networks, and research-market networks, etc. Some of these relationships are stable, while others are not. Meanwhile, institutions such as culture, norms, laws, regulations and routines also need to be identified, within the TIS, institutions are like "the rules of the game" (King et al. 1994; Edquist and Hommen 1999). Institutions must be adjusted, or "aligned", to a new technology if it is to diffuse and use (Freeman 2002). Actors, interactions, and institutions jointly constitute the configuration of a TIS (Carlsson et al. 2002). Scholars suggest the functionality of TIS is relates with configuration (Nelson and Nelson 2002; Carlsson 2006; Hekkert and Negro 2009; Zhang and Liang 2012).

Furthermore, scholars also introduce the concept of innovation systems functions. With the aim to map the dynamics of the innovation system, Carlsson et al.

Table 10.1 Functions of technological innovation system

Functions	Indicators	Description
1. Knowledge development and diffusion	Instance bibliometrics; Number and size of R&D	Providing base of scientific and technical knowledge for the production and exploitation of innovations. Normally formed by sponsored research institutes
2. Research direction	Beliefs in growth; price; pressure; users interests	Providing sufficient incentives or pressures for organizations to involve into the innovation progress
3. Entrepreneurial experimentation	Number of new entrants, applications, customers	Activities that aim to reduce the uncertainty in terms of new technologies, applications, and markers
4. Market formation	Market size and customer groups, purchase process	Through stages of nursing, bridging and mature, develop market, articulate users' potential demand and capability, enhance performance of technology
5. Legitimation	Legitimacy in eyes of actors; activities in system	Activities that aim to increase social acceptance and compliance to changes, not given, formed by organizations in the process of legitimation
6. Resource mobilization	Change in capital; change in human resource; assets	Activities and capabilities to mobile different resources, like competence, human and financial capital, and relevant assets
7. Positive externalities development	New entrants; labour markets; specialized products, services	Both pecuniary and non-pecuniary external economies and free utilities count. The generation of positive external economies is a key process in TIS formation and growth

Sources Hekkert et al. (2007), Bergek et al. (2008)

(2002) suggest the necessity of mapping relevant activities. They view the activities in innovation systems relevant if they can influence the targets of the system. As introduced, the targets of innovation system are to develop, apply, and diffuse the new technological knowledge. Therefore, no matter positive or negative, the activities that contribute to the targets of innovation system are summarized as the functions of innovation system (Hekkert et al. 2007). By conducting a historical review on innovation system functions studies, Hekkert et al. (2007) propose seven functions of innovation system with indicators which especially suitable for technological innovation systems (see Table 10.1). According to Hekkert and Negro (2009), both individual achievement in TIS and the interactions between these functions are significant, as functions influence each other, and the fulfilment of a certain function is likely to take its effects on the fulfilment of others. The positive relationships between these functions may lead to reinforce the positive dynamics, and further to enhance the system performance and achieve the targets. Based on summarized functions, they also introduced a scheme of function-based process analysis for TIS. This process analysis approach views TIS as dynamic from its formation, emphases the significance of dynamic TIS configurations in each stage, and suggests to allocate the seven functions in sequence by mapping key events in the innovation process.

In terms of measuring the performance of TIS, scholars suggest a consideration on both analysis level and maturity of the system (Nelson and Nelson 2002; Markard and Truffer 2008). On macro level, the performance of the system can be intuitively judged through whether the system targets—generation, diffusion and use of knowledge, are well achieved. However, to only measure the performance via these three aggregative targets is not accurate enough, therefore, based on these three targets, Richne introduces a number of indicators to measure each of them. For instance, the ability of TIS to generate innovation knowledge is assessed via four indicators, as the number of patents, number of scientists, mobility of professionals, and technological fields. Similarly, to measure the diffusion of knowledge, indicators are timing/the stage of development, regulatory acceptance, and number of partners/number of distribution licenses. Finally, conventional indicators of the use of knowledge are normally applying the value of employment, turnover, growth, and financial assets (Bergek et al. 2008).

Associate with distinguished components and characteristics, scholars suggest different approaches to conduct analysis about TIS. For instance, as introduced, Hekkert et al. (2007) suggest the approach of process analysis, with aims to understand processes of technological change and innovation; and Bergek et al. (2008) demonstrate a scheme of analysis with six steps, for understanding TIS especially with the aim to issue appropriate policies to facilitate the development of TIS. The approaches of analysis and the distinctions of TIS configurations, functions, and performance have set a standard or a platform, which makes comparison between different innovation systems possible and more operational, especially those with many different institutional set-ups. According to the literature, it has been well studied how technology innovation is promoted by the innovation system, and the contributions of technology innovation to sustainable socio-technical change are also well explained. Nonetheless, studies about the relationships between the TIS and the sustainability of technological change are still limited, and it is also important to understand what kind of TIS is helpful for improve the sustainability, especially for innovation practices. Literature about TIS and the sustainability of socio-technical change has provided a solid foundation for this work to address this divide in current research.

Conceptual Framework

In this work, we adopt the function-based process analysis that suggested by Hekkert et al. (2007), and the model of analysing socio-technical change that introduced by Lyytinen and Newman (2008) to explore how TIS can influence the sustainability of industry by impact the sustainability of socio-technical change (RQ1). The conceptual framework is developed by combining these two analytical

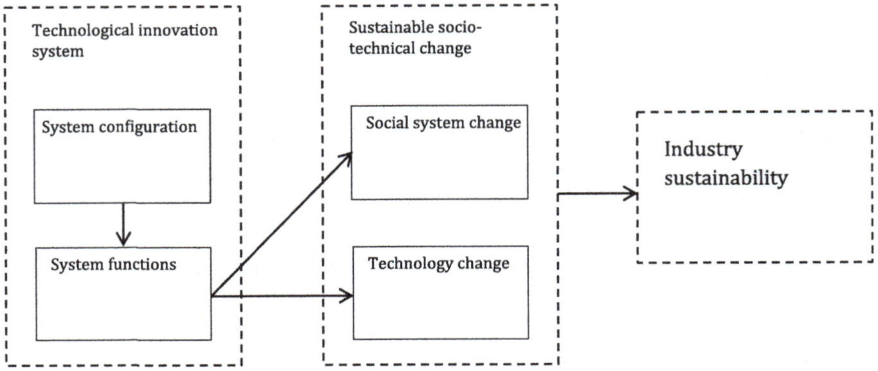

Fig. 10.2 TIS and industry sustainability (derived from Lyytinen and Newman 2008; Hekkert and Negro 2009)

models (Fig. 10.2). Further, through empirical case studies that based on the framework, this work then answer the question of what a TIS should be if aims to enhance the sustainability of industry (RQ2).

According to literature, configuration of technological innovation system is composed by involved actors, their relationships, and institutions. Configuration sets the foundation for the system (Carlsson et al. 2002). Besides, the technological innovation system normally undergoes a process of formation to operation, along with the process of technology development and diffusion. In the different stage of technology innovation, configuration of the system is not static but dynamic. Therefore, the analysis about system configuration must be distinguished and mapped with the stage of technology innovation. Moreover, as Hekkert et al. (2007) indicate, seven functions of TIS take place with a time sequence along with technology innovation, and also significantly determined by configuration of the system. Then a well functioned TIS ensures the performance of the system, which could thereby facilitate process of "…initiating, importing, modifying and diffusing new technologies" as expected (Lundvall 2007).

The model of socio-technical change suggests that a socio-technical change includes the transformation in terms of four components: tasks, technologies, structures, and actors (Lyytinen and Newman 2008). In this work, we summarize the change of structures, actors, and tasks as the change in terms of social system, and the transformation of technology is viewed as the process of technology change. The model of social-technical change itself has revealed the significance of TIS functions in terms of maintaining sustainability of the transformation process. To be more specific, seven TIS functions can play different roles to impact the transformation of both technology and social system. For instance, knowledge development, research direction, and market formation functions of TIS could determine the social system by changing the tasks, actors, and structures; and of course, the result, or the product of TIS could directly impact the change in terms of technology. Therefore, if the TIS can be well-functioned, then the social system and technology could be sustainably transformed, then according to literature, the sustainability of industry could be ensured (Hekkert and Negro 2009).

Developed conceptual framework could be applied to answer the question of how sustainability of industry is impacted by a technological innovation system (RQ1). To apply the conceptual framework, we can first distinguish the process of technology innovation into stages of technology development and diffusion; then following the strategies that suggested by Hekkert et al. (2007), to map different configurations of the system in each of these two stage; next, along with the process of technology innovation, to identify and measure the seven function of the system based on the indicators that summarized; at last, by mapping the changes in social system and technology, then we could address how these functions have contributed to the perceived transformations. Meanwhile, with the help of empirical case studies, the analysis about configurations and functions of the system could help to answer the question of what kind of TIS is better for enhancing the industry sustainability (RQ2). In this work, the conceptual framework is employed to analyze a comparative case study of TD-SCDMA and TD-LTE innovation in China. As demonstrated, the comparative case study could not only provide a theoretical duplication for achieving a better understanding how industry sustainability is impacted by the innovation system, but also help to summarize what a proper technological innovation system should be like with the aim to enhance the sustainability of IT industry.

Methodology

The method of qualitative case study was applied in this research (Kaplan and Maxwell 1994; Yin 2009). According to conceptual framework, we first identified the key events for each technology innovation, generated a timeline for the process, and divided these events into stage of technology development and technology diffusion. Secondly, we summarized the configuration of both TD-SCDMA and TD-LTE innovation system. Then associated with the events that identified, we mapped and measured different functions of TD-SCDMA and TD-LTE innovation system. At the same time, contrast with the functions of TIS, we captured the variations of the socio-technical transformations in terms of TD-SCDMA and TD-LTE innovation within China's telecommunication industry. To achieve this purpose, documentary research and semi-structured interviews were applied (Baxter and Jack 2008; Zucker 2009). Through documentary research, an overall picture of TD-SCDMA and TD-LTE innovation system were roughly delineated, include actors, interactions, institutions, and other factors that need to concern. Then for acquiring in-depth view of the cases that we exam, executives in different organizations were interviewed. Since TD-SCDMA as a 3G mobile technology that diffused around 2008, had been relatively well studied, relevant data are easy to access and quite sufficient, thus semi-structured interviews in this research were more focus on understanding the case of TD-LTE innovation.

For documentary research, firstly, some official websites of actors were visited as most general information could be found, like websites of Ministry of Industry and Information Technology (www.miit.gov.cn) and Datang Telecom (www.datanggroup.cn). Secondly, mainstream media and internet portals were particularly focused. For instance, the technology specials in Sina (tech.sina.com.cn) and Sohu (tech.sohu.com), two leading Internet portal were applied. Both of them have special blogs and discussion areas about TD-SCDMA and TD-LTE innovation, from where update information about China's telecommunication policies, technologies and markets could be easily found. Thirdly, many valuable insight and information were also collected from academic publications on China's telecommunication area with both Chinese and English. These articles hold different perspectives, and many of them have provided very detailed descriptions about TD-SCDMA and TD-LTE innovation (Kshetri et al. 2011; Xia 2011; Kwak et al. 2012; Yu et al. 2012).

For getting in-depth view about the case, semi-structured interviews were conducted with key persons who had been involved in TD-SCDMA and TD-LTE innovation. In practice, we selected the interviewees from different interest groups that been categorized, as government officials, both domestic and foreign technology vendors, service operators, industry alliances and research institutes. Specifically 45 executives in 13 relevant organizations have been interviewed in total. Since one author of this work used to work in China's telecommunications sector for years, and experts in technology innovation especially in China's telecommunication industry as a scholar, thus his close connection within the industry has promised the accessibility of data for collection. The strategy of triangulation was applied both in data collection and result analysis, with the aim to ensure validity and reliability of this research (Patton 2002; Baxter and Jack 2008; Yin 2009).

Empirical Case Studies

This section first introduces the wireless mobile system innovation in China and background of China's telecommunication industry. Then the case of TD-SCDMA and TD-LTE innovation in China is reviewed based on key events in their innovation processes. At last, according to key criteria in the framework, the dynamics of TD-SCDMA and TD-LTE innovation system, and the transformations in terms of socio-technical change are summarized in Tables 10.2 and 10.3, respectively.

Table 10.2 TD-SCDMA innovation process

Stages and milestones	TIS configuration	TIS functions	Socio-technical transformation
Stage 1: development ***Mid-1990s to 1999.11*** • *System development was almost finished* • *Selected as international standard by ITU*	***Main actors***: *MPT, Cwill, CATT, Siemens Xinwei Telecom Technology* ***Relationships***: • *Government-research institutes;* • *Research institutes-tech vendors;* ***Institutions***: • *Initiated by government, with strong government intervention*	***Knowledge development and diffusion*** • *R&D project number and size (medium)* • *R&D orientation (medium)* ***Research direction*** • *Beliefs in growth potential (weak)* • *Incentives from price (weak)* • *Extent of regulatory pressures (strong)* • *Interest by leading customers (weak)*	***Technology change*** • *Increased patents* *Total: TD 148 + SCDMA 66,* *Domestic IPRs: TD:29.7% + SCDMA 51.5%* • *New technology is developed* ***Social system change*** • *Number of scientists* *Around 5000 scientists increased* • *Number of partners* *Domestic firm:38; Foreign firm: 8* • *Number of licenses* *1 TD-SCDMA license is issued* • *Employment* *Direct increase: 1.2 million* *Indirect increase: 2.7 million* • *Turnover* *Increased investment: 270 billion* *Increased consumption: 605 billion* • *Growth* *Increased customer: 0.23 billion;* *GDP growth by TD-SCDMA: 0.5%*
Stage 2: diffusion ***1998.01 to 2009.12*** • *Equipment and handsets were available* • *Network tests conducted* • *Spectrum was allocated* • *Commercial trail during 2008 Olympic games* • *Licenses were issued*	***Main actors***: *MII, Datang Group, NDRC, SASAC, TDIA, Putian, ZTE, and China Mobile company* ***Relationships***: • *Government-tech vendors;* • *Government-service providers;* • *Tech vendors-service providers;* ***Institutions***: • *Strong government intervention, with laws, regulations, decrees, subsidies,* etc.	***Entrepreneurial experimentation*** • *Increased new entrants (weak)* • *Increased new applications (weak)* ***Market formation*** • *Market size and Customer groups (weak)* • *Purchasing process (weak)* ***Legitimation*** • *Social acceptance (weak)* • *Institutions compliance (strong)* ***Resource mobilization*** • *Rising volume of capital (medium)* • *Changing of human resource (medium)* ***Positive externalities development*** • *Emergence of labour market (medium)* • *Emergence of service provider (weak)*	

Table 10.3 TD-LTE innovation process

Stages and milestones	TIS configuration	TIS functions	Socio-technical transformation
Stage 1: development 2005.03 to 2010.10 • System development was almost finished • Selected as international standard by ITU	**Main actors**: MII, RITT, Datang Telecom, Huawei, ZTE, Ericsson, Nokia, China Mobile, MediaTek, Universities, TDIA, MIIT **Relationships**: • Research institutes-tech vendors; • Research institutes-service providers; • Tech-vendors-service providers; **Institutions**: • Initiated by research institute, with strong support	**Knowledge development and diffusion** • R&D project number and size (strong) • R&D orientation (strong) **Research direction** • Beliefs in growth potential (strong) • Incentives from price (medium) • Extent of regulatory pressures (medium) • Interest by leading customers (strong)	**Technology change** • Increased patents Total: TD 148 + LTE 320 Domestic IPRs in total: 65% • New technology is developed **Social system change** • Number of scientists Around 15,000 scientists increased • Number of partners Domestic firm:30; Foreign firm: 7 • Number of licenses 3 TD-LTE licenses are issued • Employment Direct increase: 2.2 million Indirect increase: 4.5 million • Turnover Increased investment: 1000 billion Increased consumption: 1500 billion • Growth Increased customer: 0.87 billion GDP growth by TD-LTE: 2.3%
Stage 2: diffusion 2010.10 to 2015.02 • Equipment and handsets were available • Network tests conducted • Spectrum was allocated • Licenses were issued	**Main actors**: MII, RITT, Datang Telecom, Huawei, ZTE, Ericsson, Nokia, China Mobile, MediaTek, Universities, TDIA, MIIT **Relationships**: • Government-vendors and providers; • Tech vendors-service providers; • Industrial alliance-vendors and providers; • Customers-vendors and providers **Institutions**: • Medium government intervention, with laws, regulations, decrees, subsidies, etc. • Emerging demands from the market have oriented the system	**Entrepreneurial experimentation** • Increased new entrants (strong) • Increased new applications (strong) **Market formation** • Market size and Customer (strong) • Purchasing process (strong) **Legitimation** • Social acceptance (medium) • Institutions compliance (medium) **Resource mobilization** • Rising volume of capital (strong) • Changing of human resource (strong) **Positive externalities development** • Emergence of labour market (strong) • Emergence of service provider (strong)	

Wireless Mobile System Innovation and Telecommunication Industry in China

Traditionally, China is known as a latecomer with a weak radical of technology innovation and a long history of technology import. With the aim to catch up through technology innovation, the government in China has issued several "National Five-year Plan" to promote the capability of indigenous technology innovation, and takes the lead in many technology innovation projects by manoeuvring the state-controlled industry to invest in the technology development and diffusion (Kennedy 2006; Guan et al. 2009; Kwak et al. 2011; Liu et al. 2011; Tsai and Wang 2011; Zhu 2014). Driven by the government, China developed TD-SCDMA and TD-LTE technology have been officially authorized by the International Telecommunication Union (ITU) as international standards for the third and the fourth generation (3G and 4G) of mobile system.

Historically, the first generation of mobile system was launched around 1970s, only voice communication was capable. Then in the early 1990s, the 2G system was introduced. In this era, Global System for Mobile communication (GSM) and narrowband CDMA were applied as two main international standards. GSM was initiated in Europe and CDMA was issued in US (Yan 2007). In 1999, the International Telecommunication Union (ITU) approved three 3G international standards, known as WCDMA, CDMA2000, and TD-SCDMA. CDMA2000 and WCDMA were based on CDMA and GSM networks, and mainly commercialized in EU and US to replace the old system, respectively. TD-SCDMA is introduced by China, requiring completely new supporting networks (Lyytinen and King 2002). The standard was believed as an attempt to develop indigenous technology and avoid technology dependency (Gao and Liu 2012). TD-LTE and FDD-LTE are authorized as two international 4G mobile system standards by ITU. TD-LTE system is derived from TD-SCDMA in last generation, and FDD-LTE is backward compatible to WDMA and CDMA2000 (Wang and Kim 2007).

In the telecommunication industry, the government holds strong national will to promote indigenous technology innovation, with the purpose of getting rid of foreign dependency. Besides, the environment is asymmetric and complex due to the intense confliction of bureaucratic interests among different interests groups. Moreover, the industry is always dynamic with seemingly endless reconsolidations (Xia 2012). Interest groups are always compete with each other for setting up new equilibriums, and the frequency and degree vary across countries related with their history, institutions, legal systems, property rights and cultural norms (Yan 2007). Three state-own enterprises, China Mobile, Unicom, and Telecom, have constituted the service operator group. The government plays as a full controlling shareholder of these "big three", gave them licenses, located spectrums, and offered support both directly and indirectly (Kwak et al. 2011). In market, each firm has its own network with research institutes, service sub-providers, and equipment manufacturers. These equipment manufacturers could be either domestic firms or foreign companies. At last, research institutes and industry alliances like TDIA also play important roles in the innovation.

Moreover, periodical reformation is another significant characteristic about China's telecommunication industry (Gao et al. 2013). Some reforms were target oriented, while some of them were typically concurrent with the wider government reforms. For instance, around year 2008, after a serious of mergers and reorganizes, Chinese government reduced the number of main service providers from six to three, as China Mobile, China Unicom, and China Telecom in current. In this round of reform, to promote domestic TD-SCDMA was the major consideration. While in this year, the central government started "super ministry system reform". Many giant ministries were merged and reconstructed. One of the main authorities in current telecommunication field—Ministry of Industry and Information Technology, was established and responds for issuing policies, supervising, promoting innovation, and information security (Xia 2011). This revolutionary change was mainly concurrent with government reform. Nonetheless, innovations like TD-SCDMA and TD-LTE were achieved by TISs in such a dynamic industry, and it has been witnessed the industry sustainability was also significantly improved along with the innovations and its revolutions.

TD-SCDMA Innovation in China

Stage 1: technology development (Mid-1990s to November 1999)

In mid-1990s, Chinese government then determined to catching-up via developing indigenous technologies by strongly supporting its domestic technology enterprises. Initially, Ministry of Posts and Telecommunications (MPT) mandated China Academy of Telecommunications Technology (CATT) to explore the third generation of mobile technology. In 1995, manipulated by MPT, CATT and Cwill formed a joint venture named as Xinwei Telecom Technology. For solving the problem of signal transmission, technology solution issued by Siemens was selected. Earlier on, Siemens had invested a lot on the R&D of 3G, as a result, Siemens owned the patents of TD duplex signal transmission technology (Yan 2007; Gao et al. 2014). In January 1998, MPT held a meeting in Beijing to discuss practical issues of preparing China's 3G proposal. In the meeting, the MPT chief scientist stressed strong support of government to develop indigenous 3G technology. With strong interests from the government, this meeting could be counted as the beginning of China's official 3G standardization. In 5th Nov 1999, ITU officially granted China's TD-SCDMA as one of the three international 3G standards (Stewart et al. 2011).

Stage 2: technology diffusion (January 1998 to December 2009)

Initially, China's TD-SCDMA even did not generate any interests from Chinese domestic technology vendors and services operators. Understandable, Chinese network operators and technology vendors were facing great uncertain for TD-SCDMA's future, thus they took the strategy of "wait and see". Chinese government determined to make every effort to promote its indigenous TD-SCDMA standard. On 23rd October 2002, MII issued Decree No. 479, which allocated 155 MHz asymmetrical frequencies in overall spectrum to TD-SCDMA system. In contrast, WCDMA and CDMA2000 acquired 60 MHz each according to the decree (Yan 2007). This move had sent out a strong signal to everyone that Chinese government would have no hesitate in supporting TD-SCDMA. In November 2003, MII incited Datang Telecom to transfer its key IPRs of TD-SCDMA system to another two SOEs—Putian and ZTE, which was aiming to accelerate the TD commercialization by transferring their R&D attentions from WCDMA and CDMA2000 to China's own TD-SCDMA. To ensure the transfer could be finished quickly and smoothly, the government also provided substantial financial compensation to Datang (Yan 2007). On 20th January 2006, with the aim to prevent domestic firms to prepare the duplicated productions for 3G products, MII issued the No. 91 Decree to legitimize TD-SCDMA as a national standard, and published 23 technology specifications.

Moreover, the government asked China Mobile to offer TD-SCDMA services during 2008 Beijing Olympic Games, in support of the national initiative of showing newly technology achievements to the world. In March 2007, China Mobile gradually started to deploy TD-SCDMA network in eight big cities which would host Olympic Games. On 1st August 2008, a week before Olympics opening ceremony, China Mobile officially began to use TD-SCDMA network to provide 3G services like video-telephone and mobile television broadcast. On 7th January 2009, when TD-SCDMA industrial value chain was established, MII then officially issued 3G operation licenses to the market. China Mobile as the largest operator was ordered to use TD-SCDMA system, and China Unicom and China Telecom were granted the licenses for WCDMA and CDMA2000, respectively.

TD-LTE Innovation in China

Stage 1: technology development (March 2005 to October 2010)

In March 2005, with the support from government, TD-LTE was first proposed by Datang Telecom. Later in 2005, Ministry of Information Industry (MII) mandated its affiliate Research Institute of Telecommunication Transmissions (RITT) to respond for TD-LTE standardization. Several technology vendors and network operators were invited to participate in the program by RITT, like Datang, Huawei, Ericsson, and China Mobile. Meanwhile, some national Universities like Tsinghua and Shanghai Jiaotong University, were also invited. At the beginning of 2008, influenced by the sixth government reform, MII was replaced by Ministry of Industry and Information Technology (MIIT), which mainly responded for issuing industry policies, supervising, promoting innovation, managing telecommunication industry, and protecting information security. In October 2008, according to an interviewee's recall, the then premier WEN Jiabao had four times written instructions for TD-LTE standardization, and listed TD-LTE development as one of the most significant approach to stimulate domestic economy. After a year's intensive R&D, in the end of 2009, MIIT launched the first time large-scale tests of TD-LTE utilization. Later in October 2010, TD-LTE with FDD-LTE were officially selected as two international 4G standards by ITU (Stewart et al. 2011).

Stage 2: technology diffusion (October 2010 to February 2015)

On 15th October 2010, at World Telecommunication Conference, the deputy director of State Radio Administration, XIE Cun disclosed that Chinese government had decided to grant in total 190 MHz spectrum to TD-LTE. While in contrast, only 40 MHz for FDD-LTE, which has obviously shown the preferential strategy. Then on 19th December 2012, China Mobile launched the commercialization of TD-LTE first at Hong Kong, and achieved the data roaming with Shen Zhen's TD-LTE network. Technology vendors and network operators interested in 4G era have shown enough enthusiasm to participate. For instance, on 27th February 2013, at GTI Summit (Global TD-LTE Initiative), China Mobile published 4 LTE smartphones and 4 LTE MIFI products cooperated with HTC, LG, Huawei, and ZTE. Moreover, China Mobile had invested over 200 billion RMB in procurement, with more than 207 thousand bases were purchased. The other two major operators China Unicom and China Telecom still put their emphasis on FDD-LTE system, and took the strategy of "wait and see" as they did in the 3G era.

In October 2013, SASAC and MIIT jointly launched TD-LTE Industrialization Special Program (TISP) to improve the TD-LTE R&D capability and industrialization. With a budget of 34 billion RMB, TISP offered subsidy for domestic firms, joint ventures, and research institutes to invest in TD-LTE industrialization. The formation of TISP had shown the determination of Chinese government on promoting indigenous 4G development, which had passed a significant signal to the TD industry and financial market. Moreover, Chinese government spent nearly 20 billion RMB on the acquisition of two domestic chip manufacturers, Spreadtrum and RDA Microelectronics, in order to form a powerful technology vendor to participate in global competition on TD chip manufacturing. On 4th December 2013, MIIT officially issued TD-LTE licenses to three network operators but with different spectrum allocation. China Mobile was granted with 130 MHz bandwidth in total, China Unicom and China Telecom each had 40 MHz bandwidth. However, the license of FDD-LTE was granted at 27th February 2015.

Discussion, Implication and Conclusion

Socio-technical Transformation with TD-SCDMA and TD-LTE Innovation System (RQ1)

According to the case of TD-SCDMA and TD-LTE innovation, the whole innovation process is divided into the stage of technology development and technology diffusion. In different stages, the innovation system has different configurations, hence impact the functions of the system. Along with the process of innovation, the TIS is dynamic, and the functions of TIS have directly and indirectly influenced the process of technological change. For instance, as Table 10.3 indicates, TD-LTE is developed with totally 468 relevant patents increased, which should be own to the well-performed functions of knowledge development and diffusion, as well as research direction in terms of technology change. Moreover, due to the well-functioned TIS in terms of conducting entrepreneurial experimentation, formatting the market, mobilizing the resource and legitimating, the social system of TD-LTE innovation has been significantly affected. For instance, more scientists (around 15,000) and organizations (37) are involved, and the tasks of growth in terms of innovation are remarkably achieved (6.7 million increased employment, 2500 billion increased turnover, 0.87 billion increased customers, and 2.3% increased GDP). As the result, along with the innovation, technology is developed, industry is well promoted, and domestic vendors like Huawei, ZTE and MediaTek had not only broken the dependency with foreign technologies, but also gradually grown into international giants in telecommunication field. Although the examples here are taken from the case of TD-LTE innovation, the case of TD-SCDMA innovation also reveals the same dynamics. Therefore, the theoretical duplication that formed by two case studies have confirmed that, the sustainability of China's telecommunication industry has been significantly enhanced by TD-SCDMA and TD-LTE innovation systems, due to their significant contribution to the sustained socio-technical change.

Apart from theoretical duplications that the cases provided, the distinctions in terms of degree and effect of sustainability change are also highlighted by TD-SCDMA and TD-LTE innovation. The distinction maintains a great significance, as the socio-technical transformation that observed is mainly driven by the technological innovation system. Which means, the reason that differences between TD-SCDMA and TD-LTE's socio-technical transformation can exist, is because there exists distinctions between the TIS for each of them. To explore such kind of differences could contribute to improve the understanding of how sustainability of the industry relates with different characterised technological innovation systems. Associating with differences of socio-technical transformations that shown in Tables 10.2 and 10.3, we then make a brief comparison between these two innovations from the perspectives of social system change and technology change.

Considering from the perspective of socio-technical change, the process is well-sustained from TD-SCDMA to TD-LTE. However, it is also obvious that, the transformation in 4G innovation is far more efficient and better achieved than the 3G. For instance, in terms of technology changes, the development and diffusion cycle of TD-LTE has been significantly shortened if compared with TD-SCDMA. If considering from the situation of social system change, the numbers of participants, employments, and turnovers that increased by TD-LTE innovation are nearly three times more than TD-SCDMA (see socio-technical transformation volume in Tables 10.2 and 10.3). Moreover, it is also noteworthy that, at 3G era, China Mobile took more than three years to boost its 3G subscribers from 10.5 to 87.9 million. In contrast, TD-LTE has attracted more than 50 million users within just ten month. Therefore, the comparison between two innovations has shown that, although the transformation from 3G to 4G is well-sustained, the TD-LTE innovation is more efficient and better achieved than the other. As discussed, the differences are mainly caused by the differences between the two innovation systems, thus this distinction could be helpful to understand what kind of technological innovation system is better in such kind of cases.

TIS Comparison Between TD-SCDMA and TD-LTE (RQ2)

The comparison between Tables 10.2 and 10.3 has revealed the differences between the effects of TIS functions in each innovation. In general, TIS of TD-LTE functions better than TD-SCDMA. As the tables indicate, the number and scale of R&D in TD-LTE is more and larger than TD-SCDMA; undergone the era of 3G, beliefs in TD-LTE's growth potential and interests by leading customers are completely stronger than TD-SCDMA; even in capital and financial market, the investment and consumption relates with TD-LTE is nearly three times more than TD-SCDMA. Therefore, through comparing the function effects between the two TISs, it is not difficult to draw the conclusion that TIS of TD-LTE functions better than TD-SCDMA, and the TIS in current have shown more potential in terms of enhancing the sustainability of industry.

As suggested by reviewed literature, differences in terms of TIS functionality are mainly caused by the differences in the configuration. First of all, the main actors of TD-LTE are more stable and have been clarified at the very beginning stage; while the actors of TD-SCDMA are relatively dynamic. For instance, the technology vendors like Huawei and ZTE, and service provider like China Mobile are not involved in the system until the diffusion stage; while in TD-LTE innovation, the core participants, like government institutes (MIIT), technology vendors (Huawei, ZTE, MediaTek, Ericsson), service operator (China Mobile), industrial alliance (TDIA), and research institutes (Universities) are mostly enrolled in the system at the very beginning stage. Second, relationships in TD-SCDMA innovation system are mostly composed by formal networks, and relatively deficient if compared with the later system. For instance, at the 3G era, the innovation was initialed by the government, and only two kinds of core networks were maintained in the system (government-research institutions networks and research institutions-technology vendor's networks). In contrast, the relationships in TD-LTE innovation system are much more diversified. For instance, many informal networks like industrial alliance and customers with technology vendors and service providers are maintained and active in TD-LTE system. Besides, core networks are all built up at the initial stage of innovation, even if the networks that mainly function at the diffusion stage. At last, the differences also reflect at the institutions in the system. In terms of the 3G TIS, the innovation was mainly pushed by the government with strong institutional interventions, while in the 4G TIS, the interventions from the government are slightly lighten than the 3G era, and the demand powers from the market have taken effects.

In fact, the result from case studies have confirmed the suggestion from Bergek et al. (2008), that early enrollment of main actors could reduce the uncertainty of innovation, hence improve the performance of TIS. This is also appropriate to explain why early built networks in TD-LTE innovation system could facilitate the function of system from formation to maintenance. By far, based on the function approach of TIS analysis, the TD-SCDMA and TD-LTE innovation systems are critically compared in terms of the differences of configurations and effects of functions. The 4G innovation system is approved to be more efficient and better functioned than the 3G innovation system.

Findings

After analysing the result of comparison between the 3G and 4G innovation systems, a serious of findings are summarized as follows. Firstly, a well-functioned technological innovation system can significantly contribute to the sustainability of IT industry, as it can significantly push forward the process of socio-technical transformation (RQ1). Secondly, the configuration of technological innovation system determines the functionality of the system. For enhancing the sustainability of industry, a technological innovation system must have an appropriate configuration, which can be characterised as: constitutes by stable and early enrolled core actors, who connected with diversified and early built networks, and influenced by both regulative powers like institutional intervention and normative incentives like demands from the market (RQ2). Thirdly, compared with TD-SCDMA innovation system, the improvement of TD-LTE innovation system reveals that along with sustainable socio-technical transformation (from 3G to 4G), both actors and networks in industry get matured and diversified, which could significantly facilitate the formation and maintenance of technological innovation system, hence the sustainability of industry.

Research Implications

This work contributes to innovation studies in IS research in four ways: Firstly, for innovation literature, this work extent current literature by employing the model of sustainable socio-technical change to bridge the gap between functions of technological innovation system and sustainability of industry, and summarizing what kind of TIS is better for industry sustainability through comparing two related innovation systems in terms of mobile system innovations in China. Secondly, based on the model of socio-technical change and approach of TIS functions analysis, the conceptual framework that presented in this work has demonstrated an original thinking about how industry sustainability can be enhanced by the well-functioned TIS. Thirdly, the socio-technical change model and TIS function scheme of analysis have been applied to study the TD-SCDMA and TD-LTE innovation cases in this work, which to some extent, have broaden the understanding of how these analytical schemes can be applied in practice. At last, for practice, the case studies of technology innovation in China's telecommunication industry provide rich descriptions about how new technology is developed and diffused. For other late-coming countries with the aim to establish a sustainable IT industry through indigenous technology innovation, China has offered a valuable reference for them.

Conclusion

Underpinning by the model of socio-technical transformation and the frame of technology innovation system, this work uncovers how sustainability of IT industry can be impacted by technological innovation systems, and what a technological innovation system should be if aims to enhance the industry sustainability. Qualitative case study method with documentary research and semi-structured interviews as the strategies for data collection is applied. Cases of TD-SCDMA and TD-LTE innovations in China are comparatively examined, with several findings are discussed accordingly. This work argues that, a well-functioned technological innovation system can significantly contribute to the sustainability of IT industry, by significantly pushing forward the process of socio-technical transformation. Besides, a well-configured technological innovation system could be characterised as: constitutes by stable and early enrolled core actors, who connected with diversified and early built networks, and influenced by both regulative powers and normative incentives.

Acknowledgements Guanyu Liu is a researcher, at the Institute for Development Policy and Management (IDPM), University of Manchester, United Kingdom. His research interest is technology innovation in China.

Ping Gao is a senior lecturer in Development Informatics, at the Institute for Development Policy and Management (IDPM), University of Manchester, United Kingdom. His current research focus is technology innovation in developing countries.

References

Baxter, P., & Jack, S. (2008). Qualitative case study methodology: Study design and implementation for novice researchers. *The Qualitative Report, 13*(4), 544–559.

Bergek, A., Jacobsson, S., Carlsson, B., Lindmark, S., & Rickne, A. (2008). Analyzing the functional dynamics of technological innovation systems: A scheme of analysis. *Research Policy, 37*(3), 407–429.

Carlsson, B. (2006). Internationalization of innovation systems: A survey of the literature. *Research Policy, 35*(1), 56–67.

Carlsson, B., Jacobsson, S., Holmén, M., & Rickne, A. (2002). Innovation systems analytical and methodological issues. *Research Policy, 31*(2), 233–245.

Chang, P. L., & Shih, H. Y. (2004). The innovation systems of Taiwan and China: A comparative analysis. *Technovation, 24*(7), 529–539.

Choung, J., Hameed, T., & Ji, I. (2012). Catch-up in ICT standards: Policy, implementation and standards-setting in South Korea. *Technological Forecasting and Social Change, 79*(4), 771–788.

Chung, C.-C. (2013). Government, policy-making and the development of innovation system: The cases of Taiwanese pharmaceutical biotechnology policies (2000–2008). *Research Policy, 42*(5), 1053–1071.

Crossan, M. M., & Apaydin, M. (2010). A multi-dimensional framework of organizational innovation: A systematic review of the literature. *Journal of Management Studies, 47*(6), 1154–1191.

Crowston, K., & Myers, M. D. (2004). Information technology and the transformation of industries: Three research perspectives. *The Journal of Strategic Information Systems, 13*(1), 5–28.

Currie, W. L., & Guah, M. W. (2007). Conflicting institutional logics: A national programme for IT in the organisational field of healthcare. *Journal of Information Technology, 22*(3), 235–247.

Damsgaard, J., & Lyytinen, K. (2001). The role of intermediating institutions in the diffusion of Electronic Data Interchange (EDI) how industry. *The Information Society, 17,* 195–210.

Edquist, C., & Hommen, L. (1999). Systems of innovation theory and policy for the demand side. *Technology in Society, 21*(1), 63–79.

Fagerberg, J. (2005). Innovation a guide to the literature. In J. Fagerberg, D. Mowery, & R. R. Nelson (Eds.), *The Oxford handbook of innovation.* Oxford: Oxford University Press.

Fagerberg, J., & Srholec, M. (2008). National innovation systems, capabilities and economic development. *Research Policy, 37*(9), 1417–1435.

Freeman, C. (2002). Continental, national and sub-national innovation systems-complementarity and economic growth. *Research Policy, 31,* 191–211.

Funk, J. L., & Methe, D. T. (2001). Market- and committee-based mechanisms in the creation and diffusion of global industry standards the case of mobil. *Research Policy, 30*(4), 589–610.

Gao, P., Lyytinen, K., & Somasundaram, R. (2013). Strategy of China's telecommunication Transformation. In *AMCIS.*

Gao, X., & Liu, J. (2012). Catching up through the development of technology standard: The case of TD-SCDMA in China. *Telecommunications Policy, 36*(7), 531–545.

Gao, P., Yu, J., & Lyytinen, K. (2014). Government in standardization in the catching-up context: Case of China's mobile system. *Telecommunications Policy, 38*(2), 200–209.

Geels, F. W. (2002). Technological transitions as evolutionary reconfiguration processes a multi-level perspective and a case-study. *Research Policy, 31*(8–9), 1257–1274.
Geels, F. W., & Schot, J. (2007). Typology of sociotechnical transition pathways. *Research Policy, 36*(3), 399–417.
Guan, J. C., Yam, R. C. M., Tang, E. P. Y., & Lau, A. K. W. (2009). Innovation strategy and performance during economic transition: Evidences in Beijing, China. *Research Policy, 38*(5), 802–812.
Hekkert, M. P., & Negro, S. O. (2009). Functions of innovation systems as a framework to understand sustainable technological change: Empirical evidence for earlier claims. *Technological Forecasting and Social Change, 76*(4), 584–594.
Hekkert, M. P., Suurs, R. A. A., Negro, S. O., Kuhlmann, S., & Smits, R. E. H. M. (2007). Functions of innovation systems: A new approach for analysing technological change. *Technological Forecasting and Social Change, 74*(4), 413–432.
Howcroft, D., Mitev, N., & Wilson, M. (2004). What we may learn from social shaping of technology approach. In J. Mingers & L. Willcocks (Eds.), *Social theory and philosophy for information systems*. London: Wiley.
Iyer, G. R., LaPlaca, P. J., & Sharma, A. (2006). Innovation and new product introductions in emerging markets: Strategic recommendations for the Indian market. *Industrial Marketing Management, 35*(3), 373–382.
Kaplan, B., & Maxwell, J. A. (1994). Qualitative research methods for evaluating computer information systems. In J. G. Anderson, C. E. Aydin, & S. J. Jay (Eds.), *Evaluating health care information systems, methods and applications*. Thousand Oaks, CA: Sage.
Kennedy, S. (2006). The political economy of standards coalitions: Explaining China's involvement in high-tech standards wars. *Asia Policy, 2*(1), 41–62.
King, J. L., Gurbaxani, V., Kraemer, K. L., McFarlan, F. W., Raman, K. S., & Yap, C. S. (1994). Institutional factors in information technology innovation. *Information System Research, 2*(5), 139–169.
Klein, H. K., & Hirschheim, R. A. (1989). Legitimation in information systems development: A social change perspective. *Office Technology and People, 5*(1), 29–46.
Kshetri, N., Palvia, P., & Dai, H. (2011). Chinese institutions and standardization: The case of government support to domestic third generation cellular standard. *Telecommunications Policy, 35*(5), 399–412.
Kwak, J., Lee, H., & Chung, D. B. (2012). The evolution of alliance structure in China's mobile telecommunication industry and implications for international standardization. *Telecommunications Policy, 36*(10–11), 966–976.
Kwak, J., Lee, H., & Fomin, V. V. (2011). Government coordination of conflicting interests in standardisation: Case studies of indigenous ICT standards in China and South Korea. *Technology Analysis & Strategic Management, 23*(7), 789–806.
Lee, H., & Oh, S. (2006). A standards war waged by a developing country: Understanding international standard setting from the actor-network perspective. *The Journal of Strategic Information Systems, 15*(3), 177–195.
Liu, F.-C., Simon, D. F., Sun, Y.-T., & Cao, C. (2011). China's innovation policies: Evolution, institutional structure, and trajectory. *Research Policy, 40*(7), 917–931.
Lundvall, B.-Å. (2007). National innovation systems—Analytical concept and development tool. *Industry and Innovation, 14*(1), 95–119.
Lundvall, B.-Å., Johnson, B., Andersen, E. S., & Dalum, B. (2002). National systems of production, innovation and competence building. *Research Policy, 31*(2), 213–231.
Lyytinen, K., & King, J. L. (2002). Around the cradle of the wireless revolution: The emergence and evolution of cellular telephony. *Telecommunications Policy, 30*(11), 587–604.
Lyytinen, K., & Newman, M. (2008). Explaining information systems change: A punctuated socio-technical change model. *European Journal of Information Systems, 17,* 589–613.
Markard, J., & Truffer, B. (2008). Technological innovation systems and the multi-level perspective: Towards an integrated framework. *Research Policy, 37*(4), 596–615.

Montealegre, R. (1999). A temporal model of institutional interventions for information technology adoption in less-developed countries. *Journal of Management Information Systems, 16*(1), 207.

Nelson, R. R., & Nelson, K. (2002). Technology, institutions, and innovation systems. *Research Policy, 31*(4), 265–272.

Orlikowski, W., & Robey, D. (1991). Information technology and the structuring of organizations. *Information System Research, 2*(2), 121–143.

Patton, M. Q. (2002). *Qualitative evaluation and research methods* (Third Edit ed.). Thousand Oaks: Sage Publications.

Scott-Morton, M. S. (1991). *The corporation of the 1990s: Information technology and organizational transformation*. New York: Oxford University Press.

Siu, W., Lin, T., Fang, W., & Liu, Z. (2006). An institutional analysis of the new product development process of small and medium enterprises (SMEs) in China, Hong Kong and Taiwan. *Industrial Marketing Management, 35*(3), 323–335.

Stewart, J., Shen, X., Wang, C., & Graham, I. (2011). From 3G to 4G: Standards and the development of mobile broadband in China. *Technology Analysis & Strategic Management, 23* (7), 773–788.

Teo, H. H., Wei, K. K., & Benbasat, I. (2014). Predicting intention to adopt interorganizational linkages: An institutional perspective. *MIS Quarterly, 27*(1), 19–49.

Tilson, D., & Lyytinen, K. (2006a). The 3G transition: Changes in the US wireless industry. *Telecommunications Policy, 30*(10–11), 569–586.

Tilson, D., & Lyytinen, K. (2006b). Coordination of technology and diverse organizational actors during service innovation—The case of wireless. *Telecommunications Policy, 30*(10–11), 569–586.

Tsai, C., & Wang, J. (2011). How China institutional changes influence industry development? The case of TD-SCDMA industrialization. In *Innovation, strategy, and structure-organization, institutions, systems and regions*, 2011 Copenhagen, Denmark. DRUID.

Wang, J.-H. (2007). From technological catch-up to innovation-based economic growth: South Korea and Taiwan compared. *Journal of Development Studies, 43*(6), 1084–1104.

Wang, J., & Kim, S. (2007). Time to get in: The contrasting stories about government interventions in information technology standards (the case of CDMA and IMT-2000 in Korea). *Government Information Quarterly, 24*(1), 115–134.

Xia, J. (2011). The third-generation-mobile (3G) policy and deployment in China: Current status, challenges, and prospects. *Telecommunications Policy, 35*(1), 51–63.

Xia, J. (2012). China's telecommunications industry in the era of 3G and beyond: Market, technology, and institutions. *Telecommunications Policy, 36*(10–11), 793–797.

Xiao, X., Califf, C. B., Sarker, S., & Sarker, S. (2013). ICT innovation in emerging economies: A review of the existing literature and a framework for future research. *Journal of Information Technology, 28*(4), 264–278.

Yan, H. (2007). Appropriability, proximity, routines and innovation: The 3G standard setting strategy and indigenous innovation policy in China: IS TD-SCDMA a Flagship? In *Appropriability, proximity, routines and innovation*, 2007 Copenhagen, CBS, Denmark (pp. 1–24). DRUID.

Yin, R. K. (2009). *Case study research: Design and methods* (4th ed.). Thousand Oaks: Sage Publications.

Yu, J., Zhang, Y., & Gao, P. (2012). Examining China's technology policies for wireless broadband infrastructure. *Telecommunications Policy, 36*(10–11), 847–857.

Zhang, J., & Liang, X.-J. (2012). Promoting green ICT in China: A framework based on innovation system approaches. *Telecommunications Policy, 36*(10–11), 997–1013.

Zhu, X. (2014). Mandate Versus Championship: Vertical government intervention and diffusion of innovation in public services in authoritarian China. *Public Management Review, 16*(1), 117–139.

Zucker, D. M. (2009). *How to do case study research*. Massachusetts, US: School of Nursing Faculty, University of Massachusetts.

Chapter 11
Structures and Strategies of Chinese Companies in Key Enabling and Advanced Manufacturing Technologies

Rainer Frietsch and Peter Neuhäusler

Abstract While at the EU-level there are many programmes and efforts to increase the interaction and collaboration with China, policies have also been set up and (partially) implemented to keep Europe's competitive edge over China, but also other competitors. A number of technological fields are nominated by the European Commission as an important input or precondition for Europe's future competitiveness, among them the so called Key Enabling Technologies (KETs). This chapter examines where Chinese companies stand in terms of national and international competitiveness in these Key Enabling Technologies. A more general question is whether Europe is not taking a realistic view of its current and future position with regard to the KETs. Our empirical analysis shows that Europe's current position in AMT seems to be good—mainly due to a high performance of Germany, but also France and the UK—while it is rather poor in KETs. Concerning the potential threat from Chinese companies, it seems that they are shortening the gap. Recently, the vast majority of patent applications, both in KETs and in AMT, at SIPO stem from Chinese applicants. The answer to the question "How does China perform?" is quite clear at the moment. It does not yet perform very well on the international stage, but the national market for technologies is mostly dominated by Chinese inventors/companies. The answer to the second research question whether Europe is daydreaming about its current and especially its future positioning in KETs and AMT is: "Most probably yes". The good news for Europe is that it still holds strong positions in Societal Grand Challenges, which will contribute even more to jobs and growth in Europe than KETs and AMT alone. The idea that KETs and AMT not only provide direct input to this goal of growth, but also indirectly help to keep the competitive edge in the Grand Challenges, is a reasonable one.

R. Frietsch (✉) · P. Neuhäusler
Fraunhofer Institute for Systems and Innovation Research, Karlsruhe, Germany
e-mail: Rainer.Frietsch@isi.fraunhofer.de

R. Frietsch
Institute for Policy and Management, Chinese Academy of Sciences, Beijing, China

P. Neuhäusler
Innovation Economics, Berlin University of Technology, Berlin, Germany

T. Clarke and K. Lee (eds.), *Innovation in the Asia Pacific*,
https://doi.org/10.1007/978-981-10-5895-0_11

Keywords Key enabling technologies · KET · Advanced manufacturing technologies · AMT · China · Competitiveness · Patent

Introduction

Without any doubt, the most dynamic country of the past decade in terms of its economic development and its science and innovation system is China. For some, this development is an opportunity, while others see it as a threat. Those who see the opportunities refer to the growing market and to a new division of labour in international production and value chains. Those who see the threat are mainly worried about China challenging their basic competences and invading their established markets and taking their market shares.

Proponents and opponents of the Chinese thread can be found in Europe, and in many countries, not only in science and industry, but also among policymakers. While at the EU-level there are many programmes and efforts to increase the interaction and collaboration with China, policies have also been set up and (partially) implemented to keep Europe's competitive edge over China, but also other competitors—mainly the USA, Japan, or South Korea. The Innovation Union—the European Union's new innovation policy strategy—aims high to take the lead in certain technological areas and innovation-driven sectors, with the intention to create jobs and wealth in Europe: "By improving conditions and access to finance for research and innovation in Europe, we can ensure that innovative ideas can be turned into products and services that create growth and jobs." (European Commission 2013, p. 8).

Horizon 2020, the EU's current funding programme, continues previous efforts to keep the competitive edge. All the framework programmes so far have had similar aims, mainly striving to stay scientifically and economically ahead of the US and also Japan, and delivering the message to member states that there is clear priority for science and technology. But the current programme sends a different signal, to some extent, as it is explicitly stated that scientific excellence takes priority over the equal distribution of funds. In addition, it is intended to make a stronger differentiation between research funding and structural funds, which could result in a higher efficiency and more value for money of the European innovation system (Veugelers et al. 2015).

In addition, a different approach and idea underlies this new programme, namely that of a mission orientation. Similar to several other countries, the Societal Grand Challenges (SGCs) guide policy making and agenda setting in terms of science funding and innovation policy. Europe has formulated seven such Societal Grand Challenges including energy, mobility, climate, health, food, and security.[1] The challenges are (effectively maybe not intentionally) defined according to existing

[1]The seventh challenge is called "Inclusive, innovative and reflective societies", but is not analysed in this chapter as its technological foundations are rather limited so it cannot be analysed with the tools and approach applied here.

strengths in Europe and the intention is to keep or even enhance them. A number of technological fields are named as an important input or precondition for competitiveness in these Societal Grand Challenges. Crucial technologies are listed under the acronym of LEIT—Leadership in Enabling and Industrial Technologies, for example, advanced computing, robotics, or new electronic components. As a particular subfield of LEITs, the Key Enabling Technologies (KETs) have already played an outstanding role since FP7—the seventh framework programme of the EU. KETs comprise nanotechnology, photonics, industrial biotechnology, advanced materials and micro- and nano-electronics. Advanced Manufacturing Technologies (AMT) are seen as a cross-cutting area that supports the other five KETs and therefore plays a special role within this group. AMT cover process technologies that are used to produce any of the other five KETs. These typically include production apparatus, equipment and procedures for the manufacture of specific materials and components (IDEA Consult et al. 2015).

This chapter examines where Chinese companies stand in terms of national and international competitiveness in these Key Enabling Technologies as defined by the European Commission. A more general question is whether Europe is not taking a realistic view of its current and future position with regard to the KETs. The main task therefore is to provide empirical evidence for the role of innovation in AMT and KETs of Chinese companies on their home market, but also abroad. We try to do this by linking the innovation output of companies with their input in terms of R&D expenditures. We mainly rely on previous work analysing the general positioning of Europe in KETs (Neuhäusler et al. 2015). This chapter analyses China's positioning and puts Europe's position into perspective. For this purpose, the basic questions are: Which are the Chinese firms responsible for most of the patent filings in AMT and KETs? Where were their inventions made? Where do Chinese firms protect their intellectual property and which technology markets do they address? Our approach is based on matching firms on the EU R&D Scoreboard (including subsidiaries) with patent applicants from the PATSTAT database at the level of company/applicant names.

The chapter is structured as follows. In the next section we briefly describe the methods, before providing general empirical evidence from our patent database analyses in section three. Section four provides empirical data employing the matched dataset between the R&D Scoreboard companies and the patent database, with a special focus on Chinese firms. Section five discusses the results against the background of European policies and concludes.

Methods

Patent Data

The patent data for the study were extracted from the "EPO Worldwide Patent Statistical Database" (PATSTAT). PATSTAT contains information about published patents from 83 patent authorities worldwide, dating back to the late 19th century. It includes all the information that is stated on a patent application, i.e. application authorities (patent offices), several patent relevant dates (priority-, filing-, and publication date), the type of application (invention patent, utility model, etc.), inventor and applicant addresses, patent families, patent classifications (IPC and ECLA), title and abstract of a patent filing, technical relations and continuations, as well as citations to patents and to non-patent literature. We used the automated tool developed by the K.U. Leuven for name cleaning and applicant name harmonization (Du Plessis et al. 2009; Magerman et al. 2009; Peeters et al. 2009). The patents in our analyses are counted according to their year of worldwide first filing, which is commonly known as the priority year. This is the earliest registered date in the patent process and is therefore closest to the date of invention. To allow international comparability of technological/inventive capabilities, we follow a concept suggested by Frietsch and Schmoch (2010) called transnational patents, which is able to overcome the home advantage of domestic applicants, so that a comparison of technological strengths and weaknesses becomes possible—beyond home advantages and unequal market orientations. In detail, we count all patent families that have at least one PCT or EPO application as a member.

A harmonized version of the data from the PATSTAT database was matched at the level of patent applicants with data from the R&D Scoreboard at the level of individual companies (including subsidiaries).

The EU Industrial R&D Investment Scoreboard

The European Union's R&D Scoreboard[2] collects data from the publicly available audited accounts of companies, as they are provided, for example, in BvD's Orbis database. The approach of the R&D Scoreboard is considerably different[3] from that of statistical offices like Eurostat or the OECD, which provide data on Business Enterprise Expenditure on R&D (BERD). The R&D Scoreboard data are used for benchmarking company commitments and performance. In the vast majority of cases (99%) the accounts do not include the location of R&D so that the companies total R&D investments are assigned to the country in which its headquarter is registered.[4] BERD data, on the other hand, are used for the analysis of R&D

[2]The R&D Scoreboard was provided by Commission Services in response to the Commission's Research Investment Action Plan. See: "Investing in research: an action plan for Europe", COM (2003) 266, http://europa.eu.int/eur-lex/en/com/cnc/2003/com2003_0226en02.pdf.

[3]The R&D Scoreboard covers all R&D financed by a company's internal funds, regardless of where the R&D is performed. BERD, on the other hand, are all R&D activities that are performed by the business sector within a country, regardless of the sources of funds. The Scoreboard uses data from audited financial accounts and reports, whereas BERD is survey based.

[4]The registered office is the company address notified to the official company registry. It is normally the place where a company's books are kept.

performance and R&D expenditures of territorial units defined by (political) boundaries, mainly countries or regions.

The 2013 version of the Scoreboard is used here covering the world's top 2000 R&D investors, and a share of almost 90% of the total business expenditure on R&D worldwide.[5] The dataset provides information like R&D investment, net sales, capital expenditures, operating profits or the number of employees to enable the assessment of R&D and economic performance of companies. Companies' behavior and performance can be analysed over longer time periods using the database, which contains information on the top R&D companies starting from 2004.

Matching R&D Scoreboard and Patent Data

It is necessary to link the R&D Scoreboard and PATSTAT to assess the technological output of industrial sectors in AMT and KETs and any input-output relation. To establish the link between the two datasets, a probability matching was performed of harmonized patent applicant names with company names from the R&D Scoreboard. Two thousand worldwide companies are listed in the 2013 Scoreboard, for which information on subsidiaries is available.

The aim of the matching procedure is to locate information on patent applicants in PATSTAT that corresponds or has a high similarity to a company name entry in the R&D Scoreboard. For this purpose, the similarity between applicant names in PATSTAT and each entry of company names in the R&D Scoreboard was calculated, including the names of the subsidiaries of these companies, using the method of Levenshtein distance. The Levenshtein distance is a calculation of how many edits would be needed in order to align two text strings. Edits can mean: insertion, deletion or replacement of a character. Thus, the Levenshtein distance itself measures the dissimilarity between two text strings. For a normalized similarity measure, the result of the Levenshtein distance is divided by the number of characters of the longer of the two text strings and subtracted from 1. In that way, the resulting similarity function is restricted to the range between 0 and 1. The lower the number of edits necessary to align two text strings, the higher the similarity between the two.

In the case of name variations, name changes and the like, as well as information on subsidiaries, it may happen that several PATSTAT entries were assigned to one entry in the R&D Scoreboard list of company names. In this case, the PATSTAT entries were treated in an aggregated form.

Although we already employed a pre-cleaned patent applicant name version, a further cleaning of text-strings is the first step within the matching procedure (e.g. treatment of lowercase letters, umlauts or special characters, removal of the legal

[5]According to the latest figures reported by Eurostat, i.e. BERD financed by the business enterprise sector in 2009 compared with R&D figures in the 2010 Scoreboard.

form of the companies, removal of country and city names). The applicant names from PATSTAT as well as the company names from the R&D Scoreboard were cleaned employing the same procedure to ensure conformity.

To select our matched pairs, we ran the matching algorithm twice. In the first step, companies as well as their subsidiaries in both datasets were matched only if they share the same country information, i.e. we included a country criterion. If the country information was not the same, the similarity value was set to 0. In the second step, the country criterion was excluded for all companies that were not assigned a corresponding entry in the first run. This was only done for the company headquarters, i.e. without subsidiaries, which had not been matched in the first run. The second step is to prevent that some potential correct matches are included that were missed due to the country criterion in the first step. This is particularly valid for companies with branches in multiple countries.

Of the 2847 firms in the R&D Scoreboard (including their subsidiaries), 2670 could be assigned a corresponding patent applicant in PATSTAT, i.e. 93% of the firms listed in the R&D Scoreboard are matched. The 2670 matched Scoreboard firms correspond to a share of 58% of worldwide transnational patents filed in 2011. The remaining 42% are patents filed by universities or public research institutes, single inventors or firms that are not covered by the R&D Scoreboard. Within the fields of KETs and AMT, 61 and 57%, respectively, of all transnational patent filings are included in the matches, i.e. the firms in the R&D Scoreboard are responsible for 61% of all transnational KETs filings in 2011 (57% in AMT).

For the analysis of the R&D Scoreboard companies from China, we were able to identify 146 companies directly registered in China and another 31 Chinese companies registered in the Cayman Islands. The country code information from the Scoreboard was used to identify the companies directly registered in China. A manual Internet search was conducted to identify Chinese companies registered in the Cayman Islands. All Cayman Islands' companies that could be identified as undoubtedly Chinese were classified as such.

China's Patent Applications at Home and Abroad

The total numbers of transnational and SIPO patent filings in KETs and AMT are displayed in Fig. 11.1. No country differentiation has been made yet, so these are total numbers at these offices. What can be seen are rather stable trends between 2000 and 2009 at the transnational level, with slight increases since 2009. While KETs reach around 42,000 patents in 2012, AMT are about one fifth of that, with around 9000 patents in 2012. The corresponding numbers of patent applications at the Chinese patent office (SIPO) are much more dynamic and even accelerate from 2009 onwards. Within KETs, the Chinese numbers—as can be seen from the right axis—are more than double the corresponding numbers at the transnational level. In case of AMT, the number of patents that are filed at the national office in China are even triple the corresponding numbers at the transnational level.

Figure 11.2 then differentiates the shares of KETs patent applications at the transnational level and at the SIPO for a selected set of countries. The shares in totals per office are displayed. The USA is the largest patent filing country until 2006, but shows the steepest decline from more than 35% in the year 2002 to about

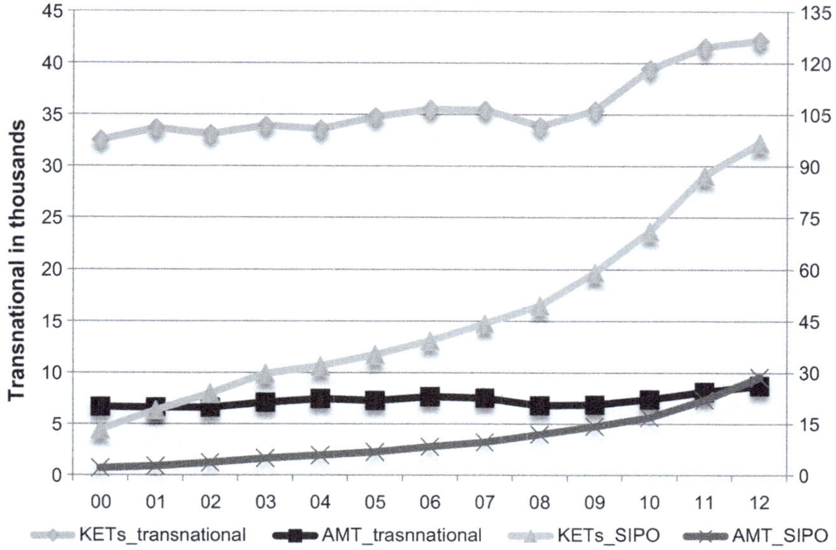

Fig. 11.1 Total number of Transnational* and SIPO patent filings in KETs and AMT. *Source* EPO–PATSTAT; Fraunhofer ISI calculations

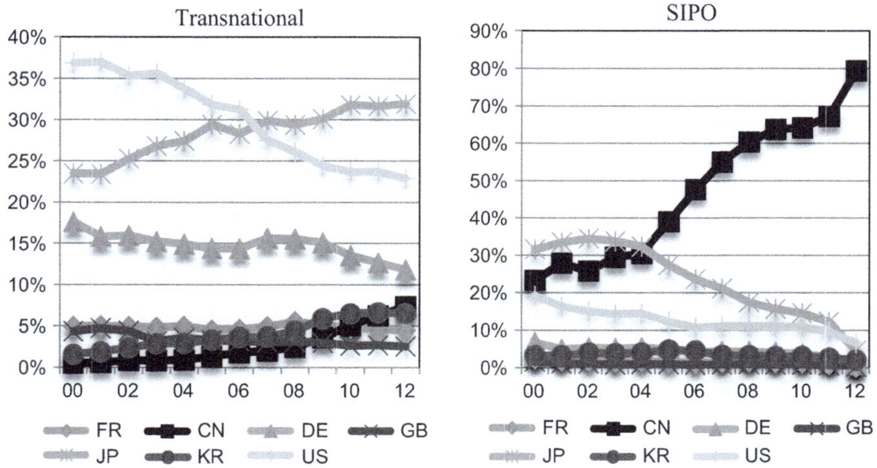

Fig. 11.2 Country-specific shares of KETs filings. *Source* EPO–PATSTAT; Fraunhofer ISI calculations

23% in 2012. The Japanese were able to increase their shares from below 25% to more than 30% in the most recent years and overtook the USA in 2007. Germany ranks third with a rather stable share of around 15% until 2009, but a declining trend since then. This decline can be explained, first of all, by the surge in Chinese applications, but South Korean filings also increased, especially between 2007 and 2010. Other European countries like France or Great Britain also show slightly decreasing trends, but have recently seemed able to almost keep their levels, which are, however, well below 5%. Chinese inventors ranked fourth in 2012 with about 7% of transnational filings, slightly ahead of South Korea. For Europe as a whole, this implies decreasing trends, but also limited total shares of less than 30% of worldwide patent applications in Key Enabling Technologies.

The right-hand graph shows the corresponding trends for the Chinese patent office (SIPO), where we see a completely different picture. Japan was in the lead until about 2004, but a very steep increase of Chinese inventors now dwarfs the other countries to a marginal total of about 20%, while Chinese inventors account for almost 80% of filings.

Advanced manufacturing technologies—which are seen as an enabling group of crosscutting technologies for the other KETs—shows a similar picture at the Chinese patent office SIPO, with China again dwarfing all the other countries, in this case to about 17% in total (Fig. 11.3). A different pattern is displayed in the left-hand panel on transnational patent applications. The USA was not that dominant here and its position deteriorated from 2005 already. It was overtaken by Germany in 2007, which itself has declined since 2009 and now has about 20% of worldwide patent applications at the transnational level. This means it ranks third behind the USA and Japan. Japan started from a level of 20% and decreased slightly until 2010, but has increased its shares strongly in recent years. China's surge is

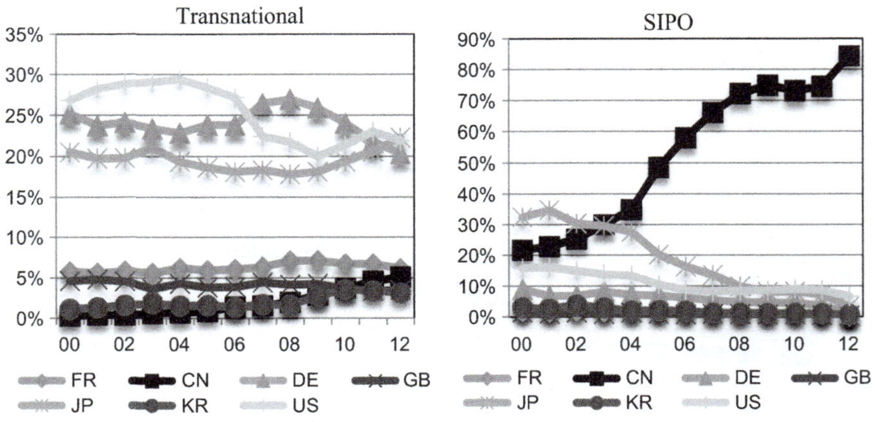

Fig. 11.3 Country-specific shares of AMT filings. *Source* EPO–PATSTAT; Fraunhofer ISI calculations

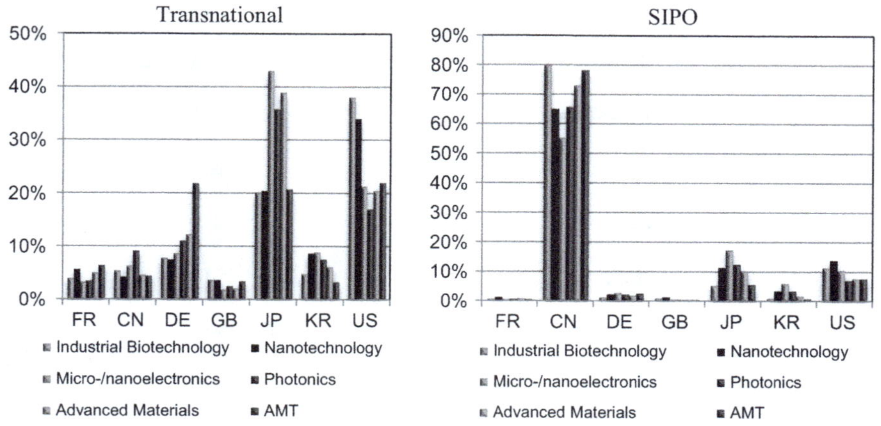

Fig. 11.4 Technology-specific shares of countries within KETs, 2010–2012. *Source* EPO–PATSTAT; Fraunhofer ISI calculations

also clearly visible and has even accelerated since 2009, but it still plays a rather marginal role with about 5% of worldwide patent applications.

Further differentiating the patent applications by technological subfields (see Fig. 11.4) reveals the Japanese focus on microelectronics, photonics and advanced materials, while the USA is strong in industrial biotechnology and nanotechnology. Germany has a strong position in AMT, as do France and the UK. China focuses on photonics and microelectronics at the transnational level, which puts it in direct competition with Japan. At the Chinese patent office, on the other hand, Japan is able to retain its highest shares in microelectronics and photonics, where China has its lowest shares together with nanotechnology of 55 or 65% respectively.

All this leads to specialization indices in KETs and AMT that prove the strong position of Japan and Korea in the case of KETs and of Germany and France in the case of AMT (Fig. 11.5). The technological profiles of the USA, Germany, France and also the UK at the Chinese patent office exhibit an above average role of KETs, which does not reflect their particular strengths on the transnational level. So the profile here is clearly different. China's technological profile does not show any particular strength in KETs or AMT, either at the transnational level or at their home office SIPO. This means, even though they dominate the absolute numbers in China, they do not have a particular focus on these technologies. This also means that they have higher shares and a stronger focus on other areas (e.g. communication technologies).

When looking at the worldwide growth rates and the technology market share (share of patent applications at the particular office), it is interesting to note that Chinese inventors have not only increased their numbers of patent applications in general, but have also focused on areas with high growth and rather large fields in absolute terms (Fig. 11.6). China's largest market shares are in photonics with more than 6% of worldwide patent applications. Total patent applications grew by about

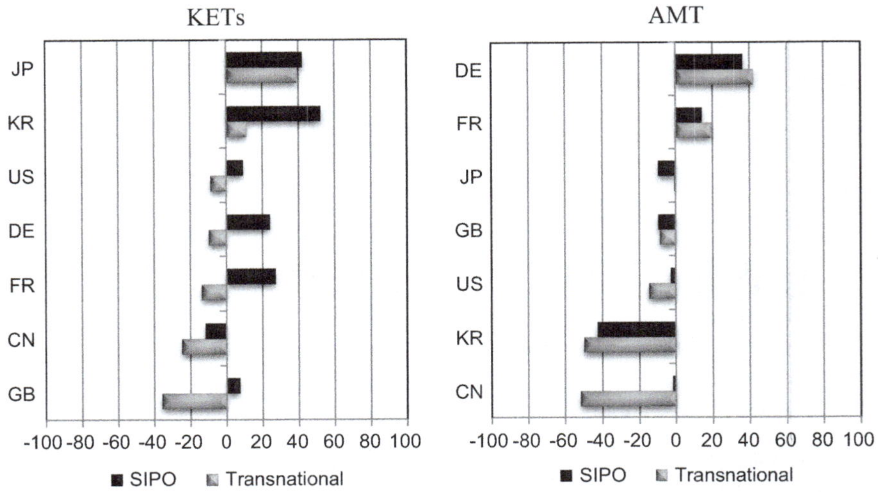

Fig. 11.5 Specialization Indices (RPAs) in the years 2009–2011. *Source* EPO–PATSTAT; Fraunhofer ISI calculations

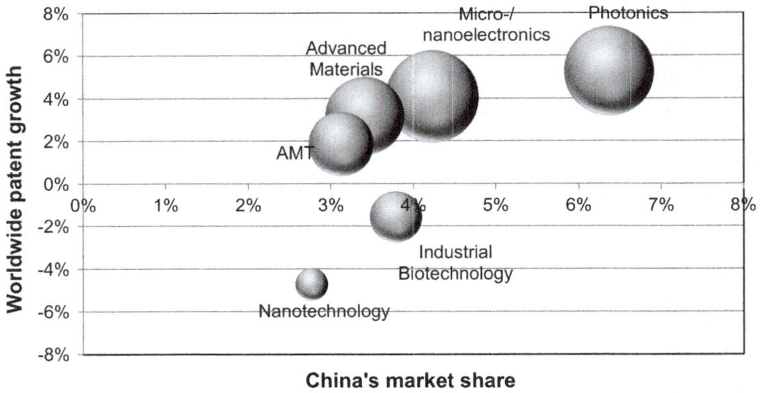

Fig. 11.6 Worldwide patent growth and China's share of all patents, transnational, 2006–2012. *Source* EPO–PATSTAT; Fraunhofer ISI calculations

5% between 2006 and 2012. Nanotechnology and industrial biotechnology actually declined—driven by the downturn in the USA in the aftermath of the economic crisis. Here, China's shares are below 3 and 4%, respectively. In AMT Chinese also have limited market shares. This is the third smallest field under observation here, which has only grown by about 2% since 2006. The Chinese shares are not very high so far in any of these areas, but given the worldwide growth, a strategy or at least a taking of opportunities seems to be emergent.

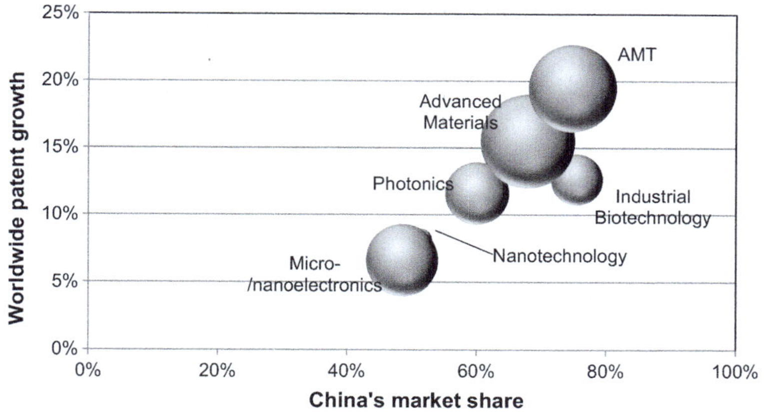

Fig. 11.7 Worldwide patent growth and China's share of all patents, SIPO, 2006–2012. *Source* EPO–PATSTAT; Fraunhofer ISI calculations

It is also interesting to note (see Fig. 11.7) that the changes in the shares are very different at the Chinese patent office. Advanced materials and advanced manufacturing technologies are the largest technological fields here. They have grown the strongest since 2006 and Chinese inventors hold high shares. In microelectronics and nanotechnology—these fields have grown rather slowly in China—the Chinese shares of total patent filings were only around 50% in the period 2006–2012. Industrial biotechnology grew at a medium rate, but the Chinese shares here are quite high.

All these results can be interpreted in two directions. First, Chinese inventors are not yet ready for international competition in most of the technological fields that are in the scope of this analysis, with the exception of microelectronics and photonics. There also seems to be a domestic market for these technologies, so that other countries, first of all Japan, but also the USA, compete with China on their national market. This results in rather low shares for China compared to their average shares. Second, Chinese inventors dominate the scene at the Chinese patent office in AMT and also in advanced materials so that one can expect them to quickly improve their technological capabilities and to benefit from economies of scope and especially economies of scale. They can be expected to enter the international scene with the experience made at home in the coming years. European countries obviously try to retain their position in China in terms of advanced manufacturing—they are not in the best position with respect to the other KETs—but the market seems to be restricted so far so that they are obviously struggling to do this and prepare for future developments. Whether they are able to prevail, given the Chinese efforts, remains to be seen.

The top-10 applicants for KETs patents by Chinese inventors on the transnational level are mainly large companies, but also three public research organizations: the Chinese Academy of Sciences, Tsinghua University and Peking University

Table 11.1 Top Chinese Applicants in KETs—Transnational and SIPO

Transnational		SIPO	
Applicant name	# Filings	Applicant name	# Filings
Shenzhen China Star Optoelectronics Technology Company	557	Ocean's King Lighting Science & Technology Company	5811
Chinese Academy of Sciences	500	SMI Semiconductor Manufacturing International	1948
BOE Technology Group Company	332	Foxconn	1848
Huawaei Technologies Company	192	China Petroleum & Chemical Corporation	1667
CSMC Technologies FAB 1 Company	131	Tsinghua University	1505
BASF (China) Company	104	Zhejiang University	1409
Tsinghua University	98	Hongfujin Precision Industry (Shenzhen) Company	1350
Ocean's King Lighting Science & Technology Company	96	Chinese Academy of Sciences	1279
Peking University	78	Harbin Institute of Technology	947
BYD Company	71	Shanghai Jiao Tong University	937

Source EPO–PATSTAT; Fraunhofer ISI calculations

(see Table 11.1). The Chinese branch of a German company (BASF) is also among the top 10. The absolute number of filings by these 10 companies/organizations varies widely, with 557 for the Shenzhen Optoelectronic Technology Company and 71 for BYD. At the State Intellectual Property Office the top 10 list (see right columns of Table 11.1) is slightly different with only three overlapping actors: Oceans King Lighting Science and Technology Company, Tsinghua University and the Chinese Academy of Sciences. On the national level, there are even more public research organizations among the top 10 applicants. In addition, Zhejiang University, the Harbin Institute of Technology, and Jiaotong University show up.

This pattern reflects two different issues. On the one hand, it underlines the previous statement that, in general, Chinese inventors are not yet ready for international competition. Only three of them appear in both lists and only a few have really high numbers of patent applications in this field. On the other hand, it underlines the outstanding role of public research organizations for the technology portfolios of China. In Western countries the shares of university patents are rather low (Lissoni et al. 2008). The main reason is that public research is not able or at least does not have the competence or duty to commercialize its research findings. A lot of R&D expenditures in the Chinese system are spent by public research. Even though the statistics on R&D expenditures show that the share of BERD is about 75% in China (OECD 2016), this imbalance in the patent output raises doubts about the statistics or at least about the effectiveness and efficiency of the expenditures. What can be derived from this imbalance of public and private patent

Table 11.2 Top Chinese Applicants in AMT—Transnational and SIPO

Transnational		SIPO	
Applicant name	# Filings	Applicant name	# Filings
Zoomlion Special Vehicle Company	85	Southeast University	509
Sany Heavy Industry Company	43	Foxconn	504
Huawei Technologies Company	33	Harbin Institute of Technology	464
ZTE Corporation	27	Zhejiang University	431
Positec Power Tools (Suzhou) Comp.	14	Beihang University	409
SGCC (State Grid Corp. of China)	14	SGCC (State Grid Corp. of China)	404
Ecovacs Robotics (Suzhou) Comp.	13	Tsinghua University	387
Shenzhen China Star Optoelectronics Technology Company	12	Shanghai Jiao Tong University	357
Gao Song	12	Tianjin University	308
Shanghai Boiler Works	9	Hongfujin Precision Industry (Shenzhen) Company	297

Source EPO—PATSTAT; Fraunhofer ISI calculations

output, however, is the big challenge facing technology transfer and commercialization in China. This is even bigger than it appears at first sight given the background of high patent filing subsidies by the government, which particularly benefit public research organizations and state-owned enterprises. In other words, Chinese applicants file a lot of patents on the national and especially the international level due to the fact that they get direct funds for the fees and not due to market expectations or reasonable commercial interests.

There is a different pattern of the top-10 applicants in advanced manufacturing technologies (Table 11.2). On the international level there are no public research institutions. On the national level, on the other hand, there are seven universities and one state-owned enterprise among the top 10. The absolute numbers of filings are much lower and only a few big companies reach a reasonable absolute level of transnational patents, namely Zoomlion, Sany, Huawei, and ZTE. On the national level at the SIPO, a toll manufacturer (Foxconn) for multinational companies appears on the list, next to the universities and state-owned enterprises.

Chinese Companies: R&D Expenditures and Patents

In this section we restrict our analyses to China-owned companies with the highest spending on R&D, including those registered for example in the Cayman Islands. The data are taken directly from matching the R&D Scoreboard and the patent database PATSTAT. This matched dataset offers two advantages. On the one hand,

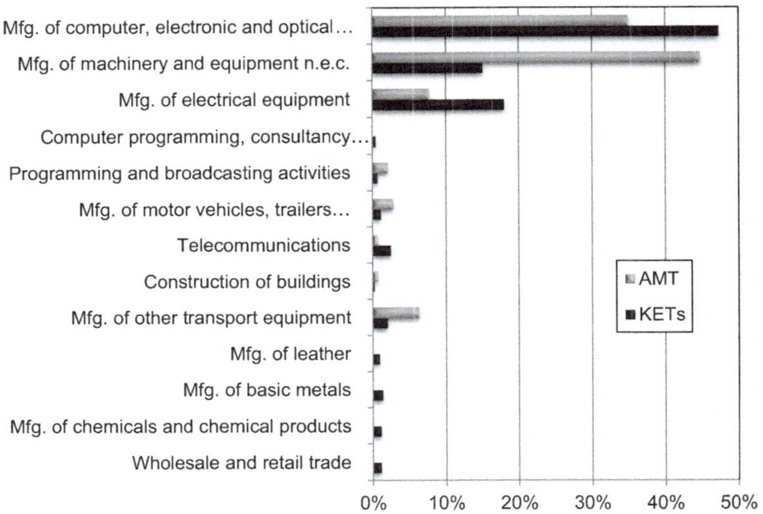

Fig. 11.8 Shares of patent filings by sectors, Chinese R&D Scoreboard firms only, 2009–2011. *Source* EU–R&D Scoreboard; EPO–PATSTAT; Fraunhofer ISI calculations

it allows an integrated perspective of R&D and patents. On the other hand, it enables the analysis not only of technological areas, but also of industrial sectors.

Figure 11.8 shows the shares of patent filings by sectors of the Chinese R&D scoreboard firms. Manufacturing of computer, electronic and optical products is responsible for almost 50% of the transnational patent applications in KETs filed by Chinese enterprises. At the same time this sector accounts for 35% of AMT patents. The manufacturing of electrical equipment sector is responsible for less than 20% of KETs and less than 10% of AMT. Manufacturing of machinery and equipment, on the other hand, plays an important role for AMT, and a significant role in KETs. The other sectors have marginal shares in patenting, except for transport (other transport equipment and motor vehicles and trailers), which has notable shares in AMT. This means that the technological origins of KETs and AMT are generally in sectors, where this can be expected. For many other countries—for example Germany—the shares of the peripheral sectors are higher. In other words, the data shows the limited horizontal diversification of Chinese companies. From another analysis (Frietsch and Schüller 2010) we know, however, that Chinese companies prefer deep vertical diversification and try to cover as much of a value chain as possible.

In Figs. 11.9, 11.10, 11.11 and 11.12 the patent intensity—this is the number of total filings per €1 million R&D expenditure—is plotted against the shares of KETs and AMT filings for a set of 20 Chinese companies. Zoomlion has the highest patent intensity, with almost 6 patents per €1 million R&D expenditures. This might be one result of their acquisition strategy and also of the fact that the data stem from

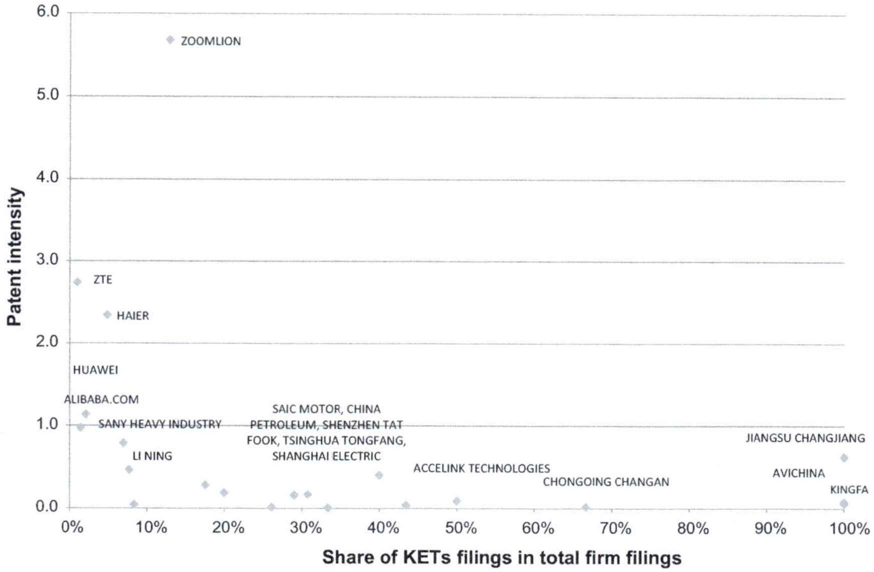

Fig. 11.9 Patent intensity (total filings/R&D exp.) and shares of KETs filings, transnational, 2011. *Source* EU–R&D Scoreboard; EPO–PATSTAT; Fraunhofer ISI calculations

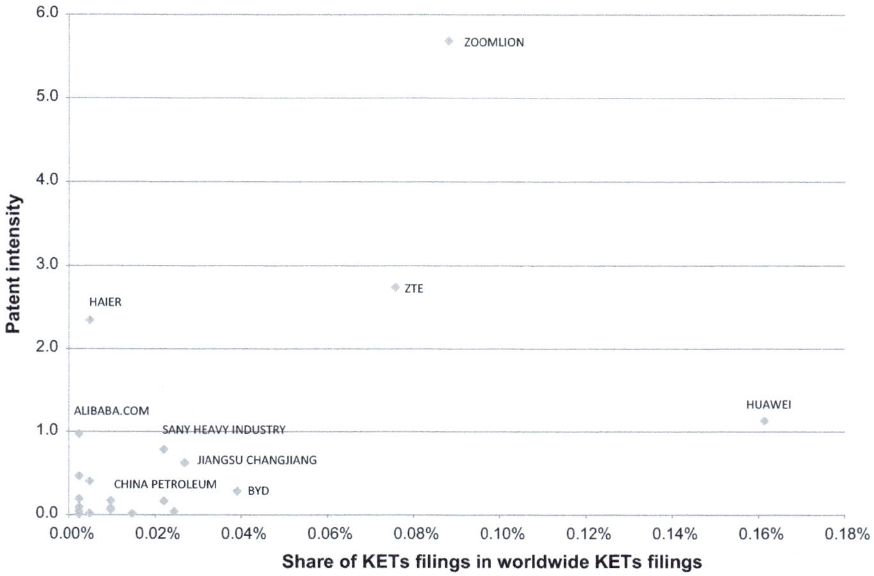

Fig. 11.10 Patent intensity and shares of KETs filings in worldwide KETs filings, transnational, 2011. *Source* EU–R&D Scoreboard; EPO–PATSTAT; Fraunhofer ISI calculations

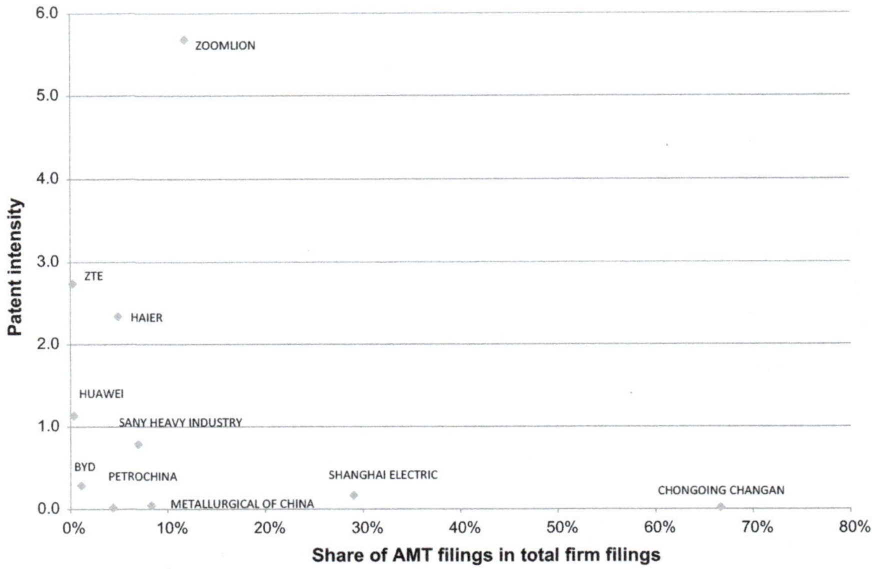

Fig. 11.11 Patent intensity and shares of AMT filings in total filings, transnational, 2011. *Source* EU–R&D Scoreboard; EPO–PATSTAT; Fraunhofer ISI calculations

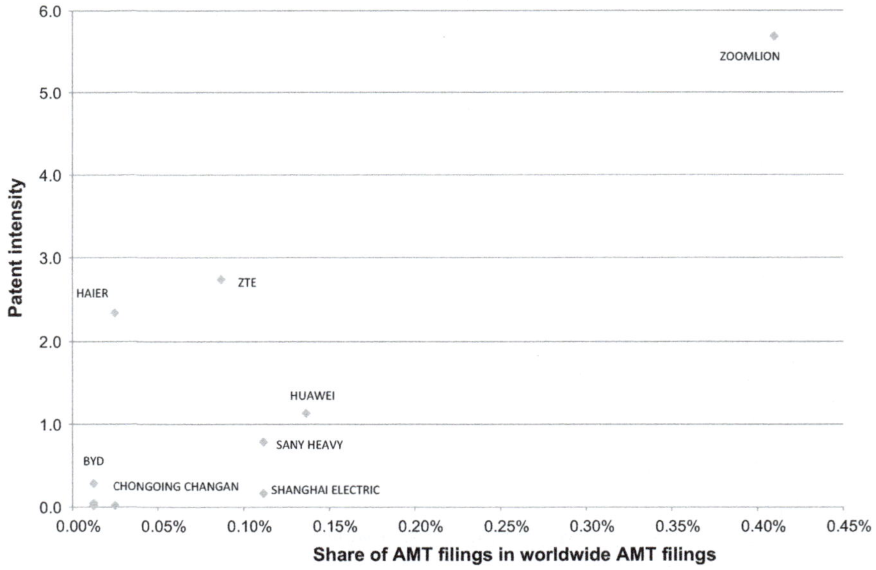

Fig. 11.12 Patent intensity and shares of AMT filings in worldwide AMT filings, transnational, 2011. *Source* EU–R&D Scoreboard; EPO–PATSTAT; Fraunhofer ISI calculations

before they were hit by the Chinese real estate and construction bubble.[6] ZTE and Haier had quite high intensities of between two and three patents per €1 million R&D expenditure. A number of other well-known companies including Huawei, Alibaba and Sany also have high intensities that deviate from the majority. However, all these companies have rather low shares of KETs filings in their portfolio, indicating that their activities have other focal points. In contrast, there are several companies which focus only or almost only on KETs. These are Kingfa, Jiangsu Changjiang, Avi China and Chongqing Changan. These companies may not be that well-known in the West so far, but are already among the biggest R&D spenders in the world. Their numbers of transnational patents might be limited currently and they seem to have a strong focus on the Chinese market, but they might be able to grow quickly and benefit from the economies of scale offered by the huge Chinese market.

We do not find any exclusively specialized companies that only patent AMT, but again Chongqing Changan has rather high shares,[7] even though it only has a very small fraction of transnational AMT applications. Zoomlion clearly stands out again with respect to worldwide shares, and already had more than 0.4% of the transnational patent applications of the priority year 2011. The other Chinese big R&D spenders also reach high shares in AMT on the transnational level. Huawei, for example, has 0.14% of the AMT patents, and 0.16% of KETs.

A clear learning curve can be derived from Fig. 11.13, which shows the filings by Chinese inventors of the Chinese R&D Scoreboard companies listed in four periods. At the beginning of the 2000 s, the shares of Chinese among all inventors within the filings by Chinese companies are rather low at about 65% in the case of KETs and none at all in the case of AMT. The shares of Chinese inventors then increased rapidly over time and the shares of foreign inventors—European, North-American, Asian, Rest of the World (RotW)—have decreased respectively. Already by the middle of the previous decade Chinese inventors held a much higher share that has increased even further to a level well above 90% by the beginning of this decade.

It seems that Chinese companies went abroad and collaborated with foreign inventors (or bought the technologies). They then climbed up the learning curve so that less and less external knowledge became necessary and has since been substituted by national knowledge. The strong position of Chinese companies in communication technologies is well known and they have extended this to information and network technologies as well, by following a similar learning curve and have quickly caught up with their competitors. The accelerated increase in the worldwide market shares of Chinese companies in these technological fields may

---

[6]See, for example, www.china-investiert/zoomlion; https://en.wikipedia.org/wiki/zoomlion; en.zoomlion.com.

[7]The overlap of IPC classes between KETs and AMT is rather limited, but the fact that one patent on average has about 2.5 different IPC classes (4-digit level) leads to an overlap of patents. Chongoing Changan is obviously patenting many inventions that fit both definitions, so the enabling idea of AMT for KETs seems to be justified in this case.

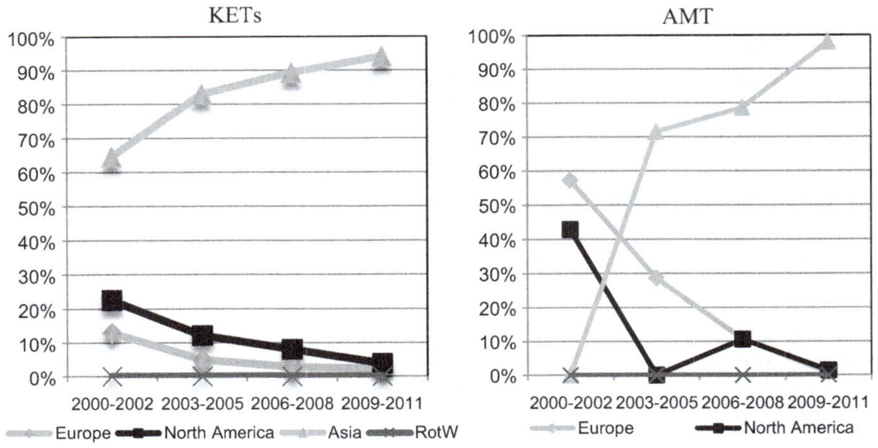

Fig. 11.13 Filings by foreign inventors, Chinese R&D Scoreboard firms only. *Source* EU–R&D Scoreboard; EPO–PATSTAT; Fraunhofer ISI calculations

have been supported by the framework conditions and the changing nature of the markets—from technology/innovation-driven markets to price competition with still short, but less radical technology cycles. There might be clear differences to KETs and especially to AMT. However, the huge demand on the national market and the meanwhile high capital endowment of the Chinese customers, especially in B2B sales, are also an asset for Chinese companies in these technologies. In other words, what worked for communication and information technologies in general might also work for KETs and AMT, even though the framework conditions are different. At least the learning strategy of Chinese enterprises seems to be similar.

Discussion and Conclusions

We started with the European idea that KETs and AMT are of high relevance for growth and jobs in Europe. This implies a reasonably strong positioning of European-based companies in these technological fields. These fields are supposed to be of particular relevance not only as drivers of growth in the technology markets themselves (of KETs and AMT), but also as enablers for a strong positioning of the EU in the so called Societal Grand Challenges—mainly fields where Europe is currently strong and with existing and future global markets. These challenges include transport, energy, health, climate, security, food and also "Inclusive, innovative and reflective societies".

Our empirical analysis showed that Europe's current position in AMT seems to be good—mainly due to a high performance of Germany, but also France and the UK—while it is rather poor in KETs. About 50% of transnational patent applications in AMT originate in Europe—and 50% of these alone in Germany, which therefore accounts for 25% of worldwide AMT filings (Gkotsis 2015; Neuhäusler et al. 2015). Another 25% of AMT originate in Asia and in North America, respectively. For KETs the global picture is completely different, with 50% of the applications originating in Asia—mainly in Japan, but with growing shares of South Korea and China—while 25% again stem from North America and only 25% from Europe. It therefore seems reasonable to conclude that Europe is strongly competitive in AMT and weaker in KETs.

Generally speaking, with respect to our research question of the potential threat from Chinese companies, it seems that they are shortening the gap. They are responsible for an increasing share of patents at SIPO and more recently for the vast majority of patent applications, both in KETs and in AMT. Japan plays an outstanding role at the international level and dominates KETs here, and is still attempting to keep its competitive edge on the Chinese market as well.

The biggest R&D spenders have a broad portfolio, where KETs and AMT play a relevant role. Furthermore, some of the big spenders focus explicitly on KETs and AMT and might be preparing for large numbers of filings nationally and also internationally. The example of Zoomlion suggests such a strategy. However, the most interesting finding was that we were able to identify general strategies of Chinese firms over time. They started at the level of low or almost no activity and then learned abroad, collaborating with foreign inventors or even hiring them. In the next stage, knowledge was re-shored and the national market developed. Assuming this process continues along the lines of other technological sectors like communication and information technologies, the next step is to enter the world market and become strong and competitive players on a global scale. The Chinese might be aiming even higher given their huge national market that makes economies of scale and scope possible as well as the cultural belief that failure can lead to improvements. In the field of Key Enabling Technologies China will mainly have to compete with Japan and South Korea. In AMT it is Europe that will be challenged. So the answer to one of our research questions, namely "How does China perform?" is quite clear at the moment. It does not yet perform very well on the international stage, but the national market for technologies is mostly dominated by Chinese inventors/companies.

The second research question was whether Europe was daydreaming about its current and especially its future positioning in KETs and AMT. The answer here is: "Most probably yes", with the exceptions of Germany and maybe France (as well as some smaller countries in Europe, e.g. the Netherlands or Belgium), who currently have a solid portfolio and a good position, especially in Advanced Manufacturing Technologies, but also partly in KETs, where Scandinavian countries still retain the competitive edge in certain parts.

The good news for Europe is that it still holds strong positions in Societal Grand Challenges, which will contribute even more to jobs and growth in Europe than KETs and AMT alone. The idea that KETs and AMT not only provide direct input to this goal of growth, but also indirectly help to keep the competitive edge in the Grand Challenges, is a reasonable one. Insofar, and this is a still open and ongoing process, the concrete parts of KETs and AMT that are necessary preconditions for this competitiveness need to be identified and then pursued with greater intensity.

References

Du Plessis, M., Van Looy, B., Song, X., & Magerman, T. (2009). *Data production methods for harmonized patent indicators: Assignee sector allocation*. EUROSTAT Working Paper and Studies, Luxembourg.

European Commission. (2013). *Innovation Union. A pocket guide on a Europe 2020 Initiative*. Luxembourg: Publications Office of the European Union.

Frietsch, R., & Schmoch, U. (2010). Transnational patents and international markets. *Scientometrics, 82,* 185–200.

Frietsch, R., & Schüller, M. (2010). Asia's catching-up: Scientific and technological competitiveness. In R. Frietsch & M. Schüller (Eds.), *Competing for global innovation leadership: Innovation systems and policies in the USA, Europe and Asia* (pp. 119–142). Stuttgart: Fraunhofer Verlag.

Gkotsis, P. (2015). *The capability of the EU R&D Scoreboard companies to develop advanced manufacturing technologies—An assessment based on patent analysis* (JRC Technical Report, Report EUR 27176 EN, European Commission). In J.R.C.I.f.P.T.S.J.R.C. (Ed.), Seville: IPTS.

IDEA Consult, ZEW, NIW, TNO, CEA, Ecorys Fraunhofer ISI. (2015). *Key enabling technologies* (First annual report: European Commission, DG Growth).

Lissoni, F., Llerena, P., McKelvey, M., & Sanditov, B. (2008). Academic patenting in Europe: New evidence from the KEINS Database. *Research Evaluation, 17,* 87–102.

Magerman, T., Grouwels, J., Song, X., & Van Loo, B. (2009). *Data production methods for harmonized patent indicators: Patentee name harmonization.* EUROSTAT Working Paper and Studies, Luxembourg.

Neuhäusler, P., Frietsch, R., Bethke, N., & Mund, C. (2015). *Assessing companies capability to develop advanced manufacturing technologies in selected industrial sectors* (Report to IPTS in the AMCAP project). Karlsruhe: Fraunhofer ISI.

OECD. (2016). *Main science and technology indicators*. OECD. http://www.oecd.org/sti/msti.htm .

Peeters, B., Song, X., Callaert, J., Grouwels, J., & Van Looy, B. (2009). *Harmonizing harmonized patentee names: An exploratory assessment of top patentees*. EUROSTAT Working Paper and Studies, Luxembourg.

Veugelers, R., Cincera, M., Frietsch, R., Rammer, C., Schubert, T., Pelle, A., et al. (2015). The impact of horizon 2020 on innovation in Europe. *Intereconomics, 50,* 4–30.

Part III
Organisational and Human Dimensions of Innovation

Chapter 12
Developing Human Capital for Knowledge Based Economies

Thomas Clarke and Soheyla Gholamshahi

Abstract In Part III of the book the organisational and human dimensions of innovation in the Asia Pacific are examined, beginning with Clarke and Gholamshahi's analysis of the significance of human capital for the development of knowledge-based economies. In the OECD countries, more than half of GDP is accounted for by knowledge-based industries, including the main producers of high-technology goods, high and medium technology manufacturing, and knowledge intensive services such as finance, insurance, business, communication and social services. This is manifest in the rising human capital levels of the population in OECD countries as measure in educational attainment, and in the increased demand for highly educated and highly skilled workers. The challenge for the Asia Pacific is to develop the human, social and institutional capital necessary for successfully competing in the knowledge economy. The *Forum for the Future* (2016) suggest a five capitals model of human capital, social capital, finance capital, manufacturing capital and natural capital. Defining human capital as people's health and well-being, knowledge, skills and motivation, and defining social capital as the institutions which sustain and develop human capital in partnership with others for example families, communities, businesses, unions, schools and voluntary organizations including the values and behaviours that allow these social forms to operate). Human capital is one of these five interdependent forms of capital, and is not a separate, substitutable item in itself (that is human capital works with and complements other forms of capital). Human and social capital become ever more critical as the knowledge economy progresses. Hoff and Stiglitz insist, "Development is no longer seen primarily as a process of capital accumulation but rather as a process of organizational change" (2001: 389). The Asian Development Bank in a report on *Moving Towards Knowledge-Based Economies* (2007) suggests a new paradigm for economic development "It is even envisaged that knowledge can eventually become a means of mass production—similar to manual labour in the industrial economy—once web-based information and communication technologies (ICTs) have reached worldwide penetration levels, allowing individuals to

T. Clarke (✉) · S. Gholamshahi
Centre for Business and Social Innovation, UTS, Sydney, Australia
e-mail: t.clarke@uts.edu.au

T. Clarke and K. Lee (eds.), *Innovation in the Asia Pacific*,
https://doi.org/10.1007/978-981-10-5895-0_12

work and provide routine knowledge in a virtually networked (global) environment" (ADB 2007: ix).

Keywords Human capital · Knowledge based economies · Skill development

Introduction

An insistent question asked in the developing world is how they might acquire the higher skills and technologies to secure entry to the social stability and economic prosperity apparently afforded by the knowledge economy? "What kind of institutional arrangements will best enable societies to generate new skills, knowledge and ideas and the networks needed to diffuse and take advantage of them?" (Evans 2006: 2; Sen 1994; Lucas 1988; Rodrik 2004; Rodrik et al. 2004; Romer 1986; Romer 1994; Shapiro and Taylor 1990). The economies of the Asia Pacific are now in direct competition with the United States, Japan, and Europe in the acquisition of the knowledge and skills to develop human capital for the knowledge economy (Acemoglu et al. 2005; Bairoch 1982; Dunning 2006; Easterly 2001; Helpman 2004; Porter 1990). There is an old adage, "Innovation walks on two legs." As Catherine Livingstone, the former Chair of Telstra, and CEO of Cochlear in Australia said, "…the starting point for any discussion on innovation must always be people: it's people who innovate, not governments, not institutions, not businesses, but the people inside them. It's an intensely human activity. It's minds rubbing on minds" (Livingstone 2017).

All of the advanced economies have committed policies to enhance their human capital for the digital era. For example the European Union launched a New Skills Agenda in June 2016 with the digital skills as a key element. The intention is to help service the digital transformation of European industry, with the explosion of mobile technology, big data, the cloud, and social media continuing to overwhelm the business environment. The solution to this immense technological transformation is people: "The biggest challenge of industrial leaders isn't technology—it is the people. While digital technologies are rapidly becoming a commodity, success largely depends on an organisation's Digital IQ" (PWC 2016: 4).

In this context many people lack skills, or are even disconnected, and there are widespread anxieties among companies regarding digital disruption of established value chains, and concerns regarding vulnerability to cyber attack. Looking to the future digitalization of products and services opens up multiple opportunities for innovation, investment and the creation of new businesses and employment. The rapid evolution of the software application economy potentially could provide millions of jobs in the future enabling leadership in web entrepreneurship. However there remain many challenges ahead, for example India has seen a rapid development of its computer services economy, and the leading Western corporations are attracted to the Indian economy, with Indian information technology corporations becoming global players. The start-up economy in India by 2015 was employing more than 80,000 people.

Yet despite the millions of Indian technology and engineering graduates India's venture capitalists claim they cannot find enough employees with the requisite skills to scale up their enterprises, and India's higher education sector is having difficulty responding to this challenge (IBM 2017).

One indicator of the intensity of national commitment towards the knowledge economy is the international comparison of research intensity survey completed by UNESCO (2016). Table 12.1 illustrates that due to its vast population and substantial national commitment to scientific research and development China now has the greatest number of science researchers in the world at approaching 1.5 million, followed by the United States with 1.25 million. However, relative to the size of their population, other countries demonstrate their commitment to R&D, with Finland, Denmark, Sweden and Korea leading the world in researchers per 1000 population.

Competing in the Knowledge Economy

The World Bank (1998) placed the advance of knowledge at the centre of world economic development in their influential annual report *Knowledge for Development*. The emergence of economies based on the production, distribution and use of knowledge and information was charted by the OECD (1996) in their report *The Knowledge-Based Economy*. The determinants of the success of enterprises, and of national economies as a whole, is ever more reliant upon their effectiveness in gathering and utilising knowledge (ADB 2007). The development and sharing of new knowledge is so rapid in the new economy, the OECD suggests innovation has developed from a linear model to a more complex, relationship based model.

Instead of discovery and innovation proceeding along a fixed and linear sequence of phases, innovation is the result of numerous actions of many players.

Table 12.1 International Comparison of Researcher Intensity 2013

	Total researchers	Researchers per 1000 employees
China	1,484,000	1.93
USA (2011)	1,252,000	8.891
Japan	660,000	10.19
Russian Federation	441,000	6.17
Germany	361,000	8.54
Republic of Korea	322,000	12.84
Sweden	62,000	13.33
Denmark	41,000	14.86
Finland	39,000	15.68
Singapore (2012)	34,000	10.17

Source Adapted from: UNESCO (2016: 671)

This has implications for the rapid emergence of global production networks of advanced technology. The promise of the knowledge economy has attracted the interest of national governments around the world, not only in the advanced industrial countries, but also in the developing economies. In many developing countries aspirations towards a knowledge economy are confounded by an increasing digital divide. For other developing countries the prospects of making an early transition seem more realistic. A number of Asian countries now have national policies committed to developing as knowledge economies over the next decade with specific investments in education and training, technological infrastructure, venture capital support, and research and development, including Singapore, Hong Kong, Malaysia, Korea, Taiwan, Thailand, India and China. Excitement is generated by the apparent potential to leap through stages of industrial development from simple commodity production to high value added knowledge based business. An additional incentive is the realisation that it is likely that resources alone will not bring prosperity to developing countries. By employing their ingenuity to better effect, countries poor in resources have regularly out-performed the resource rich countries of the world (Maddison 2000).

The challenge is to develop the human, social and institutional capital necessary for competing in the knowledge economy, as Hoff and Stiglitz put it, "Development is no longer seen primarily as a process of capital accumulation but rather as a process of organizational change" (2001: 389). In terms of the educational component of human and social advance, many developing countries have cultures that place a very high value on educational attainment. Education is of central importance in the cultures of the Asia Pacific, for example the desire for learning, and the belief in personal development through education is more profound in Chinese culture than in the West. The Chinese mode of learning has an ancient lineage and involves a classical approach to literature and science, but often is accompanied by a traditional pedagogy of rote learning of codified knowledge, an approach that will scarcely equip China for effective participation in a rapidly transforming global economy. Recognising this, the government proposed a change in the mission of the Chinese universities from 'the cultivation of knowledge' to the 'cultivation of talents and creativity' (Clarke 1999).

However for such an economically dynamic region, little of this talent and creativity is exhibited in Asia Pacific industry until relatively recently. Young (1994) and Krugman (1994) dismissed Asia Pacific's economic growth as the result of a dramatic rise in the quantity of inputs to the economic system at an early stage of industrialization. Such gains from input-driven growth cannot continue indefinitely unless there are accompanying increases in efficiency. Asia Pacific growth largely can be attributed to a great mobilization of resources, combined with a self-sacrificing level of personal savings. Lingle (1997: 85) argued "East Asian economies have been following rather than leading the rest of the developed world, by relying upon ready access to Western technology and open markets. As the 'age of mass industrialization' passes the competitive advantage of many East Asian economies will be challenged. Without producing their own domestic entrepreneurial talent and self-generated technological advance, these countries will continue to lag the developed economies in what could prove a perpetually dependent relationship".

Moreover once absolute poverty is escaped, the relentless pursuit of economic growth in pursuit of the West might prove a singularly barren goal in a resource constrained planet. As Evans (2007: 7) argues development is not just about economic growth and consumption, it is about the capacity to make choices as one of the most important human capabilities "processes of participation have to be understood as constitutive parts of the *ends* of development in themselves" (Sen 1999: 291). More fundamental orientations and objectives are necessary than the incremental increase in GDP per capita that traditionally has been the critical indicator of economic growth. "Among all the recent contributions to development theory, the capability approach takes most seriously the universally accepted proposition that growth of GDP per capita is not an end in itself, but a proxy for improvements in human well-being, to be valued only insofar as it can be empirically connected to improved well-being. Sen argues that we should evaluate development in terms of "the expansion of the 'capabilities' of people to lead the kind of lives they value—and have reason to value".

Because it rejects reduction of developmental success to a single metric, the capability approach identifies "public deliberation" as the only analytically defensible way of ordering capabilities puts political institutions and civil society at the center of developmental goal-setting" (Evans 2007: 7).

This chapter will examine theories of growth, development, knowledge and human capital, examining the process of human capital formation in developing economies. The trajectories of industrial and human capital development in the Asia Pacific region will be investigated as the most promising developing region in economic terms, posing the questions of will this region succeed in joining the advanced industrial countries in the knowledge economy, and can other developing countries and regions of the world follow this path?

Human Capital Theory

The realization of the criticality of human capital to economic growth and well-being adds significance to this form of investment: expenditure on education, health and social services become as essential as investment in physical capital (Bowman 1969). With increasing returns to organizations due to investment in human capital allowing specialization, economies with a larger stock of human capital will experience a faster rate of growth (Romer 1990). There is growing agreement on the importance of skills as the engine of economic growth, but more debate on the significance of educational attainment for broad competencies supporting life-long learning, and more specific competencies including the ability to use information and communication technologies, to solve problems, and to work in teams (OECD 2001: 100). In the OECD countries more than half of GDP is accounted for by knowledge-based industries, including the main producers of high-technology goods, high and medium technology manufacturing, and knowledge intensive services such as finance, insurance, business, communication and social services. This is manifest in the rising human capital levels of the population in OECD countries as measure in educational attainment, and in the increased demand for highly educated and highly skilled workers.

Until recently the knowledge economy deploying the most advanced skills appeared heavily concentrated in the established advanced industrial countries. According to the World Bank (2006: 4) the transition to the knowledge economy involves long-term investments in education, developing innovation capability, modernizing the information infrastructure, and having an economic environment conducive to market transactions. Four pillars of the framework of a knowledge economy are erected as:

(i) An *economic and institutional regime* providing for efficient mobilization and allocation of resources and to stimulate creativity and incentives for development, dissemination and use of knowledge;
(ii) *Educated and skilled* workers who can continuously upgrade and adapt their skills to efficiently create and use knowledge;
(iii) An *effective innovation system* of firms, research centres, universities, consultancies, and other organizations that can promote the knowledge revolution, build networks globally, and assimilate and adapt knowledge to local needs;
(iv) An *information infrastructure* that can facilitate effective communication, dissemination and processing of information and knowledge (World Bank 2006: 4).

Though the countries of the developing world generally have large populations and a commitment to education and learning, for economic advance something more is needed than skills and abilities. Educated and trained people require an appropriate environment with opportunities and incentives to utilize their acquired knowledge, and in many developing countries this is largely missing (Mizrahi 2004; Taylor and Leonard 2002). Foreign direct investment by multi-national corporations often requires a skilled workforce as a key factor, and in recent years foreign direct investment has moved towards relatively skill-intensive production and services, and less towards primary and resource-based manufacturing (OECD 2003: 24). Multinational corporations may further enhance training and development opportunities. However foreign direct investment is heavily skewed towards a relatively few developing countries, and large tracts of the developing world largely are left to their own devices.

Human Capital Formation

Porter et al. (2007: 56) suggest nations move through several stages in their economic development, each with enhanced capabilities (Fig. 12.1):

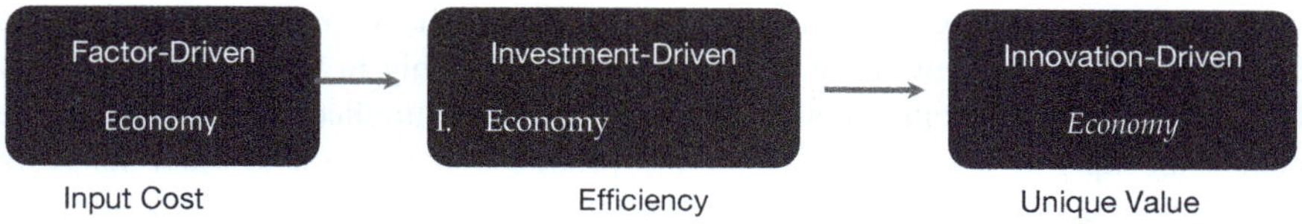

Fig. 12.1 Stages of competitive development. *Source* Adapted from Porter et al. (2007)

(i) ***Factor driven***

Basic factor conditions especially low cost labour and natural resources are critical for the production of simple commodities or products designed in more advanced countries. Technology is slowly assimilated, and companies compete on price in labour intensive manufacturing and resource extraction in industries sensitive to world economic cycles, commodity prices and exchange rate fluctuations.

(ii) ***Investment driven***

Efficiency in the production of more advanced but undifferentiated products with investment in infrastructure, skill development, incentives for investment and productivity. Though more sophisticated products both design and technology from abroad, but with a growing capacity to use and improve the technology. More extended capabilities along the value chain, still susceptible to demand shocks but with greater resilience than countries depending on commodity cycles.

(iii) ***Innovation driven***

The ability to produce innovative products and services using advanced methods, with leading technology and supporting industries. Capability is based in specialist clusters of knowledge based businesses, with supporting institutions and incentives encouraging an innovation driven economy. Distinctive products and higher level services offer greater protection from external economic shocks.

Porter et al. (2007) highlight the challenges of transition from one stage of economic development to the next necessitating the acquisition of skills and appropriate institutional support: "The sequential process of building interdependent microeconomic capabilities, improving incentives, evolving company strategies, and increasing rivalry creates important pitfalls in economic policy. The influence of one part of the business environment depends on the state of the others. Lack of improvement in any important area can lead to a plateau in productivity growth and stalled development. Worse yet, key weaknesses … can undermine the entire economic reform process…. This analysis also begins to reveal why countries find the transition to a new stage of development so difficult. Such inflection points require wholesale transformation of many interdependent aspects of competition" (2007: 56).

The hard path to growth developing economies have traditionally followed begins with simple commodity production as in assembly in the garment industry following buyer's specifications and using materials supplied by the buyer. The next stage up the value chain is for the producer to take on a wider range of manufacturing functions including sourcing and logistics (original equipment manufacture (OEM), with the buyer remaining responsible for design and marketing). With the following stage of original design manufacture (ODM) the producer carries out parts of the design process, and in the most advanced stages the buyer merely attaches his own brand to the product. Finally reaching the top of the value chain with original brand manufacture (OBM) the producer designs, manufactures and markets its own products under its own brand. Conventionally it was assumed that this pathway to securing control of the value chain had to be patiently repeated with each new industry and technology that is entered, until methods of faster cycle capability involving skipping traditional stages of the value chain, or even creating new value chains and production processes were conceived.

Trajectories of Development in the Asia Pacific

Though the Asia Pacific is widely regarded as the most successful example of economic and skill development, the route to rapid growth has not been without serious obstacles. The Asian economies learned to their cost the limitations of attempting to compete in commodity markets where over-capacity is continually driving down prices for semi-conductors and other electronic components the production of which had previously fuelled their rapid economic growth. Recovering from the Asian financial crisis of 1997/98, the South East Asian economies were reminded of the dependence of surviving as a contract manufacturer for US based companies with the downturn in technology markets from 2000. Though the return of demand in 2003/04 recovered the fortunes of the East Asian economies, the collapse in demand during the global financial crisis of 2008 and 2009 was another shock which from the West which the Asia Pacific had to absorb, and there is still a sense of dependence in many sectors on technology and expertise from the advanced industrial countries.

Until the arrival of the new economy, to become an advanced economy involved treading a long and difficult path of industrial and structural transformation from labour intensive industries (typified by textiles), to non-differentiated scale driven industries (steel, basic chemicals, and heavy machinery), to differentiated assembly based industries (automobiles, electric, electronic goods), finally to the Schumpeterian R&D intensive industries (specialty chips, biotechnology, and new materials). This conceptualization of a stages-based process of industrialization is in line with growth as Joseph Schumpeter conceived, which envisaged a sequence of stages in each of which breakthrough innovations (new technologies) create a new dominant industry as the main engine of growth. Japan joined the Western industrial countries quickly in the first three stages early in the 20th century, and more recently in the fourth stage. This prompted the East Asian countries to follow the Japanese model of growth: what the World Bank referred to as the East Asian Miracle was effectively this cultural borrowing of industrial technology (JETRO 1998; Ozawa et al. 2001).

China's rapid export expansion threatens this *flying geese* pattern of economic development in East Asia. (The *flying geese* pattern was recognised by Akamatsu Kaname in the 1930s, and refers to the process by which countries move up the product and technology ladder as they develop, leaving the rungs they vacate to be occupied by the economies following in their flight.) In the 1990s the growth of China's exports to the United States came at the expense of the newly industrialising economies of East Asia, but were largely in product lines that the NIE's (Hong Kong, Republic of Korea, Singapore and Taiwan) were abandoning including footwear, clothing, toys and household products. Meanwhile the ASEAN 4 (Indonesia, Malaysia, Philippines and Thailand) increased their share of exports to the United States in more capital and technology intensive products.

While China's comparative advantage in labour intensive industries increased during the 1990s and early 2000s and ASEAN 4 countries advantage decreased, what is of more concern to these countries is China's growing comparative advantage in an increasing number of capital intensive industries. China's mix of exports initially overlapped most with exports from Indonesia and Thailand, but the overlap in exports between China and the more advanced economies of East Asia is now growing, as China becomes more technologically sophisticated. "The competition is bound to intensify in a number of product groups unless countries make determined efforts to diversify their mix of products, to raise the technological thresholds in existing product categories, and to increase their trade in services" (Yusuf et al. 2003: 25).

The progress of trade and technological development experienced in East Asia is divided into four stages by Yusuf (2004c: 4–6) who elaborates the wider international production relations inherent in skill development:

- ***Labour intensive light manufacturing***
  In the 1960s Hong Kong, South Korea, Singapore and Taiwan began investing in light, labour intensive manufacturing industries, whose products quickly penetrated price sensitive markets in Western countries.
- ***Upgrading by newly industrialised economies***
  Export led-growth in light manufacturing was joined in the 1970s by South East Asian countries, and by 1980 by China. Meanwhile the Asian countries that were first to industrialise moved into more capital intensive and skill intensive manufacturing, attracting a rising flow of foreign direct investment from the West. Multinational corporations began dispersing production of advanced components to overseas subsidiaries in Asia.
- ***Global production networking***
  By the end of the 1980s East Asia was drawn into a developing web of relationships involving production, trade and FDI. "Japanese multinational companies are building a regional division of labour that emphasises technology-intensive

prototype production in Japan and mass production of standardised products in Asia" (Hatch 2003: 31). Rapid increases in trade, FDI and corporate restructuring in the 1990s made the light manufacturing sectors of East Asia coextensive with company activities in Japan, the United States, and Europe. Large multinational companies in automobiles, electronics, office equipment, and optical instruments invested in production facilities, followed by their parts suppliers.

- ***Technological deepening***
  With further trade liberalisation, intensifying competition from China in both product markets and for FDI, and an increasing emphasis on scale, a fourth stage in East Asian development was predicated on technological specialisation and deepening. The clear illustration of the benefits of the rapid acquisition of technological capability is China, which emerged to become the largest trading nation in the world, and the largest producer of information technology hardware.

Yusuf (2004c: 8) highlights the rigours of this pursuit "For more than a decade, upgrading has been the mantra of East Asian middle-income economies. As they have collectively struggled to reach the next rung of the ladder, economies in the region have often only succeeded in extending the embrace of commodification. Upgrading can be achieved through incremental product or process innovation that can be the source of modest rents until the competition catches up, which can occur in a matter of months. However, when upgrading is based on significant design and product innovation protected by patent rights or the products themselves are difficult to imitate, substantial rents can accrue over several years. Building a reliable base of technological capability is becoming increasingly urgent for all those East Asian economies seeking to avoid the trap of low-level growth associated with commodity production. The risk has certainly risen over the past five years, as low-cost producers in China have dramatically expanded capacity and flooded the markets for manufactured commodities."

The normal trajectory of economic development is to begin with labour intensive light industries such as textiles, to develop heavy industries such as steel and petrochemicals, then differentiated assembly industries such as electronics. Innovation intensive industries such as biotechnology and super-semiconductors are the foundations of the new knowledge economy followed by knowledge based businesses associated with software production, multi-media and other products based on intellectual capital.

The question is whether it is possible to accelerate economic development by missing some of these stages? For example the Irish economy, which enjoyed rapid economic growth in the 1990s and early 2002s, apparently successfully moved from agriculture to an information age economy, without needing to build industrial age physical plant and infrastructure. Ireland's created a favourable climate for knowledge based business through favourable tax policies, minimal regulation, and positive incentives to attract investments in high technology and pharmaceutical industries. (However Ireland's historically close cultural relations with the US, even older cultural ties with several European countries, and more recent embrace of the

European Union played an important part too in the rapid spurt of the Irish economy. Also Ireland's embrace of international finance came to disaster during the financial crisis, which badly damaged the economy).

Japan, Korea and China are now on the threshold of a new fifth stage led and driven by the digital revolution, most notably the Internet, producing *abstract goods* or *conceptual goods*. The other Asian NIEs are swiftly catching up, although they remain some way behind in R&D intensive industries, they are stepping up their investment in R&D. The ASEAN-4 countries are still largely in the non-differentiated scale driven industries, though they have entered with some success the labour-intensive, standardized lower-end segments of the assembly based differentiated industries of computer chip assembly and consumer electronics. It is the giant economies of China and India that have made the greatest strides forward. China is advancing in the assembly-based industries, including automobiles and consumer electronics, taking advantage of its huge domestic markets that can attract foreign multinationals and technologies (Evans and Staveteig 2006). Since economic liberalization India has attracted significant multinational investment in R&D centres located in high technology clusters, and progressed as the back-office data processing centre of business across the world.

As entry barriers fall, the arrival of lower income countries in commodity production forces middle income producers to diversify into other products and services, prompting a race up the value chain: "One widely pursued strategy, is for economies to upgrade to the assembly of high-technology products such as mobile handsets or digital cameras. However, most of the East Asian economies are already adept at assembling electronics equipment, and a shift to high technology items does not necessarily increase local value added by much. Moreover, earnings only increase when the growth of supply for a more sophisticated line of products lags behind demand. A large and continuous increase in value added that is more likely to result in higher earnings is becoming tied to steady technological advance in certain commodity products and in complex products or services (Hobday 1998). These include the machinery needed to produce the parts and components and to assemble the manufactures pouring out of East Asian factories, the conceptualization, design, integration, and maintenance of complex products such as plant equipment, and the supply of or high value–added services, most of which are now tradable and can command global markets" (Yusuf 2004c: 7).

The impact of the Internet could alter the dynamics of catch-up and compete among Asian economies. The NIEs are adapting to the Web as decisively as Japan, and investing in advanced broadband telecommunication networks. Moreover unlike the previous linear and sector differentiating progression of structural upgrading in which a new industry becomes dominant without significantly effecting the older generation of industries, the Internet based new economy industries impact upon all of the older generation of industries in areas of management, production, procurement, distribution and customer services. Transaction intensive sectors such as finance, telecommunications, distribution, and government, are even more dramatically impacted.

Global and Regional Integration

Integration is increasing at the global level, developing more competition as freer trade displaces previously protected domestic markets. At the regional level, Japan is no longer the economic driver of East Asia that it was in the recent past, and China is both a promising market and fierce competitor. As the technological revolution intensifies, production organisation is transformed by the growth of foreign direct investment, the emergence of international production networks bringing together component suppliers, assemblers, supply chain managers, and buyers in dynamic and changing relationships (Lasserre 2003; Krugman and Venables 1995; Lawson 1999; Lawson and Lorenz 1999; Hatch 2003; UNCTAD 2005b). In this competitive environment Yusuf et al. (2003: 18) argue:

> Countries (and firms) that are well integrated into international production networks and widely exposed to market trends abroad will be much better placed to exploit market opportunities than those that remain less integrated. But unless East Asia moves towards a technological and skill-intensive, rather than factor-intensive, mode of manufacturing, a slower increase in value added will constrain growth in the future, a tendency that could be exacerbated by a gradual cessation in the expansion of the labour force in several countries. It is imperative that East Asia prepare to move up the value chain, relying more on productivity-enhancing innovations based on science and technology for its dominant source of growth.

China has relied heavily on foreign direct investment (FDI) for inward technology transfer, and the changes in China's exports and imports have correlated with changes in inflows of FDI. In the 1980s FDI was concentrated in labour intensive industries, by the 1990s they shifted to capital intensive industries, and this trend continues. Most of China's FDI inflows come from the European Union, Japan and the United States, but a significant proportion also originates in the newly industrialising economies. Many Japanese firms have moved their production and procurement to China in the medium term to take advantage of lower production costs, to supply the expanding domestic market, and to supply parts to major customers. A significant share of recent flows are into industries producing flat screen televisions, DVD players, LCD monitors, plasma display panels, laptop computers, and digital cameras, that will significantly augment China's manufacturing capability in higher-technology areas. This shift in high tech production from Japan (and the United States) to China will continue to develop (Yusuf et al. 2003: 26). As China becomes more attractive for such relocation of production, other East Asian economies, particularly the ASEAN 4 are experiencing difficulty attracting the additional FDI inflows need to upgrade their industries, as Yusuf et al. (2003: 26) argue, "If China successfully transforms itself from the *factory of the world,* to the *design laboratory of the world* by using direct investment by Japanese corporations in research and development facilities, the pressure on Southeast Asian economies will sharpen further. For the ASEAN nations, this could drastically heighten the urgency of developing new and differentiated products and services"

Commoditization or Differentiation?

Another powerful influence upon the East Asian economies is the ongoing transformation of the structure of world production in industries such as automobile parts and consumer electronics. In a process of deverticalisation lead firms now outsource virtually all of their manufacturing operations, and restructured value chains have created geographically dispersed global production networks dominated by large contract manufacturers. Many contract manufacturers have their headquarters in the advanced industrial countries, but have specialised production facilities throughout the world including the Asia Pacific. These international production networks now orchestrate as much as two thirds of all trade in commoditized manufactures. Asian Pacific firms need to extract the best returns possible from participation in production networks, and need to develop their own differentiated products in order to avoid being marginalised and to realise their technological potential in niche markets (Yusuf et al. 2003: 27). For example in the gradual transition of the production development of the personal computer and later the tablet and iPhone from the US and Japan to China. While concept design and product planning remained in the US and Japan, and applied R&D and development of new platforms centred on Taiwanese companies, product development for mature products, and production engineering shifted to China. Ultimately this led to the sale of IBM personal computers to Lenovo of China in 2005, and later to the increasing incidence of locally designed and produced smart phones in China.

The formula for economic growth in the past 30 years in the Asia Pacific was derived from high rates of capital accumulation, technological change and the influx of young educated workers. Yusuf et al. argue that as the proportion of working age population begins to decline, it is only a leap in the region's technological capability that will permit continued advance towards catching up with the Western economies:

> Several countries in the region are finding less and less profit can be squeezed out of existing product lines. Many manufactured products (even high technology ones) have now become standardized commodities traded in intensely competitive markets, much like primary products. Commoditized manufactures offer relatively weak prospects for growth because their real prices are decreasing and they have become barely profitable despite their manufacturers efforts to raise productivity. The hard disk drive industry epitomizes the problems facing segments of East Asia's electronics industry: formerly exotic high-tech products once earning high rents are being transformed into marginally profitable commodities attractive only for companies with highly specialised technological capability and hard-won market share. Between 1988 and 2002 the price per megabyte of hard disk drives fell from $11.54 to less than $0.15, side by side with drastic reduction in the size of each unit and a miniaturization of individual components. These trends in turn have forced the industry to consolidate and to increase substantially research into areas such as microelectromechanical systems to reduce the size of storage devices and the capacity intensity of production (Yusuf et al. 2003: 28).

The escape from this cutthroat competition in commodity markets is through design skills and innovation. To move from competition based on the cost of cheap factor

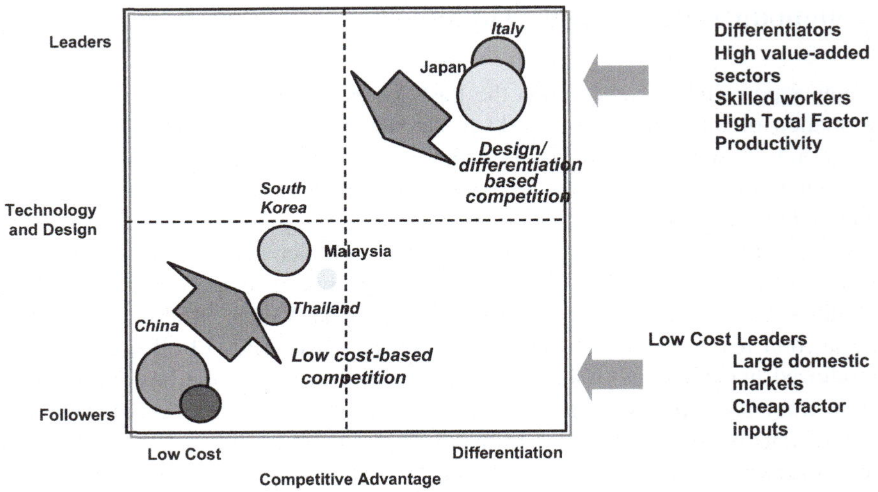

Fig. 12.2 From commodity to differentiation based competition

inputs, to competition based on the high value added of design (Fig. 12.2). These skills enable firms to differentiate their products, and in some instances, to create demand for entirely new products with a new technology that disrupts previous patterns of consumption. The added value provided by successful research and design can provide the returns to finance further growth. The countries in the region are assimilating this important lesson, China alone in increasing its R&D spending became the second highest investor in R&D after the United States, with Japan third. This initiative has received a considerable boost from 400 research centres in China established by multi-national companies.

Innovation and creativity will be critical to the regional economies of the near future. Better innovation systems, and channels for regional and global collaboration are necessary. The investment in education during the 1990s yielded high returns, but it was education geared toward a factor intensive model of the economy, today schools need to equip students not only with technical skills but with creative capabilities to question and learn independently. East Asia needs to nurture business, professional and entrepreneurial skills to foster the development of the service activities that are the basis of the new economy. (Spurred by the growth of ICT services, in Hong Kong, Singapore and Taiwan services accounted for 60% + of GDP by the early 2000s, and in the other countries of the region services form around 40% + of GDP). With the exception of Hong Kong, Japan, Singapore and Taiwan, gaps in business skills are evident in the region, and even Japan's level of legal, accounting and financial skills fall short of other OECD countries. When the economies of East Asia concentrated on manufacturing and served as suppliers to major US or European corporations the shortage of professional skills was not as apparent. But when these economies attempt to commercialise research and development, as firms seek to develop, design and market new products independently with their own brand names, and package services with higher value added services together with manufactured products to raise profit margins, the gaps in professional skills became more critical (Yusuf et al. 2003: 30).

Development Towards Knowledge Based Economies?

The World Bank in a study funded by the Japanese government once characterised East Asia's economic performance as *The East Asian Miracle* (World Bank 1993: 1), describing these as the High Performing Asian Economies (HPAEs). Though in the ensuing decade East Asia remained the global leader in terms of growth rates, since the financial crisis of 1997/98, the region has struggled to sustain the pace of earlier development in a more open, volatile, competitive and connected global markets. In a series of studies again sponsored by the Japanese government and completed by the World Bank, the questions are explored of *Can East Asia Compete* (Yusuf and Evenett 2002); *Innovative East Asia: The Future of Growth* (Yusuf et al. 2003); *Global Production Networking and Technological Change in East Asia* (Yusuf et al. 2004a); and *Global Change and East Asian Policy Initiatives* (Yusuf et al. 2004b). Sustaining rapid growth in a more competitive, integrated and changing world would depend on East Asian economies:

- Retaining the strengths of the past (macroeconomic stability, openness to trade, high rates of savings and investment, and human capital development);
- Overcoming the weaknesses of the present (in the financial sector, corporate governance, regulatory oversight, legal framework, exchange rate management, and social protection); and
- Deriving much more of the impetus for growth from innovation than from factor accumulation (Yusuf et al. 2003: 1).

The challenge is for the East Asian economies to become more innovative, and particularly the question of how the East Asian economies might achieve the transition from high tech industries towards the knowledge based economies they aspire to become (Teece 2000; Grant 1996; World Bank 2006). The momentous transition is to move from a supply driven production economy of simple mass produced products, to an innovative, customer driven knowledge economy where capability brings rewards.

In this context the promise of the knowledge-based economy is powerful indeed, and most economies of the Asia Pacific committed to ambitious policies to leap forward into this new techno-economic paradigm with the creation of knowledge economies including Korea; Malaysia; Singapore; Taiwan; Thailand; Hong Kong; Japan and China. All of these were ambitious polices with apparent limitations and possibilities (Chaminade and Edquist 2006; O'Doherty and Arnold 2003). Yoshida (2001) reviews the common vision of Asian economies to commit to the development of a knowledge economy:

- All the Asian economies share in common a vision that their continued success as leading commercial and manufacturing centres in a global knowledge-based economy depends on their ability to harness science and technology and importantly, people's capacity for innovation.
- All continue to consider information technology, especially as it relates to the Internet and electronic commerce as critical to their futures but are attempting to diversify especially into biotechnology. China and Japan already possess world-class scientific and technical expertise in a wide range of disciplines.
- All are trying to stimulate venture capital and high technology start-ups rather than relying only on existing large companies—the large Asian companies themselves are investing more heavily in start-ups than in the past.
- Most importantly China's decision to enter the World Trade Organisation, the calls for deregulation by Japanese companies and the overall concern with increasing private sector rather than just government R&D expenditure points to the determination by these countries that the recent economic success of the United States —rests with its ability to innovate, produce lots of technologically-based new companies, and adapt to an increasingly open global economy.
- All are basing their decisions on a perception that increased access to markets and knowledge is driving the pace and scope of globalisation faster and wider than ever before, and therefore, their economic success and the livelihood of the people depend on the ability of their firms and universities to take full advantage of, and contribute to, global science and technology advances.
- In the short term, the region's heavy dependence on its information technology sector and its ability to leverage its R&D investment in that sector to build up a more diversified scientific and technological infrastructure and expand further into Internet related technologies will determine how well each player is able to sustain its growth.
- In the long term, the question for each player will be whether or not their institutional reforms and the many new global business alliances will sustain and enhance domestic innovation, and enable their companies to keep pace with rapid technological changes coming from the United States and elsewhere.

The McKinsey Global Institute (MGI) offer an optimistic prognosis of the capacity of China to transform into an innovative economy: "China has the potential to meet its "innovation imperative" and to emerge as a driving force in innovation globally. The "China effect" in global innovation would be felt in several ways. As the nation with the largest population and the second-largest economy in GDP terms, China will be a growing source of innovation to serve the needs of an enormous and increasingly demanding consumer market (UNCTAD 2005a). It is also a logical location for R&D and rapid commercialization of new ideas by global companies—for China, for other emerging markets, and for the rest of the world. Finally, the Chinese model of rapid, low-cost innovation can be applied around the world, potentially disrupting a range of industries (MGI 2015).

High-Tech Clusters and Innovation Precincts

International experience suggests the most intensive innovation occurs in industrial clusters in urban communities that have capability, infrastructural support and other amenities. It is not possible for East Asian governments to wish into existence these high technology clusters, though every government has adopted ambitious policies for information and communication technology developments (Freeman 1995, 2008; Pitelis 2009; Staber 2001; Tallman et al. 2004; Sorenson 2003; Uzzi 1997). Japan, Singapore and Taiwan have laid the groundwork for such clusters by combining local capacity and international linkages forged through trade, FDI, and the movement of knowledge workers. Other countries such as China, Korea and Malaysia, each of which has a base in high-tech manufacturing industries, are attempting to induce clusters that fuse manufacturing capability with research and producer services. The expensive, high risk, state sponsored approach involves investing heavily in a transport and communications infrastructure, serviced land, research facilities and providing incentives for high tech industries to locate in the designated area. More promising environments are open urban milieu, that cultivate creativity, offer opportunities for collaboration with firms in other clusters that support innovation, and invite the circulation of human capital from overseas.

Innovation precincts are forming in urban communities across the globe, as catalysts of local creativity and innovation, globally connected, and working near the frontier of technology and applied knowledge. As Brungs (2017) explains:

> There are many types of precincts (or districts or hubs) and they are generally geographical areas with a particular focus. Some rare ones can even operate as a hub and spoke model, that is, they have connected areas that go beyond the main immediate geographical location. Innovation precincts … create a critical mass by bringing together the innovation and employment potential of forward-looking education and research institutions, high-growth small and medium-sized enterprises, and tech and creative start-ups in well-designed, amenity-rich, mixed-use environments (Brungs 2017).

Innovation precincts do not happen by accident, and successful precincts across the world all share a few core similarities, including:

- Excellent transport networks and are within 30–45 min of an international airport
- Within walking distance of, and partnering with, a research-intensive university (and not just to access the researchers and, probably even more importantly, the students)
- Encompass a high density of start-ups and companies
- Close proximity to vibrant communities, and
- Excellent infrastructure, including access to significant broadband capacity.

> As advanced economies, like Australia's, move towards innovation, companies, researchers and entrepreneurs have found the need to work in close proximity to each other. Together, they can share ideas, draw on varied expertise and grow talent. Their proximity negates the need for any one company, business or institution to master all the knowledge or own all the resources they need to be successful. Instead, they can rely on a network of

collaborators. Importantly, innovation precincts facilitate the creation and commercialisation of new ideas and support the economy by creating new jobs. They drive a higher economic contribution than that of isolated and unconnected businesses, and create a high-employment multiplier effect (for every one new high-tech job five additional local jobs are created) (Brungs 2017).

The Global Diaspara of Science and Technology Human Capital

Another advantage of East Asia is the large diaspora of skilled workers participating in leading North American clusters of innovation, who have acquired intangible capital, business contacts, and financial wealth (Turpin et al. 2010). Estimates suggest there are between 40 and 65 million overseas Chinese and 25 million overseas Indian. This great diaspora are more likely to cluster in urban centres overseas, and more likely to work in highly skilled industries and professions than the population at large. For example in Silicon Valley 53% of the science and engineering workforce is foreign born, and Indian Americans own 15% of all start-ups (Cheng 2016; Chand 2015). As in the development of Hong Kong, Singapore and Taiwan these individuals can be the nuclei for cluster development in East Asia—providing there is a welcoming institutional environment. The life-blood of dynamic clusters is the continuing innovation of firms, and the constant networking among them (Gunter and Hoevan 2004).

The internationalization of scientific and technical human capital is generated by and includes research and development (R&D) personnel, but as Turpin et al. (2010) suggest also includes the knowledge, know-how and learning capacity embedded in their knowledge networks, capturing the fluidity of this diaspora:

> The global context of the science and technology human capital movement is today often characterized as "the frequent back and forth movement of migrants, ideas, knowledge, information, and skill sets that is now a routine part of contemporary trans-nationalism" (Favell et al. 2007: 19). Mahroum (2000) has described the international mobility of scientists as both a driver and a consequence of processes of the increasingly global forms of organization of knowledge production and distribution. Thinking about transnational mobility in this context leads us toward a "network ontology" (Coe and Bunnell 2003: 454) that privileges "connections" (Meyer 2001) and focuses on the circulation of innovative personnel and knowledge over a "scalar" approach tied to fixed work sites or geographic locations (Coe and Bunnell 2003: 454).

Asia's Advantages and Disadvantages

Asia has some powerful advantages in building knowledge based businesses, but also possesses some serious economic and social weaknesses. Among Asia's advantages may be included the fact the region is already a centre of IT hardware manufacturing, with a young well educated workforce. Asian business cultures can cope with risk-taking and the Asian market represents half the world's population. Asia's disadvantages require further exploration: software, services and content are harder to create than manufacturing hardware commodities.

Although Asia is often praised for its 'entrepreneurial' culture, there is a shortage of venture capitalists. Asian governments have a poor record in financing high-tech start-ups, and high tech company start-up funds remained unused in Hong Kong and Singapore. The governments of Hong Kong, Malaysia and Singapore now direct the biggest funds for high-tech entrepreneurs through venture capitalists. However many of those who call themselves, 'venture capitalists' are really work for divisions of banks. How can these contradictions between an eager willingness to create knowledge based businesses and an apparent lack of the requisite social and economic skills be reconciled? There are some possibilities for the development of high-tech knowledge based businesses: for example the application of technology for local and regional needs represents a major opportunity as Alibaba has proved. The Asian region is the largest manufacturing centre of the world, and on-line logistics, business to business e-commerce, and trade finance are all local needs that can be served by Asian firms. Asian manufacturers are famously efficient at making things, but far less so at managing the information that feeds into and out of the process. South Korea and Taiwan, whose governments have not tried as hard to lead the Internet wave, could benefit even more from e-business than their neighbours, as their huge manufacturing sectors turn to new applications. However, the instinct of Asian governments to lead this transformation is still a danger, with governments attempting to force their economies down a path that they think will transform their economies into the technology hub of Asia.

The Limitations of Top-Down Strategies

As the OECD (2000) concludes in a survey of *Knowledge Based Industries in Asia* the national policies for becoming knowledge based economies may be inspiring, but these visions are top-down government development strategies, and may be a little unrealistic. Deficiencies in Asian economies, highlighted during the Asian financial crisis, include an overemphasis on manufacturing and large firms to the detriment of services and smaller enterprises; inadequate investment in education and innovation capabilities; and changing competitive advantages due to rising labour costs which have led to a decline in foreign investment.

APEC's (2000) assessment of the pre-conditions for developing a knowledge economy are that most essential requirement is basic education; followed by information and communication infrastructure; sustained by an entrepreneurial, innovative culture, open to new ideas especially from the outside; and supported by a policy framework offering social support, regulation of competition, and transparency. Yusuf (2004c: 17) records the existing policies of East Asian governments to initiate and support technological advance as:

- Human capital deepening;
- Creation of publicly financed research institutes;
- Grants, subsidies, and tax incentives for private R&D activities and government contracts;
- Technology licensing policies and technology transfer arrangements through FDI in high-tech industries;
- R&D by public sector firms;
- Incentives for developing and applying information technology.

At the corporate level, knowledge management is often translated into installing the technical tools and systems which can be purchased and implemented readily, with a neglect of the more difficult organizational transformation to create a more knowledge sharing culture. Similarly at the national level in the ambitious policies of the Asian economies to become knowledge based, there is an over-emphasis on equipping the information and communication infrastructures, and little focus on the kind of organizational relationships which might foster knowledge exchange. For this reason knowledge management tools and systems technologies are reported to be less effective in many Asian business cultures. Asian economies have demonstrated a determination to progress in recent decades but this may represent their greatest knowledge challenge. In countries and enterprises wedded to hierarchical authority and obedience, conceptions of the learning organisation and the questioning it gives rise to seem rather remote.

It is likely many Asian economies will continue to emphasise investment in information and communication technologies as the infrastructure of their knowledge economy to the neglect of the economic, social and organisational restructuring required to deliver the benefits of the knowledge economy. Many Asian economies are advanced in providing the tools by which information can be accessed (though a few including China are seriously behind with this). However if people are inhibited from making independent and creative use of this information, then it will be harder to translate it into useful knowledge. It is likely Asia will win the race to become the world's primary centre for manufacturing, if it has not already done so. It is far less certain that Asia is well positioned in the race to develop and succeed with knowledge economies. China will continues to advanced in high technology manufacturing, and India will excel at information and business services outsourcing, but these activities will not readily provide a strategic direction to the creative heights of the knowledge economy

Conclusions

For the economies in East Asia that have been successful developing the human, economic and technological capital for the ongoing pursuit towards a knowledge economy, there will continue to be the demanding task of encouraging the institutions and relations that will match them equally with advanced industrial countries of the West. "To a significant extent future competition will essentially be competition between alternative firm-level learning and innovation systems. While these are constructed by firms, they depend increasingly on external assets and relationships" (Scott-Kemmis 2008: 47). This will involve a concentration on developing the talents and abilities of people more than any other factor, and allowing people the freedom to define their own objectives and ideals:

> The confluence of endogenous growth theory with institutional approaches to development and the capability approach jibe nicely with the shifting historical context. Together they suggest that 21st century development will depend on generating intangible assets (ideas, skills, and networks) rather than on stimulating investment in machinery and physical assets oriented to the production of tangible goods. This makes investment in human capabilities (which include what is traditionally known as "human capital") more economically critical. At the same time, new development theories assume that economic growth depends on political institutions and the capacity to set collective goals. The capability approach sets out the political argument most firmly, arguing that only public interchange and open deliberation can effectively define development goals and elaborate the means for attaining them (Evans 2007: 2). That is the future innovation success of the Asia Pacific rests with the free expression of the creativity and ingenuity of the people of this dynamic region.

References

Acemoglu, D., Johnson, S., & Robinson, J. (2005). Institutions as the fundamental cause of long-run growth. In P. Aghion & S. Durlauf (Eds.), *Handbook of economic growth*. Amsterdam: Elsevier.

ADB. (2007). *Moving toward knowledge-based economies: Asian experiences*. Asian Development Bank

Bairoch, P. (1982). International industrialisation levels from 1750–1980. *Journal of European History, 2*, 268–333.

Bowman, M. (1969). Economics of education. *Review of Educational Research, 39*(5), 641–670.

Brungs, A. (2017). *Innovation precincts*. University of Technology Sydney.

Chaminade, C., & Edquist, C. (2006). *Rationales for public policy intervention from a systems of innovation approach: The case of VINNOVA*. CIRCLE Electronic Working Paper Series Paper no. 2006/04.

Chand, M. (2015). *Diasporas as drivers of national competitiveness*, Elsevier.

Cheng, J. (2016). *Engaging diasporas: The case of Australia and other key countries*. Consultancy Report for Securing Australia's Future Project.

Clarke, T. (1999) The development of management education in China. *Education and training, 41*(6/7), 273–276.

Coe, N., & Bunnell, T. (2003). Spatializing knowledge communities: Towards a conceptualization of transnational innovation networks. *Global Networks, 3*(4), 437–456.

Dunning, J. H. (2006). Towards a new paradigm of development: Implications for the determinants of international business activity. *Transnational Corporations, 15*(1), 173–228.

Easterly, W. (2001). *The elusive quest for growth: Economists' adventures and misadventures in the tropics*. Cambridge, MA: MIT Press.

Evans, P. (2007). *In Search of the 21st Century Developmental State*. Berkeley: University of California. Working Paper. July 27, 2007.

Evans, P., & Staveteig, S. (2006). *21st Century Industrialisation and Development in the Global South: The Chinese case in comparative-historical perspective*. Berkeley: University of California. Working Paper. January 17, 2006.

Favell, A., Feldblum, M., & Smith, M. (2007) The human face of global mobility. *Society, 44*(2), 15–25.

Freeman, C. (1995). The "National System of Innovation" in historical perspective. *Cambridge Journal of Economics, 19,* 5–24.

Freeman, C. (2008). *Systems of innovation*. Cheltenham: Edward Elgar.

Georghiou, L., Smith, K., Toivanen, O., & Ylä-Anttila, P. (2003). *Evaluation of the finnish innovation support system* (38 pp). Finland: Ministry of Trade and Industry Publications 5/2003.

Grant, R. (1996). Toward a knowledge-based theory of the firm. *Strategic Management Journal, 17,* 109–122.

Gunter, G. B., & Hoevan, R. (2004). *The social dimension of globalisation*. Working Paper Number 24. World Commission on the Social Dimensions of Globalisation. Geneva: International Labour Office.

Hatch, W. F. (2003). Agenda for Asian Regionalism. *Japanese Economy, 32*(21), 86–97.

Helpman, E. (2004). *The mystery of economic growth*. Cambridge, MA: Harvard University Press.

Hobday, M. (1998). Product complexity, innovation and industrial organisation. Mike Hobday. *Research Policy, 26*(6), 689–710.

Hoff, K., & Stiglitz, J. (2001). Modern economic theory and development. In G. Meier & J. Stiglitz (Eds.), *Frontiers of development economics*. New York, NY: Oxford University Press.

IBM. (2017). *Upskilling India: Building India's talent base to compete in the global economy*. IBM Institute for Business Value.

JETRO. (1998). *Jetero hakusho, white paper*. Tokyo: JETRO.

Krugman, P. (1994). The myth of Asia's miracle. *Foreign Affairs, 73*(6), 62–78.

Krugman, P. R., & Venables, A. J. (1995). Globalization and the inequality of nations. *The Quarterly Journal of Economics, 110*(4), 857–880.

Lasserre, P. (2003). *Global strategic management*. Basingstoke: Palgrave Macmillan.

Lawson, C. (1999). Towards a competence theory of the region. *Cambridge Journal of Economics, 23,* 151–166.

Lawson, C., & Lorenz, E. (1999). Collective learning. *Tacit Knowledge and Regional Innovative Capacity, Regional Studies, 33,* 305–317.

Lingle, C. (1997). *The rise and decline of the Asian century*. Hong Kong: Asia 2000.

Livingstone, C. (2017). *New chancellor says UTS has people focus to make innovation work*. http://newsroom.uts.edu.au/news/2017/04/new-chancellor-says-uts-has-people-focus-make-innovation-work

Lucas, R. E. (1988). On the mechanics of economic development. *Journal of Monetary Economics, 22*(1), 3–42.

Maddison, A. (2000). *The world economy: A millennial perspective*. Paris: OECD.

Mahroum, S. (2000). Scientific mobility. *Science Communication, 2*(4), 367–378.

McKinsey Global Institute. (2015). *The China effect on global innovation*. McKinsey Company

Meyer, J. B. (2001). Network approach versus brain drain: Lessons from the diaspora. *International Migration, 39*(5), 91–110.

Mizrahi, Y. (2004). *Capacity enhancement indicators*. World Bank Institute: Washington D.C.

O'Doherty, D., & Arnold, E. (2003). *Understanding innovation: The need for a systemic approach* (The IPTS Report. 71 Seville IPTS).

OECD. (2000). *Science, technology and innovation in the new economy*. OECD

OECD. (2001). *Competencies for the knowledge economy*. Paris: OECD.

OECD. (2003). *Human capital formation and foreign direct investment in developing countries*. Paris: OECD. Working Paper 211.

Ozawa, T., Castello, S., & Phillips, R. J. (2001). The internet revolution, the McLuhan stage of catch-up, and institutional reforms in Asia. *Journal of Economic Issues, 35*(2), 289–298. (Lincoln: Association for Evolutionary Economics Fiscal Office).

Pitelis, C. (2009). The sustainable competitive advantage and catching-up of nations: FDI, clusters, and the liability (Asset) of smallness? *Management International Review, 49*(1), 95–120.
Porter, M. E. (1990). *The competitive advantage of nations*. Basingstoke: Macmillan.
Porter, M., Ketels, C., & Delgado, M. (2007). The microeconomic foundations of prosperity: Findings from the business competitiveness index. In A. Lopez-Claros, M. E. Porter, X. Sali-i-Martin, & K. Schwab (Eds.), *The Global Competitiveness Report 2006–2007*.
PWC. (2016). *Industry 4.0: Building the digital enterprise*. PWC. https://www.pwc.com/gx/en/industries/industries-4.0/landing-page/industry-4.0-building-your-digital-enterprise-april-2016.pdf
Rodrik, D. (2004). *Growth Strategies*. Kennedy School of Government, Harvard University. Working Paper.
Rodrik, D., Subramanian, A., & Trebbi, F. (2004). Institutions rule: The Primacy of institutions over geography and integration in economic development. *Journal of Economic Growth, 9*, 131–165.
Romer, P. M. (1986). Increasing returns and long-run growth. *Journal of Political Economy, 94* (5), 1002–1037.
Romer, P. M. (1990). Endogenous technological change. *Journal of Political Economy, 98*(5), 71–102.
Romer, P. (1994). The origins of endogenous growth. *Journal of Economic Perspectives, 8*, 3–22.
Scott-Kemmis, D. (2008). Industry policy frameworks for a knowledge economy. In *Review of the Australian Textile, Clothing and Footwear Industry* (Vol. 2). Canberra: Commonwealth of Australia.
Sen, A. (1994). The origins of endogenous growth. *Journal of Economic Perspectives, 8*, 3–22.
Sen, A. (1999). *Development as freedom*. New York, NY: Knopf.
Shapiro, H., & Taylor, L. (1990). The state and industrial strategy. *World Development, 18*(6), 861–878.
Sorenson, O. (2003). Social networks and industrial geography. *Journal of Evolutionary Economics, 13*, 513–527.
Staber, U. (2001). The structure of networks in industrial districts. *International Journal of Urban and Regional Research, 25*, 537–552.
Teece, D. (2000). *Managing intellectual capital*. Oxford: Oxford University Press.
Tallman, S., Jenkins, M., Henry, N., & Pinch, S. (2004). Knowledge, clusters, and competitive advantage. *Academy of Management Review, 29*, 258–271.
Taylor, M., & Leonard, S. (Eds.). (2002). *Embedded enterprise and social capital*. Aldershot: Ashgate.
Turpin, T., Woolley, R., & Marceau, J. (2010). Scientists across the boundaries: National and global dimensions of scientific and technical human capital (STHC) and policy implications for Australia. *Asia Pacific Migration Journal, 19*(1), 65–86.
UNCTAD. (2005a). *China in a globalising world*. New York and Geneva: UN.
UNCTAD. (2005b). *Trade and development report: New features of global interdependence*. UN: New York and Geneva.
UNCTAD. (2007). *World Investment Prospects Survey* 2007–2009. UNCTAD. http://www.unctad.org/en/docs//wips2007_en.pdf
UNESCO. (2016). *UNESCO science report—Towards 2030*. UNESCO Publishing.http://en.unesco.org/unesco_science_report
Uzzi, B. (1997). Social structure and competition in interfirm networks: The paradox of embeddedness. *Administrative Science Quarterly, 42*, 35–67.
World Bank. (1993). *The East Asian miracle: Economic growth and public policy*. Oxford University Press.
World Bank. (2006). *The knowledge economy, the kam methodology and world bank operations*. World Bank Institute: Washington D.C.
Yoshida, P. (2001). Asian economies striving to enhance innovation capabilities. *Research Technology Management*, *44*(1), 2–6.

Young, A. (1994). Lessons from the East Asian NIE's: A contrarian view. *European Economic Review, 38*, 964–73.

Yusuf, S. (2004). *Competitiveness through technological advances under global production networking*. In Yusuf et al. (2004a).

Yusuf, S., Anjum Altaf, M., & Nabeshima, K. (Eds.). (2004a). *Global production networking and technological change in East Asia*. New York: Oxford University Press.

Yusuf, S., Anjum Altaf, M., & Nabeshima, K. (Eds.). (2004b). *Global change and East Asian policy initiatives*. New York: Oxford University Press.

Yusuf, S., & Evenett, S. J. (2002). *Can East Asia compete?*. Washington D.C.: World Bank.

Yusuf, et al. (2003). *Innovative East Asia: The future of growth*. Washington D.C.: Worlds Bank.

Chapter 13
The Creation and Disruption of Innovation? Key Developments in Innovation as Concept, Theory, Research and Practice

Michael Lester

Abstract The development of innovation across a very wide canvas is portrayed in the final chapter of the book by Michael Lester. The disruptive impact of new digital networked technologies upon the transformation of enterprises and industries extends to a disruption of the processes of innovation itself, encompassing the nature of innovation concepts, theory, research and practice. This suggests we need to rethink our ideas on innovation as we enter what has been described as the second machine-age of big data, super computers and broadband communication (Brynjolfsson and McAfee, The second machine age: work, progress, and prosperity in a time of brilliant technologies. Norton, New York, 2014). The chapter highlights the disruption of conventional wisdom on innovation processes examining the new wave of entrepreneurial start-ups in the digital age. Unprecedented opportunities exist it is claimed in the rapid expansion of creative innovation and entrepreneurship with a social as well as economic purpose. New product technology platforms and open source software have reduced the technological barriers and risks to product innovation. The evolution of big data combined and powerful data algorithms creates the capacity to discern patterns in complexity integral to the creation of new knowledge. Big data tools are being applied across all scientific disciplines and industries and businesses. The institutional foundations of this innovation and growth are examined and the importance of inclusive and open institutions stressed for accelerating innovation, conceiving of innovation as the knowledge-based outcome of complex linkages and interactions between actors and institutions including universities, businesses and government (Freeman, J Econ 19:5–24, 1995). This suggests a systems approach to the wide institutional relationships including education, taxation, law and other institutions including governments in shaping the markets of the future.

M. Lester (✉)
Centre for Business and Social Innovation, UTS Sydney, Ultimo, Australia
e-mail: melester@yahoo.com

T. Clarke and K. Lee (eds.), *Innovation in the Asia Pacific*,
https://doi.org/10.1007/978-981-10-5895-0_13

Keywords Innovation process · Innovation theory · Digital innovation · Innovation institutions · Disruptive technologies · Disruption process · Network effects · Big data tools · Networked technologies · National innovation systems · Entrepreneurship · Growth and competitiveness · Industry disintermediation · Jobless growth · Post human future · Standards wars · Open source · Global value chains · Second machine age · Venture capital · Crowd sourcing · Economic catch up · Global value chains

Introduction

Much is rightly made of the disruptive impact of new digital networked technologies and the transformation of industries and enterprises (Christensen 1997). This introductory survey and overview chapter suggests that the disruptive effect extends to the very process of innovation itself changing the nature of its concept, theory, research and practice. There is an emerging opportunity to rethink our ideas and practices of innovation as we move towards 'the second machine age' (Brynjolfsson and McAfee 2014).

This chapter poses a series of structured questions drawing on a highly selected survey of recent widely available writing on innovation. The disciplines range across economics, law, management, political science, history, philosophy, sciences, technology and engineering. At each section the questions attempt to highlight the disruption of conventional wisdom about the innovation process as a whole. The analysis and implications are international, however the case of Australia is frequently used as an example of an economy pursuing innovation by a variety of means.

Innovation, Entrepreneurship and Start-Ups in the Digital Age

Are We in a 'Golden Age' of Young, High-Tech 'Hero' Entrepreneurs and Start-Ups?

Entrepreneurs are the change agents at the heart of the innovation process: we are all of us now it seems Schumpeterians (Schumpeter 1942). It is the entrepreneurs' vision, their passion and commitment that build the bridges between opportunity and its realization. This usually involves high technological, market and financial risk taking in the establishment of start-up ventures that grow to displace and replace the dominant corporations of their day.

The new digital age technologies are simultaneously opening up unprecedented opportunities for new startups while reducing the barriers for a 'new breed' of young entrepreneurs to innovate successfully. Arguably, there has never been a better time for entrepreneurs, startups and the innovation process (Wadhwa 2015). In Australia, startups have the potential to contribute \$109 b, 4% GDP and 540,000 jobs by 2030 (Thorpe 2013). There are 1500 hubs in Sydney and Melbourne, with

2000 founders as part of a rapidly expanding ecosystem. Many of these activities are targeting information, media and telecommunications, but opportunities are being missed in finance, insurance, manufacturing and health.

The celebrity stars, and entrepreneurial leaders of the big new technology companies such as Gates (Microsoft), Bezos (Amazon), Jobs (Apple) and Zuckerman (Facebook) took their garage startup companies to global corporate leadership and astonishing personal wealth in record time. They are modern heroes for the current generation of digital-age entrepreneurs with more than 70% of 'millennials' around the world wanting to join or establish a startup venture as their preferred career choice (Deloitte 2016).

Is There Something New About the 'Digital Age' Breed of Entrepreneurs?

The new wave of digital technology innovation was driven unexpectedly by a rag tag group of hackers, geniuses and geeks rather than by the traditional, big well-funded R&D based corporations (Isaacson 2014). This new breed of entrepreneurs is often seen as missionary rather them mercenary (Stone 2013), while others argue that the real difference between them and business barons of yore isn't a matter of temperament or ethics, but rather a matter of business strategy (Heller 2013). On that view, today's entrepreneur is simultaneously ambitious business-builder and mould-breaker laboring apart, even in the absence of a unifying social narrative to tell them how.

So they make their own narratives growing their businesses not by structure but by story. For example, the battle for control of Twitter is written about as a contest for control of its story; what people needed argued leader Jack Dorsey was not a new array of Twitter functions but an account of its role in connectedness and cultural ascent (Bilton 2013). In a similar way, Bezos at Amazon atomized his company into small teams, keeping business close to points of customer contact even at the cost of internal coherence. It was agile but with no coordinating mechanism and with limited information flows to prevent overlap and collision. Ironically, Bezos quotes Nicholas Taleb's concept of 'the narrative fallacy', which is his term for turning a mess of information into a neat story, inventing hydra-headed businesses out of tidy stories is what companies like Amazon do best (Heller 2013).

How Is 'Innovation' as Competitive Efficiency Balanced with Social Purpose?

In an earlier era, innovation was portrayed as turned purposefully to a socially comprehensive, politically inflected end—a community of purpose, like an ideal 'war effort' (Drucker 1942). Subsequently, the industrial ideas of efficiency and competitiveness from the 'hot' and 'cold' wars of mid-last century and the iconoclastic ideas of the 60s community and social purpose from against the social main-stream, are now found intertwined but always in tension in the new entrepreneurs and their tech companies (Heller 2013).

The idea of the post sixties' counterculture was not simply a rejection of postwar industrialism but an attempt to develop a new corporate, organisational and entrepreneurial idealism (Turner 2006), exemplified by The Whole Earth Catalog (Brand 1984). This outsiders view of technology evolved into the dreamy sentimental stories of new corporate idealism and an associated belief, in the defining business and social heroism of creative innovation and entrepreneurship; making a difference, having an impact and changing the world for the better are the entrepreneurial motifs of today.

Is the New Digital Age 'Start Up' Different to the Traditional 'Silicon Valley' Model?

In the digital age technology risk, the chance that a company can't build what it sets out to build, is no longer the problem that it has been historically for startups; it is market risk, on the other hand, that is the killer (Reis 2011). In particular, the risks for developers of mobile apps have been reduced significantly by the development and widespread availability of product technology platforms by the new, large tech enterprises such as Google, Apple and Amazon. The 'open source' movement in software coding has also reduced the technological barriers and risks to entrepreneurial product innovation.

The 'lean startup' product development philosophy or methodology (Reis 2011) is designed to 'dispel the cloud of uncertainty around innovation' by reducing market risk. It synthesizes ideas from Japanese manufacturing, software development and scientific method. The earlier market risks arose because businesses often conceptualized, designed and produced a product before they correctly gauged market reaction. The 'lean start up' deconstructs these high-risk market bets into a plethora of low-stakes gambles that can be tested on real-world customers. A series of 'experiments' is run in-market as quickly and inexpensively as possible, so that by the time the product is launched it is reasonably certain that there will be customer demand for it.

How Do Digital Software and 'Big Data' Encourage the New 'Fail Fast' Start up Model?

The new 'fail fast' start up model can be applied to any new business and has in fact been used for years in the motion picture industry among others; it is the malleability of software that lends itself particularly well to fast prototypes and turn-on-dime evolution (Greenwald 2014). It encourages entrepreneurs to 'fail fast' and quickly abandon ideas that are not working.

The evolution of 'big data' and the tools to handle it, is also opening a multitude of new data driven entrepreneurial and business startup opportunities on an unprecedented and accessible scale (Shaw 2014). Data production in the last two years has amounted to a zettabyte (one ZB is 10 to the power 21 bytes or one billion terabytes) that dwarfs prior records of human civilization. However, it is not the quantity per se that is revolutionary but that we now also have the tools to do something with all this data (King 2013). It is improved statistical and computational methods that are the key not, in themselves, the exponential growth in storage or even in computational capacity. Moore's doubling law is nothing compared to the power of big data algorithms involving new ways of linking data sets, creative approaches to visualizing, seeing patterns and discerning patterns in complexity, that are integral to creating knowledge.

These big data tools are now available for use across a wide range of disciplines from astronomy to medical health. Data science courses are hugely popular and there is a movement of quantification rumbling across fields in academia, science, industry, governments and not for profits (Shaw 2014). It is hard to find one area not affected and there is a similar pattern in every field. These widely available data algorithm tools provide a fundamentally new way of doing experimental designs, mining unstructured data from businesses, computational biology and quantitative genetics improving public health.

Innovation, Growth, Employment and Inequality

Is Technology and Innovation Self-directed or Shaped by Society and the Economy?

The first instinct of social scientists, taking their cue from Marx, is to see technology as an exogenous driver of economic growth; as a force from outside the economy rather than inside, or endogenous to the economy, with the institutions then responding to those forces, as a form of 'superstructure' (Acemoglu 2013). The conventional and still contemporary economic models of growth treat technological change as a 'residual' or 'black box' contributor to economic growth after the driving factors of capital, labour and land are accounted for: "the handmill gives you society with the feudal lord; the steam mill, society with the industrial capitalist".

But this form of 'technological determinism' is seriously at odds with the facts (Acemoglu 2013). There are many examples of technology responding to politics, for example, the decline of the Roman empire, the inability of the Chinese historically to capitalize on their leading inventions, advances in sailing and ship building in the 15th century, space travel in the modern era. Likewise, government policy and conflict over technology is probably a first order factor in understanding the direction of technological change today, for example, distorted incentives in the

US health care system, the lack of carbon pricing or effective regulations in response to climate change. Curiously, there is very little analytical work on how politics affects endogenous technology, despite early seminal work on the question (Weisbrod 1991).

How Important Are Institutions in Promoting or Hindering Innovation and Growth?

A recent scholarly and broad ranging survey and analysis of the history and economics of the rise and fall of countries and civilizations, and of the various associated theories of change and growth, concludes that the key to sustainable growth lies in institutions that are inclusive (Acemoglu and Robinson 2012). The more people within a society who are given the opportunity to participate and contribute economically to society the more innovative and successful it will become. Vested economic interests at any given time develop political power and institutions designed to protect the *status quo* by excluding the participation of new entrants and competitors with innovative ideas. Inclusive institutions promote innovation, change and economic growth.

How Is Technology Diffusion and Adoption of New Innovations not Frictionless?

The 18th century clockmaker, John Harrison, found a mechanical solution, to the problem of determining longitude, arguably 'the greatest scientific problem of his time' (Sobel 2007), against the efforts of the combined scientific establishment from Galileo to Newton, who searched for an answer in the skies. This remarkable story of a 'lone genius' is not only a story of triumphant and lifelong dedication to successful technological innovation but also a story of institutional barriers erected by vested self-interests, including from within the scientific community. The English Parliament offered a huge reward for anyone who could find the solution, under the Longitude Act of 1714, but Harrison found nothing but self-interested resistance from the Board set up to administer the Act and was never paid the full amount of the prize.

Much as we might like to believe in or yearn for frictionless adoption of technological solutions and innovations, people talking to people is still one of the important diffusion pathways that can change norms and standards in response to innovation opportunities. For example, consider the contrasting cases within the health professions of surgical anesthesia and the antiseptic method innovations. Surgical anesthesia was demonstrated in 1846 in Boston and within seven years it was adopted by virtually every hospital in America and Britain. The antiseptic method was reported in 1867 in the *Lancet* but it took a generation before Lister's recommendations became routine practice (Gawande 2013).

Economic incentives for both innovations ran in the same direction; their technical complexity was equally difficult. But, one combated a visible and immediate problem (pain) while the other combated an invisible problem (germs), whose effects were not manifest until well after the operation was completed. Also, both made life better for patients (antisepsis), but only one made life better for doctors (anesthesia). Here we are in the first part of the 21st century still trying to figure out how to get ideas and innovations from the first part of the 20th century to take root in response to the global problem of death in childcare. Confronting innovation and diffusion, people and institutions can feel messy and anachronistic, introducing uncontrolled variability into the processes.

Are We Entering a 'Tipping Point' in the Diffusion of Digital Innovations?

The recently popular idea of 'tipping points' (Gladwell 2000) as an 'epidemic spreading of trends' and a point in the diffusion process at which it is easy to spread change finds its origins in the standard, text book theory of "diffusion of innovations" (Rogers 2003). This is a 5-step process: knowledge; persuasion; decision; implementation; confirmation. It follows an S-shaped curve over time, where individual innovation adoption decisions depend heavily on the innovation decisions of others; early adopters to laggard late adopters, all relying on well trusted 'opinion leaders'. While the mass media can be effective in eliminating an awareness deficit, opinion leaders are best at changing attitudes. Homophilous relatively closed social system values are likely to frustrate diffusion while in heterophilous open systems like America, facilitated by faster and denser communication networks, the tipping point is easier to push (Orr 2003).

Is Innovation Faltering as Implied by Falling Productivity and Economic Growth?

There is concern in the context of the poor performance of the US economy in terms of productivity, growth, inequality and competitiveness over the past ten or fifteen years, that the technological dynamic and associated 'faltering innovation' is 'fizzling out' (Cohen 2011; Gordon 2012; Vijg 2011). Others dismiss the concerns and suggest that, far from decline or stagnation "we ain't seen nothing yet…if we rethink how innovation happens" (Mokyr 1990, 2013). On this optimistic view science and technology are mutually dependent and self-sustaining, The supply side generates new tools and instruments needed for new technologies, for example, DNA sequencing, high speed computers, etc. At the same time, new, powerful computer search tools are making access to new knowledge, technology and tools even easier and quicker.

Are We Entering a New Paradigm of 'Jobless Growth' and Increasing Inequality?

The imminent disappearance of jobs is a 'rampant concern' of our digital age of 'disruption', as it was at the beginning of the industrial revolution (Levine 2015). Reputable and influential magazines such *The Atlantic* ran a cover story titled 'the end of work' while *Foreign Affairs* exclaimed simply, 'hi, robot'. Best selling books on business management carry frightening titles such as "Rise of the robots: technology and the threat of a jobless future" (Ford 2015).

Scholarly statistical analysis of 'the new machine age' shows that the nexus between growth, productivity, jobs and income equality, to which the twentieth century world had become accustomed, was broken in the 1990s, at least in the case of the US economy (Brynhoffson and Macafee 2014). This 'deskilling' technological change driven by digital, networked, data rich technologies, is affecting both skilled and unskilled workers and will lead to growth but also to inequality. It will define a new understanding of economics, technology and innovation. The new technologies are indeed creating a bounty of new opportunities and widespread benefits, caused by the novel process of 'recombinant innovation'. But they also give rise, by their nature, to a 'winner takes all' process as skills and earnings disparities widen, and as we witness the hollowing out of the 'middle classes' in our societies.

National Innovation Systems

How and to What Ends Do Countries Approach Their Innovation Policies?

Many countries have in recent years embraced the broadly based "national systems of innovation" approach to promoting and nurturing an innovative, productive and competitive national business environment and culture, supported with varying degrees of government policy intervention (OECD 1997). It conceives of innovation as the knowledge-based outcome of complex linkages and interactions between actors and institutions including universities, businesses and government (Freeman 1995).

This systems approach embraces a wide range of innovation policy components, including, education, taxation, and law. It complements earlier innovation policy paradigms involving, linear input (research spending) and outputs (patents); supply push science; research and technology premised on linear models of innovation; and buttressed by 'market failure' rationale for government intervention. The World Bank (2014) and the OECD jointly have a web site called the 'Innovation Policy Platform' (IPP) that provides access on a country basis to key policy documents that reflect this broader systems-based approach to innovation policy.

How Are Countries' Respective Innovation Policies and Performances Compared?

There is a proliferation of international comparisons and indexes that rank individual country innovation performances based on a wide range of indicators drawing on the concept of national systems of innovation. For example, the annual Global Innovation Index (GII) Report (INSEAD, Cornell, WIPO) adopts 7 pillars (institutions; human capital and research; infrastructure; market sophistication; business sophistication; knowledge and technology outputs; creative outputs) and 84 Indicators covering 142 Countries. The International Innovation Index (III) (Boston Consulting Group & NAM) ranks the 'innovation friendliness' of 110 countries and 50 US states based on a survey of 1000 senior executives who are members of the National Association of Manufacturers (NAM). Business outcomes and policy inputs are ranked using a range of input indicators (fiscal policy; education; innovation environment) and output indicators (patents; technology transfer; R&D; business performance; labor productivity; shareholder returns; migration; economic growth).

What Is the Role for the 'Entrepreneurial State' in an Innovative Economy?

A recent strong and coherent case has been made for the role of government conceived in terms of 'market failure' and the role of governments in 'national innovation systems' and creating and shaping the markets of the future (Mazzucato 2013). For example, private sector information technology companies built their businesses off the back of long term basic research and development funded and often conducted by government. While Steve Jobs was undoubtedly a genius who understood both engineering and design, Apple's products and success as a nimble innovator relied on US government Defense funded research that pioneered the Internet, GPS positioning, and voice-activated 'virtual assistants'. HTML was developed in publicly funded university research. Likewise, Google's search algorithm was financed by an NSF grant.

But it can be argued, that this logic does not sufficiently weigh some of the potential risks, and down sides in a government role, such as, pouring endless taxpayer money down 'rat-holes' with no chance of success, regulations that can be a dead hand holding back innovation and entrepreneurship. What cannot be denied is that the state has played a central role producing game-changing break-throughs, and that its contribution to the success of technology-based businesses should not be underestimated (Schumpeter 2013).

What Goals Are Driving Country Strategies for Innovation?

Most developed countries have grappled for at least the past two or three decades with evolving approaches to innovation policy to boost their increasingly sluggish productivity and economic growth performance. A growing sense of urgency has been injected into these endeavours by the accompanying falls in their global competitiveness and the accompanying, apparently inexorable rise, of a number of primarily large developing countries, especially China and India, and their emergent middle classes. These developing countries are in turn starting to focus on their own innovation strategies as they seek to transform themselves beyond their role as low labour cost manufacturing and assembly platforms.

In his State of the Union Address (President Obama 2014), President Obama announced the establishment of 'manufacturing innovation hubs' around the country to meet the challenges of productivity, growth, employment and competitiveness. He also announced funding for R&D to develop ideas for the challenges in energy, renewables and climate change. It has also been argued (Benner 2015) that in response to China's global economic emergence, including the rate at which it is turning out scientists and engineers, and its rapid climb in the global rankings of patent applications, the US needs immigration reform. Each year the highly respected NBER produces a detailed review of "*Innovation Policy and the Economy*".

Europe ministers have approved a giant, 7-year, Euro 77 billion, '*Horizon 2020*' research and innovation program (European Union 2013). It is expected to further eliminate fragmentation in the fields of scientific research and innovation. It will underpin the objectives of the *Europe 2020* strategy for growth and jobs, as well as the goal of strengthening the scientific and technological bases by contributing to achieving a European Research Area in which researchers, scientific knowledge and technology circulate freely. Horizon 2020 focuses on, generating excellent science to make the research and innovation system more competitive, fostering industrial leadership to speed up the development of technologies that will support businesses and innovation, and tackling societal challenges by supporting activities covering the entire chain from research to market. After two years of negotiations this decision was seen to demonstrate clearly that research and innovation figure high on the political agenda.

Country Case Study—Australia: What Are the Continuing Issues and Tensions in Australian Innovation Policy?

The politics of research and innovation often wax and wane with the mood, fashion and ideology of the day and this has been the case with the continuing story of innovation policies in Australia. But the underlying structural issues and challenges have remained much the same (Dodgson 2013). The Council of the learned Australian Academies of Science, Technology, Social Sciences and the Humanities recently reported on the role of science, research and technology in lifting Australia's productivity to drive prosperity (ACOLA 2014). The report is the outcome of a three-year research program through the Office of the Chief Scientist and provides a good snap shot of the long-standing issues and tensions in innovation policy in Australia. It shows that while information and communications technology has raised Australia's productivity in banking, agriculture and manufacturing, overall productivity, measured as multi factor productivity declined between 2003 and 2011. A clear link is seen between the quality of management and firm productivity, but Australian management practices rate only moderately above average globally, while a significant 'tail' number of firms are 'mediocre'. Small and medium size enterprises account for nearly half of employment but only one third of value added. Australia has a high ranking on scientific research and publications but is not good at translating these to innovative products and services.

Why Is There Scepticism About the Effectiveness of Innovation Policies?

Many reports, reviews and assessments have been made of innovation performance in Australia over the years but with little apparent sustained impact on policies or the innovation and competitiveness performance of the country. For example, the West Report (2003) was a monumental mapping of Australia's science and innovation system. A series of annual Innovation Systems Policies Reports has been published (Department of Industry) providing a descriptive catalogue of developments at the national level, as well as in the states, and overseas, but it does not provide assessments or evaluations.

Writing at the time of announced closure of Ford Australia's manufacturing operations, a leading economics journalist expressed his skepticism about a role for industry and innovation policy on the grounds that he has yet to see programs that aren't just disguised protection of favoured industries, amounting to propping up losers rather than picking winners (Gittins 2014). He concludes that most innovation programs have just been a sham. On the other hand, in the same context, science journalists cite the Industry Minister as saying that Australians are smart, innovative and creative, and that they have the ability to remake this industry sector and the time in which to do it (Wilkins and Williams 2014).

Australia's investment in high-technology industries is lower than other advanced economies (OECD 2012), and its high-technology exports are only 2.3% compared to the USA 20% (EU 2011). Australia is seen to have prospects in specialized niches, such as, medical devices, biomaterials, mining equipment and aerospace (OECD 2012) but on the other hand it lacks innovative global, mid-size firms. On some accounts little has been done to create a realistic transformation scheme for industry with lots of talk (Gillard 2012) but little or no investment by governments or business. Australia has the capacity to generate ideas but startups need more tenacity and belief to pursue ideas through to commercialization, which takes time (Wilkins and Williams 2014).

What Has Been the Impact of Innovation Policies Based on 'Market Failure'?

Australia lifted its world ranking in the most recent report of the Global Innovation Index (2014) from 19th to 17th but the index data shows Australia doing much better on the input rather than the output side of innovation, with the ratio of performance between the two, the 'innovation ratio', among the lowest of the 81 countries surveyed (Green 2014). Awareness of this issue and the need for good innovation policy and outcomes has been reflected in public discussion of the question: do we get good results for our science and research funding dollar? (Williams 2013).

Australia's approach to innovation policy has been framed in terms of the concepts of 'market failure' applied particularly to the activities of science and research. This has led to an overemphasis on the supply or input side of innovation rather than being led by the demand or output side of innovation (Dodgson et al. 2009). Innovation is about broad 'system failure' rather than the earlier simpler ideas of linear supply side push factors.

Has There Been a Failure to Renew and Revitalize the 'National Innovation System'?

The architecture of Australia's national innovation system was described nearly ten years ago in a national review, as a generation old and requiring an urgent re-appraisal and restructuring (Cutler 2008a, b). It was characterized as 'stalling not sprinting, and over 70 recommendations were made in that review, including on innovation in business, strengthening people and skills, excellence in national; research, information and market design, taxation, and governance of the national innovation system. These were subsequently responded to in a government policy launch document (DIIS 2010).

Since then, with Australia's performance in innovation and competitiveness languishing further, previous Prime Minister Abbott, did not name a science minister for the first time in decades, and removed the titles of 'innovation' and 'skills' from ministerial and agency titles, and his government cut funding to science, research and business R&D (Mather 2013; Hepworth 2013). Current Prime Minister Turnbull although of the same political party as his immediate predecessor, is a strong advocate of innovation (Tingle 2015), though appears often constrained by vested interests.

Innovation and Industry Evolution

How Are Digital Technologies Transforming Industries

The current wave of innovation in the digital or 'second machine age' is not only opening up unprecedented new business and industry opportunities, potentially disrupting and transforming all sectors of industry and the economy, but it is at the same time changing the very structure of industries. In particular, these new technologies are pushing American culture under the control of fewer and fewer corporations (Packer 2014). The digital age Amazon is seen as something new in the history of American business; not just 'the everything store' but the everything with its tentacles extending in all directions: the epitome of a successful new-economy company.

How Is Digital Transformation Impacting on Successful Established Industries?

But it is not just the new wave companies and industries that are being created driven by digital age technology and innovation. The old long established industries are also tapping into the transformational dynamic, none more obviously than the financial services industry. The role of complex, derivative based products and associated automated stock trading is both the result of technological innovation in the finance industry, especially 'high-frequency trading', and their role in contributing to the 'global financial crisis' of 2009 is widely acknowledged (Lewis 2014).

Notwithstanding that global crisis, from which many economies are still struggling to fully extricate themselves, the industry has continued on its technological innovation path. For example, the recent interim report into the Australian Financial Services Industry (Murray 2014) identifies the role of technological innovation in driving major efficiency in the system and benefit to consumers. It identifies a number of options in response: make electronic service delivery the default; amend regulation that specifies using certain technologies to become technology neutral; establish a central mechanism or body for monitoring and advising government on technology and innovation in the industry.

Why the Paradox of Simultaneous Industry 'Disintermediation' and 'Consolidation'?

Consumers are benefitting from the entry of new players into the taxi services and accommodation rental markets by the entry of new internet based services such as Uber and Airbnb respectively, who put the consumer in direct contact with the service provider by removing the traditional intermediaries. Amazon was a pioneer in such 'disintermediation' and is now trying to create a 'machine' that assumes the shape of public demand by the elimination of the 'gatekeepers' or business professionals that get in the customer's way on a large and diversified scale (Packer 2014). This is leading to massive business and industry consolidation.

The impact of Amazon on publishing is privileging the 'blockbuster' (Elberse 2013) just as in society the effect of the 'second machine age' is widening inequality with 'the rich getting richer, the poor getting poorer' (Brynjolfssohn and McKee 2014). The result in the book world is a few brand names at the top and a mass of unwashed titles down below with the middle hollowed-out.

Amazon and its technology platform are also driving restructuring and consolidation in the book retailing industry For example, independent book-stores can sell Amazon's popular Kindle reading devices. In addition to getting a small payment on each Kindle sale the independent gets a commission on all e books that the reader buys in the next two years. Many, but certainly not all, booksellers were sceptical seeing the revenue-sharing program as a Trojan horse aimed at further undermining their business. Independents make up about 10 per cent of book sales, down from as much as 25% before Amazon arrived on the scene (Streitfield 2013).

Does "Blockbuster" Success Obviate the Idea of the "Long Tail"?

It was originally fashionable to argue that the coming of the digital technology world would fragment popular culture with the conventional lowest common denominator offerings of the machine age mass markets giving way to countless niches, each 'selling less of more': "The long tail" effect (Anderson 2006). More recently, and in the light of experience, it is argued (Elberse 2013), that the traditional, mass market 'blockbusters' continue to rule the roost, most obviously in media, publishing and entertainment industries generally, giving the lie to the 'long tail', and 'selling more of less'. The former is driven, in economic terms, by an effectively zero marginal cost of distribution of a single product by Internet, while the economics of 'blockbusters' are driven by the 'increasing returns to scale' network effects available on the internet (Shapiro and Varian 1999).

Despite the competing theories, the complexities of internet-based business opportunity and resulting industry impacts are still working their way through, even in the publishing industry that has led the way. With so many writers now able to enter the market at once through on line self-publishing it is becoming increasingly difficult to be 'discovered' (Robinson 2013). It is even easier to drop into obscurity and not be heard of again and so a new industry is cropping up to market them. Publishers are consolidating in response to the digital ebook challenge, for example, the 2012 merger of Penguin and Random House, and there will continue to be such "major, earth shaking changes" as the publishing industry becomes leaner and more compact (Boog 2013). But these same major publishers are also tapping into the new class of amateur self-published writers who are turning out so much material right now; the best known example being the "50 shades of grey" phenomenon with its author E L James initially selling hundreds of thousands of copies of her self-published work before a mainstream publishing company took it on and amplified the sales to a truly global scale.

How Did the 'Paradox' of Disintermediation Play Out in the Global Financial Crisis?

The technology experience of the global financial services markets in the lead up to the 2009 crisis was in some respects paradoxical (Lewis 2013). The American stock market, traditionally a sleepy oligopoly dominated by NASDAQ and the NYSE, was by mid-2007 fragmenting to nearly 40 private exchanges by the following year, all of them trading in the same stocks. At the same time a new SEC regulation designed to protect investors from their brokers, required brokers to route client orders to whichever exchange offered the best price. Perversely, this opened up new opportunities for brokers to abuse their clients. Trading volumes soared on the back of fast computers controlled by high frequency trading firms, including Goldman Sachs, who found more opportunities to interpose themselves buyers on one exchange and sellers on another.

"The initial promise of computer technology was to remove the intermediary from the financial market, or at least reduce the amount he could scalp from that market. The reality has turned out to be a boom in financial intermediation and an estimated take for Wall Street of somewhere between $10 and $20 billion a year" (Lewis 2013). The combination of new market rules and new technology was turning the stock market into, in effect, a war of robots.

How Industry Significant Are the 'Increasing Returns to Scale' of Digital Technology?

The theory of 'increasing returns to scale' within the broad inter-disciplinary field of 'complexity studies' is well elaborated and relatively long-standing (Arthur 1994) but has not always been well received by economists. It provides a range of insights into the workings of high technology economies and industries, such as, technology lock-in, industry clustering, network effects, information contagion, self-reinforcement, human learning, and pricing. It has particular theoretical application in the digital, networked age of the Internet and was subsequently elaborated in more detail in that context (Shapiro and Varian 1999).

A case in point is the emergence of the Chinese enterprise BGI (Beijing Genomics Institute), the world's largest genetic research centre producing at least a quarter of the world's genomic data, more than Harvard or the National Institutes for Health (NIH) (Specter 2014b). Founded in only 1999, BGI intends to transform DNA into a common resource, a kind of universal reference library, freely accessible it is hoped, to anyone who wants to use it. This story is driven by the plummeting costs of mapping the human genome: the first was mapped in a decade and cost $3 billion for a team of international experts; today BGI does the same work in a few days for about $4000; by end 2015 the cost was projected to fall below $1000. New digital big data technology tools have transformed DNA sequencing into a low cost industrial process exploiting increasing returns.

Management of Technology and Innovation

How Can Management Get Value from Its R&D Investment?

A recent innovation survey of the top 1000 global companies (Jaruzelski 2012; Jaruzelski et al. 2015) underlines the finding that spending on R&D is not equivalent to financial success; rather it is the management or execution of that R&D spending. Neither, the survey finds, is creativity any guarantee of value creation or 'bang for the buck' on R&D. The survey identifies three types of R&D management strategies: need seeking; market reading; technology driven. What is important for commercial innovation success is the alignment of ideation, innovation practices and tools within each of these three strategies. Show that R&D spending is shifting from hardaware to software. At the same time, those surveys.

How Can Management Ensure an Innovation Focus Within the Firm?

Perhaps more fundamental than the effective management of R&D itself are the issues of the innovation orientation and culture of businesses and their management. For example, while less than 50% of Australian businesses are actively fostering innovation (the highest level to date), the average for the 27 EU member countries is 53%, with Germany coming in at 80% (ICAA 2013). A published annual list of the 50 'most innovative companies' in Australia (BRW Inventium 2013) highlights 'best practice' as a model and a checklist has been prepared so that Australian companies can self-assess their "innovation readiness" (Innovation Australia 2013).

How Important Is the Building An 'Innovation Culture' Within the Firm?

The concept of 'innovation culture' provides a further yardstick against which enterprises can be measured in terms of the success of their management of technology. For example, a recent report surveyed the innovation culture of Australia's leading innovative technology organizations (Burdon 2014), based on the perspectives and rankings of employers and employees, and benchmarked the results against international levels. Innovation ability was assessed against ten requirements: vision; integration; alignment; network; processes and resources; rewards; adaptability; inclusiveness; action orientation; self-improvement. The results showed a strong correlation with competitive advantage and financial success; an absence of a strong innovation culture was found to be an impediment to growth and success.

How Has the Firm-Level Management Challenge Changed in the Digital Age?

Historically, and particularly during the 'great age of American innovation', break-through technologies came from within the internal basic research laboratories of corporations, as for example, was the case with the renowned Bell Laboratories (Gertner 2012). This is quite unlike the wave of incremental, continuous innovation in the current Internet-based digital technology revolution.

This year's best business books on strategy highlight that while business leaders repeatedly say they want their companies to be more innovative, it is not companies that are innovative but people (Favaro 2015). For example, a company's ability to innovate requires rising above 'group think' through leaders that can work together effectively in a group setting (Sunstein and Hastie 2015). Experience in the business of producing movies focuses on the centrality of the individual curious and creative mind: "This isn't a science. This is a creative business" (Grazer and Fishman 2015). Or, as Steve Jobs has been quoted as saying, "Creativity is just connecting things". Which pretty much describes any successful innovative enterprise.

How Has Basic Research Been Linked to Successful Commercial Innovation?

Whether based on internal or external basic research the path to innovation is long and involves many players from the lab discovery through to successful innovation and commercialization. For example, Korean firms such as Samsung and LG lead markets in the innovation of liquid crystal display (LCD) technology and industry, but the story of the technology goes back to the first discoveries by Otto Lehman in Germany in 1888 (Castellano 2005). Despite past ongoing work by companies in Germany such as Merck, the big technology breakthrough did not come till the 1960s, this time at Princeton, which was in turn picked up but then stopped short by RCA. In the late 1970s the Japanese companies such as Hitachi built the first flat LCD screens. They were arguably the true risk takers and pioneering technology innovators but it took the Koreans to come along, copy the technology, refine the technology and products and create a whole new industry. The Koreans are now developing new technologies, such as optic organic light emitting diodes (that are emissive rather than backlit as is LCD) to replace LCD (Baker 2013).

Intellectual Property Protection for Innovation

Is China Stealing Trade Secrets and Innovations?

The US is charging members of Chinese military with espionage in the form of stealing trade secrets from American companies, particularly in the form of software (Surowiecki 2014). Similar concern was expressed in the US during the late 1970s and 80s with the success of the "Japanese miracle" orchestrated by MITI 's 'industrial policies' (Johnson 1999) when the growing global competitiveness of the Japanese economy and its corporations were perceived as a threat to American businesses and the economy. From a historical perspective (Ben-Atar 2004) that's pretty much how the Americans got their start as a manufacturing power too, by illicitly appropriating mechanical and scientific innovations from Europe, as did the English and French before them from China (Mihm 2015).

How Did America Tap into British Technology to Drive Its' "Industrial Revolution"?

Throughout the late 18th and early 19th centuries, American industrial spies roamed the British Isles, including Samuel Slater, often called "the father of the American Industrial Revolution" (Surowiecki 2014). As an immigrant in 1789 he brought an intimate knowledge of Arkwright spinning frames and set up the first water-powered textile mill in the US. Two decades later, Francis Cabot visited Britain, memorized plans for Cartwright power looms and on return built his own version, becoming the most successful industrialist of his time. In fact, the American government often encouraged such piracy. For example, as a result of Alexander Hamilton's 1791 'Report on manufactures' Americans were receiving patents for technology pirated from abroad.

What Is the Role and Extent of Compulsory Patent Licensing?

In a recent review of Australia's compulsory patent licensing system (Productivity Commission 2013) it was found that applications were made to the Federal Court under the relevant provisions in patent legislation on only a few occasions, none of which were successful. A case was substantiated for reform of the Australian provisions in the form of clearer criteria in support of the 'public interest' provision, wider awareness of the relevance of the application of Trade Practices legislation in instances of 'anti-competitive' behaviour, and clarification of the scope of the "crown use" provisions where government purchasing is involved.

Are New Technologies Such as 'Gene Testing' Likely to Change Patenting Practices?

Most countries have similar 'compulsory licensing' provisions that are also rarely used. Among developing countries, Brazil, India and Thailand have used them to access medicines at a lower price. Among developing countries, the United States uses compulsory licenses most frequently, invoking anti-competitive, anti-trust legislation. In the Australian review it was concluded that the issues of compulsory licensing were likely to become of increasing importance, particularly in regard to health care arising from the patenting of genes that are 'isolated and refined', as well as their 'associated testing methods'. Recognition of a trend to more accessibility and openness in intellectual property is reflected in an examination of the powerful new technologies enabling easy manipulation of genetic codes by a new breed of 'gene hackers' (Specter 2015). At the same time this raises a range of new ethical questions and concerns about how these technologies might be used and the resulting social and environmental dangers.

Do New Technologies Warrant Technology Specific Patenting Regimes?

The innovation process differs across different technologies and industries. Even though patent systems largely treat all innovations equally, from a patenting point of view, there are important differences between various new technologies, for example, between software and other innovative technologies (Goldman 2013). Three features of software that make it unique from a patenting perspective, and as a consequence, society is 'overpaying' when it provides patent protection for software. First, it has shorter innovation cycles, for example, a few years as against a few decades for pharmaceuticals. This means significant 'first mover' advantages, and a lifecycle that typically ends before the patent is issued, usually four years or more. Second, it will be produced without any patent incentive. Production incentives are available under Copyright and Trade Secrets provisions, software vendors can restrict competition with user technology 'lock in', and 'open source' software is widely used. These differences cause 'friction' in the patent system and difficulties for the innovation process throughout all sectors of the economy seeking to adopt software based innovations.

Is 'Open Innovation' Likely to Be of Greater Importance in the 'Digital Age'?

Sometimes accused of being just 'old wine in new bottles', the concept of 'open innovation' has been around for a while (Chesbrough 2003) and its antecedents lie in concepts of inter-firm collaboration and alliances. But its nature may be changing again and it may become even more important in the age of new digital technologies. It is characterized by increasing collaboration and knowledge exchange externally to the firm, using these relationships to leverage resources for innovation. For example, Samsung has an "Open Innovation" initiative to identify and grow the technologies and infrastructure of the future. This is a multi-pronged approach that involves participation in global consortia, forging links between the industry and top universities, coöperation with vendors and operation of successful overseas research centres.

The literature on 'open innovation' focuses on three aspects (Randawa et al. 2014): firm centric; management of networks; and cultural, with the first predominating and the other two being relatively under researched. The research focuses more on outbound rather than inbound, and on value creation rather than capture, and was found to cluster around several mature areas of research such as "absorptive capacity" and 'lead user' innovation. There appears to be scope for better integration of this 'self identified' research on 'open innovation' with other related theories of innovation, and it might be added, with the emerging evidence of new approaches to open, collaborations in the digital, software age.

How 'Open' Is Open-Source Software and Innovation?

With the emergence of more stock-market intermediation and computerized high-frequency-trading in America (see section "Innovation and Industry Evolution") in the lead up to the financial crisis of 2009, Goldman Sachs found themselves lagging their competitors. Its computers were slow and a lot of the winning strategies were of a winner-take-all variety; get in first and get all the money. They sought out programmer Serge Aleynikov to improve the speed of their system (Lewis 2013).

He found himself endlessly patching up a system that was nearly ten years old: "the existing code base becomes an elephant that's difficult to maintain", he said. He focused on decentralizing the system to make it faster and did this by resorting, every day, to open-source software, available free to anyone for any purpose. But he quickly discovered that Goldman had a one-way relationship with open-source. They took huge amounts of free software off the Web, but they did not return it after he had modified it, even when his modifications were very slight and of general rather than financial use. His bosses said it was Goldman's property. After leaving Goldman he was accused of stealing company code and convicted to eight years in federal prison.

Are the Chinese Showing the Way on a 'Open License' Approach to Innovation?

Chinese firm BGI is the world's largest genetic-research centre, producing at least a quarter of the world's genomic data by capitalizing on the technological revolution that has transformed genetic sequencing into an industrial process. BGI is betting its future on laying out the genetic codes of as many life-forms as possible. In the process it is set on transforming DNA into a common resource, a kind of freely accessible, universal data reference library. Its founder, JianWang, is quoted as saying: "For the last five hundred years, you have been leading the way with innovation. We are no longer interested in following" (Specter 2014a, b).

Following the disastrous mishandling of the 2002 SARS outbreak by the Chinese government, a different approach was adopted in response to the appearance in 2011 of a rare and deadly strain of E Coli bacteria, initially in Germany and quickly spreading to Europe and then USA. BGI quickly sequenced the infectious strain, progressively posting it on Twitter. The data were made public under an 'open license' which meant that any research team could use the information at no cost and many did. The episode underscored the weakness of sticking with the usual scientific approach via publications and patents. A British report on the future of scientific collaboration (Royal Society 2012) credited BGI with an openness that saved lives, noting that, within a week, two dozen reports had been filed on an open-source site dedicated to the analysis of the strain, producing results in time to help contain the outbreak. A leading American Professor of Genetics from Harvard Medical School is quoted as saying of BGI and its actions: If by nationalism you mean hoarding of data, that just isn't happening. I am just glad that there is somebody in the world who has the priorities and the money to do this—to hold this in place while the rest of us are getting our act together" (Specter 2014a, b).

Standards, Alliances and Consortia for Innovation

Do 'New Technology' Collaborations Support or Impede Innovation & Competition?

In a digital, networked economy most companies need to cooperate with others to establish standards and create a single network of compatible users (Schapiro and Varian 1999). Discussions of the link between firm size and innovation are outmoded in the era of high-technology and globalization as the boundaries of the firm have become more fuzzy over recent decades (Teece 1992). Strategic alliances or constellations of bilateral agreements among firms are increasingly necessary to support innovative activities. Anti trust law and competition policy need to recognise that these new organizational forms are often the functional antithesis of cartels, even though they may have certain structural similarities: in the US they have traditionally been regarded exclusively in terms of standard, anti-competitive cartel theory (Jorde and Teece 1990).

How Do Countries Differ in the Practices of Research Consortia?

Such forms of cooperation have long been important and accepted in Japan and Europe. Research consortia have played an important role in the economic success of several East Asian countries (Dodgson and Kastelle 2006). Case studies in Korea (Samsung), Taiwan (ITRI) and China (Ericsson) demonstrate the centrality of strategic learning rather than cost-saving objectives, facilitating the development then transition from innovation diffusion capabilities to innovation generation capabilities. Also notable are institutional innovations in the East Asian context such as 'patent pools' that supplement more conventional forms of R&D collaboration.

How Is the Balance to Be Struck Between Cooperation and Innovation?

An empirical study of the effects of some thirty-two industry consortia on the coordination of innovation strategies of members in the wireless telecommunications industry that led to the global UMTS standard for mobile communications identified mixed impacts (Delcamp and Leiponen 2012). Consortia are particularly prevalent in, but not limited to, industries with compatibility standards. Inventions that are likely to become part of the standard system tend, on the basis of mutual patent citations, to build on innovations by peers that were members in the same consortia. Thus, on the one hand, by internalizing to the consortia the potential innovation externalities, consortia may enhance the productivity of innovation, increase incentives to invest in R&D, and enhance efficiency of standardization. On the other hand, the consortia appear to structure and constrain the process of innovating standardized technologies. The conclusion is that policy makers need to balance these two effects, not least to ensure that such processes are truly accessible for all interested parties.

Are Formal Standards-Setting Processes More Important Than Ever?

During the industrial revolution formal standard setting procedures focused on traditional manufacturing standards, such as those needed for interchangeable parts and mass production. The digital data and telecommunications era has shifted more and more of these formal processes into the high-tech and information areas. These processes are established by hundreds of official standard-setting bodies throughout the world. Never before have such cooperative, political processes been so important to market competition. Participants often complain about how slow, political, and often wrong these processes are but history shows that the consensus process can be critical to building credibility and launching new technologies.

Why do Standards Change Competition to Co-opetition in the Digital, Networked Age?

To compete effectively in networked markets companies need carefully picked allies to promote and establish a standard and then compete against those same companies. Standards alter competition. They expand network externalities, reduce uncertainty, and reduce consumer lock-in. At the same time, they shift competition from a 'winner-take-all battle to a more conventional struggle for market share, from the present to the future, from features to prices, and from systems to components. The term 'coopetition' has been coined to capture this tension between cooperation and competition based on game theory business strategy (Brandenburger and Nalebuff 1996).

Managing open standards can be especially tricky. Unless there is an agreed and effective lead champion or sponsor the standard can stagnate, or else be prone to 'splintering' or 'fragmentation' with the emergence of multiple, incompatible versions of standardized technology. They can also be 'hijacked' by companies seeking to expand them in proprietary directions.

Are the Members of Standards' Consortia Rivals or Complementors?

Formal standard development is increasingly supplemented by standards consortia: informal and less inclusive alliances, in which firms coordinate standard-related R&D and streamline standard development. An empirical study (Baron and Pohlmann 2013) finds that standards related to consortia are characterized by a more fragmented ownership of intellectual property rights and a strong degree of technological rivalry. Technological specialists are less likely to be members. Members tend to have substitutable rather than complementary technologies and patent portfolios. The authors conclude tentatively, that a main benefit of such consortia is to reduce the cost of standard development by eliminating wasteful R&D duplication and settling conflicts of interest upfront to more formal standard setting processes.

How Important Are 'Standards Wars' in the Emerging Information-Age?

When two new incompatible technologies struggle to become a de facto standard, a 'standards war' can ensue. The most famous of recent times was that between Microsoft and Netscape Browsers (Schapiro and Varian 1999). These 'wars' can end in a truce (modems), duopoly (video games) or a fight to the death (VCRs). Such 'wars' are unique to network markets and traditional principles of strategy are not enough. A critical distinguishing feature between these 'wars' are the magnitude of 'switching costs', or more generally, the 'adoption costs' for each rival; technology. These determine how compatible each technology is with the current technology. The nature of these information-age 'standards wars' and their differing tactics and outcomes are illustrated by the cases of AMstereo (mutually destructive); cellular phones (two continuing incompatible technologies); and, 56 k modems (resolved through a standards agreement).

Is There a 'Standards War' Over the Emergence of the 'Internet of Things' Market?

Dell, Intel and Samsung recently announced a home automation alliance called the Open Interconnect Consortium that creates an open-sourced standard for machine-to-machine communication (Spring 2014). Open-source code is seen by the Open Interconnect members as allowing developers and device-makers to create devices, wearables and sensors that communicate with one another regardless of operating system or protocol. Their standards will encompass wireless technologies including Wi-Fi, Bluetooth, ZigBee and NFC (near-field communication).

Open Interconnect competes with similar home automation standards groups such as Qualcomm-led AllSeen Alliance, which includes LG and Microsoft among its 51 members. The IPSOP Alliance is another global cooperative forum "building a smarter world through the internet of things", including many Fortune 500 high tech companies, each a leader in its segment. It supports an IP-based approach to connecting smart objects. Google and Apple are pursuing their own strategies.

Home automation is a subset of the 'internet of things' market, for which is forecast explosive growth to $1.7 trillion by 2020 (IDC 2015). Major players are fiercely battling it out for a share even though the technology has not yet caught on with consumers. Home automation systems integrators are saying that while too many standards is never a good thing for customers, it is a good sign for the industry, signaling large company interest in the market and generally raising consumer awareness. Competition is seen by them as driving innovation and better than the alternative of one company calling all the shots.

Research and Innovation Funding

How to Get Value from Government Funded Research that Is Steadily Cut Back?

Governments are major and important sources of research funding that underwrites innovation, especially for basic research in universities, government research laboratories, and industry and corporate R&D (Mazzucato 2013). For example, in Australia there is evidence that public investment in basic research increases productivity, that in a 2012 study investment in basic research led to thirty times more economic growth than that from investment in physical capital such as infrastructure, and that the impact of applied research was ten times that of physical capital (Ting and Phillips 2014).

Despite such evidence, government funding of research continues under question and under threat (Bailes 2014). Australia allocates around A$9 billion a year of taxpayers' money for research but that expenditure is at its lowest level in 30 years at only 0.56% GDP in 2013 (Ting and Phillips 2014). This is however, a considerably higher proportion of total national research spending (including by the private sector) than in most OECD countries; correspondingly, Australian business expenditure on R&D as % GDP is considerably lower than in other OECD countries. This leads to repeated questions about how well this money is spent, especially at times of budget and fiscal stringency when governments threaten to decrease the amounts of research funding in the budget and make the cuts (Jensen and Webster 2014).

What Is the Role of Evaluation in Improving Research-Funding Systems?

Despite long standing criticisms of research funding in Australia there has been a lack of meaningful evaluation or change in the system which researchers see as 'arcane, overly bureaucratic and wildly inefficient (Jensen and Webster 2014). A range of improvements are called for including: aligning incentives for long term, risky but achievable research rather than short term, low risk, novel research; shifting objectives and metrics from number of publications and their quality to outcomes that tackle real problems and provide solutions; reducing the opportunity costs of the red tape involved in the grants systems from applications through to reporting; funding the full costs of research by including the time of chief investigators which are currently seen as subsidized through their teaching salaries; focusing less on equitable funding to all and concentrate on funding clusters and centres of specialized excellence. There is also no database infrastructure in Australia to support the evaluation of research funding, mechanisms and policies, and their economic impacts, as found in the US (Weinberg et al. 2014).

Should the Funding of University Research Use 'Quality' not 'Quantity' Metrics?

Unlike in other countries, including UK, USA and Canada, research funding in Australian universities is only partially covered by government granting schemes with the bulk covered by a cross-subsidy from university teaching salary budgets, including increasingly via student fees. The Excellence in Research for Australia (ERA) program (Australian Research Council 2008) adopted funding allocation criteria based on a quality ranking scale from 1 through 5, with 3 judged world standard and 5 as above world standard, but the overall value of the exercise has been questioned (Schmidt 2014). This is because, although it was planned to skew research funding towards quality, (awarding seven times the funding to grade 5 research as to grade 3 research, with no funding to grades 1 and 2), the total quantum of funding available ($116 million) represented only a small portion of total $9 billion funding in Higher Education R&D (HERD).

Can Industry-Led, Industry-Wide Research Funding Deliver Better Results?

Australia's agriculture sector does perhaps provide lessons when it comes to the successful funding of research for innovation in the form of a century long experience with collaborative research involving industry and government (Webster

2014). Some fifteen agriculture sector Research and Development Corporations (RDC) (Grains, Livestock, Cotton, etc.) operate under government legislation, with multi-year programs, funded jointly by industry levies and matching government money. These industry led bodies tackle industry wide problems and opportunities, and are backed up by an in-built-extension service that transfers the research results to the industry. A recent evaluation calculated that every $1 invested in the research yielded about $11 in benefits over 25 years, through increased productivity, better market outcomes and improved management practices (RR&DC 2008). Unfortunately, this agricultural RDC model is not likely to apply well to the development of proprietary intellectual property that is much more common in highly differentiated product markets in sectors such as manufacturing and services.

Can a Focus on the Patent System Enhance Research and Innovation Performance?

An idea was floated by the Australian government that government research grants to universities might be linked to the number of patents the university registers, rather than the number or quality of papers it gets published (Maxwell 2014). This came at a time when Australia is rapidly going backwards in the development of high technology products for export (1.5% of 2011 exports, representing only 40% growth between 2001 and 2011, against overall export growth of 270%). In Australia only a low 5.4% of businesses engage in university—industry collaboration for innovation (ABS 2010–11 data), a figure at the very bottom end of developed country practice, with the percentage at around 30% in Scandinavian countries for example.

It is argued (Maxwell 2014) that there is a 'bias against innovation' in Australia, given the poor patent record and domestic market orientation of our 20 largest listed corporations, which has a 'knock-on effect' that flows through the economy down to SMEs and universities. Universities and research organizations in Australia publish 3.18% of the world's research publications but only an estimated 0.15% of the world's patent filings. It is proposed that larger Australian companies would be encouraged into being more innovative if patents were made cheaper to create and easier to own, thereby making our underutilized patent system more valuable as an asset.

University Research and University Industry Collaboration

Can 'Innovation Districts' Link Universities and Industry Successfully?

'Innovation districts' promote close relationships between inventors of knowledge, entrepreneurs who commercialise that knowledge and institutions that facilitate commercialization (Katz and Wagner 2014). They are a recent development of the earlier concepts of corporate campuses and science parks that are now seen as spatially isolated from communities, neighbourhoods and quality of life, all of which are now seen as central to the spatial integration of innovation (Katz et al. 2015). In The US and Europe, universities that harbour pure researchers often form the 'anchor' of important industrial districts. It is in pure research that academics and applied scientists develop the skills that they will later apply to develop innovations. Applied research and patenting cannot occur in the absence of the technical literacy that pure research engenders (Rice 2014).

Is the Quantum of University Research Funding Important in Industry Collaboration?

International research that examines the linking of basic research, applied commercial research and job creating innovation adopts a number of key assumptions (Rice 2014). For example, the Triple Helix Model developed in the 1990s emphasizes the central role of universities in a new triadic relationship with government and industry as hosts for both pure and applied research in the Knowledge Economy, compared to the centrality of the dyadic relationship between government and industry in the Industrial Economy (Etzkowicz 2008). Indeed, it is the exploratory elements of puzzle solving that drive the essential creativity that underlies all innovation, especially in the digital age. The US is often seen as an exemplar of market-facing research. Yet the massive historical subsidies for pure research in materials science and information technology—initiated to assist in the development of defence-sector innovations—have created important spin offs that today form the basis of much of the US high-technology sector. The quantum of funding provided to develop and maintain a knowledge base is the big issue, regardless of how the pie is sliced up.

Can Companies Manage the 'Outcome—Impact Gap' in University Collaborations?

Studies of industry-university collaboration typically frame the analysis in terms of research project *outcomes*, defined as a result that creates an opportunity for a company, such as guidance for the direction of technology. From a business standpoint, however, research outcome is of only incidental importance. What matters is not outcome but *impact*—how the new knowledge derived from collaboration with a university can contribute to a company's performance in terms of products, processes or people. An *outcome—impact gap* has been identified (Pertuze 2010) in university-industry collaborations in the US. Promising outcomes of university projects often fail to translate into tangible impacts for the companies involved. This has resulted in development of a range of best practices that managers can follow to best carry out collaborations once the agreements are in place.

How Can Universities Improve Their Interaction with Industry?

While just about every university in Australia has a strategic plan aimed at more engagement with industry the evidence suggests that changing the culture to achieve this aim still has some way to go (CRCA 2012). Stories of success and the rewards that can be reaped still seem to be treated more as exemplars than the norm (Peacock 2012). Big differences are observed across the universities and project agreements typically do not address the respective aspirations of the parties. A recent industry produced "Innovation Barometer" (GE 2012) rates Australia as a leader in university- industry collaboration. But it notes that "surprisingly" only 64% of survey respondents said it was easy for companies to partner with universities.

Science, Technology and Innovation Policy in Developing Countries

Will Innovation Be China's Next Source of Competitive Advantage?

Innovation is seen as being China's next source of competitive advantage (Veldhoen 2012). The Chinese government recently published an ambitious fifty-year plan to advance its technical and scientific position in the world demonstrating just how serious the country is about its technological place in the world (Specter 2014a, b). China has made tremendous progress in building science and technology capabilities. For example, it is on track to be the world's top R&D spending country by 2019 spending US$257 billion (in 2012) compared to America's US$397 billion, Europe's US$282 billion and Japan's US$134 billion (OECD 2014). But to achieve its ambitions to become an innovation-oriented nation, the country has to challenge itself by establishing an enterprise-centred national innovation system, better spending the increasing sums of money on innovation, improving its intellectual property rights regime, overcoming talent shortage, and nurturing a culture of creativity (Cao et al. 2009).

How Is India Promoting Innovation to Achieve 'Inclusive Growth'?

Following receipt of a World Bank report on innovation (World Bank 2007) the President of India declared a "Decade of Innovation" (President of India 2010) for the country (Dutz 2007). The Prime Minister's Adviser on Innovation and chair of the National Innovation Council (NINC) was charged with development of a National Innovation Strategy based on the Indian economic model of 'inclusive growth' (Petroda 2010). A National Knowledge Network (NKN) was established following presentation of the Innovation Policy in 2012, establishing a decentralized institutional and governance framework for innovation involving states, industry sectors and city councils.

Can India's 'Frugal Innovation' Meet the Needs of the Poorest?

Launched in 2014 as a not-for-profit organization, the India Inclusive Fund combines innovation with entrepreneurial dynamism to solve the problems of the poorest and least privileged citizens. It leverages the venture capital model, introducing a new class of capital investment in scalable, sustainable new micro SME ventures, earning small profits while addressing social needs. 'Frugal innovation' is a system specialization; it is not just 'innovation on the cheap' but a response to the reality of Indian purchasing power and raw materials and a recognition that "creativity loves constraints" (Bound and Thornton 2012). But while the science budget has grown 25% over the past five years in India its R&D spending is still only at 1%GDP.

Can Innovation' Jumpstart and Transform Development in Poor Countries?

"Innovation is popping up everywhere in the economic development debate these days" (Bollyky 2010), embracing both technological innovation for development and innovation in the delivery of development assistance (Brookings 2011). 'Innovation' has 'sex appeal' and everyone loves the idea of a 'killer app' for global prosperity. For example, US Secretary of State Hillary Clinton and the Millennium Challenge Corporation (MCC) are looking for more innovative ways to decrease global poverty, including by using innovative funding for new compacts with developing countries. A recent high level Brookings Roundtable focused on "Innovation and technology for development", discussing new IT, web-based innovations to 'jumpstart' development and help the poor become their own agents of change (Birdsall 2012). 'But not all technology leapfrogging is the same (Moss 2014)'.

How Can Agricultural Innovations Meet the Needs of the Developing Countries?

Feeding an extra 3 billion plus people over the next four decades is seen as a major challenge requiring a great leap in agricultural innovation (Elliott 2013). It involves tackling the interrelated issues of land, water, energy, climate change and decreasing crop yields. New demand based financing mechanisms may play an important role; these 'pull mechanisms' (as opposed to more traditional 'push mechanisms' on the supply-side) would still be donor financed but would use market-based financing mechanisms. The G20 Summit recently agreed to fund a $100 million results-based initiative for agriculture assistance using these new 'pull' mechanisms (Elliott 2012).

But there is also skepticism about just how far innovation in agricultural research and science can guide development policy (Sandefur 2012). The accompanying processes of economic reform and political compromise that are necessary are essentially messy and tedious by comparison to the 'innovation' fix, for example, moving people out of agriculture while still increasing productivity. In India, this technological scepticism extends to the prominent activist Vandana Shiva sowing the 'seeds of doubt' accusing biotechnology companies such as Monsanto of imposing 'food totalitarianism' (Specter 2014a). The fiery opposition to globalised genomics articulates a case against the very idea of intellectual property rights over seeds, that is seen to promote agricultural monocultures and to put the corporations not the farmers in control.

Others believe that GMOs are the key to solving world hunger and argue that to feed the one billion hungry people in the world no single crop or approach can provide the solution; we will need to use every one of them to succeed. Meanwhile, however, the gulf between the truth about GMOs and what people say about them keeps growing wider (Specter 2015).

Can Global Climate Change Be Tackled with New 'Global Public Good' Technologies?

Intellectual property rights (IPR) are central to the ongoing debate about innovation and climate change, and in particular, how developing countries will gain access to low-carbon, clean technologies (Bollyky 2009). These are highly contentious issues that threaten long-term global climate change negotiations, dividing countries along north–south lines and were not resolved in the most recent Paris negotiations. An international development conference focused on how these new low-cost, zero-carbon technologies with the characteristics of 'global public goods' might be financed and developed (CGD 2013). This is seen by the organizers as "one of the great policy challenges of our age" involving the balancing of country ownership, funder priorities and taxpayer accountability.

What New Roles for Public Funding, 'Carbon Price' and Intellectual Property Tights?

The Copenhagen commitment by donor governments to mobilize $100 billion in climate finance for developing countries by 2020 envisioned an important role for private financing. A key question is how public funding can catalyse large scale private funding for global climate change innovation and change. The massive coordinated research and development and deployment required would be boosted by a global price for carbon and an intellectual property access regime that preserves incentives for privately financed innovation and moves beyond the issue of intellectual property rights that have dogged negotiations to date to facilitate transfer of clean technology (Bollyky 2009).

Innovation in Global Value Chains

How Are 'Global Value Chains' Increasingly Being Using by Corporations?

The 'global value chain' (GVC) framework represents an increasingly popular form of industrial organization on a global scale. It is a key way of understanding the firm-level dynamics and structuring of global industries. Initially, the 'value-added chain' international business literature (Kogut 1985) focused on which activities and technologies a firm keeps in-house and which are outsourced to other firms, and where the various activities are located (Morrison et al. 2008). Frameworks such as global commodity chains (GCC) drew specific attention to the context of globalization of industries with a focus on developing countries. They stressed the leading role played by producers and buyers such as large retailers (e.g., Walmart) and brand merchandisers (e.g., Nike) (Gereffi and Kornzeniewicz 1994) in driving the formation of globally dispersed and organizationally fragmented production and distribution networks.

What Are the Governance Drivers and Modalities of 'Global Value Chains'?

The factors determining how GVC are governed, include, transaction complexity; ability to codify transactions; and, supply-base capabilities (Gereffi et al. 2005). This gives rise to five types of GVC governance: hierarchy; captive; relational; modular; and, market. These types exhibit a variety of characteristics and impact communities in different ways, including by sector and geography. The GVC approach shifts the focus from manufacturing only to all the activities involved, including, marketing and distribution, to the relationships between the various actors, and to the relative returns along the length of the value chain. Understanding "governance" rather than the more simple ideas of "coordination" is central to that analysis.

How Are the Lines Blurred Between Exports and Imports in Global Value Chains?

The importance of GVCs is reflected in the rising trade in 'intermediate inputs', which now account for more than half the goods imported by OECD economies and close to three quarters of imports of large developing countries, such as China and Brazil) (Xing 2015). Imported inputs also account for a significant chunk of exports, blurring the line between exports and imports, as well as between domestic products and imports. Intermediate inputs account for one quarter of OECD exports and about 44% of EU exports; for China the figure is nearly 30% of their exports (OECD 2013).

Who Profits from Innovation In 'Global Value Chains'?

Analysis of the distribution of profits and jobs from innovation in GVCs shows a different picture to that presented by the commonly used measures of bilateral trade deficits (Dedrick et al. 2010). For example, a $299 Apple iPod shows up as a $144 trade deficit for the US with China, but China's input is only about $5 of labor, involved in assembly. Most of the value is created and captured elsewhere in the value chain. Various component suppliers in Taiwan, Korea and Japan capture about 10% of the profits, while Apple captures 25%, and 25% in distribution and retail. So the US through Apple captures good jobs and wages, in R&D, engineering, and management in its home country. There are losers. Apple used to manufacture in the US; those (low wage, low skill) jobs are now gone.

What Are the Implications of 'Global Value Chains' for Learning and Innovation?

Merely entering GVCs does not cause a sharp and automatic upgrading of capabilities, and associated positive impact on local producers (Morrison et al. 2008). It is not a mechanistic and risk-less process, and local firms need to invest in learning and building technological capabilities to upgrade effectively. The interaction between GVCs and innovation systems, and how this affects enterprise learning has a number of key characteristics (Pietrobelli and Rabellotti 2010): GVC governance influences learning mechanisms, for example, pressure to achieve international standards; a well-structured and efficient innovation system would help reduce transaction complexity; and, the innovation system interacts with the internal governance of the GVC determining its form and operation.

Why Is There a Geographic Shift 'in Innovation Within' Global Value Chains'?

Fundamental changes to GVCs are afoot and the location of their geography is likely to shift fundamentally, propelled by a number of driving forces (World Economic Forum 2012): cost pressures from rising energy and transport prices and growing protectionism, will promote reductions in the 'length' of value chains; increasing prices for resources for inputs along with export restrictions will further intensify upward pressure on prices; rising costs, particularly of wages, in China, the centre of GVCs in manufacturing, may be offset by already strongly improving productivity; lower information technology costs will open up opportunities to countries wishing to grab a slice of the value chain action; and, continued growth in developing country markets and relative stagnation in the developed will drive GVC reorientation and relocation, potentially in unpredictable ways.

These GVC dynamics will, among other things, drive unilateral trade policy responses centered on promoting competitiveness, efficiency and attractiveness to value chain investments. Countries that stimulate investment in innovation and intellectual capital, such as design, R&D and new business models, will help their firms and countries move up the global value chains capturing a bigger return in profits and jobs (OECD 2013).

Within GVCs business innovation power has begun to move from the US, Europe and Japan to developing countries, for example, China, Brazil and India (WEF 2012). Analysts have tended to explain this shift by concentrating on 'pull' factors within the developing countries, such as investment in high-level education, the return of migrating engineers, big and expanding internal markets, etc. In contrast, new analysis (Humphrey and Schmitz 2012) concentrates on explanatory 'push' factors that emanate from the old innovation powers, notably, the 'organizational decomposition of the innovation process' (ODIP).

Who Are the Innovation Winners and Losers in the Shift in Global Value Chains?

By way of example, in the GVCs that link Brazilian auto and Indian software suppliers with lead firms in the US and Europe (Lema et al. 2012), the 'organizational decomposition of the innovation process' (ODIP) undertaken by the lead firms contributes directly and indirectly to the accumulation of innovation activities in Brazil and India (Humphrey and Schmitz 2012). They engaged not only in 'applied' development, but also in 'systemic' development of products and services. Adopting these more sophisticated innovation strategies based on 'learning' countries can avoid the traditional 'middle income trap' as they raise the level of their development (Lee 2013). This build-up of innovation capability is only partially visible in conventional R&D statistics. It also suggests that the buildup of innovation capabilities in Brazil and India is accelerating ODIP in the US and Europe. While it is clear that the developing countries are benefiting it is not clear if the developed countries and their lead firms are suffering as a result.

What Does the 'Greening' Technology of Global Value Chains Say About Innovation?

In considering the GVC impact on innovation in developing countries it is useful to distinguish between 'emerging economies' which are already well integrated into the global economy, and the 'least-developed countries' that are not, for example, in the case of 'climate-mitigation technologies' (Glachant et al. 2013). Pushing technology transfer in emerging economies requires strengthening IP rights, lowering barriers to trade and investment, and improving technology absorptive capacities. In contrast, their role in innovation is limited. Standard tools of innovation policy, such as, public R&D, public support to private R&D, better access to finance, need to develop. Governments should also introduce more stringent environmental policies with proper enforcement to go beyond adoption of foreign technology. The least-developed countries do not import green technologies and low barriers to trade and FDI or strict IP rights are unlikely to trigger technology transfer, In these countries, the focus should be on building technological capacities.

Innovation, Dynamic Capabilities and Sustainable Strategies

How Do 'Dynamic Capabilities' Relate to Firm-Level Innovation and Strategy?

'Dynamic capabilities' refer to the firm-level organizational determinants of innovation, both enablers and inhibitors, internally and externally (Eisenhardt and Martin 2000). Although a contested concept, it is defined as the firm's ability to integrate, build, and reconfigure internal and external competencies to address rapidly changing environments (Teece 1997). These are all the more important in an increasingly globalised, competitive and knowledge economy environment. More generally, it is a resource-based view (RBV) of the firm providing a framework for understanding how competitive advantage within firms is achieved and how it might be sustained over time. It is a complement to the traditional emphasis of strategy as industry structure and strategic positioning (Porter 1979).

Can Lack of 'Dynamic Capability' Account for Failure of Innovative Companies?

In the last few years, the growing recognition of the importance of firm capabilities in management strategy and business innovation has made the original theory of 'dynamic capabilities' (Teece and Pisano 1994) particularly relevant. It was developed to explain how companies fulfill two seemingly contradictory imperatives. They must be both stable enough to continue to deliver value in their own definitive way and resilient and adaptive enough to shift on a dime when circumstances demand it (Kleiner 2013). As Teece tells it, his early work focused on why companies profited (or did not profit) from innovation and he came across many stories of historically successful and innovative companies with appropriate strategies that failed in the market place, such as EMI and Nokia. This was widely interpreted as a failure of strategy but Teece saw it as a lack of capabilities to deliver on the strategy.

How Can 'Innovation Capability' Be Characterized and Managed at the Firm-Level?

Managing the complex and risky process of innovation has been problematic and fraught with difficulty (Kanter 1989). Building an 'efficient' firm is not necessarily the same as building an 'innovative' one. It has been argued, building on the concept of 'dynamic capabilities', that the management of innovation can be viewed as a one of organizational capability (Lawson and Samson 2001). Using a conceptual model of the firm as an "innovation engine" the operating model sees substantial investment in innovation capability as the primary engine of wealth creation, rather than the possession of physical assets. The 'innovation capability' construct has seven elements: vision and strategy; harnessing the competence base; organizational intelligence; creativity and idea management; organizational structures and systems; culture and climate; and, management of technology. In this way, it is argued that the process of innovation can be managed, systematised and replicated within organizations.

Is 'Best Practice' Dynamic Capability Dependent on Specific Markets and Industries?

Although dynamic capabilities are idiosyncratic in their details and path dependent in their emergence, they have significant commonalities across firms, popularly termed 'best practice' (Eisenhardt and Martin 2000). In moderately dynamic markets, they resemble the traditional conception of routines; detailed, analytic, stable processes with predictable outcomes. In contrast, in high-velocity markets, they are simple, highly experiential and fragile processes with unpredictable outcomes. There is a need to focus on the actual processes and experiences of dynamic capability building and their outcomes, across different market and industry contexts; focusing exclusively internally and ignoring external changes is unrealistic.

Does 'Dynamic Capability' Deliver Innovation and Profitability?

Innovation is widely agreed to be a precondition for sustainable competitive advantage (Im 2004) but the consequences of dynamic capabilities including for innovation and profitability is under researched. The majority of research on dynamic capabilities is theoretical and conceptual, and in the early literature the innovation concept was not given much attention. In particular, the relationship between dynamic capabilities and product innovation performance and profitability had not been addressed. In the case of SMEs a positive relationship has been found between dynamic capabilities and innovation, but it was not possible to do so for the relationship between innovation performance and profitability, nor between dynamic capabilities and profitability (Grunbaum and Stenger 2013).

Are 'Dynamic Capabilities' for Innovation Transformed in the New Digital Age?

The 'New Dynamic Capabilities' framework focuses on the firm's ability to quickly orchestrate and reconfigure externally sourced competencies (Shuen and Sieber 2010). Successful examples range from Apple, Google, Android, IBM Linux developer ecosystems, to crowd-sourced, crowd-funded open innovations such as Obama08 mobile app. They simultaneously leverage internal resources such as platforms, know-how, user communities and digital, social and mobile networks. The framework is driven by the rise of Web 2.0 strategy, new digital, information and network economics, and the fall in transaction costs of specialized multi-party orchestration. The New Dynamic Capabilities framework for corporate strategic management bridges innovation strategy, digital strategy and multi-national strategy; experimenting, innovating and learning ten times faster while orchestrating organisational capabilities worldwide for execution in a globally networked and independent environment (Wikipedia 2015).

Finance, Venture Capital and Innovation

Is 'Financialisation' of Corporations Stifling Investment in Innovation and Jobs?

As the US economy struggles to recover from the Great Recession, the erosion of middle-class jobs, and the explosion of income inequality, how can the failure of corporations to use their substantial profits to invest in new rounds of innovation that can replace the lost jobs with new, high value-added jobs be explained? A suggested explanation lies in the 'financialisation' of the US corporation, particularly, the emergence of stock buybacks as a massive and systematic way to boost company stock prices, and hence, via stock-based compensation, their own incomes (Lazonick 2013). This 'financialised' mode of corporate resource allocation has undermined the innovation performance and prosperity of the US economy. In the lead up to the financial crisis of 2008, it was this financial manipulation and associated ideology of maximizing share-holder value (MSV), much more than innovation or speculation that drove stock prices. Once a new innovative venture comes to market, MSV ideology pretty soon takes over from innovation as the driver of stock price.

Who Is Rewarded by Successful Innovation, New-Firm Formation and Growth?

Innovation and job creation require business-government collaboration, including, investments in physical and human infrastructure that provide an essential foundation for business investment, especially in high-tech fields, alongside government subsidies to business, often through tax legislation (Lazonick 2008). In the US, government funding has been critical to the emergence and development of high-tech sectors such as computers, the Internet, biotechnology and alternative energy. But for these investments and subsidies, the US would not lead the world in venture capital, an industry devoted to new-firm formation and growth. Yet, a disproportionate share of the resulting returns accrue to entrepreneurs and financiers while neglecting the contributions of other stakeholders, especially taxpayers, who made a significant contribution to the 'cumulative innovation process' (Lazonick and Mazzucato 2012).

How Can Innovative Performance Drive Corporate Resource Allocation in Future?

A policy agenda to drive sustainable prosperity and equitable growth through corporate resource allocation in innovation and job-creation rather than driven by a financialisation ideology of 'maximising share-holder value' (MSV) would include the following reforms (Lazonick 2013): Banning stock repurchases so funds can be invested in innovation; indexing employee stock options and incentives to an indicator of innovative performance rather than having them dependent on speculation and manipulation by executives; regulating employment contracts to give contributing workers a share in the gains of innovation; implementing taxes on gains from innovation to fund government agencies for investment in the knowledge and infrastructure bases required for the next round of innovation. It will be impossible to justify these reforms if the ideology of MSV is not questioned and if a 'theory of innovative enterprise' is not accepted.

How Is the Global Venture Capital Market Performing and How Is It Changing?

As the global economy slowly continues to improve, 2013 was a turning point for global venture capital investment with a slight increase in the total level of investment (1.9%) and the emergence of a number of trends that are gaining momentum (Ernst and Young 2014). Angel investors and incubators are becoming more significant and better organised. Technology is enabling new mechanisms such as crowd-funding, which is changing and arguably democratising access to the funding environment at the early seed stages (MIT 2014). Corporates looking to fund innovation gaps or to reinvest surplus cash are pioneering new ways to collaborate with fast-growing businesses and with VCs. And governments are becoming more 'switched on' in terms of taking positive steps to create entrepreneurial ecosystems in which venture finance can thrive.

What Are the Prospects for Entrepreneurial and Innovation Funding?

Venture capital (VC) players are changing and raising their game looking more globally and with a trend to consolidation in the industry (Ernst and Young 2014). The US still accounts for nearly 70%, followed by 15% in Europe with the rest in small amounts up to 10% each. There was virtually no growth in VC investments in the US, big growth (20%) in Europe and a huge fall in Chin (30%). Angels and VCs are working together, crowd funding is building and large global corporates are becoming more involved globally in VC investments. Prospects for entrepreneurs seeking funding are stronger than they have been for some time at every stage of the funding ecosystem.

Is Venture Capital Underperforming and Putting Start up Funding at Risk?

The modern VC model has been around for 30–50 years, but there is still no Henry Ford of VC (Mclure 2012). More to the point, the VC market has performed terribly for more than a decade, using annual industry performance data, but individual VCs still get paid exceedingly well. They have no 'skin in the game' and there has been little innovation in the VC model (Mulchahy 2014). 2013 had all the signs of being a comeback year for VC and the industry realized its highest returns since the Internet boom. The overall industry's persistent inability to outperform public equities is a disappointment to investors, and a very real threat to the sustainability of the VC industry as we know it. On the other hand, perhaps we just don't have enough data to tell us how it is actually performing? (Primack 2014). The existing data confirm it is underperforming but we do not have enough data to know if it is over performing either.

What Are the Problems Underlying the VC Model and How Might Changes Be Made?

The bigger problem is perhaps how little of a problem this persistent under performance is for VCs themselves, as distinct from its investors who have arguably created and perpetuated such a structural economic misalignment (Mulchay 2014). VCs aren't paid to generate great returns and are paid by their investors as asset managers, not investors. Fees, it turns out, are their lifeblood, not the blockbuster returns and carry that the traditional VC narrative suggests. They are paid well when they under perform, making high six, and more often seven, figures in fixed, fee based cash compensation. They barely invest their own funds: the market 'standard' is about 1% of the fund size. With institutional investors contributing 99%. VCs seek a minimum, not a maximum investment for themselves. Finally, the industry has failed to innovate. Its business model and economic structure of the VC partnership has remained stagnant for the past two decades, despite enormous changes in the industry. VCs have hardly taken the lead on 'creative destruction' in their own industry. VC investing institutions have gone along with this model but they could change it by paying VCs less like asset managers and more like investors.

How Can the New Access to Crowd-Sourced Funding Support Innovation?

The Internet with its global reach has opened up completely new funding sources for innovation and new enterprises (issuers). These tap into typically into a large number of small investors (crowd) through on-line portals and a range of social media (intermediaries) to provide their cash in exchange for a relatively modest equity or ownership position in the product or enterprise. The potential of such equity funding and has likely benefits and risks (CMAC 2014). Some start-ups succeed by accessing a range of funding sources (personal savings, credit cards, family loans or donations, angel investors, venture capital) often assisted by 'incubators' or 'accelerators'. Others fail, in part due to the 'capital gap' from traditional financing sources and the inability to conduct and initial public offering (IPO). Crowd-sourced financing offers the potential to fill this gap and support the early-stage development of otherwise worthwhile creative and innovative ideas, helping to move them up the 'funding escalator'.

What Are the Potential Benefits and Risks of Crowd-Sourced Financing?

Crowd-sourced funding is still in its relatively early stages world-wide: the UK and New Zealand implemented in April 2014, Canada is at the proposals stage, and in the US, the SEC is yet to settle its rules (CMAC 2014). Its introduction could potentially lower the cost of capital, including for those not utilizing crowd-funding, if it becomes a source of increased competition between all capital providers. On the other hand, it may also divert funding and savings from other worthwhile ventures towards the many start-ups that eventually fail at a high opportunity cost for the economy as a whole. It also carries potential financial risks for crowd investors themselves who generally lack financial literacy or capacity and leading to an undermining of the confidence of those very 'crowds' upon whom it relies as a source of funding.

Innovation Challenges and Disruptive Technologies

What Are 'Disruptive Technologies' and How Do They Impact on Businesses?

The landmark book *The Innovator's Dilemma* (Christensen 1997) drew a distinction between 'sustainable technologies' that are developed and improved incrementally, gradually and at the margin of on going business, and those that he termed 'disruptive technologies' which are so new and radical that they require a fundamental rethinking of business (Hardy 2014a, b), for example, cloud technology, mobile phones, personal computers, digital photography, email, laptops. 3-D printing for example, provides a platform for innovation by a new generation of entrepreneurs or 'makers' who can take advantage of small scale, low barriers to entry manufacturing capability based on digital technologies and big data capababilities (Anderson 2014). The 'dilemma' posed is that even successful, innovative companies that are doing everything right with their customers, markets and technologies, can be blindsided and overtaken by these often unlikely, unexpected and often low-margin 'disruptive technologies'. Established businesses are uncomfortable with them and they often appear as highly risky, undeveloped and well ahead of any consumer markets. Even the best-managed companies' efforts to innovate in these circumstances are found wanting. This has lead companies to revise their strategies and look for 'breakthrough opportunities' beyond the 'business as usual' model that would give them the 'jump' on their competitors (Economist 2009).

What Are the 'Potentially Disruptive Technologies' and Their Likely Impact?

Disruptive technologies typically displace existing, often mature technologies creating new products, processes and even industries. By way of current examples, the range and number of potentially 'disruptive technologies' and their estimated impacts ($billion) can be gauged from the following recently prepared listing of 12 such 'disruptive technologies' (Manyika et al. 2013): mobile internet (3.7–10.8); automation of knowledge work (5.2–6.7); the internet of things (2.7–6.2); cloud technology (1.7–6.2); advanced robotics (1.7–4.5); autonomous vehicles (0.2–1.9); next generation genomics (0.7–1.6); energy storage (0.1–0.6); 3d printing (0.2–0.6); advanced materials (0.2–0.5); advanced oil and gas exploration and recovery (0.1–0.5); renewable energy 90.2–0.3).

Is There a Difference Between 'Disruptive Technologies' and 'Disruptive Innovation'?

While the seminal work on competitive strategy (Porter 1980) elaborated strategies for companies to win by, the work on disruptive technologies (Christensen 1997) was motivated by trying to understand why even the best of companies failed. Subsequently (Christensen and Raynor 2003) 'disruptive technology' was replaced by 'disruptive innovation', on the grounds that it was rarely the technology per se that was disruptive (or sustaining) but the use that companies made of it, that is, the innovation that it enabled them to undertake (Christensen 2007). These days it seems everyone is either disrupting or being disrupted: disruption is a predictable pattern across many industries in which fledgling companies use new technology to offer cheaper and inferior alternatives to products sold by established players (New York Times 2014).

Is 'Disruptive Innovation' Undermining the Foundations of the Scientific Method?

Concerns are increasingly being raised within the scientific community and beyond in public debate about the impact of new technologies on the methods and processes of scientific research itself (Edge 2014). A case in point is the key concept of the 'reproducibility 'of experimental results and research findings, or their independent replication as the means of verifying their correctness; a principle brought into scientific discourse in the 1660s by Robert Boyle. A case is made for its redefinition using terminology more appropriate to the different research environments scientists work within today, namely, today's pervasive use of computational methods: computers are unlike any previous scientific apparatus because they act as a *platform* for the implementation of a method, rather than directly as an instrument. This creates additional instructions to be communicated as part of Boyle's vision of replicable research—the code, and digital data (Stodden 2014).

Is 'Disruptive Innovation' a Valid 'Theory of Change' that Enables Prediction?

While most 'big ideas' have loud critics, 'disruptive innovation' has been subject to little serious criticism (Lepore 2014). This is partly because in its modern usage, 'innovation' is the idea of 'progress' jammed into a criticism-proof jack-in-the-box. This skirts the question of whether novelty is an improvement. Originally a word with chiefly negative connotations, 'innovation' signified excessive novelty, without purpose or end. Its redemption began in 1939 with Schumpeter's theory of 'creative destruction': the idea of 'progress' stripped of the aspirations of the Enlightenment, scrubbed clean of the horrors of the twentieth century, and relieved of its critics. Post 9/11, 'disruptive innovation' goes further, holding out hope of salvation against the very damnation it describes: disrupt and you will be saved but it meets none of the conditions of proof required of a 'theory of change'. It is a theory built on handpicked case studies, arbitrary definitions of success, dubious sources and questionable logic. The theory explains only why companies fail but it does not explain change. It relies on a circular logic and 'disruptive innovation' cannot be predicted and can only reliably seen after the fact (Lepore 2014).

What Are the Values and Goals Underlying the Concept of 'Disruptive Innovation'?

Innovation and disruption are ideas that originated in the arena of business but which have since been applied to arenas whose values and goals are remote from those applied to business (Lepore 2014). These arenas include public schools, colleges and universities, churches, museums, government, many hospitals, and journalism that is not an industry rather than a profession. The examples and instances abound. The underlying ethos is well captured in a recent book on disruption (Linkner 2014) whose job appears to be to convince a generation of people who want to do good to learn instead, to be remorseless. Forget rules, obligations, your conscience, loyalty, a sense of the commonweal. If you start a business and it succeeds, sell it and take the cash. Don't look back. Never pause. Disrupt or be disrupted (Lepore 2014).

What Are the Issues Posed by 'Artifiicial Intelligence' as a Disruptive Technology?

After an over-hyped birth in the early years of robotics in the 1950s 'artificial intelligence' has re-emerged completely reinvigorated in the digital age of big data as potentially major disruptor and source of economy-wide innovation utilizing 'machine learning' and 'data analytics' (Knight 2016). One of the founders of robotics speaks of the 'singularity' or the 'Turing test' at which point the power of artificial intelligence overtakes human thought (Kurzweil 1999) currently set at about 2030–40. Recently appointed the director of engineering at Google he is now heading up a team there that has been described as the greatest AI laboratory on earth and Google has bought up almost every machine learning and robotics company it can find (Cadwallader 2014).

AI is already with us in the well-known forms of the pervasive consumer data algorithms on our smart phones and laptops that track our behaviour and generate 'big data' that is processed by corporations to target their merchandising. In Australian mining and agriculture 'autonomous machines' are adding to productivity in the field, and sophisticated 'data analytics' are at work in infrastructure and geology (Zelinsky 2013). Potentially more significantly, machine learning is driving new ways of doing science using Bayesian statistics, data analytics and predictive modelling to allow 'small data', that is few data about huge problems, to test billions of behavioural models for best fit model, thereby inverting the usual experimental and modelling approach which tests data against a given model for fit and creating a 'new kind of calculus' (Durrant-Whyte 2016).

Are Disruptive Digital Technologies Driving Us Towards a 'Post Human' Future?

We are still a long way from reaching the 'singularity' and nowhere remotely close to developing computerized, robotized, 'super intelligence' but the prospect is in the air more than ever before, captures the imagination of popular culture while endangering fears, and gives rise to philosophical speculation about their implications (Searle 2014) and just how society might handle the arrival of a such a possible 'existential catastrophe'? What if machines develop the ability of 'recursive self-improvement' that allows them to redesign themselves to be ever more intelligent? Why would we expect them necessarily to share our human values, ethics, preferences, moralities, and aspirations, and contribute to their development? These fundamental questions deserve at the least to be taken seriously by society and ethical guidelines need to be developed to guide our future research and innovation into these technologies: "they are quite possibly the most important and most daunting challenge that humanity has ever faced" (Bostrom 2014).

At the metaphysical philosophical level the 'infosphere' is seen as reshaping humanity reality on the basis that "reality consists of information" and vice versa (Floridi 2014). The sheer force and accelerating pace of digital disruption are pushing traditional Enlightenment conceptions of humanism aside into uncertain and unknowable post human futures (Kroker 2014). Society is marked by growing uncertainty concerning both the ultimate ends of technological innovation and the ways of understanding and negotiating the uncertain digital future. The emerging signs of this future are a 'drift' culture, recombinant technology, figural aesthetics, and distributive consciousness. Technology now seeks out and amplifies what was previously marginalized, paradoxically turning back on itself and effectively undermining traditional humanist concepts such as subjectivity, privacy and absolutist ideologies of the past century, this time in purely technocratic formulations.

Innovation, Skills and Creative Industries

What Do We Know About the Relationship Between Skills and Innovation?

It is widely accepted that innovation depends upon people who are able to generate and apply knowledge and ideas in the workplace and in society at large. Governments invest significantly in education and skill formation. But it is difficult to make explicit links between specific skills and innovation because of the broad definitions involved and the difficulties involved in measurement Countries are seeking to learn more about the broad range of skills involved, and 'soft skills' such as multicultural openness and leadership, may be increasingly important in addition to basic, technical and generic skills such as problem solving. Managerial and entrepreneurial skills are also mentioned, as are creativity and design. People also need the skills that enable them and their workplace to 'learn' (OECD 2011).

Are We Facing a New Era of 'Jobless Growth' in the 'Second Machine Age'?

The view that automation and other forms of technological progress in aggregate create more jobs than they destroy has come to dominate the discipline of economics. To believe otherwise is to succumb to the "Luddite Fallacy". For most of the two hundred years since the Luddite rebellion technology has boosted productivity enormously, and employment grew alongside productivity up until the end of the twentieth century. However, data also show that, more recently, job growth decoupled from productivity in the late 1990s. The power of exponential, digital, and combinatorial forces, as well as the dawning of machine intelligence and networked intelligence, presage even greater destruction (Brynjolfsson and McAfee 2014).

What Skills and Training Are Required in the 'Second Machine Age'?

It is difficult to know how to answer questions about the nature of skills required for the future and how to educate and train people to achieve them. Will a generation be left behind in all areas of the economy and society, or at least most of them, in an era of 'jobless', 'de-skilling' growth? There are some positive pointers as to how people might be valuable and compete with machines in the new digital age. We need to work to improve the skills of ideation, large-frame pattern recognition, and complex communication instead of just the three Rs. And whenever possible, we need to take advantage of self-organising learning environments, which have a track record of developing these skills in people (Brynjolfsson and McAfee 2014).

What Is the 'Hollowing Out' of the Middle-Class, Knowledge Workforce?

Cooks, gardeners, dog-walkers, repairmen, carpenters, dentists and others in 'touch and spatially sensitive' jobs are not about to be replaced by machines which cannot yet 'learn' such skills, even if not all of these kinds of jobs are paying well. They may however face more competition for those jobs by people from displaced middle-class, knowledge jobs such as accounting, law and even medicine whose repeatable, analytical nature to 'machine learning'; this continuing 'hollowing out' polarises the labor market in the head-to-head race against the 'intelligent' machine (CEDA 2015). This is a global phenomenon with the middle class jobs in manufacturing also increasingly outsourced and offshored, lost jobs or downshifting to lower paid jobs (Thompson 2011). The boundary between uniquely human creativity and machine capabilities continues to be fuzzy and change, and people will need to be more adaptable and flexible in their career aspirations. Those in highly creative and decision making roles will flourish and usually with high premium earnings, since these tasks are not readily automated either. We can be confident that more surprises are in store. It is very easy to underestimate the power of digital, exponential, and combinatorial innovation in the 'second machine age' and its impacts not only on our workforce but upon social structures and society as we know it (Brynjolfsson and McAfee 2014).

What Is the Role of School Education in Preparing for Innovation Skills?

"Teach the children well" (Brynjolfsson and McAfee 2014). The US was a clear world leader in primary school education in the first half of the twentieth century but over the past half century that advantage has vanished, with the a ranking no better than the middle of wealthy countries. The economic benefits of lifting the ranking are likely to be large. It has been said that America's greatest idea was mass education and that idea should still apply at all levels, not just K12 and university education, but also preschool, vocational and life-long learning. Education can be delivered differently by adopting new digital technologies, in which the sector is a relative laggard.

One clear and consistent finding from educational research is that teachers matter, and higher teacher salaries and accountability would be a grand bargain. It is important in the process not to drive out important but less measurable forms of learning, including creativity, and to ensure that access and participation in new technology based education is as broad as possible. While there is no hard evidence linking technology use and better school outcomes, the evidence does show better outcomes associated with effective use of technology; it is not the technology that matters but the teachers and how it is used (Morrison 2014).

How Can Universities Better Deliver the Skills Necessary for Innovation?

An innovation-capable workforce is critical to achieving the goal of increasing productivity (ACOLA 2014). Innovation involves more than technical skills. It also needs people who understand systems, cultures and the way society uses and adopts new ideas. Skills in both STEM and HASS are required by successful businesses, and getting the mix right between them is a critical factor in deploying innovation for efficiency and productivity at the firm level. Long-term demand for STEM skills is difficult to predict, not least with the convergence of life sciences, physical sciences and engineering in the digital age. Improving the quality of information to students and preparing them for life-long learning will help meet evolving workforce needs. Particularly in Australia, there is a need to improve entrepreneurship, and business management skills, including the ability to manage innovation, especially within STEM training and also in the Vocational Education Training (VET) level. Closer engagement in these STEM training issues is needed between universities and business.

The tremendous experimentation with 'massive online open courses' (MOOCs) is a highly promising 'disruptive' technology in tertiary education but its real impact is still mostly ahead of us (Adams 2013). To date their performance is falling short of the hype of their proponents and developers that include some of the largest, richest and most prominent universities in America (Harvard, MIT, Stanford). Despite most being provided for free, completion rates are disappointingly low. On the other hand, many thousands of students are participating and benefitting, especially in the more vocationally oriented IT programs.

Do Training Skills Investment by Enterprises Result in Improved Innovation?

An analysis of SMEs in Britain has concluded simply, that, the most innovative firms train more staff (Freel 2005). The most consistent and reliable statistical associations concern the relationship between innovativeness (in both products and processes, and in manufacturing and services) and firm-level training intensity (Benoit 2014). The findings underline the importance of intermediate 'technical' skills, rather than higher level 'technology skills'. However, perhaps the most fundamental observation is the recognition that labor quality has a dynamic component, in addition to the static elements commonly measured. In other words, it is not just the initial formal qualifications that matter but their continuous effective deployment within the firm, and their regular updating. Innovation and training in modern economies are inextricably linked (Campbell and Warner 1987). There is indeed, a positive association between investment in training and firm performance (ACOLA 2014).

Does 'Creativity' Cause 'Balkanisation' of Innovation and Neglect of 'Imagination'?

"This false divide between the arts and science, between arts and industry, between the arts and the economy: we've actually got to put that to bed. As if creativity is somehow something that only applies to the arts, and innovation is this thing over here that applies uniquely to the sciences or design. This is actually a false dichotomy: it is just not like that", according to the then Prime Minister of Australia (Cutler 2008a, b). It was argued that there is a 'balkanisation of innovation' with too many, disconnected systems all pulling in opposite directions. There is a 'hole in the centre' of the innovation system 'donut', and we need to tear down the fences around innovation's 'gated communities' need to be torn down and stronger linkages and platforms built for collaboration. The arts provide "windows into realities under construction" that serve to highlight the role of 'imagination' in the innovation process. This imaginative solution-seeking role needs to complement the role of analytic problem solving, by helping us to envision alternative futures (Cutler 2008a, b).

What Are 'Creative Industries' and How Do They Contribute to Innovation?

The creative industries are now increasingly identified as key drivers of modern 'knowledge-based' economies, as well as being the providers of cultural offerings worthy of subsidy on 'market failure' grounds, and a high-growth industry (film, tv, publishing, video games) in their own right warranting the development of their own new industry development plans and assistance (Cultural Ministers Council 2008). As well as being among the most innovative of sectors in the economy, and important source of demand for innovative digital technology products, they support innovation in a variety of other sectors through creative inputs, such as ideas for new products and services, or marketing support for product and service innovations. They are no homogeneous sector however. While software and advertising show the strongest links to industrial innovation, architecture and content providers contribute rather little (Potts 2009).

Governments have generally been slow to recognize and support the creative industries as a platform for innovation but there are signs of growing awareness and interest in Europe, especially the UK where it has been recognized as providing more jobs than sectors such as finance and construction and a 'manifesto' has been proposed for its development (Bakhshi et al. 2013). Interest is emerging in Australia with the establishment of university-based centres such as those at Queensland Institute of Technology and the University of Technology Sydney (Cunningham 2013).

How Do Embedded 'Creative Workers' Contribute to Innovation Across the Economy?

Creative workers are employed in sectors outside the creative industries often in greater numbers than within the creative field and policy makers are increasingly interested in how to develop their contribution to economic growth (Potts 2011). Relatively little is known about the work life of these 'embedded creatives', which companies seek to employ them and why, and the implications for education and training of creative workers (Hearn et al. 2014). Creative industry workers are at the cutting edge of digital business and disruption. In particular, the film, video and photography industries have pioneered the emergence of new business models, and new modes of collaboration with 'the crowds', customer co-creation, and managing 'long-tail' markets, in the process, deepening our understanding of constant digital disruption, business strategy and innovation (De Fillippi and Wikstrom 2014). The creative industries are an 'enabling platform' for national innovation in a digital age, knowledge-based economy (Cutler 2008a, b).

Are Cities the Most Important Innovation Platform for 'Collaborative Creativity'?

Cities bring opportunities for wealth and for the creative inspiration that can only result from face-to-face contact, and can now help solve the world's most pressing problems of poverty, energy shortages, and climate change (Glaeser 2011). Innovation, most of all, is a messy business, driven by random collisions and taking more than just smart people, but diversity as well (Satell 2013). Vibrant cities are crucial to our continued ability to innovate. Contrary to early expectations that computers and the internet would free people to live and work wherever they chose, away from large corporate offices and congested cities, the new, creative, 'machine age' workers prefer to cluster together in attractive inner urban 'hubs'.

Interest in the innovation performance of cities is reflected in a number of global 'innovation city' systems of comparative metrics and rankings (Innovation Cities Program 2013). Culture and associated creativity is now recognized as a prime driver of innovation, and if the best and brightest can go anywhere, why wouldn't they go to a place they will enjoy living in? As Steve Jobs noted, creativity is about connecting things. He designed the his Apple HQ to facilitate such interactions, and its why cities need not only office buildings and research parks, but more cafes, music festivals, art shows and other places where creative people can meet and exchange ideas (Satell 2013).

Bibliography

Acemoglu, D. (2013, December 3). Politics and technology. *Why nations fail blog*.

Acemoglu, D., & Robinson, J. (2012). *Why nations fail: The origins of power, prosperity, and poverty*. New York: Crown Business, Random House.

Adams, S. (2013, December 11). Are MOOCs really a failure? *Forbes*.

Anderson, C. (2006). *The long tail: Why the future of business is selling less to more*. New York: Hyperion Press.

Anderson, C. (2014). *Makers: The new industrial revolution*. USA: Crown Business Press.

Arthur, W. B. (1994). *Increasing returns and path dependence in the economy*. Ann Arbor: University of Michigan Press.

Australian Council of Learned Academies (ACOLA). (2014). *The role of science, research and technology in lifting Australian productivity*. Canberra: Securing Australia's Future.

Australian Research Council (ARC). (2008). *Excellence in research for Australia (ERA)* (Annual Reports). Canberra: AGPS.

Bailes, M. (2014, May 12). The state of Australia: Science, innovation and research. *The Conversation*.

Baker, N. (2013, July 8). A fourth state of matter: Inside South Korea's LCD revolution. *The New Yorker*.

Bakhshi, H., et al. (2013, April 23). *A manifesto for the creative economy*. London: NESTA.

Baron, J., & Pohlmann, T. (2013). Who cooperates in standards consortia—Rivals or complementers? *Journal of Competition Law and Economics, 9–4*, s905–s929.

Ben-Atar, D. S. (2004). *Trade secrets: Intellectual piracy and the origins of American industrial power*. New Haven, Connecticut: Yale University Press.

Benner, K. (2015, January 22). Obama, immigration and Silicon Valley. *Bloomberg View.com*.

Benoit, D. (2014, September). *Innovation, productivity and training* (35pp). Discussion Paper, Institute for Study of Labor (IZA), Bonn.

Bilton, N. (2013). *Hatching twitter: A true story of money, power, friendship and betrayal*. Portfolio Reprint.

Birdsall, N. (2012, August 6). Clicks to policy bricks: Can innovation jump start development transformation? *CGDE blog*.

Bollyky, T. J. (2010). Innovation in economic development.

Bollyky, T. J. (2009, December). *Principles for innovation and access to low-carbon technology*. Center for Global Development (CGD) Notes, Washington DC.

Boog, J. (2013, January 28). Publishing trends for 2013: As a writer, how will they influence you? *GalleyCat, NYICD*.

Boston Consulting Group & National Association of Manufacturers (BCG & NAM). *International innovation index (III)* (Annual survey report). Boston, MA.

Bostrum, N. (2014). *Superintelligence: Paths, dangers, strategies* (352pp). Oxford: Oxford University Press.

Bound, K., & Thornton, I. (2012, July). *Frugal future: Lessons from India's innovation system*. London: NESTA.

Brand, S. (1984). *Whole earth catalog*. San Francisco.

Brandenburger, A., & Nalebuff, B. (1996). *Co-opetition: A revolutionary mindset that combines competition and cooperation*. New York: Currency/Doubleday.

Brookings Institute Roundtable. (2011). *Innovation and technology for development*. Washington, DC.

Brynjolfsson, E., & McAfee, A. (2014). *The second machine age: Work, progress, and prosperity in a time of brilliant technologies*. New York: Norton.

Burdon, S. (2014, March). *Survey of Australia's leading innovative technology organizations*. Sydney: Australian Information Industries Association (AIIA).

Business Review Weekly (BRW). (2013). Inventium: The 50 most innovative companies.

Cadwallader, C. (2014, February 23). Are the robots about to rise? Google's new director of engineering thinks so…". *The Observer*.

Campbell, A., & Warner, M. (1987, March). New technology, innovation and training: An empirical study of selected British firms. *New Technology, Work & Employment, 2*(2), 86–99.

Cao, C., et al. (2009). China's innovation challenge. *Journal of Innovation Management, Policy and Practice, 11*(2).

Capital Markets Advisory Committee (CMAC). (2014). *Crowd sourced equity funding*. Canberra: Treasury, AGPS.

Castellano, J. A. (2005, January). *Liquid gold: The story of LCD and the creation of an industry*. London: World Scientific Publishing Company.
Center for Global Development (CGD). (2013). *How to spend it (if we had it): Priorities for allocating international climate change finance*. Conference, Washington, DC.
Chesbrough, H. W. (2003, April). *Open innovation: The new imperative for creating and profiting from technology*. Mass: Harvard Business School Press.
Christensen, C. M. (1997). *The innovator's dilemma: When new technologies cause great firms to fail*. Cambridge, MA: Harvard Business School Press.
Christensen, C. M. (2007, May–June). Disruption driven growth: Ten years after 'the innovator's dilemma'. *Strategy and Innovation, 5*(3).
Christensen, C. M., & Raynor, M. E. (2003, September). *The innovator's solution: Creating and sustaining successful growth*. Cambridge, Mass: Harvard Business School Press.
Cohen, T. (2011, January). *The great stagnation: How America ate all the low-hanging fruit of modern history*. USA: Dutton.
Committee for Economic Development of Australia (CEDA). (2015, June 16). *Australia's future workforce* (Report). Sydney: CEDA.
Cooperative Research Centres Association (CRCA). (2012, January 19). *Are we crap at university—Industry collaboration, or do we just think we are?* CRCA.
Cultural Ministers Council. (2008). Building a creative innovation economy. Australia and New Zealand, February.
Cunningham, S. (2013, October 30). The creative economy could fuel Australia's next boom. *The Conversation*.
Cutler, T. (2008a, September 9). Venturous Australia: Building strength in innovation. *National Innovation Systems Review*. Canberra: AGPS.
Cutler, T. (2008b, August 19). Creativity, the arts and innovation. *A Currency House Conversation*.
Davis. (2014). Monash, cited in Wilkins.
Dedrick, J., et al. (2010). *Who profits from innovation in global value chains: A study of the iPod and Notebook PCs?* In Industry Studies, Alfred P Sloan Foundation Conference, Boston, MA.
Delcamp, H. R., & Leiponen, A. (2012). *Innovating standards through informal consortia: The case of wireless telecommunications*. NBER Working Paper 18179, Washington, DC.
Deloitte. (2016). *The Deloitte millennial survey* (Department of Industry, Annual innovation systems policies reports). Canberra, ACT: AGPS.
Department of Industry, Information and Science (DIIS). (2010, May, 12). *Powering Ideas: An innovation agenda for the 21st century, 2009–20*. Canberra: AGPS.
De Fillippi, R., & Wikstrom, P. (2014). *International perspectives on business innovation and disruption in the creative industries: Film, video and photography*. Cheltenham: Edward Elgar.
Dobinson. (2014). cited in Wilkins.
Dodgson, M. (2013, November 28). *Australia on the global innovation stage*. Warren Centre Lecture, Sydney University.
Dodgson, M., et al. (2009, December). *Systems thinking, market failure, and the development of innovation policy: The case of Australia* (41pp). Working Paper 397, Centre for Business Research, University of Cambridge.
Dodgson, M., & Kastelle, T. (2006). The evolving role of research Consortia in East Asia' innovation: Management. *Policy and Practice, 8*(1–2), 84–101.
Drucker, P. (1942). *The future of industrial man*. New York: John Day.
Durrant-Whyte. (2016). *Rise of the machines* (Public lecture). Australian Academy of Science, Canberra, ACT, February 9, 2016.
Dutz, M. A. (Ed.). (2007). *Unleashing India's innovation: Towards sustainable and inclusive growth*. Washington, DC: World Bank.
Economist. (2009, May 11). *Disruptive technologies and innovation*.
Edge Foundation. (2014). What scientific idea is ready for retirement? *Egde.org*.
Eisenhardt, K. M., & Martin, J. A. (2000, October/November). Dynamic capabilities: What are they? *Strategic Management Journal, 21*(0–11).

Elberse, A. (2013). *Blockbusters: Hit-making, risk-taking and the big business of entertainment.* New York: Henry Holt & Company.

Elliott, K. A. (2012, September 6). Win for agriculture in Cabos: Introducing the AgResults Development initiative. *CDG blog, cddev.org*, Washington, DC.

Elliott, K. A. (2013, March 25). *Agricultural innovation in action: What's next for the AgResults initiative? CDG blog, cddev.org*, Washington, DC.

Ernst & Young. (2014). *Adapting and evolving: Global venture capital insights and trends.*

Etzkowicz, H. (2008). *The triple-helix: University-industry-government innovation in action*. New York: Routledge.

European Union (EU). (2011). *Innovation statistics*. Brussels.

European Union (EU). (2013, December 3). *Council adopts 'Horizon 2000': The EU's research and innovation program for 2014–2020*. Brussels: Press release 510, 16939/13.

Favaro, K. (2015, November 2). Best business books 2015: Strategy. *Strategy & Business*.

Floridi, L. (2014). *The fourth revolution: How the infosphere is reshping humanity* (248pp). Oxford: Oxford University Press.

Ford, M. (2015). *Rise of the robots: Technology and the threat of a jobless future*. New York: Basic Books.

Freel, M. S. (2005, February). Patterns of innovation and skills in small firms. *Technovation, 25*(2) (Elsevier).

Freeman, C. (1995). The national system of innovation in historical perspective. *Cambridge Journal of Economics, 19,* 5–24.

Gawande, A. (2013, July 29). Slow ideas: Some innovations spread fast: How do you speed ones that don't? *The New Yorker*.

General Electric (GE). (2012, January). *Global innovation barometer* (Global research report, Annual, Strategy One).

Gereffi, G., et al. (2005, February 12). The governance of global value chains. *Review of International Political Economy*.

Gereffi, G., & Kornzeniewicz, M. (1994). *Commodity chains and global capitalism*. Santa Barbara: ABC-CLIO.

Gertner, J. (2012). *The idea factory: Bell Labs and the great age of American innovation*. London: Penguin Press.

Gillard. (2012). *Smarter manufacturing for a smarter Australia* (94pp) (Manufacturing task force report). Canberra: AGPS.

Gittins, R. (2014, February). The jobs will come, just as they always do. *Sydney Morning Herald*.

Glachant, M., et al. (2013, May). *Greening global value chains: Innovation and the international diffusion of technologies and knowledge*. Policy Research Working Paper 6467, World Bank, Washington, DC.

Gladwell, M. (2000). *The tipping point: How little things can make a big difference, Little*. New York: Brown & Company.

Glaeser, E. L. (2011). *Triumph of the city: How our greatest invention makes us richer, smarter,* .... New York: Penguin Putnam.

Goldman, E. (2013). *Fixing software patents*. Santa Clara Law Digital Commons, Faculty Publication 1-1-2013, Santa Clara University.

Gordon, R. (2012, August). *Is US economic growth over? Faltering innovation confronts the six headwinds*. NBER Working Paper 1835, Washington DC.

Grazer, B., & Fishman, C. (2015). *A curious mind: The secret to a bigger life*. New York: Simon & Schuster.

Green, R. (2014, July 21). Australia ranks on innovation—But indolence could cost us. *The Conversation*.

Greenwald, T. (2014, January 22). Startups embrace a way to fail fast. *MIT Technology Review*, MIT, MA.

Grunbaum, N. N., & Stenger, M. (2013). *Dynamic capabilities: Are they profitable*? 1st Annual International Interdisciplinary Conference, AIIC, Proceedings, Azores, Portugal, April 24–26.

Hardy, Q. (2014a). *The era of cloud computing*. Bits blog: New York Times.

Hardy, Q. (2014b, August 2). Where tech is taking us: A conversation with Intel's Genevieve Bell. *New York Times, Bits blog*.

Hearn, G., et al. (Eds.). (2014). *Creative work beyond the creative industries: innovation, employment and education*. Cheltanham: Edward Elgar Publishing.

Heller, N. (2013, November 25). Naked launch: What's really new about the big new tech companies? *The New Yorker*.

Hepworth, A. (2013, November 7). Business bemoans loss of R&D tax break. *The Australian*.

Humphrey, J., & Schmitz, H. (2012). How does insertion into global value chains affect upgrades in industrial cluster? *Regional Studies, 36*(9), 1017–1027.

IDC. (2015, June 2). *Explosive internet of things spending to rise to $1.7 trillion*. Framingham, MA: IDC Press Release.

Im, P. (Jr. Workman). (2004). Market orientation, creativity and new product performance in high technology firms. *Journal of Marketing, 68*(April), 114–132.

Innovation Australia (IA). (2013). *Innovation readiness self assessment tool*. Canberra: AGPS.

Innovation Cities Program. (2013). *Innovation cities global index*. 2thinknow, annual, innovation-cities.com.

Institute of Chartered Accountants Australia (ICAA)., & Innovation Australia (IA). (2013). *20 issues in business innovation: Results of survey*. Business Briefings Series, December, Canberra.

INSEAD., Cornell University., & WIPO. (2013, 2014). *Global innovation index report*, Geneva, Switzerland.

Isaacson, W. (2014). *The innovators: How a group of hackers, geniuses and geeks created the digital revolution*. New York: Simon & Schuster.

Jaruzelski., B. et al. (2015). *"Innovations new world order", Global innovation 1000 survey*. Booz Allen, Boston, MA: Strategy-Business.

Jaruzelski. (2012). *Annual global innovation survey*. Boston, MA: Booz Allen.

Jensen, P., & Webster, E. (2014, July 21). Let's spend more wisely on research in Australia. *The Conversation*.

Johnson, C. (1999). In P. Drysdale & L. Gower (Eds.), *"The Japanese miracle", Technology, foreign investment and competition policy* (Vol. VII, pp. 3–33). The Japanese Economy 1998–1999, 8 Volumes, New York: Routledge.

Jorde, T., & Teece, D. (1990). Innovation and cooperation: Implications for competition and anti-trust. *Journal of Economic Perspectives, 4*(3), 75–96.

Kanter, R. M. (1989). Swimming in new streams: Mastering innovation dilemmas. *California Management Review, 31*(4), 45–69.

Katz, B., & Wagner, J. (2014). *The rise of innovation districts: A new geography of innovation in America*. Washington, DC: Brookings Institution.

Katz, B., et al. (2015). *One year after: Observations on the rise of innovation districts*. Washington, DC: Brookings Institution.

King, G. (2013). *"Big data is not about the data New England Artificial Intelligence Meet up!", slide presentation, 14 May*. Cambridge, MA: Harvard.

Kleiner, A. (2013, November 11). The 'dynamic capabilities' of David Teece: Interview. *Strategy & Business*.

Knight, W. (2016, January 2). Could AI solve the world's biggest problems? *MIT Technology Review*.

Kogut, B. (1985, July 15). Designing global strategies: Comparative and competitive value-added chains. *MIT Sloan Management Review*, Summer.

Kroker, A. (2014). *Exits to the posthuman future*. Cambridge, UK: Polity Press.

Kurzweil, R. (1999). *The age of spiritual machines: When computers exceed human intelligence*. New York: Viking Press.

Lawson, B., & Samson, D. (2001). Developing innovation capability in organizations: A dynamic capabilities approach. *International Journal of Innovation Management, 5*(3), 377–400.

Lazonick, W. (2013). The financialisation of the US corporation: What has been lost and how it can be regained. *Seattle Law Review, 36*, 857–890.

Lazonick, W., & Mazzucato, M. (2012). *The risk-reward nexus: Innovation, financialisation and inclusive growth*. Discussion Paper, Policy Network Linkner, 2014, The road to reinvention: How to drive disruption, London.

Lazonick, W. (2008). *The new economy business model and sustainable prosperity*. Annual Industry Studies Conference, Alfred P Sloan Foundation, May MIT, Boston, MA.

Lee, K. (2013). *Schumpeterian analysis of economic catch-up: Knowledge, path-creation, and the middle-income trap*. Cambridge: Cambridge University Press.

Lema, R., et al. (2012). *Shifts in innovation power to Brazil and India: Insights from the auto and software industries* (IDS research Report 73). Denmark: Aalborg University.

Lepore, J. (2014). The disruption machine: What the gospel of innovation gets wrong. *The New Yorker*.

Levine, S. (2015). Best business books of 2015: Disruption. *Strategy & Business*, November 2, 2015.

Lewis, M. (2014). *Flash boys: A wall street revolt*. New York: W W Norton & Company.

Lewis, M. (2013, September). Did Goldman Sachs overstep in criminally charging its ex-programmer? *Vanity Fair*, Lewis.

Linkner, J. (2014, May). *The road to reinvention: How to drive disruption and accelerate transformation*. New York: Josey-Bass/Wiley.

Manyika, M., et al. (2013, May). *Disruptive technologies: Advances that will transform life, business and the global economy* (McKinsey Global Institute Report).

Mather, J. (2013, September 18). Prime Minister Abbott dumps 'science', 'innovation', and 'skills'. *Financial Review*, Sydney.

Maxwell, I. (2014, August 7). Grants aren't helping Australian technology, but patent reform could. *The Conversation*.

Mazzucato, M. (2013). *The entrepreneurial state: Debunking public v private sector myths*. New York: Anthem Press.

McLure, D. (2012, April). Scaling venture capital? We suck. We can do better. *Blog Post*.

Mihm, S. (2015, May 26). China didn't invent industrial espionage. *BloombergView*.

MIT Innovation Initiative. (2014, May 19). Can crowd funding democratize access to capital?, Roundtable Discussion, *Innovation@workBlog*. Cambridge, MA: MIT Sloan School of Management.

Mokyr, J. (1990). *The lever of riches: Technological creativity and economic progress*. Oxford: Oxford University Press.

Mokyr, J. (2013, September 8). Is technological progress a thing of the past?. *Voxeu.org*. Center for Economic Policy Research (CEPR).

Morrison, A., et al. (2008). Global value chains and technological capability: A framework to study industrial; innovation in developing countries. *Oxford Development Studies, 36*(1), 39–58.

Morrison, N. (2014, October 22). It's time to rethink our use of technology in schools. *Forbes*.

Moss, T. (2014, November 24). All technology leapfrogging is not the same: Why phones and energy are different. *CGD blog*, Washington, DC.

Mulcahy, D. (2014, August 5). Venture capitalists get paid well to lose money. *Harvard Business Review*, Harvard, MA.

Murray, D. (2014, July 15). *Australian financial services industry* (Interim Report). Canberra: AGPS.

National Bureau of Economic Research (NBER). Innovation policy and the economy. *Annual Reviews*, Washington, DC.

New York Times. (2014). Annual Innovation Report. *New York Times*, New York.

Obama, P. (2014). *State of the union address*. Washington, DC: US Congress.

OECD. (1997). *National Innovation Systems (NIS)*. Paris: OECD.

OECD. (2011). *Skills for innovation and research*. Paris: OECD.

OECD. (2012). Innovation statistics.

OECD. (2013). *Interconnected economies: Benefitting from global value chains. G20 Seminar*. Paris: OECD.

OECD. (2014). *China headed to overtake EU, US in science and technology spending. Science, technology and industry outlook 2014*. Paris: OECD.
Orr, G. (2003, March 18). Diffusion of innovations by Everett Rogers. *Review*.
Packer, G. (2014, February). Cheap words: Amazon is good for customers but is it good for books? *The New Yorker*.
Peacock, T. (2012, January 19). *Are we crap at university-industry collaboration, or do we just think we are*? Cooperative Research Centres Association (CRCA), blog.
Pertuze, J., et al. (2010). Best practices for industry-university collaboration. *MIT Sloan Management Review, 51*(4), 83 (Summer, MIT, Boston, MA).
Petroda, S. (2010). *National innovation strategy*. New Delhi: NINC.
Pietrobelli, C., & Rabellotti, R. (2010). *Global value chains meet innovation systems: Are there learning opportunities for developing countries*? (24 pp). IDB Working Paper 232, Inter American Development Bank, November.
Porter, M. E. (1980). *Competitive strategy: Techniques for analyzing industries and competitors*. Harvard: Free Press.
Porter, M. E. (1979). How competitive forces shape strategy. *Harvard Business Review*.
Potts, J. (2011). *Creative industries and economic evolution*. Cheltenham, UK: Edward Elgar.
Potts, J. (2009). The role of creative industries in industrial innovation", Innovation: Management. *Policy and Practice, 11*(2), 148–168.
President of India. (2010). *Decade of innovation 2010–20 statement*. New Delhi.
President Obama. (2014). State of the Union Address, Washington DC.
Primack, D. (2014). Venture capitalists suck but there's a way you could prove me wrong. *Fortune*.
Productivity Commission. (2013). *Inquiry into Australia's compulsory patent licensing system*. Canberra, ACT: AGPS.
Randawa, K., et al. (2014). *Review of 'open innovation' literature 2003–13*. Working Paper, University of Technology Sydney (UTS), NSW.
Reis, E. (2011). The lean start up: How today's entrepreneurs use continuous innovation to create radically successful businesses. *Crown Business*.
Rice, J. (2014, August 13). Fund R&D, then maybe universities can support industry. *The Conversation*.
Robinson, D. (2013, January 15). How and what we will read in 2013. *My Metro*, p. 14.
Rogers, E. (2003). *Diffusion of innovations* (5th ed.). Macmillan, New York: The Free Press.
Royal Society. (2012). *The future of scientific collaboration*. London, UK: Royal Society.
Rural Research & Development Corporations (RR&DC). (2008). *Measuring economic, environmental and social returns on RR&DC's investments*. Canberra, ACT: AGPS.
Sandefur, J. (2012, March 2). The epistle of Gates and the gospel of agricultural innovation. *CGDBlog*.
Satell, G. (2013, November 9). Why cities are our most important innovation platforms. *Forbes*.
Schmidt, B. (2014, July 25). Rewards not enough to encourage excellence in research. *The Conversation*.
Schumpeter, J. A. (1942). *Capitalism, socialism and democracy*. Abingdon: Routledge.
Schumpeter, J. (2013, August 31). The entrepreneurial state. Book review blog. *The Economist*.
Searle, J. R. (2014, October 9). What your computer can't know. *New York Review of Books*, New York.
Shapiro, C., & Varian, H. (1999). *Information rules: A strategic guide to the network economy*. Boston, MA: Harvard Business School Press.
Shaw, J. (2014, March–April). Why big data is a big deal: Information science promises to change the world. *Harvard Magazine*, Boston, MA.
Shuen, A., & Sieber, S. (2010). Orchestrating the 'new dynamic capabilities' framework. *IESE Insights*.
Sobel, D. (2007). *Longtitude: The true story of the lone genius who solved the greatest scientific problem of his time*. London: Walker Books.

Specter, M. (2014a, August 16). Seeds of doubt: An activists controversial crusade against genetically modified crops. *The New Yorker.*
Specter, M. (2014b, January 6). The gene factory: A Chinese firm's bid to crack hunger, illness, evolution—And the genetics of human intelligence. *The New Yorker.*
Specter, M. (2015, November 9). The gene hackers: A powerful new technology enables us to manipulate our genetic code with ease. How will we use it? *The New Yorker.*
Spring, T. (2014, July 8). Standards war?: Dell, Intel & Samsung forge their own Internet of Things alliance? *CRN.com.*
Stodden, V. (2014). What scientific idea is ready for retirement: Reproducibility? *Edge Foundation.*
Stone, B. (2013). *The everything store: Jeff Bezos and the age of Amazon.* New York: Little, Brown and Company.
Streitfield, D. (2013, November 8). Booksellers divided over Amazon's e-book deal. *Sydney Morning Herald, Business Day,* p. 29.
Sunstein, C. R., & Hastie, R. (2015). *Wiser: Getting beyond groupthink to make groups smarter.* Brighton: Harvard Business Review Press.
Surowiecki, J. (2014, June 9, 16). Spy versus spy. *New Yorker.*
Teece, D. (1992). Competition, cooperation, and innovation: Organizational arrangements for regimes of rapid technological progress. *Journal of Economic and Behavioural Organisation, 18*(1), 1–25.
Teece, D. (1997). Dynamic capabilities and strategy. *Strategic Management Journal.*
Teece, D., & Pisano, G. (1994). Dynamic capabilities: An introduction. *Industrial and Corporate Change, Oxford Journals, Oxford, UK, 3*(3), 537–556.
Thompson, D. (2011, September 20). The global hollowing out of the middle class. *The Atlantic.*
Thorpe, J. (2013). *The start up economy: How to support tech startups and accelerate Australian innovation.* Sydney: PWC Google Report.
Ting, I., & Phillips, N. (2014, September 29). Australian government spending in science reaches 30-year low. *Sydney Morning Herald,* Sydney, NSW.
Tingle, L. (2015, December 7). Innovation statement: Malcolm Turnbull takes risks. *Australian Financial Review,* Sydney.
Turner, F. (2006). *From counterculture to cyber culture: The rise of digital utopianism* (354pp). Illinois: University of Chicago Press.
Veldhoen, S. (2012). *China innovation survey: Innovation—China's next advantage?.* Boston, MA: Booz and Company.
Vijg, J. (2011). *The American technological challenge: Stagnation and decline in the 21st century.* New York: Knopf.
Wadhwa, V. (2015, June 23). Why there has never been a better time to be an entrepreneur. *The Huffington Post.*
Webster, E. (2014, April 22). Rural Australia has innovation lessons to teach us all. *The Conversation.*
Weinberg, B., et al. (2014, April 4). Science funding and short term economic activity. *Science Magazine, 344,* 41–43.
Weisbrod, B. (1991). The healthcare quadrilemma: An essay on technological change, insurance, quality of care and cost containment. *Journal of Economic Literature, 29*(2), 523–552.
West Report. (2003). *Mapping Australia's science and innovation system.* Canberra, ACT: Department of Education, Science and Technology (DEST), AGPS.
Wikipedia. (2015). Dynamic capabilities for innovation.
Wilkins, G., & Williams, R. (2014, February 15–16). Smart thinking will help clever country to reinvent itself. *Sydney Morning Herald, Business,* p. 6.
Williams, R. (2013, July 17). *Ockham's Razor, "Innovation policy: Do we get good results for our science and research funding dollar and good innovation policy outcome*? ABC Radio National.
World Bank., & OECD. (2014). Innovation Policy Platform. website.
World Bank. (2007). India Innovation Report.

World Economic Forum (WEF). (2012). The shifting geography of global value chains: Implications for developing countries and trade policies, Geneva.
Xing, Y. (Ed.). (2015). *Uncovering value added trade: New approaches in analyzing global value chains*. Japan: Asian Development Bank Institute.
Zelinsky, A. (2013). *Think big and then make it happen* (Annual Innovation Lecture). Sydney, NSW: The Warren Centre, University of Sydney.

The manufacturer's authorised representative in the EU is Springer Nature Customer Service Centre GmbH, Europaplatz 3, 69115 Heidelberg, Germany. If you have any concerns regarding our products, please contact ProductSafety@springernature.com

Printed and bound by CPI Group (UK) Ltd, Croydon, CR0 4YY
30/09/2026
02225447-0012